ECONOMIC ISSUES, PROBLEMS AND PERSPECTIVES SERIES

GOVERNMENT INTERVENTIONS IN ECONOMIC EMERGENCIES

ECONOMIC ISSUES, PROBLEMS AND PERSPECTIVES SERIES

Trust, Globalisation and Market Expansion
Jacques-Marie Aurifeille, Christopher Medlin, and Clem Tisdell
2009. ISBN: 978-1-60741-812-2

TARP in the Crosshairs: Accountability in the Troubled Asset Relief Program
Paul W. O'Byrne (Editor)
2009. ISBN: 978-1-60741-807-8

TARP in the Crosshairs: Accountability in the Troubled Asset Relief Program
Paul W. O'Byrne (Editor)
2009. ISBN: 978-1-60876-705-2 *(Online book)*

Government Interventions in Economic Emergencies
Pablo Sastre (Editor)
2010. ISBN: 978-1-60741-356-1

ECONOMIC ISSUES, PROBLEMS AND PERSPECTIVES SERIES

GOVERNMENT INTERVENTIONS IN ECONOMIC EMERGENCIES

PABLO SASTRE
EDITOR

Nova Science Publishers, Inc.
New York

For permission to use material from this book please contact us:
Telephone 631-231-7269; Fax 631-231-8175
Web Site: http://www.novapublishers.com

LIBRARY OF CONGRESS CATALOGING-IN-PUBLICATION DATA

Government interventions in economic emergencies / [edited by] Pablo Sastre.
p. cm.
Includes index.
ISBN 978-1-60741-356-1 (hbk.)
1. Finance--Government policy--United States. 2. Financial crises--Government policy--United States. 3. Global Financial Crisis, 2008-2009. 4. Monetary policy--United States. 5. United States--Economic policy--2009- I. Sastre, Pablo.
HG181.G68 2009
339.5'30973--dc22

2009034030

Published by Nova Science Publishers, Inc. ✝ New York

CONTENTS

PREFACE

There is no precise definition of "financial crisis," but a common view is that disruptions in financial markets rise to the level of a crisis when the flow of credit to households and businesses is constrained and the real economy of goods and services is adversely affected. Since mid-2007, governments have tried with limited success to keep downturn in U.S. subprime housing from developing into such a crisis. In response to the ongoing financial turmoil, the federal government intervened financially with private corporations on a large scale that resulted in the government receiving significant debt and equity considerations three times since the beginning of 2008. On October 3rd 2008, the Troubled Assets Relief Program (TARP) was signed into law, giving Treasury the option of purchasing or insuring up to $700 billion of assets from financial firms. This book looks at the global financial crisis here and abroad and the government interventions to stave off economic emergencies.

Chapter 1 - To address the turmoil in financial markets, the Emergency Economic Stabilization Act (EESA; H.R. 1424, P.L. 110-343), enacted on October 3, 2008, authorizes purchases of "troubled assets." The act passed the Senate on October 1, 2008, passed the House on October 3, 2008, and was signed into law the same day.

The Administration proposed using reverse Dutch auctions to purchase troubled assets — primarily mortgage-related securities from financial institutions. In reverse Dutch auctions, a buyer purchases multiple objects from private parties at a price set by the last accepted bid. The government has used reverse auctions since the Revolutionary War. Designing efficient reverse Dutch auctions may present some tradeoffs between enhancing competition among bidders and overpaying for assets relative to their quality. Careful auction design, however, can help minimize these problems.

Auctions are especially useful for selling assets whose value to potential owners is unknown to the seller. Reverse auctions are useful when a buyer does not know what value sellers place on assets. Auction results could clarify the market value of troubled assets. The price discovery properties of auctions could stimulate trading by reducing private traders' uncertainty about the value of troubled assets.

Chapter 2 - The federal bank regulatory agencies — the Office of the Comptroller of the Currency, the Federal Deposit Insurance Corporation, the Board of Governors of the Federal Reserve System, and the Office of Thrift Supervision — have extensive authority to enforce various legal and regulatory standards with respect to the banking institutions that they supervise. Similarly, the Securities and Exchange Commission (SEC) has a wide range of tools to enforce the securities laws. This chapter provides a brief sketch of these authorities and identifies the organizational entities within each agency that Congress assigns enforcement responsibilities. It includes a table comparing the formal enforcement tools that the banking agencies may use with those of the SEC.

Chapter 3 - In March 2008, Bear Stearns, the nation's fifth largest investment banking firm, was battered by what its officials described as a sudden liquidity squeeze related to its large exposure to devalued mortgage-backed securities. On March 14, the Federal Reserve System announced that it would provide Bear Stearns with an unprecedented short-term loan. This was rendered essentially moot when, on March 16, a major commercial bank, JP Morgan Chase, agreed to buy Bear Stearns in an exchange of stock shares for about 1.5% of its share price of a year earlier, a price that translated to $2/share. To help facilitate the deal, the Federal Reserve agreed to provide special financing in connection with the transaction for up to $30 billion of Bear Stearns's less liquid assets.

During the weekend of March 22, in the wake of criticism from Bear shareholder and employees (employees own about one-third of the firm's outstanding stock) over the $2/share price, Bear Stearns and JP Morgan renegotiated the terms of the deal: JP Morgan will purchase 95 million newly issued shares of Bear's common stock at $10/share in a stock exchange. In response to the changed deal conditions, the Fed altered the terms of its financial involvement: it got JP Morgan to agree to absorb the first $1 billion in losses if the collateral provided by Bear for a loan proves to be worth less than Bear Stearn's original claims. Instead of its original agreement to absorb up $30 billion, the Fed will now be responsible for up to $29 billion.

The Fed's unprecedented role has generated a widespread debate on the implications of such an intervention. Some, including Senate Banking, Housing, and Urban Affairs Committee Chairman Chris Dodd, have argued that in order to avoid potential systemic financial risk, the involvement made sense. But others, including Senator Richard Shelby, ranking member of the Senate Banking Committee, have concerns that it tells the market that the Fed is willing to help a large and failing financial enterprise, setting a bad precedent in terms of corporate responsibility.

The Senate Banking Committee held a hearing on April 3, 2008, solely devoted to issues surrounding the acquisition of Bear Stearns.

Chapter 4 - There is no precise definition of "financial crisis," but a common view is that disruptions in financial markets rise to the level of a crisis when the flow of credit to households and businesses is constrained and the real economy of goods and services is adversely affected. Since mid-2007, governments have tried with limited success to keep the downturn in U.S. subprime housing from developing into such a crisis.

Subprime mortgage problems, and the financial shock they caused, were widely anticipated, but the spread of turmoil into many seemingly unrelated parts of the global financial system was not. Many of the losses occurring in diverse firms and markets — often quite severe — have common features: the use of complex, hard-to-value financial instruments; large speculative positions underwritten by borrowed funds, or leverage; and the use of off-the-books entities to remove risky trading activities from the balance sheets of major financial institutions. Because of the prevalence of innovative financial arrangements, the housing downturn appears to have triggered market dynamics that amplify the effects of financial shocks and generate self-reinforcing, downward financial and economic spirals.

The Federal Reserve and foreign central banks have cut short-term interest rates dramatically and injected trillions of dollars into the banking system to keep credit flowing.

The Fed and Treasury have engaged in a series of extraordinary interventions to shore up failing financial institutions. The Fed provided $29 billion to underwrite the rescue-through-acquisition of Bear Stearns, a leading investment bank, and loaned billions to AIG, a leading insurer. Fannie Mae and Freddie Mac have been placed in government conservatorship, with the Treasury pledging to stand behind the $5 trillion in bonds the two firms sold or guaranteed. In September 2008, as market conditions appeared to worsen, Congress passed a $700 billion rescue plan (P.L. 110-343), authorizing the Treasury to purchase securities to shore up bank balance sheets. In October, as conditions appeared to worsen, the Fed entered the commercial paper market and purchased tens of billions in short-term corporate debt. Simultaneously, trillions of dollars in private debt now carries government guarantees. The duration of the current instability is in marked contrast to financial shocks of recent decades, when the central bank was able to contain market problems quickly with little or no interruption of U.S. economic growth.

Depending on how soon normal market conditions are restored, and on the severity of the economic slowdown, Congress may view the social costs of failed financial speculation as sufficient to warrant new restrictions to reduce the incidence of losses that have system-wide impacts or to put the markets and the economy in a better position to weather such shocks. The Treasury has already proposed a sweeping restructuring of financial regulation.

This chapter supplements CRS Report RL34 182, *Financial Crisis? The Liquidity Crunch of August 2007*, by Darryl Getter et al., which describes in greater detail the channels through which subprime problems cascaded through the financial system.

Chapter 5 - In response to ongoing financial turmoil, the federal government intervened financially with private corporations on a large scale that resulted in the government receiving significant debt and equity considerations three times from the beginning of 2008 until the middle of September 2008. The firms affected were Bear Stearns, Fannie Mae and Freddie Mac, and AIG. Dissatisfaction with the case-by-case approach that had been pursued up to that point led to Treasury's decision to propose a more comprehensive solution to the turmoil on September 19, 2008. On October 3, 2008, P.L. 110-343 was signed into law, authorizing the Troubled Assets Relief Program (TARP). TARP gave Treasury the option of purchasing or insuring up to $700 billion of assets from financial firms. On October 14, 2008, Treasury announced it was purchasing up to $250 billion in financial firms' preferred stock under the TARP authority.

These interventions have prompted questions regarding the taxpayer costs and the sources of funding. The sources of funding are relatively straightforward, the Federal Reserve (Fed) and the U.S. Treasury. The costs, however, are difficult to quantify at this stage. In most of the interventions, all the financial outflows that are possible have yet to occur, and the ultimate value of the debt and equity considerations received from the private firms is uncertain. At this point, the federal government has the option to own nearly 80% of Fannie Mae, Freddie Mac, and AIG. Depending on the final proceeds from the various debt and equity considerations, the federal government may end up seeing a positive fiscal contribution from the recent interventions, as was the case in some of the past interventions summarized in the tables at the end of this chapter. The government may also suffer significant losses, as has also occurred in the past.

Chapter 6 - Since the financial crisis began in August 2007, the federal government has become increasingly involved with U.S. banks and other financial institutions and U.S.

financial markets. The Federal Reserve has greatly expanded the size, duration, and scope of its credit facilities (see Appendix). The Department of the Treasury has agreed to (1) inject up to $100 billion of taxpayer funds into Fannie Mae and another $100 billion into Freddie Mac, (2) purchase up to $250 billion of preferred shares in banks, and (3) purchase $40 billion of preferred shares in American International Group (AIG). Now, Chrysler, Ford, and General Motors along with the United Auto Workers (UAW) union are seeking emergency financing to help these automakers to avoid reorganizations under Chapter 11 of the federal bankruptcy code.

Although central governments play a large role in allocating capital in many Asian and European economies (1) through government-owned banks, government pension funds, and other government-owned financial institutions, or (2) through industrial policies that direct credit to and encourage investment in favored firms, industries, regions, or groups, a historical strength of the U.S. economy has been the relatively small role that the federal government has played in allocating credit and making investment decisions. The limited number and scope of government-owned financial institutions and the absence of an industrial policy in the United States has allowed private investors, private banks, and other private financial institutions to allocate credit and make investment decisions based on economic criteria without undue political interference. Subject only to general laws and regulations, private investors, banks, and other financial institutions may seek the highest returns consistent with their risk tolerance.

Chapter 7 - Prominent economists and policymakers invoke Keynesian economics in support of proposals for dramatic federal spending increases of $800 billion or more by the next administration to stimulate the economy. The federal government is intervening in the private sector on a large scale already to combat the economic crisis. Is Keynesianism, which had been discredited in the 1 970s, truly the answer to our economic ills? Upon examination, federal policy to date has not fully embraced Keynesianism, which does not offer assurance of lasting prosperity and indeed may pose grave risks to it.

Chapter 8 - The Emergency Economic Stabilization Act of 2008 (EESA, Division A of H. R. 1424, P.L. 110-343) provides authority for the Secretary of the Treasury to purchase and insure “troubled assets” to provide stability and prevent disruption in the economy and financial system. The act established two organizations to provide broad oversight for the stability program — a Financial Stability Oversight Board (FSOB) and a Congressional Oversight Panel (COP). The act also placed audit responsibilities for the program with two individuals a new Special Inspector General (IG) for the Troubled Asset Relief Program (TARP), and the Comptroller General (CG) ofthe United States, who heads the Government Accountability Office (GAO). The duties and responsibilities of both oversight panels and both auditors overlap in some areas, but are different in other areas.

Several aspects of the FSOB do not appear to be clearly delineated in the act, including where the FSOB is “established” within the federal government, whether it is covered by a variety of general management laws, and how the FSOB is to be funded and staffed. The act is also unclear regarding certain aspects of the Special IG for the TARP, including where the Office of the Special IG is to be “established” or housed, how or when its authorized appropriation is to be provided, and its specific investigative authorities.

The duties of both oversight panels and both audit organizations overlap in several key areas, and some of the reporting requirements also overlap. Although 18 types of EESA reports are required, none of them specifically require disclosure of how the funds are used by the recipients, and only one is required to be madc to the public. The Special IG for the TARP and members of the COP were not named until mid-November 2008. Also, the nature of the "troubled assets" being purchased have changed, perhaps necessitating reassessment of the act's oversight mechanisms. Finally, it is unclear what effect the various oversight and audit mechanisms will have on the balance of power between Congress and the executive branch. Congress gave itsclf expedited legislative procedures to disapprove actions by the Secretary, but only after the first $350 billion has been obligated.

Several specific requirements in the act appear to contemplate that the "troubled assets" being purchased and insured are primarily residential or commercial mortgages and instruments based on those mortgages. However, recent proposals to deal with the financial crisis are different than these mortgage-based transactions. While the oversight and audit responsibilities of the COP, the FSOB, the CG, and the Special IG still apply, the nature of their specific responsibilities may need to be reconsidered and redefined in light of the type of "troubled assets" that are initially being purchased. It is also unclear how effective all of these oversight and audit requirements will be in ensuring transparency and a balance of power between Congress and the executive branch.

Chapter 9 - Chairman Spratt, Ranking Member Ryan, and Members of the Committee, thank you for inviting me to testify this morning on the budgetary and economic implications of the recent turmoil in financial markets and the Administration's proposal to address it.

Since August 2007, the Federal Reserve and the Treasury have been attempting to address a series of severe breakdowns in financial markets that emanated from the bursting of the housing bubble, leading to substantial losses on mortgage-related securities and great difficulty in accurately ascertaining the financial condition of the institutions holding such securities. Those problems generated significant increases in risk spreads (or the interest rates charged on risky assets relative to Treasury securities) but, more important, contributed to a broader collapse of confidence, with the result that financial institutions became increasingly unwilling to lend to one another.

Over the past several weeks, the collapse of confidence in financial markets has become particularly severe. Short-term loans between financial institutions have fallen off sharply. Instead, the Treasury and the Federal Reserve have become the financial intermediaries for them. In other words, rather than financial institutions with excess money lending to institutions needing short-term funding, many institutions with excess short-term money have purchased Treasury securities, the Treasury has placed the proceeds on deposit at the Federal Reserve, and the Federal Reserve has then lent the money out to those institutions needing short- run funding.

Thus far, turmoil in the financial markets has had less impact on macroeconomic activity than may have been expected, and, indeed, economic growth was relatively strong in the second quarter of this year—in part because of the stimulus package enacted earlier this year. A modern economy like the United States', however, depends crucially on the functioning of its financial markets to allocate capital, and history suggests that the real economy typically slows some time after a downturn in financial markets. Moreover, ominous signs about credit difficulties are accumulating. The issuance of corporate debt plummeted in the third quarter, and the short-term commercial paper market has also been hit hard. Bank lending, which has thus far remained relatively strong, will undoubtedly be severely curtailed by the difficulties that banks are facing in raising capital. Such a curtailment of credit means that businesses and individuals will find it increasingly difficult to borrow money to carry out their normal activities. In sum, the problems occurring in financial markets raise the possibility of a severe credit crunch, which could have devastating effects on the U.S. and world economies.

Chapter 10 - Chile experienced a banking crisis from 1981-84 that in relative terms had a cost comparable in size to that perhaps facing the United States today. The Chilean Central Bank acted quickly and decisively in three ways to restore faith in the credit markets. It restructured firm and household loans, purchased nonperforming loans temporarily, and facilitated the sale or liquidation of insolvent financial institutions. These three measures increased liquidity in the credit markets and restored the balance sheets of the viable financial institutions. The Central Bank required banks to repurchase the nonperforming loans when provision for their loss could be made and prohibited distribution of profits until they had all been retired. Although the private sector remained engaged throughout the resolution of this crisis, the fiscal costs were, nonetheless, very high.

The U.S. Congress is contemplating a $700 billion government assistance package to arrest the financial crisis in the United States. President Bush argued that failure to enact legislation quickly could result in a wholesale failure of the U.S. financial sector. As discussion of the Administration's plan unfolded, however, questions in Congress arose over issues of magnitude and management of the "bailout," the need for oversight, and the possibility that less costly and perhaps more effective alternatives might be available.

In this light, Chile's response to its 1981-84 systemic banking crisis has been held up as one example. The cost was comparable relative to the size of its economy to that facing the U.S. Government today. In 1985, Central Bank losses to rescue financially distressed financial institutions were estimated to be 7.8% of GDP[1] (equivalent to approximately $1 trillion in the United States today). The policy options Chile chose had similarities as well as differences from those contemplated in the United States today. Their relevance is debatable, but they do highlight an approach that succeeded in eventually stabilizing and returning the Chilean banking sector to health, while keeping the credit markets functioning throughout the crisis.

Chapter 11 - Japan's five bank bailout packages in the late 1990s may hold some lessons for the United States. Most of the packages were administered by the Deposit Insurance Corporation of Japan (DICJ). The packages had an announced value of $495 billion. The DICJ reports that it provided $399 billion to Japan's troubled financial institutions of which it has recovered $195 billion. Overcoming the crisis in Japan's banks took a combination of capital injections, new laws and regulations, stronger oversight, a reorganization of the banking sector, moderate economic recovery, and several years of banks working off their non-performing loans. When the U.S. Treasury planned the $700 billion bailout package (Emergency Economic Stabilization Act of 2008, H.R. 3997) to address the U.S. financial crisis, it reportedly examined the experience of Japan as it grappled with its banking crisis in the1990s.[1] This chapter reviews the major actions by the Japanese government in dealing with its crisis and highlights some of the lessons learned from their experience.

Like the current U.S. financial crisis, Japan's began with stock market and real estate bubbles. During the latter half of the 1980s, Japan's monetary authorities flooded the market with liquidity (money) in order to enable businesses to cope with the rising value of the yen. Businesses did invest in new capital equipment to become more competitive in international markets, but the excess liquidity also found its way into speculation in Japan's stock market, in real estate ventures, and in foreign investments. At that time, the market value of both land and equities was rising so fast that investors and speculators could hardly miss. Investors tended to ignore risks. The larger mistake for them was not to borrow and invest and consequently not be positioned to reap the returns from rising markets. Banks considered most loans with real estate as collateral as being unquestionably secure. Then the bubbles burst.

Chapter 12 - In the early 1990s, Sweden faced a banking and exchange rate crisis that led it to rescue banks that had experienced large losscs on their balance sheets and that threatened a collapse of the banking system. Some analysts and others argue that Sweden's experience could provide useful lessons for the execution and implementation of the Emergency Economic Stabilization Act of 2008[1]. The banking crisis facing the United States is unique, so there are no exact parallels from which to draw templates. Sweden's experience, however, represents a case study in how a systemic banking crisis was resolved in a developed country with democratic institutions. The Swedish central bank separated out good assets, which it left to the banks to oversee from bad assets, which it placed in a separate agency with broad authority to work out debt problems or to liquidate assets. Four lessons that emerged form Sweden's experience are: 1) the process must be transparent; 2) the resolution agency must be politically and financially independent; 3) market discipline must be maintained; and 4) there must be a plan to jump-start credit flows in the financial system. This chapter provides an overview of the Swedish banking crisis and an explanation of the measures Sweden used to restore its banking system to health.

Chapter 13 - Financial markets continue to experience significant disturbance and the banking sector remains fragile. Efforts to restore confidence have been met with mixed success thus far. After attempting to deal with troubled institutions on a case-by-case basis, Treasury has proposed a plan to purchase mortgage-related assets to alleviate stress in financial markets and in the banking system. This chapter provides answers to some frequently asked questions concerning the financial disruptions of September 2008 and the Troubled Asset Relief Program (TARP) in H.R. 3997.

Chapter 14 - Chairman Frank, Ranking Member Bachus, and members of the Committee, I appreciate this opportunity to discuss recent developments in financial markets and the economy. As you know, the U.S. economy continues to confront substantial challenges, including a weakening labor market and elevated inflation. Notably, stresses in financial markets have been high and have recently intensified significantly. If financial conditions fail to improve for a protracted period, the implications for the broader economy could be quite adverse.

The downturn in the housing market has been a key factor underlying both the strained condition of financial markets and the slowdown of the broader economy. In the financial sphere, falling home prices and rising mortgage delinquencies have led to major losses at many financial institutions, losses only partially replaced by the raising of new capital. Investor concerns about financial institutions increased over the summer, as mortgage-related assets deteriorated further and economic activity weakened. Among the firms under the greatest pressure were Fannie Mae and Freddie Mac, Lehman Brothers, and, more recently, American International Group (AIG). As investors lost confidence in them, these companies saw their access to liquidity and capital markets increasingly impaired and their stock prices drop sharply.

The Federal Reserve believes that, whenever possible, such difficulties should be addressed through private-sector arrangements—for example, by raising new equity capital, by negotiations leading to a merger or acquisition, or by an orderly wind-down. Government assistance should be given with the greatest of reluctance and only when the stability of the financial system, and, consequently, the health of the broader economy, is at risk. In the cases of Fannie Mae and Freddie Mac, however, capital raises of sufficient size appeared infeasible and the size and government-sponsored status of the two companies precluded a merger with or acquisition by another company. To avoid unacceptably large dislocations in the financial sector, the housing market, and the economy as a whole, the Federal Housing Finance Agency (FHFA) placed Fannie Mae and Freddie Mac into conservatorship, and the Treasury used its authority, granted by the Congress in July, to make available financial support to the two firms. The Federal Reserve, with which FHFA consulted on the conservatorship decision as specified in the July legislation, supported these steps as necessary and appropriate. We have seen benefits of this action in the form of lower mortgage rates, which should help the housing market.

The Federal Reserve and the Treasury attempted to identify private-sector approaches to avoid the imminent failures of AIG and Lehman Brothers, but none was forthcoming. In the case of AIG, the Federal Reserve, with the support of the Treasury, provided an emergency credit line to facilitate an orderly resolution. The Federal Reserve took this action because it judged that, in light of the prevailing market conditions and the size and composition of AIG's obligations, a disorderly failure of AIG would have severely threatened global financial stability and, consequently, the performance of the U.S. economy. To mitigate concerns that this action would exacerbate moral hazard and encourage inappropriate risk-taking in the future, the Federal Reserve ensured that the terms of the credit extended to AIG imposed significant costs and constraints on the firm's owners, managers, and creditors. The chief executive officer has been replaced. The collateral for the loan is the company itself, together with its subsidiaries.[1] (Insurance policyholders and holders of AIG investment products are, however, fully protected.) Interest will accrue on the outstanding balance of the loan at a rate of three-month Libor plus 850 basis points, implying a current interest rate over 11 percent. In addition, the U.S. government will receive equity participation rights corresponding to a 79.9 percent equity interest in AIG and has the right to veto the payment of dividends to common and preferred shareholders, among other things.

Chapter 15 - **Washington, DC**— Chairman Frank, Congressman Bachus, members of the committee, thank you for the opportunity to appear before you today. I appreciate that we are here to discuss an unprecedented program, but these are unprecedented times for the American people and our economy. I also appreciate that Congress and the Administration are working closely together so that we can help the American people by quickly enacting a program to stabilize our financial system.

We must do so in order to avoid a continuing series of financial institution failures and frozen credit markets that threaten American families' financial well-being, the viability of businesses both small and large, and the very health of our economy.

The events leading us here began many years ago, starting with bad lending practices by banks and financial institutions, and by borrowers taking out mortgages they couldn't afford. We've seen the results on homeowners – higher foreclosure rates affecting individuals and neighborhoods. And now we are seeing the impact on financial institutions.

These bad loans have created a chain reaction and last week our credit markets froze up – even some Main Street non-financial companies had trouble financing their normal business operations. If that situation were to persist, it would threaten all parts of our economy.

Chapter 16 - This chapter summarizes and analyzes four previous government market interventions (Home Owners Loan Corporation in 1933, Continental Illinois in 1984, the savings and loan insurance fund shortfall in 1989, and the Latin American debt crisis in 1989), in light of current mortgage market conditions. Current proposals to help delinquent homeowners share many features in common with all of these actions.

The Home Owners Loan Corporation (HOLC) purchased delinquent mortgages at a discount and worked with homeowners to restructure the mortgages into more manageable terms. HOLC accepted slightly more than one million applications from homeowners to refinance their homes between June 1933 and June 1935. It rejected 488,000 applications, most for "inadequate security" and "lack of distress." HOLC foreclosed on 194,000 of those it was attempting to assist. At the time, many had serious concern that HOLC could be a costly undertaking, but when it disbanded in the early 1 950s, HOLC returned a small profit to the government. HOLC successfully conceived and implemented new ways to contact delinquent homeowners and, in some cases, help homeowners find new jobs.

In 1984, Continental Illinois National Bank suffered a run after loans that it had not properly underwritten failed. The Federal Reserve and the Federal Deposit Insurance Corporation led intervention efforts. There were concerns that allowing the bank to fail could have serious repercussions throughout the financial system. This led to the FDIC Improvement Act of 1991.

In the 1980s, the Federal Savings and Loan Insurance Corporation approached insolvency because of the failure of member savings and loan institutions, also known as thrifts. Working together, Congress and the George H. W. Bush administration established the Resolution Trust Corporation (RTC), which was funded by the Resolution Funding Corporation (REFCORP). The thrift industry is still paying off the intervention operation, which is estimated to have cost $152.9 billion.

In 1989, Brady bonds helped less developed countries, mostly in Latin America, restructure their debt by renegotiating terms and writing down some of the loans. The plan, proposed by then-U.S. Treasury Secretary Nicholas F. Brady, overcame coordination problems in previous restructuring efforts. In addition to writing down some loans, the plan included some interest rate reductions, and having debtor nations post U.S. Treasury bonds as collateral with the Federal Reserve. Approximately $91.8 billion was refinanced under the plan. Repayment continues today.

H.R. 5818 and H.R. 5830 are among the bills before Congress that would intervene in economic (housing) markets.

Chapter 17 - **Washington, DC**—Last night, Federal Reserve Chairman Ben Bernanke, SEC Chairman Chris Cox and I had a lengthy and productive working session with Congressional leaders. We began a substantive discussion on the need for a comprehensive approach to relieving the stresses on our financial institutions and markets.

We have acted on a case-by-case basis in recent weeks, addressing problems at Fannie Mae and Freddie Mac, working with market participants to prepare for the failure of Lehman Brothers, and lending to AIG so it can sell some of its assets in an orderly manner. And this morning we've taken a number of powerful tactical steps to increase confidence in the system, including the establishment of a temporary guaranty program for the U.S. money market mutual fund industry.

Despite these steps, more is needed. We must now take further, decisive action to fundamentally and comprehensively address the root cause of our financial system's stresses.

The underlying weakness in our financial system today is the illiquid mortgage assets that have lost value as the housing correction has proceeded. These illiquid assets are choking off the flow of credit that is so vitally important to our economy. When the financial system works as it should, money and capital flow to and from households and businesses to pay for home loans, school loans and investments that create jobs. As illiquid mortgage assets block the system, the clogging of our financial markets has the potential to have significant effects on our financial system and our economy.

Chapter 18 - The actions taken by Treasury, the Federal Reserve and the FDIC in October have clearly helped stabilize our financial system. Before we acted, we were at a tipping point. Credit markets were largely frozen, denying financial institutions, businesses and consumers access to vital funding and credit. U.S. and European financial institutions were under extreme pressure, and investor confidence in our system was dangerously low.

We also acted quickly and in coordination with colleagues around the world to stabilize the global financial system. Going into the Annual IMF/World Bank meetings in early October, I made clear that we would use the financial rescue package granted by Congress to purchase equity directly from financial institutions – the fastest and most productive means of using our new authorities to stabilize our financial system. We launched our capital purchase program the following week when we announced that nine of the largest U.S. financial institutions, holding approximately 55 percent of U.S. banking assets would sell $125 billion in preferred stock to the Treasury. At the same time, the FDIC announced it would temporarily guarantee all newly issued senior unsecured debt of participating organizations for up to three years. In addition, the FDIC provided an unlimited guarantee on non-interest bearing transaction accounts that expires at the end of next year.

As I assess where we are today, I believe we have taken the necessary steps to prevent a broad systemic event. Both at home and around the world we have already seen signs of improvement. Our system is stronger and more stable than just a few weeks ago. Although this is a major accomplishment, we have many challenges ahead of us. Our financial system remains fragile in the face of an economic downturn here and abroad, and financial institutions' balance sheets still hold significant illiquid assets. Market turmoil will not abate until the biggest part of the housing correction is behind us. Our primary focus must be recovery and repair.

Chapter 19 - Financial markets underwent severe stress during the week of September 15-22, 2008. After Lehman Brothers declared bankruptcy and AIG received a bridge loan from the Federal Reserve, policymakers reassessed their case-by-case approach to resolving financial problems. Secretary of the Treasury Paulson announced a plan to allow Treasury to purchase mortgage-related assets from U.S. financial institutions. The announced intent of the plan is to unclog financial markets, increase the health of the banking sector, and reduce ongoing risks to the economy. This chapter discusses a draft of the proposal as it stood on September 21, 2008, and analyzes frequently asked questions.

Following a week of severe stress in financial markets, the Secretary of the Treasury and the Chairman of the Federal Reserve met with congressional leaders on September 19, 2008, to ask for legislation to authorize direct intervention in the economy. An unofficial three-page draft of a specific proposal circulated over the weekend of September 20, 2008.[1] A revised draft circulated September 21. Both draft proposals allow Treasury to purchase up to $700 billion in mortgage-related assets in an attempt to reduce disruptions in the financial system.

This chapter describes the provisions of the draft legislative proposals that were circulated and provides an analysis of several questions that the proposals raise.

Chapter 20 - In a 1989 legislative response to financial troubles in the thrift industry, the Financial Institutions Reform, Recovery, and Enforcement Act of 1989 (FIRREA, P.L. 101-73) was enacted: FIRREA's principal mission was to conduct a partially tax-payer funded program to address the troubles of the nation's many insolvent thrifts. To do so, it established a new entity, the Resolution Trust Corporation (RTC), whose mission was to address troubled thrifts by arranging their sale to other institutions or shuttering them and disposing of their assets. The RTC would eventually obtain $105 billion in funding but a major part of its principal funding came from an off-budget entity, the Resolution Funding Corporation (REFCORP). REFCORP was created by FIRREA as a publicprivate partnership, which acquired the funds that it would provide to the RTC through proceeds from its sale of U.S. Treasury bonds. During its years of operation, 1989 to 1995, the RTC was alternately criticized for dumping thrift assets and for taking too much time to dispose of them. It subsequently began selling block assets, it partnered with private entities in the joint ownership of some assets, and it issued securities backed by commercial mortgages. When shut down in 1995, the RTC had closed 747 insolvent thrifts and recovered about 85% of the value of the assets it had seized. Estimates vary but several observers cite direct and indirect governmental costs totaling about $150 billion for the undertaking.

Chapter 21 - Recent policies have sought to contain damages spilling over from housing and financial markets to the broader economy, including monetary policy, the responsibility of the Federal Reserve, and fiscal policy. Legislators and the President adopted an economic stimulus package (P.L. 110-185) on February 13. Another stimulus package, H.R. 7110, has passed the House. Over the past few months, the government has also intervened in specific financial markets, including financial assistance to troubled firms. Legislation authorizing a massive intervention in financial markets was adopted on October 3 (P.L. 110-343); it includes authority to purchase $700 billion in troubled assets. In addition, the Fed has lent directly to financial institutions through an array of new facilities, and the amounts of loans outstanding have risen into the hundreds of billions of dollars. President-Elect Obama has proposed a much larger stimulus package than that in H.R. 7110.

The estimated budget cost of the stimulus enacted in February was about $150 billion for FY2008. The largest provision (in terms of budgetary cost) was a tax rebate for individuals. The Senate committee bill also included an extension in unemployment compensation benefits; the Iraq/Afghanistan supplemental appropriations completed June 26 included a 13-week extension, signed on June 30. The current stimulus proposal would increase spending on infrastructure, unemployment benefits, Medicaid, and food stamps by $50 to $60 billion; unemployment was extended by an additional seven weeks on November 21, 2008.

The need for additional fiscal stimulus depends on the state of the economy. The National Bureau of Economic Research (NBER) has declared the economy in recession since December 2007. Growth rates, after two strong quarters, were negative in the fourth quarter of 2007, positive in the first and second quarters of 2008, and a negative 0.5% in the third quarter. According to one data series, employment fell in every month of 2008. The unemployment rate, which rose slightly in the last half of 2007, declined in January and February of 2008, but began rising in March and in November stood at 6.7%. Some forecasters believe that the ongoing financial turmoil will result in a recession that is deeper and longer than average.

Fiscal policy temporarily stimulates the economy through an increase in the budget deficit. There is a consensus that proposals that result in more spending, can be implemented quickly, and leave no long-term effect on the budget deficit would increase the benefits and reduce the costs of fiscal stimulus. Economists generally agree that spending proposals are somewhat more stimulative than tax cuts since part of a tax cut will be saved by the recipients. The most important determinant of the effect on the economy is its size. The recent stimulus package increased the deficit by about 1% of GDP.

The broad intervention into the financial markets has been passed to avoid the spread of financial instability into the broader market but there are disadvantages, including leaving the government holding large amounts of mortgage debt.

Chapter 22 - The Federal Reserve (Fed) has been central in the response to the current financial turmoil that began in August 2007. It has sharply increased reserves to the banking system through open market operations and lowered the federal funds rate and discount rate on several occasions. As the turmoil has progressed without signs of subsiding, the Fed has introduced new policy tools to try to restore normality.

Through new credit facilities, the Fed first expanded lending to the banking system and then extended lending to non-bank financial firms. Lending to non-banks is a major departure from past policy, for it is the first time that financial institutions that are not member banks of the Federal Reserve System have been allowed to borrow directly from the Fed on a routine basis. As the crisis worsened, the Fed began providing credit directly to markets for commercial paper and asset-backed securities. As a result of these programs, the Fed's outstanding loans and private asset purchases have ranged from $0.5 trillion to $1 trillion in recent months. The Fed's authority and capacity to lend is bound only by fears of the inflationary consequences, which have been offset by additional debt issuance by the Treasury.

In March 2008, JPMorgan Chase agreed to acquire Bear Stearns. As part of the agreement, the Fed made a $28.82 billion loan to a limited liability corporation (LLC) it created to buy $29.97 billion of assets from Bear Stearns. The Fed has also agreed to make loans and purchase assets through an LLC from the American International Group (AIG) worth up to $112.5 billion. In November 2008, the Fed and federal government agreed to guarantee losses on $306 billion of assets owned by Citigroup. In all of these agreements, the Fed is exposed to downside financial risk if the assets purchased or guaranteed fall in value.

The statutory authority for most of the Fed's recent actions is based on a clause of the Federal Reserve Act to be used in "unusual or exigent circumstances" that had not been invoked in more than 70 years. All loans are backed by collateral that reduces the risk of losses. Any losses borne by the Fed from its loans or asset purchases would reduce the profits it remits to the Treasury, making the effect on the federal budget similar to if the loans were made directly by Treasury. It is highly unlikely that losses would exceed its other profits and capital, and require revenues to be transferred to the Fed from the Treasury.

The primary policy issues raised by the Fed's actions are the issues of systemic risk and moral hazard. Moral hazard refers to the phenomenon where actors take on more risk because they are protected. The Fed's involvement in stabilizing Bear Stearns, AIG, and Citigroup stemmed from the fear of systemic risk (that the financial system as a whole would cease to function) if either were allowed to fail. In other words, the firms were seen as "too big (or too interconnected) to fail." The Fed's regulatory structure is intended to mitigate the moral hazard that stems from access to government protections. Yet Bear Stearns and AIG were not under the Fed's regulatory structure because they were not member banks.

Chapter 23 - Short sellers borrow stock, sell it, and hope to profit if they can buy back the same number of shares later at a lower price. A short sale is a bet that a stock's price will fall. A short sale is said to be "naked" if the broker does not in fact borrow shares to deliver to the buyer. When executed on a large scale, naked short sales can equal a large portion of total shares outstanding, and can put serious downward pressure on a stock's price. Critics of the practice characterize it as a form of illegal price manipulation. The Securities and Exchange Commission (SEC) in 2004 adopted Regulation SHO, a set of rules designed to control short selling abuses, focusing on small-capitalization stocks where the number of shares held by the public was relatively small. Until the current financial crisis, the SEC did not view short selling of large, blue-chip stocks as a problem. In July 2008, however, the SEC temporarily banned naked short sales of the stock of Fannie Mae, Freddie Mac, and 17 other large financial institutions. On September 18, 2008, the SEC banned all short selling of the shares of more than 700 financial companies in an emergency action that expired on October 8, 2008. On October 1, the SEC adopted a rule requiring short sellers' brokers to actually borrow shares to deliver to buyers, within the normal three-day settlement time frame.

Short selling was best described by Daniel Drew, the Gilded Age speculator and robber baron: "He that sells what isn't his'n, must buy it back or go to prison." Short sellers borrow shares from a broker, sell them, and make a profit if the share price subsequently drops, allowing them to buy back the same number of shares for less money. In other words, short selling is a bet that the price of a stock will fall.

Short sellers have always been unpopular on Wall Street. Like skeletons at the feast, they seem to stand against rising share values, expanding wealth, and general prosperity. However, most market participants recognize that they provide a valuable service to the extent that they identify companies and industries that are overvalued by investors in the grip of irrational exuberance. By bringing such valuations down to earth, short selling can prevent economically wasteful over-allocation of resources to those firms and sectors.

In: Government Interventions in Economic Emergencies
Editor: Pablo Sastre
ISBN: 978-1-60741-356-1

Chapter 1

AUCTION BASICS: BACKGROUND FOR ASSESSING PROPOSED TREASURY PURCHASES OF MORTGAGE-BACKED SECURITIES

D. Andrew Austin

SUMMARY

To address the turmoil in financial markets, the Emergency Economic Stabilization Act (EESA; H.R. 1424, P.L. 110-343), enacted on October 3, 2008, authorizes purchases of "troubled assets." The act passed the Senate on October 1, 2008, passed the House on October 3, 2008, and was signed into law the same day.

The Administration proposed using reverse Dutch auctions to purchase troubled assets — primarily mortgage-related securities from financial institutions. In reverse Dutch auctions, a buyer purchases multiple objects from private parties at a price set by the last accepted bid. The government has used reverse auctions since the Revolutionary War. Designing efficient reverse Dutch auctions may present some tradeoffs between enhancing competition among bidders and overpaying for assets relative to their quality. Careful auction design, however, can help minimize these problems.

Auctions are especially useful for selling assets whose value to potential owners is unknown to the seller. Reverse auctions are useful when a buyer does not know what value sellers place on assets. Auction results could clarify the market value of troubled assets. The price discovery properties of auctions could stimulate trading by reducing private traders' uncertainty about the value of troubled assets.

A reverse auction program essentially swaps Treasury securities for troubled mortgage-backed securities. If Treasury securities are exchanged for troubled assets at prices close to those assets' current market prices, costs to the taxpayer would be minimized. Financial institutions, however, may gain some liquidity, but might not receive much additional capital. Some economists have argued that other means of injecting capital into the financial sector, such as purchases of preferred stock or capital injections balanced by equity warrants (i.e., options to claim an equity stake), might be a better strategy. Since passage of EESA, the U.S.

Treasury has been working to design methods to inject capital into firms and restore market liquidity.

The heterogeneity of troubled assets may present challenges to the Treasury auction program. The reverse Dutch auctions would need to be adapted to buy highly diverse and relatively small-volume securities, in a way that minimizes risks of trading manipulation. Reverse Dutch auctions may be vulnerable to adverse selection, meaning that the average credit quality of submitted assets of a given type may be systematically worse than the average credit quality of all assets of that type. Auction mechanisms might be designed that could mitigate these problems.

Recent academic research in auction theory and in experimental economics has examined how various types of auctions work. Auctions may capture higher revenues for governments and can often allocate scarce resources more efficiently than traditional methods of selling or purchasing. Different policy problems, however, call for different types of auctions. Government economists involved in designing reverse auctions to buy troubled assets have drawn upon academic research and internal Treasury research.

To address the turmoil in financial markets, Congress passed and the President signed the Emergency Economic Stabilization Act (EESA; H.R. 1424, P.L. 110-343) on October 3, 2008. The act authorizes the Secretary of Treasury "to restore liquidity and stability to the financial system of the United States" (Sec. 2) by purchasing or insuring "troubled assets." The Secretary will design the mechanism for purchasing the troubled assets and methods for pricing and valuing these assets. The act broadly defines troubled assets as (1) mortgages and any securities based on such mortgages whose purchase the Secretary determines will promote financial market stability, and (2) any other financial instrument whose purchase the Secretary and the Federal Reserve Board Chairman determines will promote financial market stability.

The act authorizes Secretary Paulson to use $700 billion to enhance liquidity and to inject capital into financial markets by purchasing (1) mortgages and pools of mortgages, (2) preferred stock in ailing financial institutions, and (3) troubled mortgage-backed securities (MBSs).1 The Secretary has indicated that reverse auctions will be used to purchase mortgage-backed securities from troubled financial institutions. A well-designed auction could help determine the price and value of these assets in an efficient manner.

The act establishes a Congressional Oversight Panel to review the current state of financial markets, the regulatory system, and the administration of the Troubled Asset Relief Program (TARP) by the Secretary. This chapter provides Congress with information on the uses, design, and functions of auctions. It reviews some common types of auctions used by the federal government and some of the complexities of auction design that the Secretary will have to deal with in the TARP.

Dutch Auctions and Reverse Dutch Auctions

The Administration has proposed using reverse auctions to purchase mortgagerelated securities from financial institutions, which are similar to the multiple-unit Dutch auctions that the Treasury uses to sell government securities. In a reverse auction, a buyer accepts bids from multiple potential sellers. In reverse multi-unit Dutch auctions, a buyer (e.g., the U.S.

Treasury) buys a given number of units from private parties (e.g., financial institutions) at a price set by the last accepted bid.[2] **Figure 1** below contains a hypothetical example of a reverse Dutch auction.

Suppose a government agency wished to purchase 1,000 desktop computers of a given specification. Potential sellers would submit sealed bids with a price and a number of units. The agency would then sort bids by price in ascending order. The agency would accept bids, starting with the lower price, and continuing until units offered in bids reached 1,000. Hypothetical bids are shown below.

Bids for a Hypothetical Government Procurement Reverse Auction

Hypothetical Firm	Bid Price (Per Unit)	Number of Units
Hang-10 IT	$450	400
Crash Computers	$470	500
Macrohard Inc.	$510	200
HAL Systems	$525	300

The agency would accept the bid from Hang-10 IT and buy 400 units because it had the lowest bid price, although Hang-10 IT's bid price ($450) would not be the purchase price. The agency would also accept Crash Computers' bid for 500 units, because its bid price was the second lowest. Finally, the agency would buy 100 computers from Macrohard Inc. to reach the total of 1,000 computers. Because Macrohard was the last successful bidder, all computers would be bought at a unit price of $510. HAL Systems would sell no computers to the agency.

Some may wonder why the government agency would not force firms to sell computers at their bid prices, which might seem to save the agency money. Such a strategy would probably be unsuccessful in saving money because firms would change their bidding strategies if they knew that they would have to sell at their bid prices. In particular, sellers would tend to shade their bids upwards, which might raise costs to the agency.

Specific rules and operation details for reverse Dutch auctions used by governments and private firms have varied. Some central banks use multiple-price or pay-your-bid auctions to sell securities, others use uniform-price auctions, and some have used both. Differences between multiple-price and uniform price auctions are discussed in more detail

Figure 1. A Hypothetical Reverse Dutch Auction

Auctions provide a means of selling objects whose value to potential owners is unknown to the seller. Many different auction mechanisms are in common use. A large research literature in economic theory and experimental economics examines how different types of auctions work. On the one hand, well-designed auctions can provide an expeditious and efficient method for selling or acquiring objects. On the other hand, poorly designed auctions have caused governments to forego large amounts of revenue. Moreover, poorly designed auctions may increase the likelihood that valuable resources are allocated to buyers who value those resources less than others — a source of inefficiency.[3] In particular, auctions suitable for some applications may be unsuited for other applications.

The American government has used reverse auctions since Robert Morris, who headed the Treasury Department, used them to procure supplies for troops in the Revolutionary War.[4] In recent decades, the Treasury Department has used auctions to sell federal securities.[5] Over time, the federal government has gained valuable experience in conducting and designing auctions, which has reduced costs and increased revenues compared to other methods.

Current U.S. Treasury auctions, which use a multi-unit Dutch auction mechanism to sell securities, have apparently provided a starting point for Administration proposals to buy "troubled assets" via reverse Dutch auctions. Because the reverse Dutch auction process would, in approximate mirror fashion, resemble Treasury auctions of government securities to primary dealers, key market participants could quickly familiarize themselves with new bidding procedures. Those administering Treasury reverse auctions, however, recognize that differences between Treasury securities and troubled assets have consequences for auction design.[6] Designing reverse Dutch auctions may present some tradeoffs between enhancing competition among bidders and overpaying for assets relative to their quality. Careful auction design, however, can help minimize these problems.

In the Dutch auction mechanism used to sell U.S. Treasury securities, all successful buyers pay the same price; in other words, it is a *uniform-price* mechanism. Uniform-price mechanisms, according to some experts, may encourage more aggressive bidding, which raises expected revenues.[7]

While details of the Treasury reverse Dutch auctions remain unspecified, the U.S. Treasury would probably announce that it wished to buy a given amount of mortgage-related securities (MBSs) of specific types or issues for a given auction. Bidders would then list securities they wish to sell and specify prices. The Treasury would then buy the securities listed at the lowest prices until the specified amount was reached. The price offered by the last successful bidder would then be paid to all successful bidders.

Quality Differences of Troubled Assets Presents Challenges for Auctions

The diversity or heterogeneity of troubled assets may present challenges to the Treasury auction program. The mortgage-backed securitization process was intended to create marketable assets with credit characteristics that could be readily assessed by credit agencies and buyers. Credit rating agencies claimed that the rating process sorted asset-backed securities and other assets into categories with essentially homogenous profiles. All assets of a specific type receiving a given rating were supposed to embody essentially similar risk characteristics.

Confidence in the credit rating process has deteriorated over the past two years, however. Credit rating agencies, according to the Securities and Exchange Commission (SEC), struggled to keep up with more complex types of securities and had difficulty assessing risks embedded in subprime mortgage-backed assets. In addition, according to the SEC, none of the rating agencies examined had specific written procedures for rating residential MBSs and collateralized debt obligations.[8] Thus, some buyers may doubt that credit ratings represent a true gauge of asset quality. Tightened market liquidity in capital markets since August 2007 may stem in part from potential buyers' uncertainty about the credit quality of MBSs and other assets. Buyers may worry that sellers could have incentives to sell assets with difficult-to-detect risks before assets without such hidden hazards.

Similar problems may occur with reverse Dutch auctions used to buy troubled assets. A typical Treasury auction sells a large volume of identical government securities whose characteristics are well understood. The reverse Dutch auctions used by the Treasury would need to be adapted to buy highly diverse and relatively small-volume securities, whose characteristics may not be well understood by many buyers. A typical mortgage-backed security issue, while enormous relative to a single housing mortgage, is small when compared to the size of a typical Treasury security issue, and individual tranches (slices) of MBSs are smaller still.[9] Different MBSs and related structured finance assets are very diverse, although their structures and pricing follow some general principles.[10] Thus, selling Treasury securities is like selling commodity steel; buying mortgage-backed securities is like buying used cars.

If the Treasury were to run a large number of narrowly defined reverse auctions, it would be more difficult to prevent certain types of market manipulation.[11] For example, a bidder who gains control of a large proportion of an issue might exert influence on auction outcomes. But, if a wider variety of securities or assets were allowed in the same auction, which would sharpen competition, sellers may have an incentive to submit bids for those assets with hidden flaws.

Reverse Dutch auctions may therefore be vulnerable to adverse selection, meaning that the average credit quality of *submitted* assets of a given type may be systematically worse than the average credit quality of *all* assets of that type. In addition, if assets submitted to an auction were on average worse than other assets of a given type, then auction prices might be biased downwards. Some empirical research has found that adverse selection problems can lower prices on eBay auctions.[12] If reverse auctions for troubled assets generated downwardly biased prices, that could affect valuations of assets held by other firms through mark-tomarket accounting requirements. Thus, a downward bias in auction prices due to adverse selection could affect the market value or even solvency of some firms, whether or not they participated in auctions.

Moreover, managing a portfolio bought via reverse Dutch auctions susceptible to adverse selection could present financial risks to the federal government. While adverse selection could push prices down (relative to prices appropriate for the average of *all* assets of a given category), the quality of assets accepted by the Treasury through the reverse auction mechanism could also be lower (relative to average quality of *all* assets of a given category). To the extent that Treasury overpays for assets relative to their quality due to adverse selection, costs to the taxpayer rise. Whether this effect presents a significant financial risk to the taxpayer is difficult to determine before the reverse Dutch auctions have been running for some time.

Auction mechanisms, however, might be designed that could mitigate these adverse selection problems.[13] Analysts close to government auction design discussions have outlined a design in which several similar securities could be listed for an auction.[14] Price offsets or "handicaps" could be applied relative to a benchmark security. For instance, an auction might encompass a specified set of MBSs, underwritten by the same investment bank in the same month. Bids offering a specific MBS issue with a higher average default rate on the underlying mortgages would be reduced by an offset calculated using a financial asset pricing model.

Other auction mechanisms might also mitigate these problems. For example, a firm could be required to let the government select an asset randomly from all of its holdings of a specific type of asset if its bid were successful. Or participating firms could be required to post a performance bond that could be used to compensate the government if a firm's assets sold in auctions turned out to be systematically worse than average.[15] Charles Plott, a pioneer in auction design, has designed and tested a reverse Dutch auction that was able to mitigate adverse selection concerns in another context.[16]

Adverse Selection and Firms' Asset Holdings

Uncertainty about the composition of firms' holdings could be an additional source of adverse selection in the administration of the Troubled Asset Relief Program. Some claim that financial institutions have avoided offering to sell large amounts of subprime and other troubled assets out of a concern for the institution's reputation. Other market participants might infer that a would-be seller has a large inventory of subprime and other troubled assets and thus may be a risky counterparty.[17] That inference could adversely affect a potential seller's stock price and its ability to raise capital, thus providing a reason for firms to hold troubled assets. In other words, some firms may worry that attempting to sell troubled assets may damage its reputation, market value, and ability to trade. However, many view the former investment bank Merrill Lynch's sale of troubled assets as a sound strategic move.[18]

Reputational Issues and Participation

If financial markets were to associate participation in the Troubled Asset Relief Program (TARP), including bidding in Treasury reverse auctions, with financial weakness, then firms might be less willing to participate. Reputational issues, in the view of many financial experts, have discouraged some firms from participating in certain federal government or Federal Reserve programs. For example, in recent years some have viewed firms using the Federal Reserve's discount window as "desperate."[19] The Federal Reserve Term Auction Facility (TAF), in the view of some, was designed to provide liquidity to firms while avoiding the stigma that some might perceive to be associated with the discount window.[20] U.S. Treasury, however, has stressed that TARP is "not targeted at failing firms," but instead is designed to attract broad participation among financial institutions.[21]

The effectiveness of the reverse auction asset purchase program could be reduced if reputational issues caused some firms to forego participation in TARP. Factors that reduce the number of active bidders in an auction can decrease expected revenues and can dampen competition among bidders. The choice of how auction results are released and how much detail is disclosed may affect firms' willingness to submit bids. For example, if firms believe that market analysts can observe or infer from announced auction results that the firm holds large inventories of troubled assets, then that firm may become reluctant to participate in the auction. Designing Treasury reverse auctions for troubled assets and associated announcements of results to avoid any such possible reputational effects may enhance firms' willingness to participate.

Sequencing Issues

The order or sequencing in which reverse securities auctions take place may affect the results of auctions. First, the initial reverse auctions might be a learning process for both bidders and the U.S. Treasury. This might imply that smaller, simpler auctions should precede larger and more complex auctions. In the past, new auction designs have sometimes presented unanticipated operational problems or unforeseen strategic vulnerabilities. Careful design and testing of auction mechanisms, however, can minimize such problems. Second, if the Treasury interventions in financial markets do start to unfreeze credit markets as intended, then asset prices will change. Bidders' anticipation that asset prices will rise after the initial auctions (or because of other types of government intervention) could induce bidders to submit fewer assets in earlier auctions. Third, sequencing may raise operational issues because of the large number of asset types, and because of the intrinsic complexity of some mortgage-related securities.

Will Auctions Unlock Credit Markets?

The September 20, 2008, Treasury proposal suggested that reverse auctions would play a central role in restoring liquidity to credit markets. It argued that uctions could help stabilize asset and credit markets in two ways. First, firms with illiquid assets would sell them at prices determined by a competitive process, which would supply firms with liquid proceeds of those sales. Second, auction results could provide pricing benchmarks that might stimulate trading in other assets. Some believe that this could improve liquidity conditions in credit markets; others, however, are skeptical.[22]

The reverse auction program essentially swaps Treasury securities for troubled mortgage-backed securities. If the prices at which Treasury securities are exchanged for troubled assets are close to current market prices for those assets, then financial institutions may gain liquidity, but might not receive much additional capital.

What prices the "troubled" mortgage-related assets will sell at is, therefore, a key question. Merrill Lynch, for example, sold a large stake of senior mortgagerelated collateralized default obligations (CDOs) to Lone Star Funds, a private capital fund, for about 22 cents on the dollar.[23] If other assets sold at Treasury reverse auctions at prices reflecting similar discounts, the solvency of some financial institutions might be put in doubt.

Some commentators, however, have suggested that Treasury might believe that such assets are underpriced in current conditions.[24] Assets might be underpriced, relative to fundamental factors, because of the rapid deleveraging of financial institutions, which increased the supply of assets and the demand for liquidity.[25] As the price of liquidity rises, measured as the cost of overnight interbank borrowing relative to comparable Treasury rates, highly leveraged financial institutions may come under additional pressure to sell assets. Thus, deleveraging and falling asset prices may create a self-reinforcing spiral. To the extent that buying assets via a reverse auction process might strengthen the link between assets and their underlying values, more normal market conditions might be restored. But others argue that the low prices of "troubled" assets reflect their intrinsic value, and that previous prices were above those justified by fundamentals.[26]

Federal Reserve Chairman Ben Bernanke spoke of "hold to maturity" valuations of assets, which would seem to imply that prices above current market levels might be paid.[27] While paying above-market prices for assets would inject capital into financial institutions, it would also increase the costs and risks to taxpayers. How auctions could be designed to ensure "hold to maturity" valuations of assets is unclear. One economist with knowledge of auction design discussions has said that reverse auctions would be designed in a hard-nosed manner to minimize taxpayer costs. But, if current asset prices accurately reflect fundamental value and if the Treasury reverse auctions are run efficiently, comparatively little capital would be injected into the financial sector. While this would minimize costs and risks to taxpayers, such an auction program might provide limited support for financial institutions.

Some economists have argued that other means of injecting capital into the financial sector, such as purchases of preferred stock or capital injections balanced by equity warrants (i.e., options to claim an equity stake), might be a better strategy.[28] On October 8, 2008, the U.S. Treasury emphasized that EESA gives it authority to directly inject capital into firms, and is developing strategies to do so.[29]

Asset purchases and direct capital injections may have different implications for affected firms. Proceeds of asset purchases would presumably be counted as trading profits, which firms can use without restriction. Capital injections, however, generally provide firms with financial resources that are subject to restrictions. For example, capital injections might provide the U.S. Treasury with the right to demand management changes or equity warrants. Treasury purchases of preferred equity shares would probably commit firms to make regular, specified payments back to the Treasury. Proceeds from asset purchases, however, might be available for dividends, executive compensation, reducing debt, or other purposes.

Costs and Risks to Taxpayers

Federal interventions to restore more normal conditions to financial markets would provide substantial benefits to those connected to the financial sector, either directly or indirectly. Of course, some may receive greater benefits than others from a resuscitation of the financial sector. A large-scale federal intervention could impose substantial costs and risks on taxpayers and federal program beneficiaries, although the scale and nature of those costs and risks may depend on how interventions are structured and administered.

If Treasury reverse auctions were conducted in a hard-nosed and efficient manner, direct costs to taxpayers and beneficiaries could be minimized. Furthermore, the federal government might well eventually sell assets for more than their purchase price. Such auctions, however, might supply little extra capital to the financial sector, and thus may fail to achieve a normalization of market conditions. Other measures, such as debt/equity swaps, purchases of preferred stock, or trading stock warrants for capital injections, might present the taxpayer with greater financial risks, but might also be better suited to addressing current financial conditions.

AUCTION DESIGN

Auctions in recent years have been used to address a wide range of policy issues. Auctions may capture higher revenues for governments and can allocate scarce resources more efficiently than traditional methods. Different policy issues, however, may require different types of auctions to achieve reasonable results. To provide a basis for evaluating the reverse auction mechanisms that may be used in TARP, this section discusses potential problems that may arise in using auctions, and how those problems can be minimized by careful design of auction mechanisms.

Single-Unit Auctions

The most common auction mechanisms used to sell single items are the firstprice sealed-bid auction, the English or ascending-price open-bid auction, and the Dutch or descending-price auction. In the first-price sealed-bid auction, bidders submit bids to the seller, who then selects the highest bid when selling an item or the lowest bid when buying an item. In the English or ascending-price auction, bidders announce prices that must exceed previous prices by a set amount. The last bidder to remain receives the object at her last announced price. In flower markets in Amsterdam and other trading centers in the Netherlands, bidders watch a price clock that starts at a high price and descends at a constant rate. The first bidder to press a button buys the lot of flowers at the price indicated on the price clock.[30] Similar descending-price mechanisms are called Dutch auctions.[31]

Why are Treasury Auctions Called Dutch Auctions?

Treasury auctions for government securities, which use sealed-bid rules, are often described as "Dutch" auctions even though they do not use a descending-price mechanism as in flower auctions. Treasury securities auctions, however, are strategically equivalent to a particular descending-price (Dutch) auction. An auction mechanism is strategically equivalent to another auction mechanism when bidders' incentives, the identity of the winner, and the final sale price are the same for both. Some auction rules, however, may be operationally easier to carry out. For example, bidders can mail in responses for a sealed-bid auction, while English auctions require bidders (or their agents) to gather in the same place.

A descending-price (Dutch) auction, under certain conditions, is strategically equivalent to a sealed-bid, first-price auction. A rational bidder calculates what the item for sale is worth to her.[32] If a bidder bid her value, however, she would make zero gain in a first-price auction because the price paid would exactly match the item's value to her. A rational bidder therefore shades her bid downwards, trading off a larger gain (value minus price paid if she wins the auction) against the possibility that she would lose the item by lowering her bid.[33] The same calculation applies to both the sealed-bid, first-price auction and to the descending-price auction, so the two auctions may be considered strategically equivalent. An English (ascending-bid) is strategically equivalent to a second-price sealed-bid auction when bidders know what the object up for auction is worth to them.[34]

Imperfect Information: Common Values and the Winner's Curse

When bidders have imperfect information about the value of an item, an English or ascending-bid auction may force better-informed bidders to reveal valuable information to less well informed bidders.[35] For example, the value of an antique may depend on who made it, how rare it is, and on who owned it before. A knowledgeable bidder, who may know more about an item's value, will attempt to use bidding strategies that conceal private information.

The value to bidders of some auctioned items may be linked. For example, the value one energy company places on an Offshore Continental Shelf (OCS) lease that would allow exploration and extraction of oil and gas will correlate to the value other energy companies place on the same lease. Different companies might have strengths and weaknesses in exploration and extraction techniques, so the value of the lease will not be the same to each company. Any company that got the lease, however, would sell oil and gas on the same world markets. Auctions that sell items whose value to bidders is correlated are called common-value auctions.

Bidders in a common-value auction may have different indications of an item's value. For example, many energy companies may have private information about the geological structures of areas covered by an OCS lease. A company holding an OCS lease in a nearby area that had run seismic tests might have more precise information about those geological structures, and thus would have a more precise estimate of the value of the OCS lease up for auction.

When bidders have imperfect signals of value, bidders with overly optimistic signals are likely to win auctions. Such bidders, however, will suffer losses because the true value of the item is less than their optimistic estimate. This is the winner's curse: such auction winners would have been better off losing. Sophisticated bidders in common-value auctions shade their bids downward to account for the winner's curse. Sophisticated auction designers release as much information as possible about an item's value so that revenues are not reduced by bidders who shade their bids downwards.[36] That is, bidders with better information bid more aggressively.

Revenue Equivalence

Certain auction mechanisms, as noted above, are functionally equivalent to certain other auctions run using different rules. The auctions discussed above (Dutch, English, first-price and second-price sealed bid) in theory deliver the same profits to bidders and the same revenues to sellers. Moreover, any (independent private value) auction that awards the item to the highest bidders and attracts the same pool of participants also in theory provides the same profits to bidders and the same revenues to sellers.[37] This result, known as the Revenue Equivalence Theorem, implies that to affect expected revenues requires changing who participates in an auction. For example, minimum bid rules can raise expected revenue, but may lower an auction's economic efficiency. Experimental research has found that some expected auction equivalences hold, while others do not.[38] Experimental testing of revenue equivalence of auction mechanisms is an active research area.

Multiple-Unit Auctions

Auctions in which multiple units are sold simultaneously are more complex than single-unit auctions. Computing optimal bidding strategies in multiple-unit auctions may be complex and difficult. Designing multiple-unit auctions so that government revenue is maximized and so that scarce resources are likely to be assigned to those who value them the most can be challenging. The federal government, however, has successfully used complex multi-unit auctions to allocate electromagnetic spectrum for wireless communication and related uses.

Manipulation and Demand-Reduction Strategies

Bidders in some situations can benefit by strategically withdrawing bids on some items in order to lower prices on other items.[39] The logic of this strategy is analogous to standard monopoly or oligopoly pricing models. A monopolist or a firm with some market power can raise profits by reducing output below the level that would prevail in a competitive market. Just as entry by new competitors can reduce the market power of existing firms, auction designs that encourage many bidders to participate can limit the effect of demand-reduction strategies.

Complementarities

Auctions that sell complementary goods can be extraordinarily complex.[40] Items are considered complements when groups of items are more valuable than the sum of individual items. For example, take-off rights from a specific airport that a government might auction off will be more valuable if the airline can obtain landing rights at a different airport. Federal Communications Commission auctions of electromagnetic spectrum involve complementarities because a license in one geographic area may be more valuable to a telecommunications firm that holds a license in an adjacent area.

Complementarities among troubled assets may complicate current reverse auctions implemented as part of TARP. For instance, some assets backed by subprime loans were often linked to collateralized default obligations(CDOs), which provided something akin to insurance to investors holding those assets. In that case, the asset backed by a pool of sub-prime loans and the associated CDO would share a strong complementarity, which could affect behavior in a reverse auction.

Dutch Auctions with Multiple Units

The U.S. Treasury, as noted above, uses a multi-unit Dutch auction mechanism to sell government securities to primary dealers. The federal government and some corporations have used reverse Dutch auctions for some procurements. Treasury auction mechanisms can, under certain circumstances, be vulnerable to manipulations related to the demand-reduction strategies discussed above.[41] The U.S. Treasury and many entities that use auctions, however, have developed methods designed to detect or mitigate manipulation strategies.

Uniform-Price vs. Individual Price Auctions

In some multiple-unit auctions, such as Dutch auctions, all successful bidders pay the same price. Such auctions are called uniform-price auctions. In other auctions, such as first-price auctions, in which successful bidders pay their bids, different bidders pay different prices for identical items. Such auctions are often called discriminatory or multipleprice auctions. A 2002 International Monetary Fund report found that 10 of 18 advanced industrial countries surveyed used uniform-price auctions, and 15 of 18 used multiple-price auctions.[42] The U.S. Treasury claims that a uniform-price auction raises slightly more revenue than a multiple-price auction because it reduces winner's curse risks.[43]

End Notes

[1] MBSs are debt obligations representing claims to the cash flows (principal and interest) from pools of mortgages primarily on residential property. The main use of MBSs is to transform relatively illiquid financial assets (mortgages owned by mortgage originators) into liquid and tradable capital market instruments. Given the problems with the housing market and subprime mortgages, it is difficult to know the true value of MBSs. Consequently, MBSs have become illiquid.

[2] Dutch auctions usually refer to falling-price auctions, which are described in more detail below. The reverse multi-unit sealed-bid auction outlined by the Treasury is strategically equivalent to a certain falling-price multi-unit auction, which is why the former is usually called a Dutch auction.

[3] Paul Klemperer, "Using and Abusing Economic Theory — Lessons from Auction Design," *Journal of the European Economic Association*, 2003, available at [http://www.paulklemperer.org/]. In some situations, auction designers may face a tradeoff between maximizing expected seller revenue and maximizing the likelihood that resources are allocated to those who value them the most.

[4] Robert E. Wright, *One Nation Under Debt: Hamilton, Jefferson, and the History of What We Owe*, (New York: McGraw-Hill, 2008), p. 61.

[5] Various federal agencies have used different auction mechanisms for many years. The Department of Interior has run auctions to distribute Outer Continental Shelf (OCS) oil and gas leases since 1954. Since 1994, the Federal Communications Commission has used complex auction mechanisms to license slices of electromagnetic spectrum for use in wireless communications.

[6] Discussion with government official, Sept. 26, 2008.

[7] The U.S. Treasury has run multiple-price (in which buyers pay their bids) and uniformprice auctions in the past. In particular, multiple-price auctions may be more susceptible to the winners' curse, which may cause bidders to shade their bids downwards. The winners' curse and other issues relating to differences between multiple-price and uniform-price auctions are discussed below.

[8] U.S. Securities and Exchange Commission, *Summary Report of Issues Identified in the Commission Staff's Examinations of Select Credit Rating Agencies*, July 2008.

[9] Most Treasury issues are generally sized in the tens of billions of dollars range, although cash management and other concerns may lead to smaller issues (U.S. Department of Treasury, *Treasury Bulletin*, various issues). Structured product issues (i.e., asset- or mortgage-backed securities, or collateralized default obligations (CDOs)) are generally sized in the hundreds of millions of dollars range, and are often divided into a half dozen or so tranches. Tranche comes from the French verb *tranchez* meaning to slice or to carve.

[10] The Bond Market Association and American Securitization Forum note that "(e)ach product sector is distinct based on issuers, investors, origination, servicing and collateral management, trading and pricing systems, and type and volume of available information. These differences lead to distinct pricing and valuation conventions, liquidity levels and risk exposures and sensitivities." *An Analysis and Description of Pricing and Information Sources in the Securitized and Structured Finance Markets*, Oct. 2006, p. 1, available at [http://www.miacanalytics.com/fs/AboutMIAC/PR/Pricing-Informaton_Sources_Study_ 1006.pdf].

[11] Manipulation in auctions is discussed below.

[12] Sanjeev Dewan and Vernon Hsu, "Adverse Selection in Electronic Markets: Evidence from Online Stamp Auctions," *Journal of Industrial Economics*, vol. 52, no. 4, pp. 497-516, Dec. 2004.

[13] Justin Lahart, "Economists Look at Ways to Structure Auctions," *Wall Street Journal*, Sept. 25, 2008.

[14] Discussion with government official, Sept. 26, 2008.

[15] Matthew O. Jackson and Hugo F. Sonnenschein, "Overcoming Incentive Constraints by Linking Decisions," *Econometrica*, vol. 75, no. 1, Jan. 2007, pp. 241-257.

[16] Charles Plott and P.J. Brewer, "A Decentralized, Smart Market Solution to a Class of Back-Haul Transportation Problems: Concept and Experimental Test Beds," *Interfaces,* vol. 32, no. 5, pp. 13-36, 2002.

[17] Jonathan Carmel, "Pitfalls of the Paulson Plan," *Economists' Voice*, vol. 5, no. 5, Oct. 2, 2008, available at [http://www.bepress.com/ev/vol5/iss5/art14].

[18] Merrill Lynch, "Merrill Lynch Announces Substantial Sale of U.S. ABS CDOs, Exposure Reduction of $11.1 Billion," Press release, July 28, 2008, available at [http://www.ml.com/index.asp?id =7695_7696_8149_88278_101366_103431].

[19] Allan Sloan, "The Fed's Thaw," *Washington Post*, Dec. 25, 2007, p. D1.

[20] The Term Auction Facility was created in December 2007. For details, see the Federal Reserve Bank's TAF webpage, available at [http://www.federalreserve.gov/monetarypolicy/ taf.htm].

[21] Neel Kashkari, Assistant Treasury Secretary for International Economics and Development, "SIFMA Conference Call," Sept. 28, 2008, available at [http://www.youtube.com/watch?v=uXmFADm61Rc]. On Oct. 6, 2008, Mr. Kashkari was named Interim Assistant Secretary of the Treasury for Financial Stability and will oversee TARP. U.S. Treasury, Press release hp-1184, Oct. 6, 2008, "Kashkari Appointed Interim Assistant Secretary for Financial Stability, available at [http://www.treas.gov/press/releases/hp1184.htm].

[22] Paul Krugman claims that Treasury Secretary Paulson has "never been able to explain clearly why buying up bad mortgage assets at market prices will solve the credit crunch." "Bailout Narratives," *New York Times* blog, Oct. 1, 2008, available at [http://krugman.blogs.nytimes.com/].

[23] Merrill Lynch, "Merrill Lynch Announces Substantial Sale of U.S. ABS CDOs, Exposure Reduction of $11.1 Billion," Press release, July 28, 2008, available at [http://www.ml.com/index.asp?id=7695_7696_8149_88278_101366_103431].

[24] Paul Krugman, "A $700 Billion Slap in the Face," *New York Times* blog, September 24, 2008, available at [http://krugman.blogs.nyt imes.com/2008/09/24/a-700-billion-slap-in-the-face/].

[25] Leverage is the value of a firm's assets relative to its debts. Deleveraging typically means selling assets or restructuring positions to reduce debt levels.

[26] Nikki Kahn "Away from Wall Street, Economists Question Basis of Paulson's Plan," *Washington Post*, Sept. 26, 2008.

[27] Testimony of Federal Reserve Chairman Ben Bernanke, in U.S. Congress, Senate Committee on Banking, Housing, and Urban Affairs, *Turmoil in U.S. Credit Markets: Recent Actions Regarding Government Sponsored Entities, Investment Banks and Other Financial Institutions*, 110th Congress, 2nd sess., Sept. 23, 2008.

[28] Nikki Kahn "Away from Wall Street, Economists Question Basis of Paulson's Plan," *Washington Post*, Sept. 26, 2008; Paul Krugman, "A $700 Billion Slap in the Face," *New York Times* blog, September 24, 2008.

[29] Secretary Paulson, in an Oct. 8, 2008, press statement, mentioned capital injections before he mentioned asset purchases. Henry Paulson, Secretary of the U.S. Treasury, Press release hp1189, Oct. 8, 2008; Edmund L. Andrews and Mark Landler, "U.S. May Take Ownership Stake in Banks," *New York Times*, Oct. 8, 2008, p. A1.

[30] For details, see [http://www.flora.nl/en/AboutFloraHolland/Auctioning/Pages/ default.aspx].

[31] Falling-price auctions were invented to avoid Napoleonic-era taxes on rising-price auctions.

[32] "Rational" here only means that a bidder has internally consistent preferences and is selfinterested, so that the bidder can compute bids that best achieve her ends.

[33] Bidders here are assumed to keep the object and cannot resell it. In technical terms, values are private and independent. When values are linked or common, results can differ.

[34] When the value of objects are linked, such as when an auctioned object will be resold, some of these equivalences may not hold. For example, in an English auction among wholesalers, bidders may learn about an object's resale value in retail markets through the bids of others. In that case, the equivalence of an English auction to a second-price sealedbid auction would not hold.

[35] For example, in eBay auctions, informed bidders often use "sniping" strategies, in which bids are submitted seconds before the auction closes. This prevents less informed bidders from gleaning information from the bidding behavior of an informed bidder. For details, see [http://www.esnipe.com].

[36] John H. Kagel and Dan Levin, *Common Value Auctions and the Winner's Curse*, (Princeton, 2002).

[37] This result assumes that bidders are risk-neutral when values are uncertain. Auction revenues will not in general be equivalent when bidders are risk-averse. Elmar Wolfstetter, *Topics in Microeconomics: Industrial Organization, Auctions, and Incentives*, (Cambridge, 1999), pp. 186-188; For a more detailed discussion, see Paul Milgrom, *Putting Auction Theory to Work*, (Cambridge, 2004), ch. 3.

[38] David Lucking-Reiley, "Using Field Experiments to Test Equivalence Between Auction Formats: Magic on the Internet," *American Economic Review*, vol. 89, no. 5, pp. 1063-1080.

[39] Lawrence M. Ausubel and Peter Cramton, "Demand Reduction and Inefficiency in Multi-Unit Auctions," Univ. of Maryland working paper, July 27, 2002, available at [http://www.cramton.umd.edu/papers1995-1999/98wp-demand-reduction.pdf].

[40] Paul Milgrom, *Putting Auction Theory to Work*, (Cambridge, 2004), ch. 5.

[41] Yongdong Shi and Xianfeng Jiang, "Manipulation in the Treasury Auction Market," working paper, July 26, 2004, available at [http://ssrn.com/abstract=575441].

[42] International Monetary Fund, "Guidelines for Public Debt Management," Aug. 4, 2003, Table 1.2, available at [http://www.imf.org/external/pubs/ft/pdm/eng/guide/080403.htm].

[43] Paul F. Malvey and Christine M. Archibald, *Uniform-Price Auctions: Update of the Treasury Experience*, U.S. Treasury Study, Oct. 1998.

In: Government Interventions in Economic Emergencies ISBN: 978-1-60741-356-1
Editor: Pablo Sastre

Chapter 2

BANKING AND SECURITIES REGULATION AND AGENCY ENFORCEMENT AUTHORITIES

William D. Jackson, Mark Jickling, Gary Shorter, M. Maureen Murphy and Michael V. Seitzinger

SUMMARY

The federal bank regulatory agencies — the Office of the Comptroller of the Currency, the Federal Deposit Insurance Corporation, the Board of Governors of the Federal Reserve System, and the Office of Thrift Supervision — have extensive authority to enforce various legal and regulatory standards with respect to the banking institutions that they supervise. Similarly, the Securities and Exchange Commission (SEC) has a wide range of tools to enforce the securities laws. This chapter provides a brief sketch of these authorities and identifies the organizational entities within each agency that Congress assigns enforcement responsibilities. It includes a table comparing the formal enforcement tools that the banking agencies may use with those of the SEC.

BACKGROUND

In the United States, following several decades of divergence, the businesses of commercial banking and securities activities have converged.[1] Yet the regulatory framework for them, crafted largely in the 1930s, remains mainly under different statutory roofs.[2] This chapter summarizes the enforcement and compliance programs of federal banking regulators and those of the Securities and Exchange Commission (SEC). It begins by discussing the key objectives of banking and securities regulation, which shed light on why enforcement programs differ. There follow brief overviews of the statutory basis for enforcement, the major enforcement tools, and, finally, how regulators organize enforcement programs.

This chapter focuses on the primary goals of bank and securities regulation respectively. Banks are to be run in a safe manner, seeking to avoid risk and thus losses. Their regulation is largely in the background, "opaque." Although banking operations are subject to penetrating examinations by federal regulators, agencies do not make most of the details public. The SEC, on the other hand, requires securities firms and securities issuers to disclose various details of their operations, including all material information that may generate losses as well as expected profits. In contrast to bank regulation, therefore, SEC regulation of securities businesses may be labeled "transparent," that is, although sources of volatility are acceptable in the industry, they must be adequately and accurately revealed or disclosed.

In both sectors, other goals are promoted by industry standards or self-policing and by government regulation. Among these are the following: business continuity planning in case of natural and unnatural (terrorist) disasters that could weaken operations;[3] preventing use of financial institutions as conduits for money laundering or terrorist financing;[4] providing consumer protection against fraud and misconduct; safeguarding data security and the privacy of customer information; and supervising technological service providers. Banking and securities regulators and institutions have long cooperated, both nationally and internationally, informally and formally, and share cooperative arrangements of many kinds, often extending beyond U.S. borders.[5]

An Overview of Banking and Securities Regulation

Banking

Banking is one of the most heavily regulated businesses in the United States.[6] The reasons for this lie in the economics of banking. A typical bank balance sheet features long-term assets (loans and investments) and short-term liabilities (deposits). This means that banks face liquidity problems if depositors suddenly choose to withdraw their funds. Furthermore, a run on a single bank can become an industrywide problem, if cautious depositors at otherwise healthy banks — understanding that only some withdrawal claims can be satisfied — decide to get in line early. Banks are monitored closely through regulatory systems that require governmental chartering; periodic reporting on virtually every aspect of their business; systematic examination and supervision; independent auditing; and annual reports to shareholders, depositors and the public.[7] Under the dual banking system, banks may be chartered by a state government or by the federal government.

Although the chartering authority — state or federal — prescribes the requirements that a banking institution must meet with respect to the basic aspects of its business, an array of federal laws and regulations provide for close federal supervision of nearly all depository institutions in the United States. A major component of federal regulation of banking is the deposit insurance system. To discourage runs on banks and reduce the risk of contagion, Congress began federal deposit insurance during the Great Depression, following collapses of statesponsored deposit guaranty schemes.[8] Because under the deposit insurance program, the federal government assumes part of the financial risk of bank failure, federal law requires that banking regulators have access to confidential business data and gives them broad powers to assure that the managers of insured depository institutions operate them in a safe manner.

Nearly every aspect of the operation and management of an insured institution is subject to close regulatory supervision. In an economic sense, bankers and regulators are business partners: a bank that becomes insolvent is not just a business failure; it also represents a failure of regulation. As vigilant as the regulators may be, bad business decisions are inevitable, as are downturns in the economy that may result in negative effects flowing from risks that are otherwise acceptable. In other words, depositories cannot completely avoid risks. With federal insurance of deposits, however, comes a safety net that lessens the impact of bank failure on depositors and, consequently, on the entire monetary economy.

Congress divides federal regulatory authority over banking institutions among five regulators. The Federal Deposit Insurance Corporation (FDIC), besides administering the federally guaranteed insurance fund that covers any insured deposit losses, regulates state-chartered banks (and savings associations), except those belonging to the Federal Reserve System (FRS). The Board of Governors of the FRS (Fed) regulates such "member banks." The Office of the Comptroller of the Currency (OCC) regulates federally-chartered "national banks." The Office of Thrift Supervision (OTS) regulates federally-chartered and state-chartered savings associations. Besides federal regulation, all state-chartered banking institutions are subject to state banking laws and to supervision by state supervisory agencies.[9] Federal regulators also have authority to monitor safety and soundness in various related organizations, known as bank "affiliates," [10] which may be bank subsidiaries, bank service companies, or other entities related to the bank through corporate family structures known as "holding companies." Regulation of holding companies and their subsidiaries depends on what kind of firm is at their core. The Fed regulates bank-based holding companies; OTS regulates savings institution-based complexes; and the SEC, securities-based "investment bank holding companies."[11]

Securities

The federal securities laws require companies that sell securities to the public to register with the SEC. In contrast to bank regulation, however, the act of registration with the SEC does not mean that the government has deemed a corporation's securities to be a safe investment. Registration documents, known as "prospectuses," state in bold type at their beginning that these securities have not been approved or disapproved by the SEC, and any representation to the contrary is a criminal event. The prospectus for even a high-quality stock or bond issue sets forth a long list of risk factors, some of which are unlikely to occur, while others such as weather, labor cost, and raw material conditions are intuitively obvious. In fact, the standard prospectus for a high-yield (junk) bond offering usually includes statements to the effect that it is highly unlikely that the issuing corporation will be able to pay interest on the bonds, let alone repay the principal. Under federal securities law, such an offer is entirely legal if all material information is fully and accurately disclosed to the public. All parties concerned expect the value (price) of traded securities to fluctuate, unlike bank deposits of fixed value.

In other words, there is no securities law term equivalent to safety and soundness, the central notion of banking regulation. No one sees failure of a publicly-traded corporation or the decline of its share price as a SEC failure if the firm has disclosed all material risks fully and accurately. The SEC seeks to protect investors from fraud, not risk. Banking regulation transfers the risk of bank failure, including any failure resulting from fraud, from the customer to the government.

The SEC also regulates and requires registration of broker/dealers, investment advisers, mutual fund operators, and other members of the securities industry. Although the SEC exercises regulatory authority over the securities industry, its authority is somewhat limited. An illustrative comparison is between the capital requirements imposed upon banks and the SEC's net capital rule, which requires brokerage firms to maintain a minimum level of capital above mere solvency. Lawmakers intend bank capital requirements to permit institutions to weather unexpected losses or unfavorable market developments. The net capital rule, on the other hand, is a liquidation rule — it seeks to ensure that failing brokerages are shut down while they have money left to meet customer claims. Even in such cases, the brokerage industry's self-funded protection arrangement — the Securities Investor Protection Corporation — may have to cover many account shortfalls.[12]

As in banking, state securities supervisors retain certain oversight power over securities businesses.[13] Unlike the banking agencies, which supervise without intermediary organizations, the SEC has delegated significant authority to privatesector bodies. For corporation accounting, it has granted the Financial Accounting Standards Board and Public Company Accounting Oversight Board major decisionmaking capabilities. For securities firms, it has allowed many oversight responsibilities to be carried on by the National Association of Securities Dealers (NASD), a "self regulatory organization" (SRO). The stock exchanges are also SROs and thus exercise certain regulatory authority over their membership and over the corporations whose shares they list. The SEC, however, may veto rulings of these nongovernmental bodies, may require them to modify their rules (or adopt new ones), and exercise further oversight over them.

MAJOR ENFORCEMENT-RELATED STATUTES

Banking

Although Congress has scattered provisions delegating various enforcement authorities to federal banking agencies under specified circumstances throughout U.S. laws, a full range of the civil enforcement powers of the federal banking agencies is set out in section eight of the Federal Deposit Insurance Act.[14] Banking violations are also punishable under federal criminal laws, and banking regulators often refer suspected violations to the Department of Justice for possible prosecution. Many prosecutions involving banks or banking officials are based on charges under general criminal statutes, such as the federal laws against mail fraud, wire fraud, racketeering, false statements, and money laundering. In addition, many federal criminal laws apply more narrowly to banking. These include:

18 U.S.C. § 215	bank bribery
18 U.S.C. § 656	theft or embezzlement of bank funds
18 U.S.C. § 709	false advertising or misuse of federal terms such as "federal deposit insurance"
18 U.S.C. § 1005	false entries by bank employees or false statements to regulators
18 U.S.C. § 1014	false statements on a loan or credit application
18 U.S.C. § 1029	access device fraud

18 U.S.C. § 1344	bank fraud
18 U.S.C. § 2113	bank robbery.

Because both banking and securities companies operate as intermediaries in financial transactions, law requires them to make anti-money laundering and antiterrorist financing procedures to monitor and report on certain types of currency and foreign transactions under various federal laws and under regulations issued by the Department of the Treasury's Financial Crimes Enforcement Network.[15] They also must report suspicious transactions.[16] Violation of these requirements is subject to potential criminal and civil penalties.[17] In addition, Congress requires them to institute procedures to comply with the various economic sanction programs administered by Treasury's Office of Foreign Assets Control (OFAC) and subjects them to potential civil and criminal penalties for failure to comply with the requirements that include blocking assets of designated entities and persons and notifying OFAC of that.[18] Of course, banks and banking officials may be prosecuted under criminal laws of general applicability, such as those covering bribery of public or foreign officials and tax fraud and evasion.

Securities

The securities laws give the SEC a range of administrative sanctions that it can apply to violators. Like the banking regulators, the SEC cannot bring criminal charges itself but makes recommendations for prosecutions to the Justice Department. The principal securities statutes are four, as follows.

The Securities Act of 1933,[19] called a "truth-in-securities" law, requires that securities be registered with the SEC before a sponsor/issuer sells them to the public. Registration requires disclosure of detailed information about the issuing corporation's business, management, and financial condition. Failure to make complete and accurate disclosures creates liability for civil and criminal penalties.

The Securities Exchange Act of 1934[20] created the SEC and gave it broad authority to adopt rules and regulations to maintain fair and orderly securities markets. This act requires ongoing disclosure and gives the SEC control over the form and content of corporate financial statements (quarterly and annual reports, etc.). The act also applies to exchanges where securities are bought and sold — stock, bond, and stock option markets must submit their rules for SEC approval. Brokers, the firms that employ them, and other industry professionals must register; revocation of registration may prevent them from working in the securities industry. The Exchange Act also governs communications between firms and their shareholders as well as certain merger transactions.

The Investment Company Act[21] provides for regulation of defined investment companies such as mutual funds. As securities, mutual funds must be registered before public sale, a process that requires public disclosures regarding the fund and its managers. The law also places certain limits on the type of investments that funds are permitted to make and on various other business practices.

The Investment Advisers Act of 1940[22] applies to persons engaging in the business of advising others, either directly or through publications, as to the advisability of the purchase or sale of securities. Advisers whose assets under management exceed specified thresholds must register with the SEC. In 2004, the SEC required hedge funds to register as advisers.[23]

Organization of Enforcement Programs

Banking

Congress has vested enforcement of federal banking laws generally in an institution's primary federal regulator. Each of the federal banking agencies issues regulations applicable to the entities under its authority. Typically, these are coordinated through the Federal Financial Institutions Examination Council (FFIEC).[24] It is an interagency body composed of the heads of the federal banking agencies, which is charged with making "uniform principles and standards and report forms for examination of financial institutions,"[25] encouraging "application of uniform examination principles and standards by State and Federal supervisory agencies,"[26] and reviewing all federal banking regulations at least once every 10 years "to identify outdated or otherwise unnecessary regulatory requirements."[27]

Federal banking regulators have both considerable enforcement options and wide discretion in choosing among them. Besides the formal enforcement tools specifically authorized by statute, each of the federal banking agencies employs informal methods of insuring that regulated institutions meet safety and soundness standards as well as regulatory and statutory standards. These range from moral suasion to written requirements that corrective action be taken. Much of the information upon which informal enforcement actions are based derives from periodic bank examinations. Each banking agency has its own examination force that detects violations during recurring safety and special-purpose examinations of bank books and operations. Upon completion of a bank examination, the regulator will present a Report of Examination to the institution's board of directors, which is to order remedial action or present information refuting the findings. Other forms of informal enforcement tools to correct perceived weaknesses in an institution include supervisory directives, board-of-director resolutions drafted by the regulator, and written instructions or agreements from the regulator.[28]

Institutions usually make correction and remediation voluntarily following the examination process and consider such self-correction a normal part of their business because of the multiplicity and complexity of banking laws and regulations. If this informal process of enforcement is unavailing, the banking agencies resort to the formal mechanisms available to them. They, thus, typically issue progressively stricter enforcement decrees against more serious weaknesses: memoranda of understanding, civil money penalties, cease-and-desist orders, and orders requiring the removal of officials. Should errant practices continue, an institution may be closed either by charter revocation or termination of its deposit insurance.

Enforcement units within each agency are as follows.

1. OCC, the primary regulator of nationally chartered banks, which is organizationally placed within the U.S. Department of the Treasury, assigns bank supervision and enforcement operations to the Office of the Chief National Bank Examiner, within

which there are "Large Bank Supervision" and "Midsize/Community Bank Supervision" units and four district offices.

2. Fed, the primary regulator of state-chartered member banks and bank holding companies including financial holding companies, conducts supervisory and enforcement activities through its Division of Banking Supervision and Regulation and delegates to 12 regional Federal Reserve Banks certain supervisory and enforcement powers.
3. FDIC, the primary federal regulator of state-chartered banks not belonging to the Fed, allocates enforcement to its Division of Supervision and Consumer Protection, which has Risk Management, Policy and Examination Oversight, and Compliance and Consumer Protection units within eight regional offices.
4. OTS, the primary federal regulator of savings or thrift institutions, and their savings and loan holding companies, organizationally within the U.S. Department of the Treasury, allocates its supervisory and enforcement activity to its Office of Examinations, Supervision, and Consumer Protection, with certain line supervisory responsibilities delegated to four regional offices.
5. State-chartered banks are subject to regulation by state banking agencies. Each state has a banking agency and usually designates an administrative position, Chief Examiner, Deputy Commissioner, or Supervisory Examiner, to enforce banking laws applicable to state banks.[29] They usually make examinations on alternating cycles under general cooperative agreements with federal banking agencies, often negotiating them through the FFIEC.[30]

Securities

Two units within the SEC have enforcement responsibilities: the Division of Enforcement and the Office of Compliance, Inspections, and Examinations. They may operate via 11 regional SEC offices.

The Division of Enforcement conducts investigations into possible violations of federal securities laws and oversees civil suits and administrative proceedings.[31] The division conducts two levels of investigations:

Informal investigations, which rely primarily on the voluntary cooperation of witnesses and/or the target of the investigation,[32] and

Formal investigations, in which it uses subpoenas to compel testimony or the production of documents. To obtain subpoena authority, the division submits a memorandum to the commissioners (via the General Counsel). The memorandum is a justification for the proposed investigation and the need for subpoenas. A majority of commissioners, or the single commissioner then serving as the duty officer, may then authorize a formal order authorizing administrative action or filing in federal court.[33]

Normally, the agency conducts investigations on a nonpublic basis; the SEC generally refuses to comment on whether an investigation is in progress. It announces enforcement actions to the public, but not all investigations result in enforcement actions. Before bringing an action, division staff may send out a "Wells Call," suggesting intent to bring an action, giving the target the opportunity to respond in writing before bringing formal charges.[34] Disclosure requirements of the securities laws ensure that the recipient will likely have to publicize a Wells Call, since news that an action is forthcoming is normally considered material to investors.

The Office of Compliance, Inspections, and Examinations (OCIE) is responsible for examinations and inspections of registered entities — broker-dealers, investment companies, investment advisers, transfer agents, clearing agencies, and selfregulatory organizations. This office conducts inspections to attempt to assure compliance with the securities laws, to detect violations, and to apprise the SEC of developments in the regulated community. When OCIE detects deficiencies, it issues a "deficiency letter" which identifies problems that should be corrected, and the office will monitor the situation until it believes that compliance has occurred. If the office believes that violations are too serious for its process of correction, it will refer the violations to the Division of Enforcement.[35]

As in banking, each state continues to have its own set of securities laws, called blue sky laws; state agencies are responsible for enforcing these laws. SROs also have enforcement roles. For example, the National Association of Securities Dealers (NASD) oversees the registration of broker/dealers and their personnel and may bring a variety of sanctions against those who violate its rules and standards. The stock exchanges, as SROs, are required to conduct market surveillance and maintain and enforce rules to protect their public customers. SROs must submit proposed new rules to the SEC for approval.[36]

Comparison of Enforcement and Compliance Tools

Beyond the informal enforcement methods mentioned above, banking regulators have a wide array of statutorily authorized formal enforcement tools that range from civil administrative fines and orders to civil suits for damages and referrals to the Department of Justice for criminal prosecution. Among the laws delegating civil enforcement authorities is Section 8 of the Federal Deposit Insurance Act, which delegates to the federal banking regulators authority to issue cease and desist orders, prohibition and removal orders, civil money penalties, and orders canceling an institution's insured status.[37]

Likewise, the SEC has a wide range of enforcement tools. For example, it may use its discretion in investigating possible violations of the securities laws and in obtaining injunctions against practices that may constitute violations.[38] It has the authority to impose civil penalties for insider trading violations[39] and to impose civil penalties in administrative proceedings for violations of the laws.[40] The SEC may also, after notice and opportunity for hearing, begin cease-and-desist proceedings.[41]

A brief sketch of the formal enforcement tools available to federal banking regulators and to the SEC is set out in the following table.[42]

Enforcement Tools of Federal Bank Regulators and the SEC

Tools	Bank Regulators	SEC
Cease and desist order (C&D)	May be imposed on insured depository institution (IDI) or institution-affiliated parties (IAP) for (1) unsafe or unsound practice, or (2) violation of any law, rule, regulation, or any written agreement. C&D order may include affirmative order to correct conditions resulting from practices or violations, or limitations on the activities of an IDI or IAP.	May be imposed on any person who violates federal securities laws. Respondent may be ordered to disgorge ill-gotten funds.
Removal and prohibition	May be taken against any IAP who violates law, regulation, final C&D order, or written agreement; engages in unsafe or unsound practices or breach of fiduciary duty, where actual or probable financial loss occurs, or where dishonesty or mental culpability is involved; or if necessary to protect an institution or depositors. Additional grounds for removal or prohibition apply to officers and directors in violation of specific banking statutes, and to an IAP involved in criminal proceedings.	For registered entities (such as brokers, dealers, and investment advisers, the SEC may institute administrative proceedings to suspend or revoke registration, or to impose bars or suspension from employment in the securities industry. Section 305 of the Sarbanes-Oxley Act gives the SEC the authority to bar a person from serving as an officer or director of a publicly-traded company if that person committed a securities law violation and has demonstrated unfitness to serve.
Civil money penalties	Three tiers of money penalties exist: (1) for violation of law, regulation, final enforcement order, written condition or agreement, temporary C&D order, removal or suspension order, or violation of transaction reporting requirements; (2) violation of law, etc., unsafe or unsound practice, or breach of fiduciary duty that is part of a pattern of misconduct, causes more than a minimal loss, or results in pecuniary gain to the violator; (3) knowing violation of law, etc., engaging in unsafe or unsound practice, breach of fiduciary duty *and* knowingly or recklessly causing substantial loss or substantial pecuniary gain. Fines range from $5,000 per day (tier 1) to $1,000,000 per day (tier 3).	The SEC often seeks civil money penalties and disgorgement of illegal profits in civil suits. In certain cases, fines imposed on single firms and individuals have run into the hundreds of millions of dollars.
Injunctions and consent agreements	Bank regulators have authority to seek court injunctions, but in the vast majority of cases, pursue administrative remedies.	The SEC often files civil suits seeking injunctions to prohibit future violations. Many cases are settled out of court, with consent agreements, whereby the target of the investigation

Enforcement Tools of Federal Bank Regulators and the SEC (Continued)

Tools	Bank Regulators	SEC
		does not admit to wrongdoing but agrees not to commit violations in the future. Consent agreements are used in many major cases, and may involve the payment of fines and/or prohibition and suspension orders.
Termination of insurance	FDIC may terminate deposit insurance based on (1) unsafe or unsound practices by an IDI, its directors, or trustees, (2) unsafe or unsound conditions to continue operations, or (3) violation by IDI, directors, or trustees of any applicable law, regulation, etc., or written agreement between the IDI and the FDIC.	No insurance, thus no comparable authority.
Prompt corrective action and liquidation authority	As a bank becomes undercapitalized, significantly undercapitalized, or critically undercapitalized, regulators can take progressively more intrusive steps to monitor banks, restrict certain transactions, require significant changes in business operations, or replace management. Ultimately, regulators may appoint a receiver or conservator and close the institution.	No directly comparable authority. Registered broker/dealers must comply with a net capital rule, and cease operations if their capital falls below the specified level.

For Further Reading

Insurance Information Institute and The Financial Services Roundtable. *The Financial Services FactBook 2005* , at [http://www.financialservicesfacts.org/financial].

Spong, Kenneth. *Banking Regulation: Its Purposes, Implementation, and Effects*, at [http://www.kc.frb.org/BS&S/publicat/PDF/RegsBook2000.pdf].

U.S. Securities and Exchange Commission. "The Investor's Advocate: How the SEC Protects Investors and Maintains Market Integrity," at [http://www.sec.gov/about/whatwedo.shtml]

End Notes

[1] CRS Report RL30516, *Mergers and Consolidation Between Banking and Financial Services Firms: Trends and Prospects*, by William Jackson.

[2] CRS Report RL32672, *Financial Institutions and Markets: Major Federal Statutes,* by M. Maureen Murphy.

[3] CRS Report RL31873, *Homeland Security: Banking and Financial Infrastructure Continuity,* by William Jackson.

[4] CRS Report RL33020, *Terrorist Financing: U.S. Agency Efforts and Inter-Agency Coordination*, coordinated by Martin Weiss, especially section "Financial Regulators and Institutions."

[5] Institute of International Bankers, "Global Survey 2005, Regulatory and Market Developments," at [http://www.iib.org/GS2005.pdf].

[6] See Jonathan R. Macey and Geoffrey P. Miller, BANKING LAW AND REGULATION 73 (2d ed. 1997).

[7] See Patricia A. McCoy, BANKING LAW MANUAL § 12.03 [Matthew Bender, 2d ed.].

[8] CRS Report RS20724, *Federal Deposit and Share Insurance: Proposals for Change*, by William Jackson.

[9] Conference of State Bank Supervisors, "State Banking Department Links," at [http://www.csbs.org/links/state_links.asp].

[10] CRS Report RS21680, *Affiliates in Banking, Finance, and Commerce: Development and Regulatory Background*, by William Jackson.

[11] The most recent structural legislation governing financial holding companies is the Gramm-Leach-Bliley Act, 113 Stat. 1138, P.L. 106-102.

[12] CRS Report RS21741, *Securities Investor Protection Corporation*, by William Jackson and Gary Shorter.

[13] North American Securities Administrators Association, "About Nasaa," at [http://www.nasaa.org/About%5FNASAA].

[14] 12 U.S.C. § 1818.

[15] 31 C.F.R., Part 103.

[16] 31 C.F.R. § 103.19 (brokers and dealers); 31 C.F.R. § 103.18 (banks).

[17] See, e.g., 31 U.S.C. §§ 5321, 5322.

[18] See U.S. Department of the Treasury, Office of Foreign Assets Control, "Foreign Assets Control Program for the Financial Community," at [http://www.treas.gov/offices/enforcement/ofac/regulations/t11facbk.pdf].

[19] 15 U.S.C. §§ 77a *et seq.*

[20] 15 U.S.C. §§ 78a *et seq.*

[21] 15 U.S.C. §§ 80a *et seq.*

[22] 15 U.S.C. §§ 80b *et seq.*

[23] CRS Report 94-511, *Hedge Funds: Should They Be Regulated?*, by Mark Jickling.

[24] U.S. Federal Financial Institutions Examination Council, "About the FFIEC," at [http://www.ffiec.gov/about.htm].

[25] 12 U.S.C. § 3305.

[26] 12 U.S.C. § 3306.

[27] 12 U.S.C. § 3310.

[28] See Patricia A. McCoy, BANKING LAW MANUAL § 13.02 (2d ed.).

[29] 12 U.S.C. § 484 prohibits states from examining national banks except for compliance with state laws on unclaimed property and escheat.

[30] Under 12 U.S.C. § 1820(d)(6)(A)(iii), federal banking agencies are to coordinate examinations with state bank supervisors.

[31] See [http://www.sec.gov/divisions/enforce.shtml].

[32] A.A. Sommer, Jr. (ed.) 6 SECURITIES LAW TECHNIQUES § 87.03 (2005).

[33] Id. at § 87.04.

[34] Sommer, at § 88.10.

[35] See [http://www.sec.gov/about/offices/ocie.htm].

[36] See, e.g., 15 U.S.C. § 78s.

[37] 12 U.S.C. § 1818.

[38] See, e.g., 15 U.S.C. § 78u.

[39] See, e.g., 15 U.S.C. § 78u-1.

[40] See, e.g., 15 U.S.C. § 78u-2.

[41] See, e.g., 15 U.S.C. § 78u-3.

[42] The tabular description of the formal enforcement tools available to bank regulators in the first column of the table closely follows information found in a table compiled by the Government Accountability Office (GAO) letter to Chairman Baker of the Subcommittee on Capital Markets of the House Financial Services Committee. "Comparison of Financial Institution Regulators' Enforcement and Prompt Corrective Action Authorities," GAO-01-322R, Jan. 3, 2001, pp. 13-21.

In: Government Interventions in Economic Emergencies
Editor: Pablo Sastre
ISBN: 978-1-60741-356-1

Chapter 3

Bear Stearns: Crisis and "Rescue" for a Major Provider of Mortgage-Related Products

Gary Shorter

Summary

In March 2008, Bear Stearns, the nation's fifth largest investment banking firm, was battered by what its officials described as a sudden liquidity squeeze related to its large exposure to devalued mortgage-backed securities. On March 14, the Federal Reserve System announced that it would provide Bear Stearns with an unprecedented short-term loan. This was rendered essentially moot when, on March 16, a major commercial bank, JP Morgan Chase, agreed to buy Bear Stearns in an exchange of stock shares for about 1.5% of its share price of a year earlier, a price that translated to $2/share. To help facilitate the deal, the Federal Reserve agreed to provide special financing in connection with the transaction for up to $30 billion of Bear Stearns's less liquid assets.

During the weekend of March 22, in the wake of criticism from Bear shareholder and employees (employees own about one-third of the firm's outstanding stock) over the $2/share price, Bear Stearns and JP Morgan renegotiated the terms of the deal: JP Morgan will purchase 95 million newly issued shares of Bear's common stock at $10/share in a stock exchange. In response to the changed deal conditions, the Fed altered the terms of its financial involvement: it got JP Morgan to agree to absorb the first $1 billion in losses if the collateral provided by Bear for a loan proves to be worth less than Bear Stearn's original claims. Instead of its original agreement to absorb up $30 billion, the Fed will now be responsible for up to $29 billion.

The Fed's unprecedented role has generated a widespread debate on the implications of such an intervention. Some, including Senate Banking, Housing, and Urban Affairs Committee Chairman Chris Dodd, have argued that in order to avoid potential systemic financial risk, the involvement made sense. But others, including Senator Richard Shelby, ranking member of the Senate Banking Committee, have concerns that it tells the market that the Fed is willing to help a large and failing financial enterprise, setting a bad precedent in terms of corporate responsibility.

The Senate Banking Committee held a hearing on April 3, 2008, solely devoted to issues surrounding the acquisition of Bear Stearns.

INTRODUCTION

On March 14, 2008, Bear Stearns (Bear), the nation's fifth largest investment banking firm, was verging on bankruptcy from what its officials described as a sudden liquidity squeeze related to its large exposure to devalued mortgage-backed securities. On that day, it also received word that it was getting an unprecedented loan from the Federal Reserve System (Fed). The funding would take the form of a 28-day Fed loan to be channeled through the large commercial bank, J.P. Morgan Chase (JP Morgan). The decision was unprecedented: never before had the Fed committed to "bailing out" a financial entity that was not a commercial bank. The action was criticized by some Members of Congress, but gained support from Chairman Christopher Dodd of the Senate Banking Housing, and Urban Affairs Committee, which has Fed oversight.[1]

Bear's liquidity crisis and the resulting Fed intervention, largely viewed as an effort to stabilize the firm and to avert a wider financial panic, sent alarms throughout the stock markets over Bear's fragility and more broadly over the potential precariousness of other major financial institutions. The day of the announcement, Bear's stock lost almost half of its value, and the stocks of other major Wall Street firms also tumbled. These concerns then spilled over into the broader universe of stocks: the Dow Jones Industrial Average, a broad index of the overall stock market, lost nearly 200 points, slightly more than 1.5% of its value.

The Fed's actions were characterized as a short-term fix; at the same time, Bear executives were also seeking a buyer to purchase the highly-leveraged firm, which was also one of the nation's largest underwriters of now-troubled mortgage-backed securities. On March 16, two days after the announcement of the Fed intervention, JP Morgan agreed to buy it.

This chapter provides an overview of Bear Stearns, examines the Fed's "rescue plan," and JP Morgan's subsequent agreement to acquire the firm.

BACKGROUND ON BEAR STEARNS

With about 14,000 employees worldwide, 85-year-old Bear is a diversified financial services holding company whose core business lines include institutional equities, fixed income, investment banking, global clearing services, asset management, and private client services.

As is also the case for its Wall Street and commercial banking peers, as housing prices took off and the mortgage industry surged earlier in this decade, Bear became actively involved in aspects of this market. It was a vertically integrated involvement that ranged from the purchase and operation of residential mortgage originators to packaging and underwriting vast pools of mortgages into "structured" securities products broadly known as mortgage-backed securities (MBS). Such products would in turn be sold to institutional investors, such as hedge and pension funds, while some were retained by the bank itself.

With the collapse of the housing market, Bear began facing very dramatic financial travails in June 2007: the firm announced that two of its hedge funds that were significantly invested in subprime mortgages were in trouble. In an attempt to keep them afloat, Bear poured $1.6 billion into the funds. Nonetheless, soon afterwards, the funds lost all of their value and were allowed to wind down. By various accounts, the funds' meltdown signaled the start of a collapse in the vital element of trust that must exist between a firm like Bear and its many customers. In October 2007, Bear agreed to a needed $1 billion capital investment from China's government-controlled Citic Securities. Later, in the fourth fiscal quarter of 2007, having written down more than $2 billion in devalued mortgage securities,[2] the company reported its first-ever quarterly loss, an unexpectedly high deficit of $859 million.

At the heart of Bear's problems have been MBS, which Bear and other Wall Street firms such as Merrill Lynch were actively engaged in packaging, underwriting, trading, and investing in for themselves. What follows is a brief primer on MBS.

Mortgage-Backed Securities

In an overview of the general credit market doldrums that are a product of problems that originated in the housing and mortgage markets, CRS Report RL34182, *Financial Crisis? The Liquidity Crunch of August 2007*, described MBS:

> Securitization allowed mortgage lenders to bypass traditional banks. Securitization pools mortgages or other debts and sells them to investors in the form of bonds rather than leaving loans on lenders' balance sheets. The MBS market developed in part because long-term fixed rate mortgages held in banks' portfolios place banks at significant risk if interest rates rise (in which case, the banks' interest costs could exceed their mortgage interest earnings). MBS were popular with investors and banks because it allowed both to better diversify their portfolios. But because the MBS market was growing rapidly in size and sophistication, accurate pricing of its risk was difficult and could have been distorted by the housing boom.
>
> There are several forms of MBS. The simplest are called pass-throughs — interest and principal payments from homeowners are collected by the lender (or a service firm) and passed through to the owner of the MBS. More complex securities are created by pooling MBS as well as mortgages, and by giving investors a menu of risk and return options. A mortgage pool may be split into parts (called tranches) to allow cautious investors to purchase safer portions and aggressive investors to purchase the riskier, high-return tranches (e.g., tranchesthat bear initial losses). Finally, mortgage cash flows may be combined with derivative instruments that link payment levels to the performance of financial variables, such as interest rates or credit conditions. These securities — combinations of traditional bonds and derivatives — are called structured products.
>
> The growth of securitization meant that more loans could be originated by non-banks, many of which are not subject to examination by federal bank examiners and not subject to the underwriting guidances issued by federal financial regulators....[3]

Bear Stearns and The Initial Fed "Rescue"

A little more than a week before the Fed's announced rescue on March 14, 2008, fixed income traders reportedly began hearing rumors that European financial institutions had ceased doing fixed income trades with Bear. Fearing that their funds might be frozen if Bear wound up in bankruptcy, a number of U.S.-based fixed-income and stock traders that had been actively involved with Bear, had reportedly decided by March 10 to halt such involvement.[4]

That development placed firms that still wanted to do business with Bear in a quandary: in the event that Bear did succumb, they were likely to be in the difficult position of explaining to their clients why they had ignored the rumors; on March 11, a major asset-management company ceased doing trades with Bear.[5] The same day, however, the Bear's Chief Executive Officer, Alan Schwartz, wrote that the firm's "balance sheet, liquidity and capital remain strong."[6]

That same week, many other firms began exercising extreme caution in their dealings with Bear, as the firm saw the exodus of a growing number of its trading counterparties. Some hedge fund clients, demanding that Bear provide cash as collateral on trades they had done with the firm, withdrew funds from their accounts with the firm. Hedge funds that had used Bear to borrow money and clear trades were withdrawing cash from their accounts. Some large investment banks stopped accepting trades that would expose them to Bear, and some money market funds reduced their holdings of short-term Bear-issued debt. Concerned that the firm's ability to pay claims was looking less assured, a number of institutional investors with credit default swaps (insurance policies that protect against corporate bond defaults) purchased from Bear, were attempting to undo those trades. (Bear had developed a sizeable market in swaps.)

This ongoing activity contributed to a precipitous and alarming drop in Bear's cushion of liquidity reserves. By the afternoon of March 13, the firm's CEO was convinced of the severity of the problem. After deliberating with other senior company staff and company lawyers, a call was made to James Dimon, CEO of JP Morgan, the nation's second largest bank in stock market capitalization. As the clearing agent for Bear's trades, JP Morgan was familiar with Bear's collateral position and thus seemed like a good prospect for lending to the firm.[7]

Later, JP Morgan's CEO and other JP Morgan senior officials held conversations with representatives from the Fed. The conclusion was that something needed to be done because a failure at Bear could have widespread financial repercussions.

By the evening of March 13, Bear had been unable to secure emergency financing or negotiate a strategic acquisition deal. Officials from the firm and the Securities and Exchange Commission, the principal Bear regulator, then informed officials from the Fed that Bear had lost far more of its liquidity than it had previously been aware of. The Fed then sent a team of examiners to look at Bear's books overnight. Early on the morning on March 14, a cadre of financial regulators, including New York Fed Chief Timothy Geithner, Fed Chairman Ben Bernanke, and U.S. Treasury Department Secretary Henry Paulson conducted a conference call. At 7:00 a.m., at the call's conclusion, the Fed decided it would offer a short-term "discount window" loan.[8]

Through the discount window, the Fed can make direct short-term loans to commercial banks. A 1932 provision of the Federal Reserve Act allows it to lend to non-banks if at least five of its seven governors approve, a provision that has not been used since the Great Depression. With two governors' seats vacant and one governor out of the country and inaccessible, the Fed invoked a special legal clause, allowing it to approve an overnight loan to Bear with only four governors. The arrangement would involve providing collateral-based financing to Bear through JP Morgan, which would be used as a conduit, since as a commercial bank, it already has access to the discount window and is also under the Fed's supervision. Exact terms were not disclosed, but the loan amount would only be limited to the amount of collateral Bear could provide. JP Morgan would have incurred no risk from the transaction but the Fed would.[9]

JP Morgan Initially Agrees to Acquire Bear Stearns with Fed Assistance

On Monday, March 17, the $13 billion back-to-back non-recourse loan through JPMorgan Chase to Bear was repaid to the Fed (with weekend interest of nearly $4 million). This event, however, was eclipsed when on Sunday, March 16, two days after the announcement of the loan lifeline, JP Morgan, one of the only major banks not to be significantly battered by the mortgage meltdtown, agreed to acquire Bear for $236 million. In the preceding days, Bear executives were both preparing for a possible Chapter 11 bankruptcy filing and pursuing a purchaser for either all or parts of the firm. The idea was that securing an immediate acquirer before trade resumed on Monday, March 17 would allow the firm to avoid likely mass withdrawals by its clients in early opening markets like Japan. After intense negotiations between Bear and JP Morgan with the active encouragement of the Fed and Treasury officials, JP Morgan signed on as Bear's purchaser.

JP Morgan's stock-for-stock buyout was valued at $2 a share for Bear stock, the closing share price on March 15, which represented a 94% discount to Bear's closing share price of $30 on March 14, and slightly over 1% of the $170 share price that Bear stock had fetched a year earlier. The boards at both Bear Stearns and JP Morgan quickly approved the deal, as did the Fed, and the Office of the Comptroller of the Currency.

The deal needed the approval of shareholders at both Bear and JP Morgan. At Bear, a schism between its bondholders and its shareholders had reportedly arisen after the announced sale. Interested in keeping the firm out of bankruptcy, and protecting their investment in it, bondholders were generally said to be supportive of the sale. But many shareholders, including some employees with an equity interest in the firm, were said to be opposed to the $2 a share offer. In heavy trading on Tuesday, March 18, the firm's share price closed at $5.91.[10]

A release from JP Morgan said that, "effective immediately, JP Morgan Chase is guaranteeing the trading obligations of Bear Stearns and its subsidiaries and is providing management oversight for its operations.... The transaction is expected to have an expedited close by the end of the calendar second quarter 2008...."[11]

An integral part of the initial merger deal was that the Fed would agree to provide what is described as a non-recourse loan to JP Morgan for up to $30 billion of Bear's less-liquid assets.[12] The Fed would then be in a position to liquidate the assets. If they rose in value before they are sold, the Fed will make money. If they fell in value, the Fed would lose. The Fed's role in this was reportedly deemed necessary to overcome JP Morgan's reluctance to taking on much of Bear's risky portfolio of complex mortgages and other questionable investments.[13]

As JP Morgan CEO James Dimon told the Senate Committee on Banking, Housing, and Urban Affairs on April 4, we "could not and would not have assumed the substantial risk" of buying Bear without the Fed's involvement.[14]

THE AMENDED BUYOUT OFFER

Reportedly responding to Bear shareholders and employees (who own about one-third of Bear stock) angry over the $2 a price share offer and to avert the attendant threat of shareholder litigation, Bear and JP Morgan renegotiated the terms of the merger during the weekend of March 22. The ensuing stock-for-stock merger agreement would value Bear stock at $10 a share. JP Morgan will also buy 95 million new shares of Bear Stearns for the offering price. Under the new terms of the stockfor- stock deal, JP Morgan will pay 0.21753 of a share for each share of Bear, up from the original exchange ratio of 0.05473.[15] Under the new terms, Bear would be valued at about $1.2 billion up from the earlier $236 million.

Also under the terms of the agreement, before April 8, Bear would sell 39.5% of 95 million shares of newly issued stock to JP Morgan, allowing the transaction to avoid a law in the state of Delaware, where both firms are headquartered. Delaware state law states that a shareholder vote is not necessary for the particular transaction if a company is selling up to 40% of its holdings. JP Morgan and Bear officials probably hoped that between the roughly 8% of Bear shares it acquired on the open market and the 5% of Bear shares held by members of its board, the 39.5% vote would give them the majority votes required for eventual shareholder approval.

Generally, the New York Stock Exchange (NYSE), where JP Morgan and Bear shares are listed and traded, requires shareholder approval if an issue of new shares are convertible into more than 20% of a listed company stock. But the rule has an exception if adherence to the procedure delays or seriously jeopardizes the financial viability of the listed company. Bear and JP Morgan invoked the exception and the NYSE accommodated them. On April 8, the shares were issued.

JP Morgan Chief Executive Jamie Dimon said that "... we believe the amended terms are fair to all sides and reflect the value and risks of the Bear Stearns franchise and bring more certainty for our respective shareholders, clients, and the marketplace." Bear's CEO, Alan Schwartz, observed "...our board of directors believes the amended terms provide both significantly greater value to our shareholders, many of whom are Bear Stearns employees, and enhanced coverage and certainty for our customers, counterparties, and lenders."[16]

A number of shareholder lawsuits have been filed over the proposed sale. For example, during the last week of March, the Wayne County Employees' Retirement System of Michigan and the Police and Fire Retirement System of the City of Detroit sued Bear Stearns, its directors, and JP Morgan, and asked the Delaware Chancery Court to initially issue a temporary restraining order blocking Bear's plan to issue stock representing a 39.5% of its stake. The court refused to do so. And after the shares were issued on April 8, the pension funds changed their request and asked for a preliminary injunction to stop JP Morgan from voting any of the newly acquired shares. On April 9, a judge on the court responded by ordering a temporarily pause to the lawsuits, accepting the investment banks' argument that fighting simultaneous lawsuits in Delaware and New York (where other suits are pending) would be wasteful and burdensome.

The Altered Terms for the Fed and the Debate over Moral Hazard and Systemic Risk

When asked about whether they had encouraged the far smaller original offer, Fed Chairman Ben Bernanke said there was no "interjection" by the Fed "to my knowledge." Treasury Undersecretary Robert Steel indicate that "there was a view... [that]... the price should not be very high." But he noted that "with regards to the specifics, the actual deal was negotiated."[17]

With respect to the amended buyout, the Fed arranged for a more favorable role for itself.

Summarizing the terms of the Fed's involvement, the CRS Report, *Financial Turmoil: Federal Reserve Policy Responses*, reports that "As part of the [buyout] agreement, the Fed announced a $29 billion loan to a corporation it created to buy $30 billion of assets from Bear Stearns. In the event that the proceeds from the asset sales exceed $30 billion and the outstanding interest, the Fed will keep the profits. In the event that the loan principal and interest exceed the funds raised by the liquidation, the first $1 billion of losses would be borne by JP Morgan Chase, and any subsequent losses would be borne by the Fed. The statutory authority for the loan was based on a clause of the Federal Reserve Act to be used in "unusual or exigent circumstances" that had not been invoked in more than 70 years.[18]

Explaining the terms in greater detail, the report observed:

> As part of the agreement, the Fed will purchase up to $30 billion of Bear Stearns' assets through a Limited Liability Corporation (LLC) based in Delaware that it has created and controls. Upon its creation, two loans will be made to the LLC: the Fed will lend the LLC up to $29 billion, and JP Morgan Chase will make a subordinate loan to the LLC worth $1 billion. The Fed's loan will be made at an interest rate set equal to the discount rate (2.5% when the terms were announced, but fluctuating over time) for a term of 10 years, renewable by the Fed. JP Morgan Chase's loan will have an interest rate 4.5 percentage points above the discount rate.
>
> Using the proceeds from that loan, the LLC will purchase assets from Bear Stearns worth $30 billion at marked to market prices by Bear Stearns on March 14. The Fed reported that The portfolio supporting the credit extensions consists largely of mortgage-related assets. In particular, it includes cash assets as well as related hedges. The cash assets consist of investment grade securities (i.e. securities rated BBB- or higher by at least one of the three principal credit rating agencies and no lower than that by the others) and residential or commercial mortgage loans classified as "performing." All of the assets are current as to principal and interest (as of March 14, 2008).
>
> All securities are domiciled and issued in the U.S. and denominated in U.S. dollars. The portfolio consists of collateralized mortgage obligations (CMOs), the majority of

which are obligations of government-sponsored entities (GSEs), such as the Federal Home Loan Mortgage Corporation ("Freddie Mac"), as well as asset-backed securities, adjustable-rate mortgages, commercial mortgage-backed securities, non-GSE CMOs, collateralized bond obligations, and various other loan obligations.
The LLC will own these assets, and will liquidate them in order to pay back the principal and interest owed to the Fed and JP Morgan Chase. The LLC's assets (purchased from Bear Stearns) are the collateral backing the loans from the Fed and JP Morgan Chase. A private company, BlackRock Financial Management, has been hired to manage the portfolio. Neither Bear Stearns nor JP Morgan Chase owe the Fed any principal or interest, nor are they liable if the LLC is unable to pay back the money the Fed lent it. The New York Fed explained that the LLC was created to "ease administration of the portfolio and will remove constraints on the money manager that might arise from retaining the assets on the books of Bear Stearns." JP Morgan Chase and Bear Stearns will not receive the $29 billion from the LLC until the merger is complete. In the meantime, JP Morgan Chase and the Fed have delegated control of the assets to the LLC, including the right to liquidate them before the merger.[19]

The unprecedented Fed intervention has triggered a widespread debate over the action's merits. The two predominant and opposing views are as follows:

Intervention made sense because of the threat of increased market instability if Bear went down. It was argued by some, including Treasury Secretary Henry Paulson,[20] that the Fed's intervention was wholly justified in pursuit of the larger goal of ensuring financial stability by averting potentially far reaching spillovers into the larger financial world if Bear were to collapse — often called systemic risk. One concern was that such a failure would unleash additional lack of confidence into markets already fraught with substantial pessimism and uncertainty. Another concern involved the $46 billion in mortgages, mortgage-backed and asset-backed securities (as reported on November 30, 2007) held by the firm. If Bear failed, it would likely have to liquidate such assets, a large fraction of which held somewhat questionable valuations based on what it said were estimates derived from "internally developed models or methodologies utilizing significant inputs that are generally less readily observable."[21] A large stream of such assets released into risk-averse markets with leery and anxious buyers would be likely to force many institutions with similar assets into substantial asset write downs. The outcome of all of this could be a financial meltdown.

The intervention helps shield the firm and the markets from the consequences of running a badly performing firm. Moral hazard occurs when entities do not bear the full cost of their actions, thus becoming more likely to repeat them. And a major concern here is that with Fed intervention, neither Bear nor the markets in general, would benefit from the painful but important lesson that failed firms should simply be left to their own fate. For example, if, after the Bear intervention, another Wall Street firm like Lehman also found itself "on the ropes" — would there be an expectation that it also would be rescued? These kind of arguments are often used to challenge the widely held belief in "Too Big to Fail" — the idea that the largest and most powerful financial institutions are too large a part of the financial system to let fail. In the case of Bear Stearns, a more aptly put variation on this might be that "it was too widely connected (to clients and counterparties) to fail."

Defending the Fed's role during April 2nd testimony before the Joint Economic Committee, Fed Chairman, Ben Bernanke, observed:

> ... Our financial system is extremely complex and interconnected, and Bear Stearns participated extensively in a range of critical markets. With financial conditions fragile, the sudden failure of Bear Stearns likely would have led to a chaotic unwinding of positions in those markets and could have severely shaken confidence. The company's failure could also have cast doubt on the financial positions of some of Bear Stearns' thousands of counterparties and perhaps of companies with similar businesses. Given the current exceptional pressures on the global economy and financial system, the damage caused by a default by Bear Stearns could have been severe and extremely difficult to contain. Moreover, the adverse effects would not have been confined to the financial system but would have been felt broadly in the real economy through its effects on asset values and credit availability. To prevent a disorderly failure of Bear Stearns and the unpredictable but likely severe consequences of such a failure for market functioning and the broader economy, the Federal Reserve, in close consultation with the Treasury Department, agreed to provide funding to Bear Stearns through JPMorgan Chase. Over the following weekend, JP Morgan Chase agreed to purchase Bear Stearns and assumed Bear's financial obligations...

Some congressional observers such as Senate Banking Committee Chairman Christopher Dodd and Joint Economic Committee Chairman Charles Schumer, have said that given the potentially negative consequences of letting Bear Stearns fail, the Fed's action appears to have been justified.[22]

Several Members of Congress have publicly expressed some concerns over the merits of the Fed's role. For example, Senator Sam Brownback commented that "the Federal Reserve acted swiftly and decisively during the Bear Stearns-JP Morgan marriage. However, I am concerned when taxpayer money is used to rescue sophisticated private investment and commercial banks from the consequences of the banks' own strategic decisions. I am interested in learning more about how the Federal Reserve will quantify the financial risk to the taxpayer resulting from the Fed's recent and any future actions to help private companies."[23]

Echoing this theme, Representative Scott Garrett observed that "... Government isn't supposed to be in the business of picking winners and losers."[24] And, at an April 3 Senate Banking Committee hearing on Bear Stearns, Senator Richard Shelby, ranking member of the Senate Banking Committee, reportedly expressed general concern that the Fed's actions would create a "moral hazard" which "encourages firms to take excessive risk based on the expectations that they will reap all the profits while the federal government stands ready to cover any losses if they fail."[25]

Outside of Congress, a number of observers have also criticized the Fed. For example, writing in the *Dow Jones Capital Market Report*, financial columnist Jim Murphy, rebutted the assertion that rescuing Bear Stearns was necessary to avoid systemic repercussions. He observed that “Here is the problem with the bailout of Bear Stearns: The assumption behind the operation is that Bear Stearns is a global investment bank and brokerage that offers goods and services not offered by the many other global investment powerhouses. This is simply untrue. Bear Stearns offered nothing and offers nothing that isn’t offered by, say, JP Morgan Chase and Merrill Lynch, to name but two huge investment banks and brokerages. Had Bear Stearns been allowed to fail, the damage would have been limited to Bear Stearns shareholders, including the firm’s employees. The collapse of Bear Stearns didn’t really put much of a dent in the capital of the blueblood investors and institutions who were said to be the mainstays of the firm. In fact, of course, it was the flight of the big plungers to other wire houses that triggered the near collapse of Bear Stearns.”[26]

Former Fed Chairman Paul Volcker is similarly critical, observing that “...the Federal Reserve has judged it necessary to take actions that extend to the very edge of its lawful and implied powers, transcending in the process certain long-embedded central banking principles and practices ... . What appears to be in substance a direct transfer of mortgage and mortgage-backed securities of questionable pedigree from an investment bank to the Federal Reserve seems to test the time-honored central bank mantra in time of crisis: lend freely at high rates against good collateral; test it to the point of no return.”[27]

But in an essentially “middle ground” view on the Fed’s intervention, Vincent Reinhart, a former Fed official who is now with the American Enterprise Institute, noted that “it is a serious extension of putting the Federal Reserve’s balance sheet in harm’s way. That’s got to tell you the economy is in a pretty precarious state.”[28]

RELATED CONGRESSIONAL CONCERNS

Congressional interest in the Bear Stearns buyout is manifesting itself in a number of ways, which are described below.

On April 3, 2008, the Senate Banking, Housing, and Urban Affairs Committee held a hearing 3 solely devoted to the issue of Bear Stearns’ acquisition and Fed involvement. The Senate Finance Committee has also shown some interest in the acquisition. On March 26, Committee Chairman Max Baucus and Ranking Member Senator Charles Grassley wrote to Fed Chairman Ben Bernanke, Treasury Secretary Henry Paulson, New York Fed Chairman Timothy Geithner, and the Bear Stearns and JP Morgan CEOs, requesting details of the sale agreement, how and by whom it was negotiated, and all the parties involved.[29]

In making the request, Chairman Baucus observed, “Americans are being asked to back a brand new kind of transaction, to the tune of tens of billions of dollars. With jurisdiction over the federal debt, it’s the Finance Committee’s responsibility to pin down just how the government decided to front $30 billion in taxpayer dollars for the Bear Stearns deal, and to monitor the changing terms of the sale...”[30]

Additionally, on April 2, Chairman Baucus and Senator Grassley asked the SEC to provide them with complete details on the role of it regulatory oversight leading up to the acquisition, including information on the conduct of business, the influence of outside parties, the potential role of hedge funds, and the compensation of the firms’ executives. The letter also requested information on whether, with respect to Bear Stearns, the SEC’s capital and liquidity standards had been adequate and whether the company had avoided adhering to such standards.[31]

The same day, the Senators also wrote Bear Stearns and JP Morgan, requesting information on compensation and severance arrangements provided to their top management prior to and as a result of the merger agreement. They specifically requested data on various forms of compensation, including stock options, deferred compensation arrangements, and health care and other employee benefits. The letter also cited news reports that the SEC had previously been investigating Bear Stearns for improperly valuing mortgage securities. It also asked whether the probe represented a lost opportunity for the agency's Enforcement Division to discover the presence of systemic market risks.[32]

In early April 2008, Henry Waxman, chairman of the House Oversight and Government Reform Committee, wrote to New York Fed Governor Timothy Geithner, a key figure in the Fed's involvement in the merger, to inquire about the Fed's selection of BlackRock Financial Management Inc. as the asset manager for the deal that allowed JP Morgan Chase & Co. to purchase Bear Stearns at bargain-basement price.

Chairman Waxman observed, "Only limited details are known about the Federal Reserve's understandings with BlackRock. It appears, however, that BlackRock is now directly responsible for managing a $30 billion portfolio on behalf of the American taxpayer ... If BlackRock does its job well, the taxpayers will be made whole or even experience a gain. If BlackRock is not successful, the taxpayers stand to lose billions of dollars. In effect, it appears that BlackRock is serving as a government contractor providing complex financial services to the Federal Reserve."

The chairman also inquired about how the Fed selected BlackRock, which he said appears to have gotten a long-term deal with the Fed without the competition that is usually found in a government bid. The chairman also asked about the nature of the compensation BlackRock will receive as reimbursement for its involvement.[33]

End Notes

[1] In recent memory, the Fed only approached this kind of specific non-bank intervention in 1998 when it helped organize a rescue of Long-Term Capital Management (LTCM), a large U.S.-based hedge fund. Concerned about the possible dire consequences for world financial markets if the failing LTCM collapsed, Fed officials were instrumental in convincing a group of U.S. and European financial institutions to inject several billion dollars into the hedge fund. They did so, and in exchange collectively received a majority share.

[2] David Smith and Dominic Rushe, "Bear Stearns: The Banking Twister Heading Your Way," *The (UK) Sunday Times*, March 16, 2008.

[3] CRS Report RL34182, *Financial Crisis? The Liquidity Crunch of August 2007*, by Darryl E. Getter, Mark Jickling, Marc Labonte, and Edward Vincent Murphy.

[4] Kate Kelly, Greg Ip, and Robin Sidel, "Fed Races to Rescue Bear Stearns in Bid to Steady Financial System Storied Firm," *Wall Street Journal*, March 15, 2008, p. A1.

[5] Ibid.

[6] Ibid.

[7] Ibid.

[8] This is credit extended by a Federal Reserve Bank to an eligible depository institution that must be secured by collateral.

[9] Kate Kelly, Greg Ip, and Robin Sidel, "Fed Races to Rescue Bear Stearns in Bid to Steady Financial System Storied Firm."

[10] Landon Thomas, "It's Bondholders vs. Shareholders in a Race to Buy Bear Stearns Stock," *New York Times*, March 19, 2008.

[11] "JP Morgan Chase To Acquire Bear Stearns," *J. P. Morgan News Release*, March 16, 2008.

[12] Ibid.

[13] Andrew Clark, "Bear Stearns Saved by Rock-Bottom JP Morgan Bid."

[14] Kara Scannell and Sudeep Reddy, "Officials Say They Sought To Avoid Bear Bailout," *Wall Street Journal*, April 4, 2008. P. A-1.

[15] There are reports that during a March 17, 2008, phone call with JP Morgan's CEO, the Chairman of Bear's board, James Cayne, criticized the $2-a-share price, even after voting for it. Additional reports have said that after the initial terms of the deal were made, Bear's CEO, Alan Schwartz, was privately telling people that he felt that the company had been "mugged." Robin Sidel and Kate Kelly, "J.P. Morgan Quintuples Bid to Seal Bear Deal," Dow Jones, March 25, 2008, p. A-1.

[16] Peter Coy, "A Sweeter Bear Bid May Sour the Fed, JP Morgan Raises its Offer in Hopes of Winning over Shareholders. Is the Federal Reserve too Cozy with Wall Street?" *BusinessWeek.com*., March 25, 2008.

[17] Robert Novak, "Wall Street in D.C." *Washington Post*, April 9, 2008

[18] CRS Report RL34427, *Financial Turmoil: Federal Reserve Policy Responses*, by Marc Labonte, p. 1.

[19] Ibid, p. 7-8.

[20] Andrew Clark, "Bear Stearns Saved by Rock-Bottom JP Morgan Bid," *Guardian.co.uk*, March 16, 2008.

[21] Gretchen Morgenson, "Rescue Me: A Fed Bailout Crosses a Line," *New York Times*, March 16, 2008, p. Bus-1.

[22] William Neikirk, "Fed Action Awaited on Size of Rate Cut Markets Hope Likely Rate Cut will Stem Tide," *Baltimore Sun*, March 18, 2008. Robin Sidel, Greg Ip, Michael M. Phillips and Kate Kelly, "The Week That Shook Wall Street: Inside the Demise of Bear Stearns," March 18, 2008, *Wall Street Journal*, p. A-1.

[23] "Brownback Comments on Bernanke Testimony," *States News Service*, April 2, 2008.

[24] David Fredosso, "The Mother of All Government Bailouts." *NationalReviewOnline*, April 2, 2008.

[25] Dana Milbank, "Buddy Can You Spare a Million," *Washington Post*, April 3, 2008.

[26] Jim Murphy, "There Was No Reason to Rescue Bear Stearns," *Dow Jones Capital Markets Report*, March 27, 2008.

[27] John Brinsley and Anthony Massucci, "Volcker Says Fed's Bear Loan Stretches Legal Power," *Bloomberg*, April 8, 2008.

[28] "Fed Cuts Discount Rate, Backs Bear Stearns Deal," *Providence Business News*, March 15, 2008.

[29] "Finance Leaders Question Players in Bear Stearns Deal," *Senate Finance Committee News Release*, March 26, 2008, p. 1.

[30] Ibid.

[31] "Grassley Seeks Details of Executive Compensation, SEC Knowledge of Bear Stearns Collapse," *States News Service*, April 2, 2008.

[32] Ibid. Separately, Senator Grassley has also reportedly asked the SEC's inspector general to examine why the agency failed to pursue reports of trouble at Bear Stearns, including an assessment of allegations that it was improperly valuing mortgage-related securities. Specifically, the Senator reportedly requested information on communications between Bear Stearns and senior SEC officials and information on why SEC examiners failed to bring an enforcement action. He also reportedly asked whether there were any indications of any "improper action or misconduct" related to the SEC investigation and whether "more aggressive action" by the SEC's enforcement division might have provided an earlier sense of the conditions that may have contributed to Bear Stearns' problems. Ron Orol, "SEC, Bear Dealings Questioned," *TheDeal.com*, April 3, 2008.

[33] Letter to Timothy Geithner, President and CEO Federal Reserve of New York from Henry A. Waxman, Chairman of the House Oversight and Government Reform Committee, April 7, 2008, available at [http://oversight.house.gov/search/search.asp].

In: Government Interventions in Economic Emergencies ISBN: 978-1-60741-356-1
Editor: Pablo Sastre

Chapter 4

CONTAINING FINANCIAL CRISIS

Mark Jickling

SUMMARY

There is no precise definition of "financial crisis," but a common view is that disruptions in financial markets rise to the level of a crisis when the flow of credit to households and businesses is constrained and the real economy of goods and services is adversely affected. Since mid-2007, governments have tried with limited success to keep the downturn in U.S. subprime housing from developing into such a crisis.

Subprime mortgage problems, and the financial shock they caused, were widely anticipated, but the spread of turmoil into many seemingly unrelated parts of the global financial system was not. Many of the losses occurring in diverse firms and markets — often quite severe — have common features: the use of complex, hard-to-value financial instruments; large speculative positions underwritten by borrowed funds, or leverage; and the use of off-the-books entities to remove risky trading activities from the balance sheets of major financial institutions. Because of the prevalence of innovative financial arrangements, the housing downturn appears to have triggered market dynamics that amplify the effects of financial shocks and generate self-reinforcing, downward financial and economic spirals.

The Federal Reserve and foreign central banks have cut short-term interest rates dramatically and injected trillions of dollars into the banking system to keep credit flowing. The Fed and Treasury have engaged in a series of extraordinary interventions to shore up failing financial institutions. The Fed provided $29 billion to underwrite the rescue-through-acquisition of Bear Stearns, a leading investment bank, and loaned billions to AIG, a leading insurer. Fannie Mae and Freddie Mac have been placed in government conservatorship, with the Treasury pledging to stand behind the $5 trillion in bonds the two firms sold or guaranteed. In September 2008, as market conditions appeared to worsen, Congress passed a $700 billion rescue plan (P.L. 110-343), authorizing the Treasury to purchase securities to shore up bank balance sheets. In October, as conditions appeared to worsen, the Fed entered the commercial paper market and purchased tens of billions in short-term corporate debt. Simultaneously, trillions of dollars in private debt now carries government guarantees. The duration of the current instability is in marked contrast to financial shocks of recent decades, when the central bank was able to contain market problems quickly with little or no interruption of U.S. economic growth.

Depending on how soon normal market conditions are restored, and on the severity of the economic slowdown, Congress may view the social costs of failed financial speculation as sufficient to warrant new restrictions to reduce the incidence of losses that have system-wide impacts or to put the markets and the economy in a better position to weather such shocks. The Treasury has already proposed a sweeping restructuring of financial regulation.

This chapter supplements CRS Report RL34 182, *Financial Crisis? The Liquidity Crunch of August 2007*, by Darryl Getter et al., which describes in greater detail the channels through which subprime problems cascaded through the financial system. This chapter focuses on the efforts of regulators to restore market stability.

INTRODUCTION

In mid-2007, mounting losses in subprime mortgage markets triggered disturbances throughout the international financial system. The scale of the turmoil has been surprising, given the small size of the U.S. subprime market in relation to global financial markets.[1] Not only is subprime a comparatively small market, its problems were known well in advance: when the rapid rise in housing prices stopped in 2006, it was inevitable that many subprime borrowers would have difficulty making payments, particularly those whose adjustable mortgage rates were scheduled to reset in 2007 and 2008. A Swiss bank CEO called subprime loan losses "probably the longest anticipated crisis we have ever seen."[2]

Nevertheless, a wide range of financial institutions have been affected adversely, many of which had little direct exposure to the subprime mortgage market. Almost weekly since July 2007, the financial press has highlighted a new trouble spot, including commercial and investment banks, issuers of commercial paper, conduits for securitization of loans, credit swaps, jumbo mortgages, money market funds, consumer lenders, hedge funds, bond insurers, government-sponsored enterprises, state and local investment funds, state and municipal governments themselves, small business lending, and so on. As economic conditions deteriorate, many fear that there may be more problems ahead, possibly involving such major financial markets as commercial real estate and credit card lending. In 2008, these periodic crises grew more severe, with several leading U.S. financial institutions requiring government assistance, merging with other firms, or failing. By September, not a single "bulge bracket" investment bank remained standing: they had either failed (Lehman Brothers), merged (Merrill Lynch and Bear Stearns), or converted themselves into commercial bank holding companies (Goldman Sachs and Morgan Stanley). The links between many of these crises and subprime mortgages are not obvious, but they are correctly viewed as symptoms of a common underlying problem.

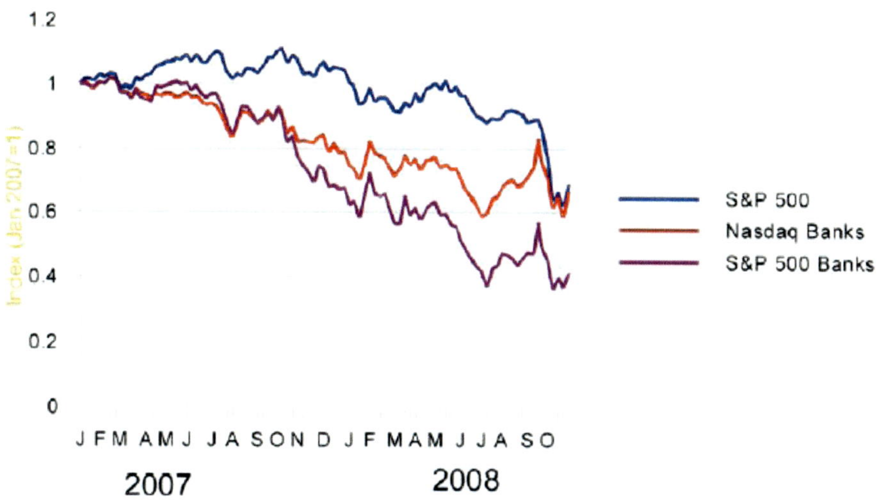

Source: Global Financial Data.

Figure 1. Bank Stock Indices and the S&P 500, Jan. 2007 - Oct. 2008

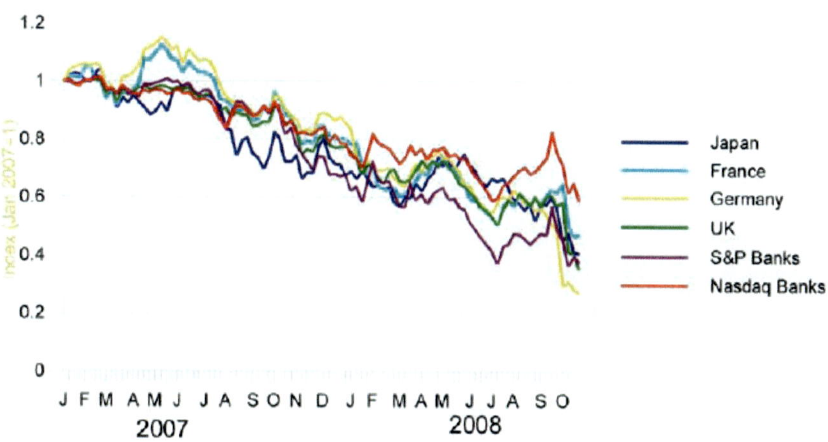

Source: Global Financial Data.

Figure 2. Developed Country Bank Stock Indices, Jan. 2007 - Oct. 2008

The stock market has certainly perceived systemic weakness across financial sectors. As **Figure 1** below indicates, share prices for commercial banks have significantly underperformed the market as a whole, as represented by the Standard & Poor's 500 index. Between January 2007 and October 2008, shares in those sectors lost over half their value. S&P 500 bank shares (including the largest U.S. banks) have done worse than banks listed on Nasdaq, probably because they are more exposed to the complex instruments, structures, and trading practices at the heart of the crisis.

Figure 2 shows that bank stocks in Japan, Germany, France, and the UK have followed the same downward trend as the U.S. indices. This should not be surprising; large banks in all these countries have significant U.S. operations, just as the major U.S. banks are active in Europe and Asia. By the end of October 2008, all these indices (except Nasdaq banks) had lost more than half their value since the beginning of 2007.

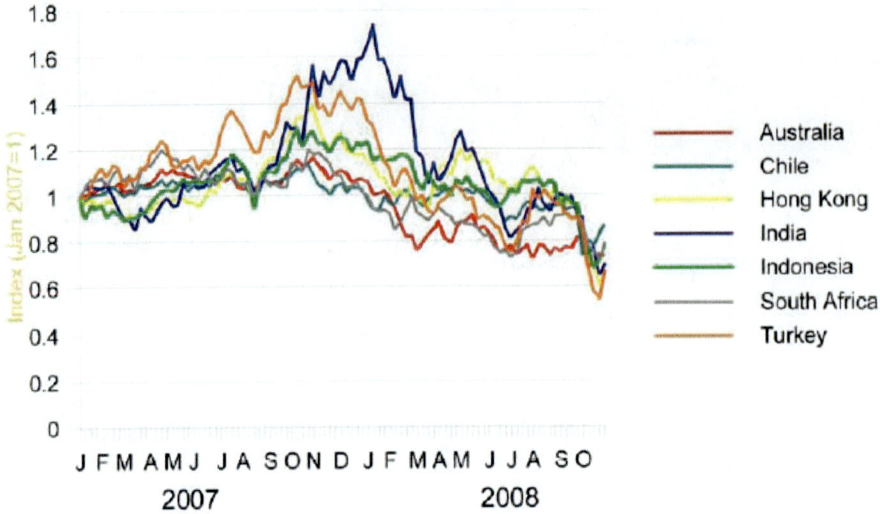

Source: Global Financial Data.

Figure 3. Bank and Financial Stock Indices, Selected Countries, Jan. 2007 - Oct. 2008

Figure 3 shows indices of bank or financial stocks from seven different countries with smaller financial markets. Again, there is a common trend, but it is a different pattern. These markets appeared to shrug off problems in the major financial centers in 2007. All seven indices showed gains over that year. Late in 2007 (or early in 2008), however, there began a steep decline, and they all dropped sharply during the panic in September 2008 (the period that led to the enactment of the $700 billion emergency package in the United States).

The mechanism that transmitted problems from the major financial centers of the developed countries to these far-flung financial systems has not been fully explained. A global economic slowdown may be a partial explanation, but the decline in stock prices began well before macroeconomic indicators turned negative. All we can say for certain is that by the beginning of 2008, stock investors around the world had decided that banking and financial intermediation had become more risky and that expectations of profits had diminished significantly.[3]

THE UNDERLYING FINANCIAL PROBLEMS

CRS Report RL34182, *Financial Crisis? The Liquidity Crunch of August 2007*, by Darryl Getter et al., describes the channels through which distress in subprime mortgages spread through the broader U.S. financial system. In addition to causing direct asset losses, the subprime crisis triggered a reassessment of financial risk that encompassed other debt markets, including leveraged loans,[4] takeover financing, credit derivatives, and commercial paper. There was — and still remains — great uncertainty regarding the true value of certain financial instruments, especially those with complex structures or for which active trading markets do not exist.

To understand how a relatively small market sector — U.S. subprime mortgages — could trigger such widespread chaos in global markets, it helps to consider ways that financial markets have evolved over decades. Innovations in financial theory, improvements in communications and computing technology, removal of barriers to international investment flows, the increasing reliance on trading markets by both businesses seeking funds and households investing their savings, and the growth of financial services relative to the rest of the economy are all factors that have transformed the financial system since World War II. The present crisis is the gravest challenge that this new system of markets has faced, and it may lead to fundamental changes in the way the business of financial intermediation is regulated.

In the 1930s, the last time this level of turmoil occurred, widespread bank failures were followed by a long economic downturn. In response, Congress recognized that banks were special: their assets tended to be long-term loans and their liabilities were primarily short-term deposits. This meant that even sound and solvent banks could be destroyed if depositors sought to withdraw their money at the same time. Their assets were illiquid. Worse, liquidity problems were contagious: if one bank failed, depositors were likely to run on healthy banks.

To stabilize the banking system, Congress instituted deposit insurance and gave bank regulators strong powers to limit the amount of risk that banks could take. Risky activities, like underwriting and sale of corporate securities, were placed off limits. Over the years, however, bank services and bank risks migrated outside of the regulatory safety net. Wall Street securities firms, for example, developed the commercial paper market, which replaced much of banks' short-term corporate lending. Investment banks like Merrill Lynch were never subject to the same kind of safety and soundness regulation as commercial banks. Newer market participants, like hedge funds, were not subject to any regulation at all. Even regulated banks were gradually allowed to own securities and insurance businesses within a holding company structure, and they were allowed to hold highly-risky speculative positions in off-balance sheet "special purpose entities."

In other words, bank-like investment strategies — such as the use of leverage (or borrowed money) and financing long-term investments with short-term debt — became common outside the safety net provided by deposit insurance and strong regulation. As a result, nonbank institutions became vulnerable to runs — if markets lost confidence in them, their sources of funds could dry up. And these nonbank runs could also be contagious, although this was not widely recognized before the current crisis.

Another notable development of the past two or three decades is the development of complex and hard-to-value financial instruments. For example, simple debt contracts like home mortgages were sold by the original lenders and packaged into bonds with a wide range of risk and reward characteristics. These bonds were often pooled again and sliced and diced into even more complex packages. Synthetic securities were created based on derivative instruments that replicate the price changes of an asset without requiring actual ownership of the asset itself. The relationship between the performance of an underlying financial asset and the complex security or derivative based on it was never simple, and under crisis conditions has proved to be completely unpredictable.

Complexity reduces transparency. Neither regulators nor market participants can easily assess the true financial condition of firms that hold or trade these newer instruments. Since large parts of derivatives markets are unregulated, there is a global web of financial claims and counterclaims that is essentially invisible to financial supervisors and market participants alike.

The new finance was based on the ability to quantify and disaggregate risks in ways that were not possible before. As derivatives markets grew, a common view was that they made the financial system more efficient and more resilient to shocks: they let risks be transferred to those who were best able to understand them and who were willing to take on risk in search of profits. Just as farmers can use grain futures to protect themselves from unexpected declines in prices, financial derivatives promised to allow many financial market participants to better manage risks arising from all sorts of financial transactions, holdings, and obligations.

The benefits, in theory, are not confined to market participants. If farm failures can be prevented by shifting market losses from producers onto speculators on the Chicago Board of Trade, the entire economy gains a valuable shock absorber. Similarly, if hedge funds and other financial speculators take on credit risk, interest rate risk, currency risk, and so on, the core institutions of the financial system ought to be able to operate in a more stable and predictable environment, with general economic benefits in terms of lower costs to borrowers and higher returns to savers.

The crisis suggests that the system has not worked as hoped. Rather than use derivatives and other innovative financial instruments to shed risk, the core institutions have employed them in speculative investment strategies, increasing their risk. The risks of these strategies appeared tolerable, but now it appears that the underlying risk assumptions or models were deficient because they were based on historical price data that prevailed during the relatively benign financial conditions of the past 40 years.[5]

The shock of losses from rising mortgage delinquencies and foreclosures, though serious, was probably not in itself sufficient to cause the crisis. It was also necessary that the financial system be structured in such a way as to multiply the initial shock and trigger dynamics that caused widening losses among financial institutions and now appear to weigh down the prospects for real economic growth. Key characteristics that produced this systemic vulnerability include

- the use of complex financial instruments, whose value is often linked by complex formulae to the value of other instruments or financial variables, and for which no active trading markets exist;
- extensive use of leverage, or borrowed funds, which permits institutions to take larger market positions with a given capital base, increasing potential profits (but also losses); and
- the practice of moving risky financial speculation off the books, into nominally independent accounting entities, so that the results do not appear in the financial accounts of the parent financial institution.

Complex Finance: The House of Cards

A result of financial innovation was the implementation of many financial strategies that were considered low risk and very likely to produce steady gains for participants. In the crisis, however, risks that were discounted have come to the fore, often producing large losses for which institutions and regulators have been unprepared. Two examples of these sorts of arrangements are set out briefly below.

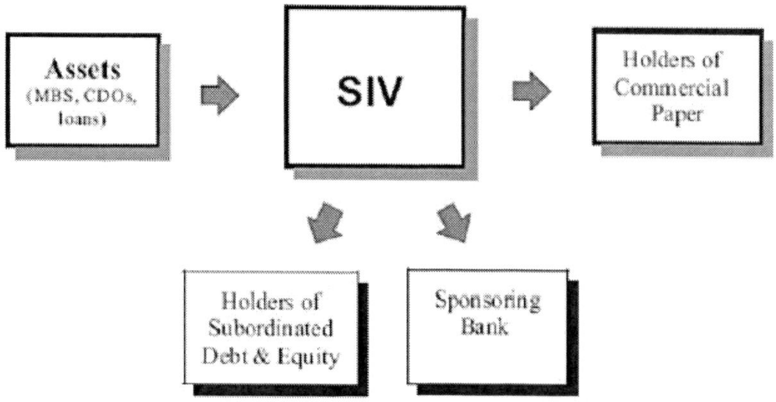

Source: CRS.

Figure 4. Structured Investment Vehicle Cash Flows

SIVs

One example is the Structured Investment Vehicle, or SIV, an entity created by banks to enable speculation on the relationship between short- and longterm interest rates. In mid-2007, commercial banks operated several dozen SIVs, with total assets of between $350 billion and $400 billion. The market leader was Citigroup. Figure 4 illustrates the basic cash flows. The SIV bought long-term debt assets, often mortgage-backed bonds, from which it received interest income. Purchase of these assets was financed by issuing short-term debt, usually commercial paper.[6] The SIV's net revenue was determined by the difference, or spread, between these two cash flows; the operation was profitable so long as the payouts from the assets exceeded interest payments to the commercial paper holders.

The profits were distributed in two ways: first as fees for services to the sponsoring institution, and second, as dividends or interest to holders of subordinated debt and equity, who were the nominal owners of the SIV. (Accounting rules require outside ownership for the SIV to be carried off the books of the sponsoring bank. In general, however, the bank was responsible for investment decisions and provided all brokerage, trade processing, and other services.)

Although data are not routinely reported or published, one estimate is that 72% of the equity in mortgage conduits, of which SIVs are a subset, was held by hedge funds.[7] Hedge funds are typically highly leveraged, which suggests that much of the equity capital in SIVs was borrowed, perhaps from the sponsoring banks themselves.

Many of the assets held by SIVs were mortgage-related, but rarely were they actual loans. Rather, they were securities backed by pools of loans, in which the interest and principal payments of homeowners are passed through to the holders of the bonds. Financial engineers also bundled mortgage-backed bonds into pools of securities called collateralized debt obligations (CDOs), and sold claims against them. CDOs were carved into various classes with different risk characteristics and yields. The portions of the pool that proved most difficult to sell might be pooled again, carved up, and resold — in a so-called CDO squared.

Despite their complexity, such securities were often able to obtain AAA ratings, and they were offered interest rates significantly higher than AAA corporate bonds. Thus, CDOs found a ready market in institutional investors seeking higher yields than traditional debt instruments offered in the early 2000s, and they were incorporated into aggressive speculative strategies such as SIVs.

As subprime defaults climbed to historically unprecedented levels in 2007, the value of mortgage-backed instruments became hard to determine, since it depended crucially on uncertain projections of future loan performance. CDOs wereparticularly affected, since by the time loans had been pooled and resold two or three times, it was difficult for investors to ascertain exactly what they owned. The assumptions about credit risk that underpinned the CDO market, which had provided the justification for those initial AAA ratings, were shown to be wildly inaccurate.

SIVs found that they were no longer able to sell the commercial paper that supported their assets. Sponsoring banks often extended credit to the SIVs (and in many cases were compelled to do so, having granted contingent lines of credit in order to secure high ratings for their SIVs' commercial paper) or took the assets onto their own balance sheets, exacerbating their own financial difficulties. Major banks did not allow SIVs to fail because of the reputational damage that would follow, but the associated losses were considerable.

SIVs are only one part of the story of liquidity problems in 2007 and 2008, but they are instructive because they include three features that contributed disturbance elsewhere. First, they involved the use of innovative securities, which were hard to value in the best of circumstances and which had little history to indicate how they might behave in a severe market downturn. Second, risks were underestimated: the SIVs were a form of highly-leveraged speculation, which was dependent on the assumption that the markets would always supply liquidity. Finally, they were off balance sheet entities: few in the markets (or perhaps in the regulatory agencies) had an accurate idea of the scope or nature of their activities until the trouble came.[8] The result of the interaction of these factors with a sharp housing market downturn is the most sustained period of instability in U.S. financial markets since the Great Depression.

Metro's Credit Enhancement

The second example is a transaction that appeared virtually risk-free at the time it was structured. Metro, the Washington, DC, area transit system, took out a long-term loan from a Belgian bank, KBC Group, to finance capital spending.[9] Metro purchased a contract from AIG, the New York insurance firm, which guaranteed timely payment on the loan. Because the loan was insured, Metro received a lower interest rate. AIG received fees. The bank was able to save on capital charges; because the loan was guaranteed by AIG, it was counted as less risky, and the bank could reduce the amount of assets it had to hold against default risk.[10]

Each of the three parties gained a little, and none expected the deal to fall apart. However, when AIG was downgraded in September 2008, the value of the insurance it provided dropped and the loan was technically in default (even though Metro itself had not missed a payment). Under the terms of the contract, the bank was able to demand immediate repayment of $43 million, placing a great burden on Metro, which sought and obtained legal relief.

What was the economic substance of the deal? The loan was low-risk to begin with, since Metro is backed by several government units, each of whose cost of capital might rise sharply if Metro were allowed to default on its debt. The purpose of the credit derivative contract was not really to reduce risk, but to permit a kind of arbitrage against capital requirements (and perhaps tax obligations). All parties expected modest gains; the chance of anything going wrong appeared remote.

With hindsight, the transaction did not reduce risk at all. In fact, it added slightly to systemic risk, or the likelihood of the entire financial system becoming unstable under certain improbable circumstances.

The Metro transaction is not isolated. Transit officials told Congress that 31 of the largest U.S. bus and rail systems face similar demands. Metro itself is said to have 14 additional deals with other lenders, involving a total of $300 million in loans.[11] Though small in terms of global financial losses, these deals are emblematic in that they promised a high probability of a small gain and a low probability of a significant loss. Throughout the world, such large losses are coming due.

What Makes a Financial Crisis?

Since August 2007, the Federal Reserve has recognized deteriorating financial markets as a principal threat to the economic outlook. The Fed has eased monetary policy, reducing its target for the federal funds rate from 5.25% (the level that was established in June 2006) to 1.00%. It has declared its willingness to provide liquidity to the financial system.[12] In the process of reaching the lower interest rate target, the Fed, in its open market operations, buys securities from depository institutions, giving them new cash to lend. Lower rates themselves, of course, stimulate demand for credit, as more investment projects become potentially profitable once they can be funded at lower cost.

Table 1. Debt Growth by Sector, 2007-2008 (Percentage Change, at Annual Rates)

Date	Households			Businesses		
	Total	Mortgage	Consumer Credit	Non-corporate Business	Non-financial Corporations	Financial Sectors
2007 Q1	7.0	7.8	5.0	10.4	11.0	10.4
2007 Q2	7.2	7.6	5.5	12.8	13.7	9.9
2007 Q3	6.2	4.9	7.5	14.2	13.6	16.8
2007 Q4	6.1	6.1	4.0	12.1	11.7	10.1
2008 Q1	3.3	2.6	5.2	7.4	6.2	5.4
2008 Q2	1.4	0.8	4.4	5.7	5.6	6.6

Source: Federal Reserve, Flow of Funds Accounts, Table D.1.

In recent years, such actions appeared to be sufficient to prevent financial shocks from developing into crises. Neither the stock market crash of 1987 (when the stock market lost 23% of its value in one day), the near collapse of the Long-Term Capital Management hedge fund in 1998 (which threatened to paralyze global bond markets), the "dot.com" crash in 2000-2001 (which again erased trillions of dollars in stock value), nor the September 2001 terrorist attacks (which closed markets and disrupted payment systems) was followed by the kind of prolonged financial stress observed in late 2007 and 2008.

It is noteworthy that through mid-2008, there was no contraction in debt outstanding to borrowers in either the household or business sectors. The rate of growth slowed, but the expansion of credit continued.[13] Emergency government actions, then, were not predicated on restoring creditflows to the real economy, but on ensuring that such flows are not disrupted in the future.[14]

Treasury Secretary Paulson stated in January 2008 that large losses reported by several major institutions were a sign that the system is working: "As markets reassess, we should not be surprised or disappointed to see financial institutions writing down assets and strengthening balance sheets. This is market discipline in action and should enhance market confidence over time."[15]

While the self-correcting properties of markets are generally acknowledged, several analysts identify forces that work in the other direction. In their models, shocks produce other shocks, multiplying the effects of an original loss.

In a recent paper, Greenlaw et al. focus on the pro-cyclical nature of leverage.[16] They assume that firms prefer to maintain a more or less constant level of leverage, or ratio of total assets to capital. As the assets that make up a firm's capital base gain in value, the firm can support more assets on the balance sheet. Balance sheet expansion, in turn, involves asset purchases, boosting asset prices further.

When prices are falling, however, the cycle works in reverse. As its capital loses value, the firm must shrink its balance sheet to maintain a given leverage ratio. As firms sell assets to reduce balance sheet exposure, asset prices are driven down. Because financial firms are typically highly leveraged, a balance sheet adjustment of any given size is multiplied. The authors assume that commercial banks have leverage ratios of about 10:1, meaning that a $1 billion capital loss requires a $10 billion reduction in their portfolio of assets, which consists primarily of loans. In other words, price shocks to a firm cause behavior that reinforces the movement of prices. These self-reinforcing cycles are illustrated in **Figure 5**.

In a 1996 paper, Bernanke, Gertler, and Gilchrist also seek a solution to the "longstanding puzzle" that large fluctuations in aggregate economic activity sometimes arise from what appear to be relatively small impulses."[17] They describe a mechanism they call the "financial accelerator." They argue that the cost of external finance to a firm — its cost of borrowing — is inversely related to its net worth. A fall in asset prices reduces the collateral value of the firm's assets, which hinders or raises the cost of borrowing. By simultaneously increasing the need for external finance and restricting its availability, a negative shock causes the firm to reduce spending and production. "To the extent that negative shocks to the economy reduce the net worth of borrowers..., the spending and production effects of the initial shock will be amplified."[18]

Source: David Greenlaw, Jan Hatzius, Anil Kashyap, and Hyun Song Shin, "Leveraged Losses: Lessons from the Mortgage Meltdown," U.S. Monetary Forum Conference Draft, Feb. 29, 2008, p. 30.

Figure 5. The Leverage Cycle

These two models describe similar effects, acting upon both the supply of and demand for credit. The models suggest that shocks to financial firms can have disproportionate impacts on real economic activity. When financial turbulence interacts with expectations of a contraction in real economic activity, the prospect of another negative spiral emerges. Martin Feldstein, chairman of the Council of Economic Advisers under President Reagan, describes the situation as a kind of Catch-22: "The credit flows needed for economic expansion require confidence in the values of financial assets, but market participants may not have such confidence while the risk of recession hangs over us."[19]

Federal Reserve Governor Frederic Mishkin elaborated on this theme in November 2007:

> The second type of risk that I consider central to the understanding of financial stability is what I call *macroeconomic risk* — that is, an increase in the probability that a financial disruption will cause significant deterioration in the real economy. Because economic downturns typically result in even greater uncertainty about asset values, such episodes may involve an adverse feedback loop whereby financial disruptions cause investment and consumer spending to decline, which, in turn, causes economic activity to contract. Such contraction then increases uncertainty about the value of assets, and, as a result, the financial disruption worsens. In turn, this development causes economic activity to contract further in a perverse cycle.[20]

This scenario, according to Mishkin, explains why the Federal Reserve is unwilling to assume that markets will self-correct without serious damage to the real economy. Financial instability, "if allowed to develop fully," could have severely negative consequences in both financial markets and the global economy.[21] To address the risk — however small — that the current situation could develop into a full-blown financial crisis, cutting off credit flows that support investment and spending, the Fed (and other central banks and regulators) have taken extraordinary steps. In one description that is perhaps not entirely hyperbolic, central bankers have decided to "tear up their rule books and established practices...to inject cash, resuscitate the interbank market, and hopefully ease the credit squeeze."[22]

GOVERNMENT INTERVENTIONS

Open Market Operations and Monetary Policy[23]

Since the fall of 2007, the Fed has made aggressive use of its monetary policy tools: cutting the federal funds rate target six times, including dramatic cuts of 75 basis points (0.75%) in January and March of 2008, and using its open market operations to inject liquidity into the banking system. Early cuts appeared aimed specifically at financial markets, but more recently, as the Fed has explicitly recognized that market conditions have become a drag on real economic activity, the distinction between actions aimed at restoring financial stability and those aimed at macroeconomic stimulus has become blurred, if it exists at all. After holding the rate steady for six months, the Fed cut rates twice in October 2008, by 50 basis points each time.

The Discount Window

In addition to open market operations, the Fed can provide liquidity by lending to individual banks through its discount window. Eligible banks can borrow shortterm (usually overnight) directly from the central bank. Whereas open market operations target the system as a whole, discount lending provides support to particular banks with a need for liquidity. Another distinction is that discount widow borrowings can be collateralized using a broader range of assets that can open market transactions, where the only acceptable collateral is U.S. Treasury or agency securities.[24]

On August 10, 2007, in its first public response to worsening financial conditions, the Fed announced a 50 basis point cut in the discount rate. (The Federal Funds rate was not cut until the next regularly-scheduled meeting of the Federal Open Market Committee in September 2007.)

A limitation of discount lending is that banks do not like to use it. Borrowing at the discount window may send a signal to the markets that a bank has liquidity problems. In an environment like that of late 2007, when interbank lending was already constrained by credit risk fears, the perceived costs of such a perception of financial weakness rise. To overcome the "stigma" of the discount window, the Fed introduced a new method for providing liquidity, the Term Auction Facility.

On March 11, 2008, the Fed took a highly unusual step: it expanded access to the discount window to primary dealers in U.S. Treasury securities. The primary dealers include large securities firms, like Merrill Lynch and Morgan Stanley, which the Fed did not regulate. (Since March 2008, all of the major U.S. investment banks have either merged with commercial banks, failed, or voluntarily placed themselves under Fed supervision.)

Term Auction Facility (TAF)

Despite the Fed's efforts to restore liquidity using its standard tools, markets continued to be tight. In December 2007, the Fed, together with the central banks of Canada, Britain, the European Union, and Switzerland, announced "measures designed to address elevated pressures in short-term funding markets."[25]

The Term Auction Facility (TAF) has conducted a series of auctions of shortterm loan funds to banks, accepting as collateral the same wide variety of assets that can be used to secure discount window borrowing. Auctions involve a fixed amount of funds, at a rate to be determined by competitive bidding. Since December, the TAF has held numerous auctions, and generally about 60 to 75 financial institutions have participated. TAF funds are loaned for periods of 28 to 35 days. The initial amount of funds provided to the bidding banks was $40 billion in December 2007, but the size of the auctions increased in 2008.

Since April 2008, the Fed has continued to operate the TAF; the total amount of loans outstanding at the end of October 2008 was about $200 billion. In November, completed and planned auctions total $600 billion.

The TAF program — and efforts to restore liquidity to the banking system generally — raise certain questions. If the current financial situation is fundamentally a reaction to a period of too-easy access to credit and of excess liquidity, is providing more liquidity the appropriate response? If market discipline operates by forcing banks to absorb losses and shrink their balance sheets, do the Fed's actions to expand credit prolong the adjustment process? Provision of liquidity lowers interest rates, which is good for borrowers and for interest-sensitive economic sectors such as housing, but not for savers, because rates of return on conservative investments like bank CDs and money market funds are depressed. It could be argued that the Fed appears to be rescuing those who caused the problem at the expense of others who had nothing to do with it.

Others question the efficacy of the mechanism: supplying liquidity to banks does not automatically translate into more lending.[26] If elevated credit risk concerns re what is causing tight credit markets, liquidity provision may be the equivalent of "pushing on a string."

Treasury's "Super-SIV" Proposal

In the fall of 2007, when public attention focused on SIVs that were suddenly unable to find buyers for asset-backed commercial paper, a number of large banks met with Treasury officials and designed a financial structure to alleviate SIV funding problems. They proposed that a consortium of private banks create a "Master Liquidity Enhancement Conduit" (MLEC), to be capitalized entirely by the banks, which would buy assets from existing SIVs and fund these purchases in exactly the same way that the SIVs had done in the past: by issuing short-term commercial paper. The expectation was that commercial paper issued by the MLEC would be viewed as safe because of the vast financial resources of the participating banks and because the Treasury had endorsed the plan (although MLEC's debt would not carry any formal government guarantee).

The MLEC concept was announced on October 15, 2007, in a joint press release from J.P. Morgan Chase, Bank of America, and Citigroup, which noted that the Treasury had facilitated the agreement.[27] (The Federal Reserve had no comment on the plan, then or later.)

Negotiations proceeded over the following weeks and months, but although press reports suggested that agreement was near, in the end banks were unwilling to commit capital to the project. The apparent coup-de-grace was delivered on December 20, 2007, when the three largest Japanese banks declined to participate.[28] A few days later, the effort to launch the MLEC was abandoned.

There are two explanations for the failure of the MLEC proposal. First, it was not clear that the concept was economically viable. The underlying problem was that the mortgage-backed assets held by SIVs had lost value and might continue to lose value unless the housing market recovered. How would transferring those assets (and losses) to a "super-SIV" help? The assumption behind the MLEC proposal was that markets were in a state of panic and that prices of mortgage-backed assets at that time were below their fundamental values. If liquidity could be restored, the super-SIV could simply hold assets until markets stabilized and rational valuations returned, and make a profit. Meanwhile, the MLEC would have given the SIVs a better price than they could have found elsewhere, allowing the sponsoring banks and other investors to cap their losses, and avoiding a "fire sale" by desperate SIVs at the brink of insolvency, which would have driven values even lower, exacerbating the general financial situation and further roiling housing markets.

In retrospect, it appears that prospective MLEC participants found this assumption and scenario less persuasive than an alternative view: that mortgage ssets were not necessarily priced below fundamental values, but might still have some distance to fall. In this analysis, the SIVs' problem was not one of liquidity, but of solvency, and the notion that they could be rescued at a profit was deemed to be unrealistic.

Second, as time went on, it became apparent that the SIVs did not in fact pose an acute threat to their sponsoring banks. By the end of 2007, over $109 billion in SIV assets had been brought back onto the sponsoring banks' balance sheets, without triggering a solvency crisis in those banks.[29] SIV assets became simply one of many sources of financial pain.

With hindsight, the SIV issue may have been overstated in the fall of 2007. It was a serious problem, and contributed to perceptions of elevated credit and valuation risk that fed the general financial turmoil, but it was not the key to the entire systemic disturbance. Rather, SIVs were one of several trouble spots that may be more properly characterized as symptoms of an underlying problem, or set of problems.

Provision of New Capital to Financial Institutions

As noted above, when banks and other financial institutions suffer declines in the value of their capital, to maintain constant leverage ratios they must either shrink their balance sheets or raise new capital. From a regulatory perspective, the latter method is usually preferable, since it does not require that new lending be curtailed. For the government to bail out troubled financial institutions through an injection of public funds is rare, although many assume that certain large institutions are "too big to fail" — that is, that the failure of such an institution could have adverse systemic consequences so severe that the government would have no choice but to intervene. The Treasury and the Federal Reserve officially deny that any such policy exists, because the moral hazard issue — which (as discussed above) may be a secondary effect of the Fed's liquidity support programs — is very clear here. If institutions believe they will be rescued from insolvency, they will take imprudent risks: the calculus becomes "Heads, I win; tails, the taxpayers lose."

Although several major financial institutions experienced severe financial stress in 2007, there were no major failures that required the U.S. government to step in to prevent a spectacular collapse. In fact, troubled U.S. institutions were able to raise significant amounts of new capital. Much of this money — over $30 billion by one estimate[30] — has come from government sources, but not the American government. Instead, sovereign wealth funds operated by China, Singapore, Abu Dhabi, and other countries have taken large equity stakes in Citigroup, Merrill Lynch, Morgan Stanley, and other firms, including leading European financial institutions.

While some find sovereign wealth fund investment to be problematic[31] and are uneasy at the prospect of foreign ownership of substantial shares of key Western financial institutions, there is little doubt that such investment has eased the adjustment process for the recipients and mitigated the systemic (and perhaps macroeconomic) impact of market turmoil. It is not known whether U.S. government officials played a role in soliciting these capital contributions.

Bear Stearns[32]

In 2008, the "too-big-to-fail" doctrine was put to the test, and various forms of government intervention were employed to prevent the disorderly liquidations of several major financial institutions.

On Thursday, March 13, 2008, it became known that the Federal Reserve had extended credit to Bear Stearns, a large investment bank whose liquidity problems had driven it to the brink of collapse. As market perceptions of Bear Stearns' weakness grew, it became unable to borrow and its customers sought to retrieve their invested funds. The Fed was unwilling to allow the firm to collapse, since a liquidation would have meant the dumping of billions of dollars in mortgage-backed and other securities on the market, at a time when demand was low. The resulting fall in prices would have exacerbated the balance sheet problems of other institutions, perhaps triggering further collapses.

Over that weekend, the Fed worked with J.P. Morgan Chase to work out an agreement by which Morgan would acquire Bear. In order for the deal to proceed, the Fed had to purchase a pool of assets that Bear valued at $30 billion, but which J.P. Morgan viewed as too risky to take onto its own balance sheet. If those assets ultimately prove to be worth less than $30 billion, the taxpayers will suffer a loss equal to the difference.[33] The final sale price was $10 per share (paid in J.P. Morgan stock), a remarkable plunge from the end of 2007, when Bear's financial statements reported a book value of $80 per share, and from January 2007, when the shares traded at a high of $172.61.

In the wake of the Bear Stearns rescue, the Fed was criticized for widening the financial "safety net" to include a firm that was neither insured by the Federal Deposit Insurance Corporation nor subject to the oversight of the Fed or any other banking agency. Bear Stearns was widely considered to have been among the most aggressive and reckless speculators in the subprime market.

Fannie Mae and Freddie Mac[34]

On September 7, 2008, the Federal Housing Finance Agency (FHFA) placed Fannie Mae and Freddie Mac, two government-sponsored enterprises (GSEs) that play a critical role in the

U.S. home mortgage market, in conservatorship. As conservator, the FHFA has full powers to control the assets and operations of the firms. Dividends to common and preferred shareholders are suspended, but the Treasury has put in place a set of financing agreements to ensure that the GSEs remain solvent and continue to meet their obligations to holders of bonds that they have issued or guaranteed. This means that the U.S. taxpayer now stands behind about $5 trillion of GSE-issued debt. This step was taken because a default by either of the two firms, which have been battered by the downturn in housing and credit markets, could have caused severe disruptions in global financial markets, made home mortgages more difficult and expensive to obtain, and had negative repercussions throughout the economy.

Like Bear Stearns, Fannie and Freddie insisted up to the last minute that they were well-capitalized and liquid. In the context of plunging stock prices and doubts about creditworthiness, however, the firms were unable to raise capital by any of the normal means. If they sold assets, the deleveraging cycle described above applied: they would have depressed the prices of mortgage loans and MBSs still further, worsening both their own balance sheet problems and those of many other financial firms. They could not use retained earnings to bolster capital because their operations had not turned a profit since 2006. Finally, rapidly falling share prices made it all but impossible to raise capital by selling new equity or common stock.

Treasury and FHFA recognized that falling values of home mortgage loans and related bonds — the only investments that the GSE charters permit them to make — meant that the two firms were effectively insolvent. Even though Fannie and Freddie maintained access to the debt markets (albeit at higher-than-usual interest rates), their inability to raise new capital cast doubts on their long-term viability. If their interest costs continued to rise, and the value of (and their income from) mortgage assets kept falling, they were doomed to collapse. Against this backdrop, the federal regulator concluded that "the companies cannot continue to operate safely and soundly and fulfill their critical public mission, without significant action" to address their financial weaknesses.[35]

In exchange for its promise to provide new capital — Treasury will buy preferred stock as needed to ensure that both firms maintain a positive net worth — the government received warrants for 79.9% of equity in Fannie and Freddie, making it the majority owner of the two GSEs.

AIG

On September 16, 2008, the Fed announced, after consultation with the Treasury Department, that it would provide a credit line up to $85 billion to American International Group. AIG, in addition to being one of the largest providers of traditional lines of insurance, was a leading participant in the market for credit default swaps (CDS), instruments that are linked to corporate credit conditions.[36] In the aftermath of the Lehman Brothers bankruptcy and the Fannie and Freddie takeover, AIG was exposed to significant CDS losses. AIG was then downgraded by credit rating agencies, triggering immediate demands for billions of dollars in collateral payments related to CDS and other financial contracts.

The Fed announced that AIG could borrow up to $85 billion over a two year period. On September 18, the Fed announced that it had initially lent $28 billion to AIG. The interest rate on the loan is 8.5 percentage points above the London Interbank Offered Rate (LIBOR), a rate that banks charge to lend to each other. In return, the government has received warrants that permit the government to take a 79.9% ownership stake in AIG.

During the weeks that followed, AIG's condition appeared to worsen. Demands for collateral and margin calls in response to losing positions increased, and it was found that speculative losses were not confined to the firm's unregulated, Londonbased trading unit, but had struck the regulated insurers as well. On October 9, the company borrowed an additional $38 billion from the Fed.

In November 2008, the Treasury announced that it was purchasing $40 billion in AIG preferred stock, pursuant to the Troubled Assets Relief Program (TARP) created by the Emergency Economic Stabilization Act (P.L. 110-343). The funds were to be used to restructure AIG's loan from the Fed. Total federal assistance to AIG now exceeds $150 billion.

The $700 Billion Troubled Assets Relief Program (P.L. 110-343)

Despite the steps taken to provide liquidity and prevent the failure of systemically important institutions, financial conditions worsened in the fall of 2008. During the week of September 22, 2008, following the bankruptcy of Lehman Brothers, markets approached full-blown panic. Investors pulled billions of dollars out of money market funds, normally considered very low-risk investments, and rushed to safety, driving the yields on Treasury bills to near zero. To the Fed and Treasury, this was a sign that the crisis had reached a new level: if financial institutions and investors viewed Treasury securities at zero percent as a good investment, who would be willing to extend credit to households and businesses? In other words, the possibility that credit markets would "freeze up," with devastating consequences to the real economy, now seemed to be at hand.

On Thursday, September 25, Chairman Bernanke and Secretary Paulson presented a proposal to leaders of Congress. They asked for authority to purchase up to $700 billion of troubled mortgage-related assets. Behind the plan lay the conclusion that the normal market self-stabilizing processes were not resolving, and would not resolve, the balance sheet problems faced by many institutions. Banks could not sell their mortgage-related assets except at fire sale prices that implied widespread insolvency throughout the financial system. Uncertainty about the fundamental value of those assets was disrupting interbank lending, as no one could judge the true condition of trading partners. The negative leverage spiral described above had taken hold, and severely constrained the ability of financial institutions to raise capital in the markets.

Waiting for asset values to recover as the housing market improved was no longer an attractive option, given the possibility of a general collapse of lending to households and businesses. The $700 billion rescue plan proposed replacing the case-by-case approach to interventions in the financial markets that had prevailed from summer 2007 through summer 2008 with a systemic program to improve the balance sheets of any institution that was holding mortgage-related assets. The government, better positioned than private firms to bear long-term risks of uncertain magnitude, would pay cash in exchange for troubled assets. The hope was that once troubled MBS no longer raised doubts about the reliability of banks' balance sheet figures, credit risk fears would subside and normal lending flows will resume.

The Troubled Assets Relief Program (TARP) was enacted on October 3, 2008, as part of the Emergency Economic Stabilization Act (P.L. 110-343). Asset purchases were expected to begin in about one month.

In fact, the TARP funds have been used not to purchase troubled mortgagerelated assets, but to inject capital directly into banks via purchases of newly-issued preferred stock. On

October 29, Treasury announced the first set of purchases: preferred stock (with warrants to acquire common stock) from nine large financial institutions[37] in exchange for $115 billion. On November 14, a second set of capital injections was announced, involving 21 banks. In addition, as noted above, $40 billion in TARP funds went to AIG.

The Treasury continues to accept applications from financial institutions for TARP funding.[38]

Increases in Government Guarantees and Insurance

In September 2008, during the panic that followed the bankruptcy of Lehman Brothers, there were massive withdrawals from money market funds. Like banks, money market funds face liquidity risk. They can only raise money by selling assets, but those sales themselves may depress assets prices further, leading to more demand for redemptions, and so on.

To stabilize the funds, the Treasury established a Temporary Guarantee Program, using the assets in a fund for foreign exchange rate stabilization. Under this program, the U.S. Treasury will guarantee to investors that they will receive $1 for each money market fund share held as of close of business on September 19, 2008. To participate in the program, eligible funds must pay a fee and sign up for the program.

In response to the crisis, the Federal Deposit Insurance Corporation (FDIC) also increased the range and amount of assets it guarantees. The TARP legislation raised the insurance ceiling for individual bank accounts from $100,000 to $250,000.

On October 14, 2008, the FDIC announced a new program — the Temporary Liquidity Guarantee Program — to strengthen confidence and encourage liquidity in the banking system by guaranteeing newly issued senior unsecured debt of banks, thrifts, and certain holding companies, and by providing full coverage of non-interest bearing deposit transaction accounts, regardless of dollar amount.

Commercial Paper

On October 7, 2008, the Fed announced that it was using its emergency authority under Section 13(3) of the Federal Reserve Act to establish a Commercial Paper Funding Facility. The facility will purchase commercial paper — short-term debt obligations used by a variety of businesses to fund their short-term operational cash needs — directly from the issuing corporations to ensure that this source of credit does not dry up. The initiative was another sign that credit conditions had not improved.

By the end of October, the Fed had purchased more than $100 billion in commercial paper.

Citigroup

On November 23, 2008, the Fed and Treasury announced a rescue package for Citigroup, the second largest U.S. bank.[39] As part of the agreement, Treasury and the FDIC will provide protection against the possibility of unusually large losses on an asset pool of approximately

$306 billion of loans and securities backed by residential and commercial real estate (and derivatives related to such assets), which will remain on Citigroup's balance sheet. Citigroup will absorb the first $29 billion in losses on the pool; the government will then cover 90% of losses that exceed that figure.

As a fee for this arrangement, Citigroup will issue $7 billion in preferred shares to the Treasury and FDIC. In addition and if necessary, the Federal Reserve stands ready to backstop residual risk in the asset pool through a non-recourse loan.

Finally, Treasury will invest $20 billion in Citigroup from the Troubled Asset Relief Program in exchange for preferred stock with an 8% dividend to the Treasury. Citigroup will comply with enhanced executive compensation restrictions and implement the FDIC's mortgage modification program.

POLICY ISSUES: ARE REGULATORS' TOOLS ADEQUATE?

This prolonged period of financial stress raises questions about the ability of regulators to monitor, prevent, or respond to market instability. Policy makers may consider a number of approaches.

Information

First, some observers believe that regulators lack comprehensive information about large areas of the markets. No federal agency has direct supervisory authority over hedge funds, nonbank lenders, over-the-counter derivatives trading, private equity funds, all of which demand liquidity and can become the trigger for systemic instability. When regulated firms create off-balance sheet entities, oversight becomes more difficult. According to Secretary Paulson, "regulators didn't have clear enough visibility with what was going on in terms of these off-balance-sheet SIVs."[40] Banking and securities laws could be amended to authorize regulators to require more disclosure and reporting from (1) currently unregulated firms and sectors and (2) about off-the-books activities of regulated firms.

U.S. financial regulation is divided among agencies specializing in single markets: futures, individual banking sectors, or securities. In today's markets, however, firms' activities regularly cross those lines. An integrated firm like Merrill Lynch or Citigroup files reports with half a dozen agencies — would a single, consolidated supervisor be better able to interpret this information and assess market conditions?

Others question whether regulators can be expected to monitor overall market conditions, when the current turmoil suggests that even market participants lack that capacity. The invention of new and complex derivative instruments and securities has been a major profit center in the financial industry for several decades. In other words, while transparency benefits regulators and public investors, opacity can be a source of income for market intermediaries and professional traders. The problem of hard-to-value assets and unverifiable trading models is likely to persist.

Another view is that regulators had plenty of information indicating that trouble was imminent, but failed to take adequate preventive measures. According to Martin Feldstein, even though "the Fed's examiners have complete access to all of the transactions of the banks that they supervise [and] can also examine indirectly what nonbank financial institutions are doing," the Fed failed to provide appropriate supervisory oversight for major money center banks, making such technical errors as understating liabilities associated with off-balance sheet activities and overstating the quality of bank asset values that were the result of the housing bubble.[41] There is a natural tendency for regulators to share industry's enthusiasm for the latest financial innovation or strategy, as long as it is generating profits that enable banks to meet capital requirements and maintain healthy levels of reserves. It is difficult, as Alan Greenspan put it, to be the one who takes away the punch bowl when the party is just getting started.[42] Federal bank agencies addressed securitization and offbalance sheet finance more than a decade ago, but characterized them as useful risk management tools.[43]

Speculation

Financial speculation presents another set of policy choices. In general, speculation is a benign and useful activity: speculators provide liquidity and help markets allocate resources efficiently. The current episode, however, illustrates that speculative excesses and errors can cause liquidity to dry up and disrupt markets.

Successful speculation rewards risk-taking. Recent developments in finance make it possible to unbundle the risks embedded in traditional financial instruments. A mortgage, for example, carries credit risk, interest rate risk, and prepayment risk, but with derivatives and CDOs, each of these risks can be disaggregated and made the basis of a financial bet. Increasingly, speculators identify financial propositions with a high probability of making a small profit, and a very small chance of a large loss. The SIV model, for example, captured the spread between short-term and longterm rates, earning a modest return that was almost risk-free unless there were to be a major disruption in the commercial paper market, which was normally very large and liquid. The CDO market relies on the narrow spread between what homebuyers pay and what investors will pay for the identical mortgages repackaged. Using derivatives, it is possible to construct similar trades based on tiny variations in observed historical relationships among a multitude of economic variables.

Of course, a strategy that promises a small but seemingly predictable return does not appeal to most investment bankers: Treasury bills offer the same risk/reward characteristics. What the bankers do is add leverage: if they borrow a high multiple of their own capital and put those funds into the same trading position, the returns to their own capital are magnified. Of course, the potential losses are magnified to exactly the same degree. Then why is leveraged speculation attractive?

One answer, put forward by Raghuram Rajan, former chief economist of the International Monetary Fund, is that compensation structures reward short-term performance and ignore long-term risk.[44] That a strategy is likely to fail spectacularly every ten or twenty years is not a disincentive to the leveraged trader: he will probably receive several large annual bonuses before the bad year comes, and even then may keep his job, since many of his peers will probably have incurred similar losses. The CEO of Morgan Stanley, for example, received no bonus for 2007, but kept the $40 million from the year before.[45] Rajan suggests that significant portions of bankers' pay could be held in escrow for long periods, and that losses be factored in before final disbursement.[46]

The combination of modern financial engineering and short-term incentives may distort or weaken market discipline and lead to excessive risk-taking. The costs of failed speculation are not always borne by the speculators themselves but may be widely distributed throughout the financial system and, in extreme cases, may fall upon the economy as a whole. Is there a case for more stringent regulation to restrain speculation or limit the potential damage from speculative losses?

Financial supervisors can impose higher capital and reserve requirements on regulated firms, and can control the amount of leverage such firms extend to their unregulated customers. Such controls would smooth out the peaks and troughs of financial industry returns: this would mean, in effect, putting a brake on periods of economic and financial expansion.

The degree of support for initiatives such as these among regulators and policy makers is likely to depend on how the current financial turmoil is resolved, and at what cost. Opposition to forms and degrees of regulation that would have seemed excessive before the crisis may be muted because the government has already established a major ownership position in the financial services industry.

End Notes

[1] About $1.2 trillion in subprime mortgages are outstanding, and most of them are being paid off. This compares to about $11 trillion in total U.S. mortgage debt, and $51 trillion in credit market debt outstanding.

[2] Brian Caplen, "Credit Suisse CEO: Clear View Curtails Crisis Fallout," *The Banker*, January 1, 2008.

[3] For discussion of the global nature of the crisis, see CRS Report RL34742, *The U.S. Financial Crisis: The Global Dimension with Implications for U.S. Policy*, by Dick K. Nanto et al.

[4] Risky bank loans equivalent to high-yield "junk" bonds, often made in support of corporate takeovers or buyouts.

[5] Contracts linked to subprime mortgages had only a few years of data on which to model performance.

[6] Commercial paper is used as a source of short-term borrowing by many firms, financial and nonfinancial. The maturity is generally between three months and one year.

[7] Adrian Blundell-Wignall, Structured Products: Implications for Financial Markets, *[OECD] Financial Market Trends*, No. 93, 2007, p. 45.

[8] For example, Citigroup's SIVs held about $100 billion in assets at the peak, yet the firm's quarterly report to the Securities and Exchange Commission for the second quarter of 2007 contained no reference to them. (The third quarter report, of course, devoted considerable space to the associated problems and potential losses.)

[9] The account of this transaction is taken from three *Washington Post* articles by Lena H. Sun: "Judge Tells Metro and Bank to Deal," Nov. 13, 2008, p. B1; "Metro, Bank Make a Deal," Nov. 15, 2008, p. B1; and "U.S. Transit Agencies Ask Congress for Help in Averting Service Cuts," Nov. 19, 2008, p. D2.

[10] The deal also produced tax savings for the participants.

[11] Ibid.

[12] Liquidity, in central banking terms, means maintaining the flow of credit. The Fed's declarations signal market participants not to allow credit decisions to be governed by fears that the opposite party may have temporary cash flow problems.

[13] As data become available for the third quarter of 2008, this picture may change. The amount of consumer credit outstanding, for example, fell in August (but resumed slow growth in September). This shift, however, was mainly due to a dropoff in car loans, which was driven by reduced buyer demand as well as tightening lending standards.

[14] V.V. Chari, Lawrence Christiano, and Patrick J. Kehoe, *Facts and Myths about th Financial Crisis of 2008*, Federal Reserve Bank of Minneapolis Research Department Working Paper 666, Oct. 2008; and Ethan Cohen-Cole, Burcu Duygan-Bump, Jose Fillat, and Judit Montoriol-Garriga, *Looking Behind the Aggregates: A Reply to "Facts and Myths about the Financial Crisis of 2008,"* Federal Reserve Bank of Boston Working Paper No. QAU08-5, Nov. 2008.

[15] Martin Crutsinger, "Paulson: No Simple Solution to Housing Crisis," *York Dispatch*, January 7, 2008.

[16] David Greenlaw, Jan Hatzius, Anil Kashyap, and Hyun Song Shin, "Leveraged Losses: Lessons from the Mortgage Meltdown," U.S. Monetary Forum Conference Draft, February 29, 2008, 47 p.

[17] Ben Bernanke, Mark Gertler, and Simon Gilchrist, "The Financial Accelerator and the Flight to Quality," Review of Economics and Statistics, vol. 78, February 1996, p. 1.

[18] Ibid., p. 2.

[19] Martin Feldstein, "Our Economic Dilemma," *Wall Street Journal*, February 20, 2008, p. A15.

[20] Frederic S. Mishkin, "Financial Instability and Monetary Policy," Speech at the Risk USA 2007 Conference, New York, November 5, 2007.

[21] Ibid.

[22] "Central Banks' Action Is Welcome But Long-Term Rethink Is Needed," *The Banker*, January 1, 2008.

[23] For a more detailed overview of the Fed's actions, see CRS Report RL34427, *Financial Turmoil: Federal Reserve Policy Responses*, by Marc Labonte.

[24] Agency bonds are those issued by government-sponsored enterprises like Fannie Mae and Freddie Mac.

[25] "Federal Reserve Actions," Press Release, December 12, 2007.

[26] See, e.g., Steven Sloan, "Fed Pushes Harder, But Sentiment Isn't Shifting," *American Banker*, vol. 178, March 10, 2008, p. 1.

[27] "Global Banks Announce Plans for Major Liquidity Facility to Bolster Asset-Backed Commercial Paper Markets," *PR Newswire*, October 5, 2007.

[28] Atsuko Fukase, "Japanese Banks Balk at Aiding SIV Fund," *Wall Street Journal*, December 20, 2007, p. C9.

[29] The exact total is unknown. The $109 billion figure represents announced transactions by five banks: Citigroup ($49 billion), HSBC ($45 billion), Rabobank ($7.6 billion), Societe General ($4.3 billion), and Standard Chartered ($3 billion). See "Bringing It All Back Home," *American Banker*, vol. 172, December 17, 2007, p. 1.

[30] Gillian Tett, "Sovereign funds face growing US pressure to address market fears," *Financial Times*, January 24, 2008, p. 1.

[31] See CRS Report RL34336, *Sovereign Wealth Funds: Background and Policy Issues For Congress*, by Martin A. Weiss.

[32] See CRS Report RL34420, *Bear Stearns: Crisis and 'Rescue' for a Major Provider of Mortgage-Related Products*, by Gary Shorter.

[33] J.P. Morgan Chase agreed to absorb the first billion dollars in losses, limiting taxpayer exposure to $29 billion.

[34] See CRS Report RS22950, *Fannie Mae and Freddie Mac in Conservatorship*, by Mark Jickling.

[35] Federal Housing Finance Agency, "Statement of FHFA Director James B. Lockhart," Press Release, September 7, 2008, p. 5.

[36] See CRS Report RS22932, *Credit Default Swaps: Frequently Asked Questions*, by Edward V. Murphy.

[37] Bank of America, Bank of New York Mellon, Citigroup, Goldman Sachs, JP Morgan Chase, Morgan Stanley, State Street, Wells Fargo, and Merrill Lynch.

[38] For news about TARP transactions, see [http://www.ustreas.gov/initiatives/eesa/].

[39] See: "Joint Statement by Treasury, Federal Reserve and the FDIC on Citigroup," online at http://www.fdic.gov/news/news/press/2008/pr08125.html].

[40] Carrick Mollenkamp, Deborah Solomon and Craig Karmin, "Call to Brave for $100 Billion Rescue; Banks Seek Investors For Fund to Shore Up Commercial Paper," *Wall Street Journal*, October 16, 2007, p. C1.

[41] Martin Feldstein, "Our Economic Dilemma," *Wall Street Journal*, February 20, 2008, p. A15.

[42] According to some sources, he was quoting his predecessor, Chairman William McChesney Martin, Jr. The remark is attributed to every Fed chairman sooner or later.

[43] See, e.g., Office of the Comptroller of the Currency, "Interest Rate Risk Management: Questions and Answers," OCC 95-28, June 20, 1995, at [http://www.occ.treas.gov/ftp/bulletin/95-28.txt].

[44] Raghuram Rajan, "Bankers' Pay is Deeply Flawed," *Financial Times*, January 9, 2008, p. 11.

[45] The firm wrote down the value of its assets by $9.4 billion in the last quarter of 2007, but increased its year-end bonus pool by 18%.

[46] Ibid.

In: Government Interventions in Economic Emergencies ISBN: 978-1-60741-356-1
Editor: Pablo Sastre

Chapter 5

THE COST OF GOVERNMENT FINANCIAL INTERVENTIONS, PAST AND PRESENT

Baird Webel, N. Eric Weiss and Marc Labonte

SUMMARY

In response to ongoing financial turmoil, the federal government intervened financially with private corporations on a large scale that resulted in the government receiving significant debt and equity considerations three times from the beginning of 2008 until the middle of September 2008. The firms affected were Bear Stearns, Fannie Mae and Freddie Mac, and AIG. Dissatisfaction with the case-by-case approach that had been pursued up to that point led to Treasury's decision to propose a more comprehensive solution to the turmoil on September 19, 2008. On October 3, 2008, P.L. 110-343 was signed into law, authorizing the Troubled Assets Relief Program (TARP). TARP gave Treasury the option of purchasing or insuring up to $700 billion of assets from financial firms. On October 14, 2008, Treasury announced it was purchasing up to $250 billion in financial firms' preferred stock under the TARP authority.

These interventions have prompted questions regarding the taxpayer costs and the sources of funding. The sources of funding are relatively straightforward, the Federal Reserve (Fed) and the U.S. Treasury. The costs, however, are difficult to quantify at this stage. In most of the interventions, all the financial outflows that are possible have yet to occur, and the ultimate value of the debt and equity considerations received from the private firms is uncertain. At this point, the federal government has the option to own nearly 80% of Fannie Mae, Freddie Mac, and AIG. Depending on the final proceeds from the various debt and equity considerations, the federal government may end up seeing a positive fiscal contribution from the recent interventions, as was the case in some of the past interventions summarized in the tables at the end of this chapter. The government may also suffer significant losses, as has also occurred in the past.

WHERE HAS THE MONEY COME FROM?

In the recent interventions, there have been two primary sources of immediate funding: the Federal Reserve (Fed) and the U.S. Treasury. The Fed has the authority under its founding statute to loan money "in unusual and exigent circumstances" to "any individual, partnership, or corporation" provided five members of the Board of Governors of the Federal Reserve system agree.[1] This authority has been cited in two of the interventions this year, Bear Stearns and AIG. The source of money loaned under this section derives from the Fed's general control of the money supply, which is essentially unlimited subject to the statutory mandates of controlling inflation and promoting economic growth.[2] Because the profits of the Fed are overwhelmingly remitted to the Treasury, the indirect source of the funds is the Treasury. In the case of Fannie Mae and Freddie Mac, the direct source of funding is the Treasury, pursuant to the statutory authority granted in the Housing and Economic Recovery Act of 2008.[3] In the case of the Troubled Assets Relief Program, the direct source of funding is the Treasury, pursuant to the statutory authority granted in the Emergency Economic Stabilization Act of 2008.[4] Treasury finances these activities by issuing bonds and increasing the federal debt.

THE COST OF FINANCIAL INTERVENTIONS

Determining the cost of government interventions, particularly those currently in progress, is not straightforward. Assistance often comes in forms other than direct monies from the Treasury, including loan guarantees, lines of credit, or preferred stock purchases.

Such assistance may have little or no up-front cost to the government, although loan guarantees in legislation are scored by the Congressional Budget Office as an up front budgetary cost. This score reflects that a loan guarantee, which can be thought of as a sort of insurance, has value even if it is never used. Many insurance policies are never used, but individuals and companies purchase them to reduce the risk of loss. In many past cases, the value to various companies of federal guarantees was to enable them to access the private credit markets, issuing bonds or obtaining bank loans that they would not otherwise have been able to obtain. In other past cases, the federal guarantee resulted in a lower interest rate on the bonds or loans.

Depending on the conditions attached to each specific intervention and how events proceed thereafter, the government may even see a net inflow of funds from the actions taken, rather than a net outflow. The summaries below address the maximum amounts promised in federal assistance and attempt to quantify the amounts that have actually been disbursed. There are also other, more diffuse costs that could be weighed. For example, many would argue that the cost to the taxpayers of any intervention should be weighed against the potential costs of financial system instability resulting from inaction, or that one intervention may lead to more private sector risk-taking, and thus necessitate additional future interventions (moral hazard). Such costs, however, are even harder to quantify than the realized cost of the interventions. This chapter does not attempt to address them.

Recent Financial Interventions

Troubled Assets Relief Program (TARP)

As the government has intervened in 2008 to prevent the failure of troubled financial firms, market conditions seemed to get worse instead of better. After the AIG intervention, Treasury argued that a more comprehensive solution was needed to restore financial calm. It proposed creating a TARP to purchase up to $700 billion of troubled assets from financial firms as a way to restore investors' confidence in the health of the financial sector. It was argued that financial firms would be unable to replenish their capital (by selling equity to private investors) unless certain assets were transferred to the government. Once financial markets stabilized, Treasury would be able to sell these assets, recouping some or perhaps all (if asset prices rose above their purchase price) of the costs.

On October 3, 2008, P.L. 110-343 was signed into law, creating TARP. In addition to an asset purchase program, P.L. 110-343 included an insurance program providing federal guarantees for troubled assets in return for premiums paid by companies. It also allowed the government to take an equity stake in companies participating in the asset purchase program. P.L. 110-343 provided broad discretion to the Treasury to design the parameters of the program, making it difficult to evaluate the ultimate costs of the program at this time. On October 14, 2008, Treasury announced a TARP capital purchase program. Under this program, rather than purchasing troubled assets, Treasury will inject capital directly into financial institutions through the purchase of preferred stock.

American International Group (AIG)

On September 16, 2008, the Fed announced that it was taking action to support AIG, a federally chartered thrift holding company with a broad range of businesses, primarily insurance subsidiaries, which are state-chartered. This support took the form of a secured two-year line of credit with a value of up to $85 billion. The interest rate on the loan is relatively high, approximately 11.5% on the date it was announced. AIG must also pay interest on the amount of the credit line that it does not access. In addition, the government received warrants to purchase up to 79.9% of the equity in AIG. On October 8, the Fed announced that it would lend up to a further $37.8 billion AIG against investment-grade securities held by its insurance subsidiaries. These securities had been previously lent out and were not available as collateral at the time of the original intervention. The Fed reported that $70.3 billion had been lent to AIG as of October 8, 2008.[5]

Fannie Mae and Freddie Mac

On September 7, 2008, the Federal Housing Finance Agency (FHFA) placed Fannie Mae and Freddie Mac into conservatorship.[6] As part of this conservatorship, Fannie Mae and Freddie Mac have signed contracts to issue new senior preferred stock to the Treasury, which has agreed to purchase up to $100 billion of this stock from each of them. The Treasury agreed to make open market purchases of Fannie Mae- and Freddie Mac-issued mortgage-backed securities (MBS). Treasury has said that it expects to profit from the spread between the interest rate that it pays to borrow money through bonds and the mortgage payments on the MBS. Fannie Mae and Freddie Mac will guarantee payment of the MBS. Treasury agreed that if the companies have difficulty borrowing money, which has apparently not been the case to date, Treasury will create a Government Sponsored Enterprise Credit Facility to provide liquidity to them, secured by MBS pledged as collateral. There are no specific limits to these purchases or loans, but they are subject to the statutory limit on the federal government's debt. In return for the Treasury support, each company issued the Treasury $1 billion of senior preferred stock without additional compensation, as well as warrants (options) to purchase up to 79.9% of each company's common stock. Treasury's authority to provide financial support will terminate December 31, 2009.

Table 1. Summary of Current and Historical Financial Interventions by the Federal Government

Beneficiary	Action	Financial Commitment	Final Cost to Treasury
TARP (October 3, 2008)	Purchase of troubled assets from financial firms	Up to $700 billion	Unknown (Assets can be sold at future date. Treasury has the option to take an equity stake in participating companies.)
	Insurance of troubled financial assets		Unknown (By law, premiums paid for the insurance are to cover losses.)
	Purchase of preferred stock		Unknown (Treasury receives dividends on stock, plus sale value of stock at the end of the program.)
AIG (September 16, 2008)	Two-Year Secured Loan from the Federal Reserve	Up to $75 billion against the general assets of AIG; up to $37.8 billion against the securities held by AIG's insurance subsidiaries	Unknown (Government receives interest on loan plus stock warrants on up to 79.9% of AIG's equity.)
Fannie Mae and Freddie Mac (September 7, 2008)	Senior Preferred Stock Purchase	Initial commitment, $100 billion each; ultimately, no set limit	Unknown (Treasury receives $1 billion (each) of preferred stock and 10% accrual on the stock.)
	Purchase of Mortgage-Backed Securities issued	No set limit	Unknown (Treasury receives interest on any MBS purchased and

Table 1. (Continued)

Beneficiary	Action	Financial Commitment	Final Cost to Treasury
	by the companies		may sell the securities in the future.)
	Credit Facility	No set limit; collateralized	Unknown (Treasury receives interest on any loans taken.)
Bear Stearns (March 14, 2008)	Asset Purchase through LLC controlled by the Federal Reserve	$28.8 billion	Unknown (The Federal Reserve LLC received $29.95 billion in relatively illiquid assets.)
U.S. Airlines P.L. 107-42 (September 22, 2001)	Loan Guarantees	Up to $10 billion	None except implicit value of loan guarantees; under $2 billion in loans made.
Savings and Loan Failures P.L. 101-73 (August 9, 1989)	Savings and Loan Failures and Insolvency of Federal Savings and Loan Insurance Corporation	Full faith and credit backing of Federal Savings and Loan Insurance Corporation	$150 billion.
Chrysler P.L. 96-185 (January 7, 1980)	Loan Guarantees	$1.5 billion	$311 million profit from sale of warrants.
New York City P.L. 95-339 (August 9, 1978)	Loan Guarantees	$1.65 billion in guaranteed bonds	None, except the implicit value of loan guarantee.
New York City P.L. 94-143 (December 9, 1975)	Short-Term Loans	$2.3 billion	None, except the implicit cost of the risk of loan.
Penn Central P.L. 93-236 (January 2, 1974)	Loan Guarantees in the wake of Railroad Bankruptcy	$125 million loan guarantees; $7 billion in federal operating subsidies	$3 billion net loss after sale of ownership stake plus the implicit value of loan guarantee.
Lockheed P.L. 92-70 (August 9, 1971)	Loan Guarantees	$250 million of loans guaranteed for five years with three year renewal; guarantee and commitment fees charged	$31 million profit from sale of warrants less the lost value of loan guarantee.

Bear Stearns

On March 16, 2008, JPMorgan Chase agreed to acquire the investment bank Bear Stearns. As part of the agreement, the Fed lent $28.82 billion to a Delaware limited liability corporation (LLC) that it created to purchase financial securities from Bear Stearns. These securities are largely mortgage-related assets. The interest and principal will be repaid to the Fed by the LLC using the funds raised by the sale of the assets. The Fed's loan will be made at an interest rate set equal to the discount rate (2.5% when the terms were announced, but fluctuating over time) for a term of 10 years, renewable by the Fed.7 In addition, JPMorgan Chase extended a $1.15 billion loan to the LLC that will have an interest rate 4.5 percentage points above the discount rate. Thus, in order for the principal and interest to be paid off, the assets will need to appreciate enough or generate enough income so that the rate of return on the assets exceeds the weighted interest rate on the loans (plus the operating costs of the LLC). The interest on the loan will be repaid out of the asset sales, not by JPMorgan Chase.

Any difference between the proceeds and the amount of the loans will produce a profit or loss for the Fed, not JPMorgan Chase. Because JPMorgan Chase's $1.15 billion loan was subordinate to the Fed's $28.8 billion loan, if there are losses on the $29.95 billion assets, the first $1.15 billion of losses will be borne, in effect, by JPMorgan Chase, however. Thus, if the assets appreciate in value by more than operating expenses, the Fed will make a profit on the loan. If the assets decline in value by less than $1.15 billion, the Fed will not suffer any direct loss on the loan. Any losses beyond $1.15 billion will be borne by the Fed.

End Notes

[1] 12 U.S.C. Sec. 343.

[2] For more information on the Federal Reserve's actions, please see CRS Report RL34427, *Financial Turmoil: Federal Reserve Policy Responses*, by Marc Labonte.

[3] P.L. 110-289, Title I.

[4] P.L. 110-343, Division A, Title 1.

[5] See Federal Reserve Statistical Release, H.4.1, dated October 9, 2008, Table 1, "Other credit extensions" available at [http://www.federalreserve.gov/releases/h41/Current/].

[6] For more information see the September 7, 2008 statement by Treasury Secretary Henry Paulson at [http://ustreas.gov/press/releases/hp1129.htm]; and CRS Report RL34661, *Fannie Mae's and Freddie Mac's Financial Problems*, by N. Eric Weiss.

[7] Federal Reserve Bank of New York, "Summary of Terms and Conditions Regarding the JP Morgan Chase Facility," press release, March 24, 2008.

In: Government Interventions in Economic Emergencies ISBN: 978-1-60741-356-1
Editor: Pablo Sastre

Chapter 6

DANGERS FROM THE POLITICAL ALLOCATION OF CAPITAL

Jim Saxton

> *In many ways some of the ideas of [Friedich] Hayek and [Milton] Friedman about how markets best provide incentives, and best provide information, and best collect information may in a sense be even more true today, because of the changes that information technology is bringing, than they were at the time when they were propounded. If you think about it, it cannot be an accident that it is the same 15-year period when communism fell, when command-and-control corporations like General Motors and IBM had to be drastically restructured, when planning ministries throughout the developing world were closed down, and when the Japanese model of industrial policy proved to be a complete failure. There is something about this epoch in history that really puts a premium on incentives, on decentralization, on allowing small economic energy to bubble up rather than a more top-down, more directed approach, that may have been a more fruitful approach in earlier years.*
>
> *Lawrence J. Summers*
> *71st Secretary of the Treasury*[1] *and Adviser to President-Elect Barack Obama*

Since the financial crisis began in August 2007, the federal government has become increasingly involved with U.S. banks and other financial institutions and U.S. financial markets. The Federal Reserve has greatly expanded the size, duration, and scope of its credit facilities (see Appendix). The Department of the Treasury has agreed to (1) inject up to $100 billion of taxpayer funds into Fannie Mae and another $100 billion into Freddie Mac, (2) purchase up to $250 billion of preferred shares in banks, and (3) purchase $40 billion of preferred shares in American International Group (AIG). Now, Chrysler, Ford, and General Motors along with the United Auto Workers (UAW) union are seeking emergency financing to help these automakers to avoid reorganizations under Chapter 11 of the federal bankruptcy code.

Although central governments play a large role in allocating capital in many Asian and European economies (1) through government-owned banks, government pension funds, and other government-owned financial institutions, or (2) through industrial policies that direct credit to and encourage investment in favored firms, industries, regions, or groups, a historical strength of the U.S. economy has been the relatively small role that the federal government has played in allocating credit and making investment decisions. The limited number and scope of government-owned financial institutions and the absence of an industrial policy in the United States has allowed private investors, private banks, and other private financial institutions to allocate credit and make investment decisions based on economic criteria without undue political interference. Subject only to general laws and regulations, private investors, banks, and other financial institutions may seek the highest returns consistent with their risk tolerance.

While recent federal interventions were designed to encourage banks and other financial institutions to replace government capital with private capital after market conditions improve, policymakers may nevertheless be tempted to use the leverage arising out of these federal interventions to affect credit and investment decisions. This raised an important question – how would the political allocation of capital affect the performance of the U.S. economy?

The political allocation of capital misdirects investment based on political criteria. Product innovation and process improvement in firms. suffer. Over time, diminishing productivity gains slow real income growth and reduce real GDP well below its potential. Economists attribute the deterioration of economic performance under the political allocation of capital to several factors:

- Inability of policymakers or bureaucrats to incorporate all of the widely diffused and rapidly changing knowledge conveyed by prices into allocating credit and making investment decisions;
- Both legal and practical restraints on political decision-making in a constitutional republic that:
  - Reduce responsiveness to changing conditions and prospects, and
  - Produce biases
    - Against entrepreneurship and innovation, and
    - For existing constituencies;
- Division of firm resources away from managing the business toward lobbying policymakers and influencing the bureaucracy; and
- Potential for corruption.

Information Problems

The knowledge necessary to allocate capital efficiently is widely diffused throughout the global economy and costly to obtain. It is impossible for any one person or organization to acquire and to update constantly all of the information necessary to allocate capital efficiently in a complex economy.

Prices reflect the collective judgment of global markets on all available information. Under the market allocation of capital, price signals from changes in interest rates and share prices allow households and firms to coordinate their investing and lending activities and rapidly adjust their behavior to reflect changing conditions or prospects.

Under the political allocation of capital, however, policymakers or government bureaucrats substitute their judgment for the collective judgment of global financial markets expressed through prices. Because of the high cost and extreme difficulty in obtaining and constantly updating information, this substitution necessarily ignores some of the information incorporated in market prices. With less than complete information, politically determined credit and investment decisions are less efficient than market-determined credit and investment decisions.

Unresponsiveness

A constitutional republic such as the United States places many restraints both legal and practical upon policymakers and bureaucrats. These restraints necessarily slow the response of policymakers or bureaucrats to changing conditions or prospects.

It takes time for policymakers to perceive funding needs. Congress must enact enabling legislation to allow a political allocation of capital. Normally, federal agencies must then devise implementing regulations before decisions can be made. While laws and regulations can be amended, change is often slow. In contrast, market participants have no such time constraints.

Bias against Entrepreneurship and Innovation

Extending credit and making investments involves risk. Loans may not be repaid, and the value of equity investments may dwindle. To reward lenders for assuming risk, riskier loans bear higher interest rates. Likewise, riskier equity investments require higher expected rates of return.

Entrepreneurs experience a high rate of failure. While only a small number of new firms grow into large prosperous multinational corporations, the rewards for investors in these few are enormous. Under the market allocation of capital, venture capital firms can provide funds to promising new firms with innovative products or breakthrough technologies because the vast returns from investing in the next Microsoft or Starbucks can offset many failed investments.

Under the political allocation of capital, neither policymakers nor bureaucrats receive large returns from successful investments in new firms. Instead, policymakers and bureaucrats that extend credit to or make investments in new firms that ultimately prove unsuccessful may suffer from press derision and public ridicule. As a result, policymakers and bureaucrats may lose their positions.

The differences in the balance between risk and returns in private firms and in government bias the political allocation of capital against funding entrepreneurship in emerging industries producing new goods and services using innovative technologies, and toward funding existing firms in established industries producing known goods and services using conventional technologies. Thus, the political allocation of capital discourages entrepreneurship, slows product and process innovation, and retards the development of new technologies.

Bias for Constituents

Under the separation of powers system with legislatures whose members are elected by separate constituencies, the public expects individual lawmakers to respond to special needs of their constituents, while the public expects the chief executive to defend general interests. Under the political allocation of capital, the natural tendency of legislative policymakers to serve the special interests of their constituents may cause such policymakers to direct or at least to influence the flow of credit and investment to their constituencies.

Struggling firms that have trouble raising funds in capital markets often seek funding from government. Because of constituency bias, many policymakers may support extending credit or investing funds to struggling firms that employ the constituents of policymakers to avoid layoffs or facility closures.

Layoffs and facility closures are never popular, but such restructuring is often necessary for struggling firms to recover. To secure governmental funding, however, firms may make popular commitments that are often not in the long-term interests of the firm or its shareholders. For example, firms may commit to maintain their current level of employment, to keep inefficient facilities open, or continue to produce unprofitable products.

Resource Diversion

The political allocation of capital encourages firms to devote management time and firm resources to lobbying activities to secure funding from policymakers or bureaucrats. At a minimum, this distracts entrepreneurs and firm managers from their business. Firms may redirect resources from product innovation and process improvement toward lobbying activities. As dependence on government funding increases, the diversion of attention and resources may become severe. Such diversions retard product innovations and process improvements. Over time, diminishing productivity gains slow real income growth and reduce real GDP below its potential.

Corruption and Crony Capitalism

Finally, the political allocation of capital may foster corruption. When policymakers and bureaucrats make credit and investment decisions, entrepreneurs and firm managers may be tempted to bribe policymakers and bureaucrats to secure funding for their firms or to prevent their rivals from securing funding. Both policymakers and bureaucrats may seek to exploit the considerable economic power that they are exercising when they allocate capital. Thus, policymakers and bureaucrats may seek bribes from entrepreneurs and firm managers.

In a number of countries, the political allocation of capital has led to crony capitalism, in which politically connected firms receive favors from the central government in exchange for various types of bribes to policymakers and bureaucrats. Under crony capitalism, politically favored firms are largely immune from competition with less well connected firms. This discourages both domestic entrepreneurship and foreign direct investment. By diminishing the incentive to innovate, productivity gains lag, reducing real GDP growth over time.

Conclusion

While the severity of the financial crisis may justify some of the recent federal interventions, these interventions, if not reversed once the crisis has dissipated, may retard the efficient allocation of capital in the United States and thus diminish its long-term growth prospects. Private firms and households make their credit and investment decisions based on economic criteria. While federal policymakers may incorporate economic criteria, federal policymakers must necessarily incorporate political criteria into their decision-making. This fundamental difference between decision-making in private financial institutions and markets and decision-making in government inevitably fosters certain biases in the political allocation of capital and creates the opportunity for corruption that reduces long-term economic growth.

APPENDIX: FEDERAL RESERVE ACTIONS

On August 17, 2007, the Federal Reserve established the Term Discount Window Facility (TDWF) to allow banks and other depository institutions to borrow at the discount window for a term of up to 90 days instead of overnight.

On December 12, 2007, the Federal Reserve established the Term Auction Facility (TAF) to allow banks and other depository institutions to bid for funds for 28 or 84 days. The size of these auctions has been increased several times.

On March 11, 2008, the Federal Reserve established the Term Securities Lending Facility (TSLF). Through the TSLF, the Federal Reserve lends up to $200 billion of Treasury securities held by the Federal Reserve to primary dealers secured for a term of 28 days (rather than overnight) by a pledge of other securities, including federal agency debt, federal agency residential-mortgage-backed securities (MBS), and non-agency AAA/Aaa-rated private-label residential MBS. On September 14, 2008, the Federal Reserve expanded the eligible collateral for the TSLF to include all investment grade securities.

On March 16, 2008, the Federal Reserve established the Primary Dealer Credit Facility (PDCF) to allow primary dealers to borrow funds overnight. Collateral may include tri-party repurchase agreements (repos) and investment grade securities.

On May 2, 2008, the Federal Reserve established temporary currency swap lines of $50 billion with the European Central Bank and $12 billion with Swiss National Bank. On July 30, 2008, the Federal Reserve increased its temporary currency swap line from $50 billion to $55 billion with the European Central Bank. On September 18, 2008, the Federal Reserve increased its temporary currency swap lines with the European Central Bank from $55 billion to $110 billion and with the Swiss National Bank from $12 billion to $27 billion. The Federal Reserve established new lines with the Bank of Canada ($10 billion), the Bank of England ($40 billion), and the Bank of Japan ($60 billion). On September 24, 2008, the Federal Reserve established temporary currency swap lines with the Reserve Bank of Australia ($10 billion), the Sveriges Riksbank ($15 billion), the Danmarks Nationalbank ($5 billion), and the Norges Bank ($5 billion). On September 29, 2008, the Federal Reserve increased its temporary currency swap with the Bank of Canada from $10 billion to $30 billion, with the Bank of England from $40 billion to $80 billion, and with the Bank of Japan from $60 billion to $120 billion, for the Bank of Japan, with the Danmarks Nationalbank from $5 billion to $15 billion, with Norges Bank from $5 billion to $15 billion, with the Reserve Bank of Australia from $10 billion to $15 billion, and with the Sveriges Riksbank from $15 billion to $30 billion, and with the Swiss National Bank from $27 billion to $60 billion. On October 13 and 14, 2008, the Federal Reserve announced that it had increased its temporary currency swap lines with the Bank of England, the Bank of Japan, the European Central Bank, and the Swiss National Bank to whatever is requested. On October 28, 2008, the Federal Reserve announced that it had established a temporary currency swap line with the Reserve Bank of New Zealand ($15 billion). On October 29, 2008, the Federal Reserve announced that it had established temporary currency swap lines with the Banco Central do Brasil ($30 billion), the Banco de Mexico ($30 billion), the Bank of Korea ($30 billion), and the Monetary Authority of Singapore ($30 billion).

On September 19, 2008, the Federal Reserve established the asset-backed commercial paper (ABCP) money market mutual fund facility to lend to banks and other depository institutions on a non-recourse basis to purchase ABCP from money market mutual funds.

On September 21, 2008, the Federal Reserve approved the applications of Goldman Sachs and Morgan Stanley to become bank holding companies.

On October 6, 2008, the Federal Reserve announced that it would begin paying interest on both required and excess reserve balances of banks and other financial institutions held at Federal Reserve Banks.

On October 7, 2008, the Federal Reserve established the commercial paper funding facility (CPFF). Through the CPFF, the Federal Reserve finances the purchase short-term unsecured commercial paper and asset-backed commercial paper that is rated at least A-1/P-1/F1 by a special purpose vehicle (SPV).

On October 21, 2008, the Federal Reserve established Money Market Investor Funding Facility (MMIFF) to finance of up to 90 percent of the purchase of up to $600 billion of U.S. dollar-denominated certificates of deposit, bank notes and commercial paper issued by highly rated financial institutions from money market mutual funds (MMMFs) by a series of private sector special purpose vehicles (PSPVs). The PSPVs will finance the remaining 10 percent of their purchases by issuing asset-backed commercial paper (ABCP).

On November 25, 2008, the Federal Reserve established the Term Asset-Backed Securities Loan Facility (TALF) through which the Federal Reserve will extend up to $200 billion of non-recourse loans to the holders of recently issued AAA-rated asset-backed securities collateralized by student loans, auto loans, credit card loans, and small business loans guaranteed by the Small Business Administration (SBA).

On November 25, 2008, the Federal Reserve announced that it would purchase up to $100 billion of Fannie Mae and Freddie Mac debt securities and up to $600 billion of residential mortgage-backed securities issued by Ginnie Mae, Fannie Mae, and Freddie Mac.

End Notes

[1] Interview with Lawrence Summers, *Commanding Heights on PBS* (conducted on April 24, 2001). Found at: http://www.pbs.org/wgbh/commandingheights/shared/minitextlo/int_lawrencesummers.html#1.

In: Government Interventions in Economic Emergencies
Editor: Pablo Sastre
ISBN: 978-1-60741-356-1

Chapter 7

DON'T SPEND TO EXCESS IN THE NAME OF KEYNESIANISM

Jim Saxton

INTRODUCTION

Prominent economists and policymakers invoke Keynesian economics in support of proposals for dramatic federal spending increases of $800 billion or more by the next administration to stimulate the economy. The federal government is intervening in the private sector on a large scale already to combat the economic crisis. Is Keynesianism, which had been discredited in the 1970s, truly the answer to our economic ills? Upon examination, federal policy to date has not fully embraced Keynesianism, which does not offer assurance of lasting prosperity and indeed may pose grave risks to it.

KEYNESIAN FISCAL POLICY

Keynesian theory treats economic output and capacity as one-dimensional, that is, it abstracts from the composition of output and the methods of production. When a gap develops between output and notional capacity, the theory postulates a need and an opportunity for government to close it. By claiming idle resources through direct intervention and putting them to use, government forces an increase in output and, in theory, raises people's incomes as well as their expectations for the future. In this way, consumers and investors supposedly become more willing and able to make purchases and invest. Such a policy could work if there were only one set of products to produce by only one method and it made no difference who produced them. Implicit in the theory is that there is no efficiency difference between government and privately managed production and investment. The size of the government sector is not thought to matter, because private and government funding are presumed to be fully interchangeable.

The problem with this view is that the definition of productive capacity relates to the past, not to what needs to be produced or how it should be produced in the future. Reductions in output—recessions—occur because too much has been produced too fast or the wrong things have been produced, which may occur either due to errors or unforeseen circumstances. A market economy will stop producing products that go unsold or that are too costly; it will reallocate resources and employ them in new ways. During the adjustment process, output will be less than nominal capacity and income may decline. If the government intervenes to support continued generation of unwanted output, it keeps the economy on the wrong path and hinders its progress toward a new production frontier. An economy set in its ways, producing a suboptimal output mix by outdated methods will suffer declining productivity. This is what caused consternation in the 1 970s when productivity slumped and stimulative tools failed to generate growth, instead only pushing up prices—an outcome called "stagflation." The experience prompted departure from Keynesian policy prescriptions in the U.S. During the 1990s, Japan also failed to restore sustained growth with a series of Keynesian stimulus packages.

Resources released from unproductive endeavors may appear to be costless but they are not. Retraining and/or relocating laid off workers positions them for renewed productive employment but preserving their old jobs or placing them in public works projects may not. The government has to tax, borrow, or print money to pay these people, and unless the value they create exceeds the income the government redistributes to them, their net contribution to the economy is zero or negative. In addition, there is a danger of large- scale misallocation of federal funds to special interests for profit or social objectives lacking public support under the guise of helping the economy recover. Invoking the Keynesian theory of job creation and income maintenance could become part of the mantra of every interest group and state government seeking to support a project with federal dollars.

Expectations of the work force and investors are not shaped by full employment forecasts alone but by opportunities for advancement and attractive returns. A growing government sector increasingly denies the private sector recuperative power and portends a future economy less responsive to changes in demand, less flexible to external shocks (such as terror attacks or oil price spikes), and slower to adopt new technologies. These prospects do not encourage consumption and investment. In reality, private and government funded enterprises are *not* interchangeable.

History Misinterpreted

The industrial expansion required to conduct World War II is credited with pulling the U.S. out of the Great Depression, but in that case (a) government spending had a clear focus and a successful outcome—victory, and (b) had to overcome profoundly counterproductive monetary and banking policies as well as untimely tax and tariff hikes. The private economy had not been recovering pre-war on its own or under the "New Deal," because it lacked monetary and financial infrastructure support. The idea that we now have to match World War II spending proportions in order to overcome a presumed recurrence of market lethargy is using a false premise. Moreover, the government could not then and cannot now assure prosperity with impulsive spending. Increased federal spending likely would raise GDP for a time, but it also may delay completion of the market clearing process (working off surpluses) and corrections to the market's functioning, developments that are necessary for private investment to return in force.

Government's Role

The government has a macroeconomic role by virtue of financing its own activities and its control over money and banking. Tax, interest rate, and banking policies can either compound or mitigate an economic downturn. Temporary tax and interest rate reductions will slow declines in income and the government's power to act as lender of last resort can keep credit flowing, especially to economic sectors that are healthy.

Federal Stimulus so Far

Earlier this year, tax rebate checks were issued that essentially offset the negative income effect of an enormous oil price spike (though that was not the initial intent). Government refrained from market intervention, allowing citizens to decide how to use the money. As a result, overall consumption did not decline, but people started driving less and turned to more fuel efficient vehicles— responses that will prompt structural adaptation to changed circumstances. Lowering marginal tax rates to increase incentives for work and investment would be still more effective in facilitating new productive output generation.

When a large part of the financial structure failed last summer, the Federal Reserve and the Treasury intervened to save several financial institutions from setting off a system wide chain of defaults. The financial system is like the electrical grid, if it goes down it takes everything else with it. The financial system is in need of repair but meanwhile hinders all parts of the economy, including those that are sound. The Federal Reserve and the Treasury have been providing capital to keep the "grid" functioning but have largely refrained from deciding how the capital is deployed, leaving that to the market. These actions differ fundamentally from Keynesianism, under which the government allocates spending.

Conclusion

The Great Depression is on everyone's mind. It feeds the fear that the economy may not pull out of the current crisis on its own. Keynesianism suggests that tax and monetary measures alone are insufficient to mobilize the economy and promises that federal spending on a large enough scale can induce the economy to grow again. Keynesians argue that World War II spending ended the Great Depression. Even accepting that premise, federal spending now merely to preserve jobs or for programs that lack sufficient public support on their own merits does not equate to winning World War II. The experience with Keynesian policies since the War suggests they may foster inefficiency, inflation, and *discourage* private investment. Congress should regard plans to push capital into politically determined channels of the economy with great trepidation. Contrary to Keynesian arguments, government cannot force the economy into sustained growth on its own terms.

In: Government Interventions in Economic Emergencies ISBN: 978-1-60741-356-1
Editor: Pablo Sastre

Chapter 8

EMERGENCY ECONOMIC STABILIZATION ACT: PRELIMINARY ANALYSIS OF OVERSIGHT PROVISIONS

Curtis W. Copeland

SUMMARY

The Emergency Economic Stabilization Act of 2008 (EESA, Division A of H. R. 1424, P.L. 110-343) provides authority for the Secretary of the Treasury to purchase and insure "troubled assets" to provide stability and prevent disruption in the economy and financial system. The act established two organizations to provide broad oversight for the stability program — a Financial Stability Oversight Board (FSOB) and a Congressional Oversight Panel (COP). The act also placed audit responsibilities for the program with two individuals a new Special Inspector General (IG) for the Troubled Asset Relief Program (TARP), and the Comptroller General (CG) ofthe United States, who heads the Government Accountability Office (GAO). The duties and responsibilities of both oversight panels and both auditors overlap in some areas, but are different in other areas.

Several aspects of the FSOB do not appear to be clearly delineated in the act, including where the FSOB is "established" within the federal government, whether it is covered by a variety of general management laws, and how the FSOB is to be funded and staffed. The act is also unclear regarding certain aspects of the Special IG for the TARP, including where the Office of the Special IG is to be "established" or housed, how or when its authorized appropriation is to be provided, and its specific investigative authorities.

The duties of both oversight panels and both audit organizations overlap in several key areas, and some of the reporting requirements also overlap. Although 18 types of EESA reports are required, none of them specifically require disclosure of how the funds are used by the recipients, and only one is required to be made to the public. The Special IG for the TARP and members of the COP were not named until mid-November 2008. Also, the nature of the "troubled assets" being purchased have changed, perhaps necessitating reassessment of the act's oversight mechanisms. Finally, it is unclear what effect the various oversight and audit mechanisms will have on the balance of power between Congress and the executive branch. Congress gave itself expedited legislative procedures to disapprove actions by the Secretary, but only after the first $350 billion has been obligated.

Several specific requirements in the act appear to contemplate that the "troubled assets" being purchased and insured are primarily residential or commercial mortgages and instruments based on those mortgages. However, recent proposals to deal with the financial crisis are different than these mortgage-based transactions. While the oversight and audit responsibilities of the COP, the FSOB, the CG, and the Special IG still apply, the nature of their specific responsibilities may need to be reconsidered and redefined in light of the type of "troubled assets" that are initially being purchased. It is also unclear how effective all of these oversight and audit requirements will be in ensuring transparency and a balance of power between Congress and the executive branch.

INTRODUCTION

One of the purposes of the Emergency Economic Stabilization Act of 2008 (EESA, Division A of H.R. 1424, P.L. 110-343) is to "immediately provide authority and facilities that the Secretary of the Treasury can use to restore liquidity and stability to the financial system of the United States."[1] Section 101 of the act ("Purchases of Troubled Assets") authorizes the Secretary of the Treasury to "establish the Troubled Asset Relief Program (or 'TARP') to purchase, and to make and fund commitments to purchase, troubled assets from any financial institution, on such terms and conditions as are determined by the Secretary, and in accordance with this Act and the policies and procedures developed and published by the Secretary." The term "troubled assets" is defined in Section 3(9) of the act as

> (A) residential or commercial mortgages and any securities, obligations, or other instruments that are based on or related to such mortgages, that in each case was originated or issued on or before March 14, 2008, the purchase of which the Secretary determines promotes financial market stability; and (B) any other financial instrument that the Secretary, after consultation with the Chairman of the Board of Governors of the Federal Reserve System, determines the purchase of which is necessary to promote financial market stability, but only upon transmittal of such determination, in writing, to the appropriate committees of Congress.

The act requires the Secretary of the Treasury to implement the program through an Office of Financial Stability within the department's Office of Domestic Finance. The office is to be headed by an Assistant Secretary appointed by the President with the advice and consent of the Senate, although the law permits the Secretary to appoint an interim Assistant Secretary without Senate confirmation.[2]

The Secretary is authorized in Section 101(c) to take "such actions as the Secretary deems necessary to carry out the authorities in this Act." However, Section 101(d) requires the Secretaryto publish program guidelines within two business days after the first purchase of troubled assets.[3] Those guidelines are required to include mechanisms for purchasing troubled assets, methods of pricing and valuing troubled assets, procedures for selecting asset managers, and criteria for identifying troubled assets for purchase. Section 115 of the act initially permits the Secretary to purchase up to $250 billion of troubled assets, and up to a total of $350 billion of assets upon a written certification by the President that the Secretary needs additional authority.[4] Subsequently, if the President submits a written plan to Congress, and if Congress does not object within 15 calendar days (through a joint resolution of disapproval described in subsection 115(c)), the Secretary may purchase up to $700 billion in troubled assets.

Section 102 of the act ("Insurance of Troubled Assets") states that if the Secretary establishes the program authorized in Section 101, then the Secretary "shall establish a program to guarantee troubled assets originated or issued prior to March 14, 2008, including mortgage-backed securities." Specifically, the Secretary is authorized to guarantee the timely payment of up to 100% of the principal and interest related to the assets.

Oversight and Audit Mechanisms

EESA established two organizations to provide broad oversight for the stability program a Financial Stability Oversight Board (FSOB) and a Congressional Oversight Panel (COP). The act also placed audit responsibilities for the program with two individuals — a new Special Inspector General (IG) for the TARP, and with the Comptroller General (CG) of the United States, who heads the Government Accountability Office (GAO).[5] Many ofthe audit and reporting responsibilities delineated in the act specifically reference the actions required in Sections 101 and 102 of the act to purchase troubled assets and to insure those assets.[6]

Questions have been raised by some observers as to whether these oversight and audit responsibilities are complimentary to one another, or are contradictory.[7] This chapter provides a preliminary comparison and analysis of the specific authorities and responsibilities of the FSOB and the COP, and also compares and analyzes the roles and responsibilities of the Special IG and the CG as described in the act.

THE FINANCIAL STABILITY OVERSIGHT BOARD AND THE CONGRESSIONAL OVERSIGHT PANEL

As described in EESA, the FSOB and the COP are similar in some respects, but different in other respects. Also, the act is unclear with regard to several key aspects of one or both of these entities. The discussion below and in **Table 1** at the end of this chapter compares the FSOB and the COP on several relevant dimensions.

Placement within the Government

The COP is described in Section 125(a) of the act as an "establishment of the legislative branch." In contrast, Section 104(a) of the act simply says that the FSOB is "established," but does not indicate whether the board is part of the executive or legislative branches. All five members of the FSOB are from the executive branch (the Chairman of the Board of Governors of the Federal Reserve System, the Secretary of the Treasury, the Director of the

Federal Housing Finance Agency, the Chairman of the Securities and Exchange Commission, and the Secretary of Housing and Urban Development). Therefore, one could reasonably presume that the FSOB is an executive branch entity.

Even if one makes that presumption, however, it is unclear whether the FSOB is intended to be a subunit within the Department of the Treasury or some other agency, or whether the board is intended to be a free-standing, independent entity. The organizational placement of the FSOB may have a number of implications, including whether the board is covered by a variety of statutory management and transparency requirements such as the Federal Records Act, the Federal Advisory Committee Act, the Freedom of Information Act, the Government in the Sunshine Act, and various human resources management and ethics requirements.[8] Legislative branch entities like the COP are generally not subject to these requirements.

Responsibilities

The listed responsibilities of the FSOB (in Section 104(a) of the act) and the COB (in Sections 125(b) and (e) of the act) are similar both in general and with regard to particular elements. For example, both entities are broadly responsible for reviewing the Secretary's actions in carrying out the requirements of the act, and both are specifically responsible for examining the effect of those actions on home ownership, financial markets, and costs to the taxpayers. As discussed in more detail below, both are also required to report to Congress on their findings. However, only the FSOB is charged with (1) making recommendations to the Secretary of the Treasury regarding the use of his authorities under the act; and (2) reporting any suspected fraud, misrepresentation, or malfeasance to the Special IG or the Attorney General of the United States. On the other hand, only the COP is specifically (1) permitted to hold hearings, take testimony, receive evidence, and administer oaths and affirmations to witnesses; and (2) required to report on the extent to which the information on transactions has contributed to market transparency. Also, if so authorized by the panel, any individual member or agent of the COP is authorized to take action on behalf of the panel; no such individualization of authority is permitted by the FSOB.

Access to Information

Section 125(e)(3) of the act authorizes the COP to obtain whatever information it needs to carry out its responsibilities from any federal department or agency, and the heads of those departments or agencies are required to provide the information requested by the chairperson of the panel. As noted previously, the COP is also permitted to take testimony and administer oaths and affirmations to witnesses. The act provides the FSOB no similar right to information from federal departments or agencies, and there does not appear to be any obligation on the part of those departments or agencies to provide that information to the FSOB. Neither the FSOB nor the COP have subpoena authority, and neither is authorized to request the Attorney General to compel agencies to provide needed information.[9]

Membership

As noted previously, Section 104(b) of the act states that the FSOB is comprised of the heads of five executive branch departments or agencies: the Chairman of the Board of Governors of the Federal Reserve System, the Secretary of the Treasury, the Director of the Federal Housing Finance Agency, the Chairman of the Securities and Exchange Commission, and the Secretary of Housing and Urban Development. No provision is made for these agency heads to allow alternates to substitute for them.

Section 125(c) of the act is less directive regarding the members of the COP, merely specifying how members are to be appointed (i.e., one each by the Speaker ofthe House of Representatives, the minority leader ofthe House, the majority leader of the Senate, and the minority leader of the Senate; and one by the Speaker and the majority leader of the Senate, after consultation with the minority leaders in each house). The act does not require that members of the COP be from Congress or even from the legislative branch, but it clearly contemplates Members of Congress as potential members; Section 125(c)(3) specifies that members of the COP who are Members of Congress or full-time officers or employees of the federal government will receive no additional pay, allowances, or benefits. The act does not require that the members of the COP be appointed by a certain date, although (as discussed below) the COP is required to submit its first "regular report" within 30 days after the first exercise of the Secretary's authority under Section 101(a) or 102 of the act, and is required to submit a "special report" on regulatory reform by January 20, 2009.[10] On November 14, 2008, Democratic congressional leaders named the first three members of the panel,[11] and Republican congressional leaders named the remaining two members on November 19, 2008.[12]

Leadership

Section 104(c) of the act specifies that the chairperson of the FSOB is elected by the members of the board, but the act excludes the Secretary of the Treasury from having a vote in that election. According to the interim Assistant Secretary for the Office of Financial Stability, on October 7, 2008, the members of the board selected the Chairman of the Board of Governors of the Federal Reserve System to be chairman of the FSOB.[13] In contrast, although a chairperson of the COP is clearly contemplated by EESA (e.g., Section 125(c)(7) of the act authorizes the chairperson to call meetings), the legislation does not indicate how that chairperson is to be selected.

Pay for Members

The act is silent regarding pay for members of the FSOB, but presumably they would simply receive their regular salaries as the heads of the five agencies. On the other hand, Section 125(c)(2) of the act states that each member of the COP shall be paid at the daily rate of basic pay for level I of the Executive Schedule (the cabinet secretary level, which is \$191,300 per year in 2008) for each day that the member is performing duties "vested in the Commission." (The act does not indicate what "commission" is referenced here, but the context suggest that the word "panel" should have been used instead of "commission.") As noted previously, members of the COP who are Members of Congress or full-time federal officers or employees are not allowed to receive additional pay, allowances, or benefits.

Meetings/Quorum

The COP is not required to meet at any specific time; Section 125(c)(7) of the act states that its meetings are held at the call of the chairperson or a majority of its members. However, because the COP is required to submit its first "regular report" within 30 days after the first troubled assets are purchased or insured, meetings of the panel are likely before the report is submitted. Section 125(c)(5) specifies that four members of the COP constitute a quorum, although the act states that a lesser number may hold hearings.

Section 104(d) of the act requires the FSOB to meet two weeks after the first exercise of purchase authority of the Secretary of the Treasury, and monthly thereafter. However, the act does not mention what constitutes a quorum for FSOB action. According to the interim Assistant Secretary for the Office of Financial Stability, the FSOB met on October 7 four days after the legislation was enacted and before the exercise of any purchase authority. In addition to selecting the Chairman of the Federal Reserve to be chairman of the FSOB, the members reportedly adopted the board's bylaws and reviewed the TARP's initial work streams.[14] The FSOB met again on October 13, 2008, and on October 22, 2008.[15] As of mid-November 2008, the FSOB had reportedly met a total of four times, and the minutes of three of those meetings were posted on the Department of the Treasury's website.[16]

Staffing/Consultants

The act does not mention whether and, if so, how the FSOB is to be staffed or paid, and does not indicate whether it can hire experts or consultants. Nevertheless, the interim Assistant Secretary for the Office of Financial Stability testified on October 23, 2008, that the FSOB had appointed staff to the Board, including an executive director, a general counsel, and a secretary.[17]

In contrast, Section 125(d) of the act permits the COP to appoint and fix the pay of "any personnel the Commission considers appropriate." (Again, the context suggests that the word "panel" should have been used instead of "commission.") The COP is also permitted to procure temporary and intermittent experts and consultants for up to one year, and use employees detailed from any federal department or agency. No limits are specified on the number of employees, consultants, or detailees that the COP may obtain, and no limits are specified regarding their pay.

Reports by the Entities

Section 104(g) of the act requires the FSOB to report to the "appropriate committees" of Congress[18] at least quarterly regarding the implementation of its responsibilities, but the act does not specifically indicate when those responsibilities begin. (For example, "quarterly" could mean every three months starting on the date the act was signed into law, or starting on the date that the Secretary of the Treasury begins exercising his authority under the act.) In contrast, Section 125(b)(1) of the act requires the COP to submit a "regular report" of the panel within 30 days after the first exercise of the Secretary's authority under Section 101(a) or 102 of the act, and every 30 days thereafter.[19]

In addition, the COP is required to submit a one-time "special report" by January 20, 2009, analyzing the current regulatory system and its effectiveness at overseeing the participants in the financial system and protecting consumers. The report is also required to contain recommendations for improvement, including whether other participants in the financial markets should be subject to the regulatory system, the rationale for such a recommendation, and whether there are any gaps in existing consumer protections.[20]

Reports to the Entities

The act does not require the FSOB to be the recipient of any reports prepared by other entities, but several provisions in the act specify that certain reports are to be sent to the COP. For example, (1) Section 104(g) of the act requires the FSOB to provide to the COP its quarterly reports to Congress; (2) Section 105(d) states that any report to Congress by the Secretary that is required by Section 105 (e.g., "tranche" reports for each $50 billion of purchases and a "regulatory modernization" report) shall also be provided to the COP; (3) Section 116(d) says that any report or audit required under Section 116 of the act (including Comptroller General reports) shall also be submitted to the COP; (4) Section 117(d) requires the CG's report on "margin authority" to be provided to the COP; (5) Section 121(f)(3) provides that reports by the Special IG for the TARP shall also be submitted to the COP; and (6) Section 129(e) states that the report to certain congressional committees on "exercise of loan authority" shall also be provided to the COP.

Funding

The act does not indicate whether and, if so, how the FSOB is to be funded. In contrast, the act specifies in Section 125(g) that the COP is authorized "such sums as may be necessary for any fiscal year," and specifies that half of the funds are to be derived from the applicable account of the House of Representatives, and half from the contingent fund of the Senate. The act goes on to state in Section 125(h) that an amount equal to the expenses of the COP shall be promptly transferred by the Secretary from time to time upon the presentment of a statement of such expenses by the chairperson of the panel. The funds are to be taken from funds provided to the Secretary under the act and sent to the applicable fund of the House of Representatives and the contingent fund of the Senate.

Termination

Section 104(h) of the act requires that the FSOB and its authority terminate 15 days after (1) the date that the last troubled asset acquired under Section 101 has been sold or transferred out of the ownership of the federal government, or (2) the date of expiration of the last insurance contract under Section 102, whichever is later. Section 125(f) of the act states that the COP is to terminate six months after the authorities provided to the Secretary expire, which is described in Section 120 of the act as December 31, 2009, subject to extension. There are no requirements in the act that either the FSOB or the COP preserve any records, or to provide a means by which the public or others can access any records.

THE SPECIAL INSPECTOR GENERAL FOR THE TARP AND THE COMPTROLLER GENERAL'S ROLE IN THE ACT

As was the case with the two general oversight bodies, the act's descriptions of the duties and responsibilities of the Special IG for the TARP and the Comptroller General are similar in some respects, but differ in other ways. Also, certain elements of the Special IG's operations appear to be undefined. The discussion below and in **Table 2** at the end of this chapter compares the roles of the Special IG and the CG with regard to several relevant dimensions.

Placement within the Government

Pursuant to the *Bowsher v. Synar* decision of the Supreme Court, it is clear that GAO is a legislative branch agency, and can have no significant executive branch functions.[21] However, although Section 121(a) of EES A "established" the Office of the Special IG for the TARP, the act does not indicate where in the government that office is to be housed. Legislation establishing other special inspectors general, while not specifying organizational placement, contains other indications of where the entity was housed. For example, the Special Inspector General for Iraq Reconstruction was established by Section 3001 of P.L. 108-106, which provided that the IG was appointed by the Secretary of Defense (after consultation with the Secretary of State), and reported to the head of the Coalition Provisional Authority.[22]

The act is also unclear where the Special IG's offices are to be located. Section 116(a)(2)(A) requires the Secretary ofthe Treasury to provide GAO with appropriate audit space and facilities in the Department of the Treasury, but the act contains no similar requirement for the Special IG. However, Section 121(d)(1) of the act says that, in carrying out the duties delineated in the act in subsection (c), "the Special Inspector General shall have the authorities provided in section 6 of the Inspector General Act of 1978." Section 6 of the Inspector General Act (codified at 5 U.S.0 Appendix) states, in relevant part, that the "head of an establishment shall provide the Office within such establishment with appropriate and adequate office space at central and field locations of such establishment, together with such equipment, office supplies, and communications facilities and services as may be necessary." Therefore, if the Special IG is determined to be located within the Department of the Treasury, then the Secretary may be required to provide the Special IG with space and facilities.[23]

Responsibilities

Section 116(a)(1) of the act describes the responsibilities ofthe Comptroller General with regard to the TARP, and Section 121(c)(1) describes the responsibilities ofthe Special IG. The general responsibilities of both the CG and the IG are similar, although stated somewhat differently. For example, once the TARP is established, the CG is to "commence ongoing oversight ofthe activities and performance of the TARP," including the performance of the TARP in meeting the purposes of this Act". The Special IG is to "conduct, supervise, and coordinate audits and investigations of the purchase, management, and sale of assets by the Secretary of the Treasury under any program established under section 101, and the management of the Secretary of any program established under section 102."

The two audit organizations' specific responsibilities are similar, but also differ in some ways. For example, while both the CG and the Special IG are required to identify the troubled assets acquired under the program, only the Special IG is charged with describing why the Secretary deemed it necessary to purchase each asset, and to list (with detailed biographical information) each person or entity hired to manage the troubled assets. The CG, on the other hand, is the only entity specifically required to examine the internal controls of the TARP, to examine the efficiency of TARP operations and contracting procedures, and to review the TARP's efforts to minimize conflicts of interest.

The act gives two responsibilities to the CG that are not given to the Special IG. Section 116(b)(1) of the act requires the CG to audit the TARP's financial statements, and Section 117 requires the CG to determine the extent to which leverage and sudden deleveraging of financial institutions was a factor behind the financial crisis, including the roles of the Board of Governors of the Federal Reserve System, the Securities and Exchange Commission, the Secretary of the Treasury, and others.

When Audits Begin

Section 121(b)(1) requires the President to nominate the Special IG "as soon as practicable after the establishment of any program under sections 101 and 102." According to an interim final rule issued by the Board of Governors of the Federal Reserve System, on October 14, 2008, the Secretary of the Treasury announced a program within the TARP to provide capital to eligible financial institutions.[24] Therefore, it appears that a "program" triggering the nomination of the Special IG has been established. The interim Assistant Secretary for the Office of Financial Stability said that Treasury officials were "working with the White House to identify candidates for possible nomination and confirmation in November."[25] Also, Section 121(e) of the act indicates that the Office of the Special IG is to be provided \$50 million from the proceeds of the sale of securities, including Treasury bills and savings bonds.[26] However, the act does not indicate when or how those funds are to be provided, so it is unclear when the Office of the Special IG will be operational.

The act says that the CG's audit functions are to begin "upon establishment of the troubled asset relief program." According to the interim Assistant Secretary and the acting CG, GAO has already begun its reviews. GAO officials and staff met with Treasury officials on October 9, and they reviewed certain contracts on October 12.[27] At least one Member of Congress has expressed support for these actions by GAO.[28]

Access to Information

The act provides both the CG and the Special IG with access to certain information, although those rights differ somewhat.[29] Section 116(a)(2)(B) states that, consistent with applicable law, the CG has access to any information or "things" belonging to the TARP, and to its officers, employees, or agents. Section 121(e)(4) requires the heads of other agencies to furnish the Special IG with any requested information or assistance that is "practicable" and not in contravention to law. Therefore, the CG appears to have specific access rights to information from the TARP, whereas the Special IG appears to have specific access only to information from other agencies. Also, the act requires that the CG be given "full facilities for verifying transactions with the balances or securities held by depositaries, fiscal agents, and custodians," and is permitted to make and retain copies of any records. No similar rights are specifically afforded the Special IG.

As noted previously, however, Section 121(d)(1) of the act says that, in carrying out the duties delineated in the act in subsection (c), "the Special Inspector General shall have the authorities provided in section 6 of the Inspector General Act of 1978." Section 6 of the Inspector General Act states, in relevant part, that each inspector general is authorized to "have access to all records, reports, audits, reviews, documents, papers, recommendations, or other material available to the applicable establishment which relate to programs and operations with respect to which that Inspector General has responsibilities under this Act." That section goes on to authorize the IGs to require by enforceable subpoena the production of all information, documents, and other evidence needed in the performance of the functions assigned by the act.

Obligation of the TARP to Respond to Audits

Section 116(b)(3) of the act requires the TARP to address deficiencies that the CG identifies, or to certify to the appropriate committees of Congress that no action is needed. The act places no similar requirement on the TARP regarding audit findings by the Special IG.

Staffing/Contracting

Section 121(e) of the act permits the Special IG to select, appoint, and employ as many officers and employees as he or she deems necessary, but the selection, classification, and pay of those employees is governed by the requirements of current civil service law in Title 5, *United States Code.* That section also permits the Special IG to employ experts and consultants at a rate not to exceed GS-15 of the General Schedule (the top end of which is currently $149,000 per year in Washington, D.C.), and to enter into contracts for other audits or studies. These authorities are similar to those provided to other statutory inspectors general under the Inspector General Act of 1978. The act contains no similar provisions for the CG, but GAO already has similar abilities under its existing statutory authorities.[30]

Reports

Both the CG and the Special IG are required to submit reports regarding their audit activities to the appropriate committees of Congress, but some of the specifics are unclear and appear to be different. For example, Section 116(a)(3) requires the CG to submit GAO's reports at least every 60 days, but does not specifically indicate when the first 60-day period begins. Section 121(f)(1) requires the Special IG's reports to include a "detailed statement of all purchases, obligations, expenditures, and revenues associated with any program established by the Secretary of the Treasury under sections 101 and 102." In contrast, the CG is simply required to submit reports of "findings under this section." The CG is required to submit GAO's reports to the Special IG, among others; the Special IG is not required to reciprocate, but is required (by Section 121(f)(3) of the act) to submit its reports to the COP. Notably, in contrast to reports from statutory inspectors general, neither the CG's reports nor the Special IG's reports are sent to the Secretary of the Treasury or any other executive branch official. It is also unclear whether the Department of the Treasury will be allowed to comment on GAO's or the Special IG's findings before the reports are sent to Congress, or whether the reports are to be made public.

Funding

Section 116(a)(2)(C) of the act requires the Department of the Treasury to reimburse GAO for the full cost of any oversight activities that are billed by the CG. Section 116(b)(1) requires the department to reimburse GAO for the full cost of the audit of the TARP financial statement — a requirement that is similar to one in the Government Accountability Office Act of 2008 (P.L. 110-323).[31]

In contrast, Section 121(g) of the act requires that $50 million of the funds from the proceeds of the sale of securities under Section 118 be provided to the Special IG to carry out his or her responsibilities. Section 118 of the act states that the Secretary "may use the proceeds of the sale of any securities issued under chapter 31 of title 31, United States Code" for the authorities granted in the act and the cost of administering those authorities. Chapter 31 of title 31 ("Public Debt") includes Treasury bills, savings bonds and savings certificates, and other instruments. However, the timing and mechanics of the transfer of funds to the Special IG are unclear (e.g., whether the Special IG gets a one-time payment of $50 million at the time the office is established, or whether that amount is to be provided over a longer period of time, as determined by the Secretary of the Treasury).

Termination

Section 121(h) of the act specifies that the Office of the Special IG terminates on the later of (1) the date the at the last troubled asset acquired under Section 101 has been sold or transferred, or (2) the date of expiration of the last insurance contract under Section 102.[32] Section 116(e) says that the CG's oversight, audit, and reporting requirements under the act also terminate on those dates. Also, Section 116(a)(2)(A) states that the Secretary of the Treasury is to provide the CG with audit space and facilities until the termination date specified in Section 120 (which is December 31, 2009, subject to extension). There are no requirements in the act that either the CG or the Special IG preserve any records or provide a means by which the public or others can access any records.

CONCLUDING OBSERVATIONS

The Secretary of the Treasury's initial proposal to purchase troubled assets was very short and contained no oversight provisions. Instead, it stated that, "Decisions by the Secretary pursuant to the authority of this Act are non-reviewable and committed to agency discretion, and may not be reviewed by any court of law or any administrative agency."' Several Members of Congress and many others, including both of the major party presidential candidates, called for increased oversight of the program. For example, Senator John McCain said, "We won't solve a problem caused by poor oversight with a plan that has no oversight."[34]

In contrast, as enacted on October 3, 2008, EESA contained an elaborate oversight system, with general oversight responsibilities given to the FSOB and the COP, and with detailed auditing responsibilities assigned to the Comptroller General and a new Special Inspector General for the TARP. Other, albeit more limited, responsibilities were assigned to OMB, CBO, and the Joint Committee on Taxation to help Congress oversee the implementation of the TARP. Together, 11 different entities are required to prepare and submit a total of 18 different types of reports to six different entities, with many of those reports required to be submitted on a recurring basis.[35] No single entity receives all of the reports.

Overlapping Responsibilities

The duties and responsibilities of both oversight panels and both audit organizations overlap in several key areas. For example, both the FSOB and the COP are broadly required to review how the Secretary of the Treasury uses the act's authorities. Likewise, the Special IG and the CG have similar general responsibilities (e.g., to "oversee the activities and performance of the TARP" and to audit the "purchase, management, and sale of assets under any Section 101 program"), as well as similar specific responsibilities.[36] Even where the entities' responsibilities differ, it is not clear why certain responsibilities were given to one organization instead of another.

Some of the EESA reporting requirements also appear to overlap, even for the same entity. For example, Section 105(a) of the act requires the Secretary of the Treasury to report to the "appropriate committees" within 60 days after the first use of his authority in Sections 101 and 102, and every 30 days afterward, on all "actions taken by the Secretary," including all agreements, transactions, and insurance contracts. Section 105(b) requires the Secretary to report to the same committees on the same transactions within seven days of each $50 billion in commitments to purchase troubled assets. Section 116 requires the Comptroller General to oversee the activities of the TARP and report on his findings at least every 60 days, which would presumably include TARP-related agreements, transactions, and insurance contracts.

Section 121 requires the Special Inspector General to report every quarter on his audits of (among other things) all "troubled assets" purchased or sold under Section 101, and the management of any insurance program under Section 102.

Congress may have wanted these overlaps and divisions of responsibility to occur, providing it with differing perspectives on the same issues. However, in practice, the areas of overlap may prove to be counterproductive, particularly if the bodies are not sharing relevant information and, as a result, are reaching different conclusions based on incomplete or variable data and methods. Also, with duplicative and uncoordinated oversight, the Secretary of the Treasury and other officials responsible for implementing the financial rescue plan may spend the bulk of their time responding to requests for information from multiple entities asking the same questions. One author commented that, once it was clear that some type of oversight was needed in EESA, "consensus seemed to have been reached by including everyone's favorite idea in the bill, with no one thinking hard about how all of them fit together and whether more oversight is necessarily better than less."[37]

Possible Additions to Reporting Requirements

These numerous oversight and audit requirements notwithstanding, it is unclear how effective they will be in ensuring that the underlying purpose of the TARP is being met, or that the program is transparent to the public. None of the reports are specifically required to address one of the central issues that have been raised about the purchases of these troubled assets — how the funds provided by the Secretary of the Treasury are being used by the recipients of those funds. Initially, the Secretary of the Treasury indicated that troubled assets would be purchased to increase lending by the banks.[38] He later said that he decided to purchase stock in financial institutions instead of bad assets because buying those assets would take too long to recapitalize the banks for lending.[39] However, a number of questions have been raised by Members of Congress and others about whether the banks that received the initial $115 billion were using the money to pay dividends to stockholders, to pay bonuses to corporate executives, or to finance the purchases of smaller banks — not to increase lending.[40]

Although none of these activities are prohibited uses of the funds, it is notable that none of the reports specifically require the disclosure of how the money is being used. Senator Richard Shelby was quoted as saying that "We don't know who's benefitting from this, [or] where the money's going."[41] The nominee to be the Special Inspector General for the TARP reportedly said he believes that he has the statutory authority needed to determine how the banks spent the money,[42] but he is not specifically required to include that information in his reports.

Also, only one of the 18 types of EESA reports is required to be made to the public.[43] All of the other reports are required to be submitted to Congress, the "appropriate" committees of Congress, or to one of the oversight or auditing bodies. While either the preparers or the recipients of these reports may be able to make them public, they are not required to do so.[44] Concerns have been raised about a perceived lack of transparency in various aspects of the financial system rescue program, including the contracts that have been awarded, and the securities being accepted as collateral for loans to the banks.[45]

A Delayed Start for the COP and the Special IG

Although the FSOB and GAO began their oversight and auditing responsibilities quickly, as of mid- November 2008 more than six weeks after EESA was enacted the COP and the Special IG have not been fully established. The act requires the leadership in the House and the Senate to select the five members of the COP. On November 14, 2008, the first three members of the panel were named,[46] and the final two members were named on November 19.[47] As of the date of this chapter, however, the panel had not met or hired staff, and a substantial portion of the $700 billion in funds had already been committed to purchase bank stock and other "troubled assets."

Also, the COP was required to submit its first "regular report" within 30 days of the Secretary's first purchase of "troubled assets." Because the first purchase of bank stock occurred on October 28, the first report may be required before, or shortly after, the COP is fully established. Also, the COP is required to submit its "special report" by January 20, 2009, "analyzing the regulatory system and its effectiveness at overseeing the participants in the financial system," and making recommendations for reform. It is unclear whether the COP can conduct this ambitious study and produce a report of this magnitude in such a short period of time.

EESA required the President to nominate the Special IG for the TARP "as soon as practicable after the establishment of any program under sections 101 and 102." Although the Secretary of the Treasury announced the establishment of such a program on October 14, 2008, the President did not nominate a Special IG until one month later, on November 14, 2008.[48] The Senate Committee on Banking, Housing, and Urban Affairs held a confirmation hearing on the nomination for November 19, 2008, and the nomination could be acted upon by the full Senate shortly thereafter.[49] EESA requires the first report by the Special IG to be submitted within 60 days after confirmation. Also, the act states that the Special IG is to be provided $50 million from the proceeds of the sale of securities to carry out the act's requirements, but it is unclear when those payments are to be made and in what amounts. At a hearing before the Senate Finance Committee on November 17, 2008, the Special Inspector General nominee said he was unsure whether $50 million would be enough to fund the office's operations.[50]

In the absence of the Special IG, the inspector general for the Department of the Treasury, Eric M. Thorson, has been attempting to oversee the implementation of EESA in addition to his regular responsibilities. He reportedly has "a few dozen" people working on the program part time, but has said that the new office should have at least 100 full time employees.[51] It is also unclear whether the Treasury IG can carry out responsibilities that Congress has specifically assigned to the Special IG. On November 13, 2008, the Treasury IG was quoted as saying, "It's a mess," and "I don't think anyone understands right now how we're going to do proper oversight of this thing."[52]

Possible Reassessment of Oversight Mechanisms

Some of the oversight and auditing requirements may need to be reassessed given the changed nature of the TARP. When EESA was enacted on October 3, 2008, the type of "troubled assets" that were generally expected to be purchased under the TARP were those fitting the first definition in Section 3(9) of the act i.e., "residential or commercial mortgages and any securities, obligations, or other instruments that are based on or related to such mortgages."[53] The composition of some of the oversight bodies, and the specific oversight and auditing responsibilities given to those entities, appear to have been predicated on this expectation.[54]

However, on October 14, 2008 — less than two weeks after EESA was enacted the Secretary of the Treasury announced that initial funds authorized by the act would be used to purchase preferred shares of stock in certain banks.[55] Congress had authorized the Secretary to take such action when it defined a "troubled asset" in Section 3(9) of EESA as both mortgage-based financial instruments as well as "any other financial instrument that the Secretary ... determines the purchase of which is necessary to promote financial stability." Subsequent developments seemed to confirm this shift in direction. On October 25, 2008, the *Washington Post* reported that the Department of the Treasury was "dramatically expanding the scope of its bailout of the financial system with a plan to take ownership stakes in the nation's insurance companies."[56] Treasury officials were also reportedly in discussions about using TARP or other funds to address liquidity problems facing state and local governments,[57] as well as U.S. automakers.[58]

Then, on November 12, 2008, the Secretary of the Treasury announced that the department no longer planned to buy troubled mortgage-based assets from financial firms, but would instead provide "aid to banks and other firms that issue student, auto and credit card loans in part by jump starting the market that provides financing for these companies."[59] Firms that reportedly could be eligible for this new round of capital purchases include insurers and specialty lenders for small businesses. The Secretary said that the department had decided that buying mortgage-based assets would take too long to recapitalize the financial institutions, and that buying equity in these firms would be a more powerful incentive for them to lend.[60]

While the oversight and audit responsibilities of the COP, the FSOB, the CG, and the Special IG may still generally apply to these new TARP-related programs, the makeup and the nature of their specific responsibilities may need to be reconsidered and redefined in light of the type of "troubled assets" being purchased and the other types of programs being considered. For example, given the current focus on purchasing bank stock instead of mortgage-based securities, members of the FSOB could be appointed based on their expertise in the banking industry (e.g., the head of the Federal Deposit Insurance Corporation or the Comptroller of the Currency) in addition to, or instead of, those appointed to the board based on their housing-related expertise. Similarly, congressional leaders have been encouraged to include state representation on the COP, in recognition of the importance financial institutions have on state economies.[61]

In addition, to the extent that the Secretary establishes programs based on statutory authorities outside of Sections 101 and 102 of EESA, the audit responsibilities of both the CG and the Special IG may need to be redefined to ensure that they cover all aspects of the program. For example, Section 116(a)(1) defines the CG's "scope of oversight" as "the activities and performance of the TARP and of any agents and representatives of the TARP (as related to the agent or representative's activities on behalf of or under the authority of the TARP), including vehicles established by the Secretary under this Act." Section 3(8) of the act defines the TARP as "the Troubled Asset Relief Program established under section 101."

Similarly, Section 121(c) of the act defines the duties of the Special IG as audits and investigations of the "purchase, management, and sale of assets by the Secretary of the

Treasury under any program established by the Secretary under section 101, and the management by the Secretary of any program established under section 102." Since all of these audit functions are geared to Sections 101 and 102 of the act, it is unclear whether the CG or the Special IG can audit or investigate programs established pursuant to other sections of the act (e.g., the proposed program to guarantee troubled mortgages under Section 109).[62] However, during Senate hearings on his nomination to be Special IG for the TARP, several Senators reportedly told Neil M. Barofsky that he should assume that he has authority for all aspects of EESA.[63]

Certain Issues Are Unclear

The information provided in the body of this chapter also suggests that certain aspects of these oversight and auditing organizations may need to be clarified. For example, it is currently unclear where the FSOB is located within the federal government, or whether it is covered by a variety of general management and transparency requirements. Also, unlike the COP, the act does not provide the FSOB with a statutory right to information from federal departments or agencies. When the FSOB meets, it is not clear whether all or a majority of members must be present to take action, as the act does not specify what constitutes a quorum. The act does not indicate whether, and if so how, the FSOB is to be funded or staffed, or whether it can employ consultants to help it carry out its mission. As a result, it may be difficult for the board to carry out some of the tasks that it has been assigned (e.g., reporting evidence of fraud or malfeasance) particularly since several members of the FSOB are likely to change at the end of this Administration. Although the FSOB is required to report "quarterly," the act does not specify when those quarterly periods begin. The FSOB also does not appear to receive any of the various reports that are provided to the COP (e.g., reports by the Special IG or the CG).

In addition, although the act states that the Office of the Special IG is "established," it does not indicate where the office will be housed, and (in contrast to the provisions regarding GAO) there is no specific requirement in the act that the Secretary of the Treasury or any other department or agency provide the office with space or facilities. (However, if the Office of the Special IG is considered part of the Department of the Treasury, then the Secretary may be required by the Inspector General Act of 1978 to do so.) Finally, the act indicates that both the Office of the Special IG and GAO's audit and reporting responsibilities under the act terminate on the date that the last asset is sold or the last insurance contract expires, whichever is later. It is therefore unlikely that reports of the Special IG will reflect all relevant transactions, as some period after those dates will likely be needed to summarize the information and provide a complete historical record. GAO's final report, however, could address those transactions under the CG's general authority in 31 LT. S .C. §§712 and 717.[64]

Oversight and the Balance of Power

It is unclear what effect the various oversight and audit mechanisms will have on the balance of power between Congress and the executive branch. EESA gave the Secretary of the Treasury broad authority to purchase "troubled assets," and defined that term to include any financial instrument that the Secretary deems "necessary to promote financial market stability." Congress gave itself expedited legislative procedures to disapprove actions by the Secretary, but only after the first $350 billion has been obligated.[65] Congress can use its regular legislative procedures to disapprove actions regarding the first $350 billion of asset purchases, but a presidential veto of any congressional action (whether through regular or expedited procedures) would require a two-thirds vote of both houses of Congress to prevent the Secretary's actions from taking effect. Also, legislation has been introduced in the 110th Congress to reverse the presumption and require Congress to *approve* any expenditure over $350 billion,[66] but the President could veto this type of initiative as well again requiring a two- thirds majority in both houses of Congress for enactment.

Senate confirmation of agency officials is another means by which Congress can provide oversight of executive branch actions, and that authority will be particularly relevant regarding the nomination of the Assistant Secretary of the Treasury for the Office of Financial Stability. However, the legislation permits the Secretary of the Treasury to appoint an interim Assistant Secretary, and places no limit on how long that appointee may serve. Given the scope of the Assistant Secretary's responsibilities and the need for immediate action, a nomination for the position may not be submitted during the remaining days of the 110th Congress. The only other position established by EESA that requires Senate confirmation is the Special Inspector General for the TARP. As noted previously, the Senate Committee on Banking, Housing, and Urban Affairs held a confirmation hearing on the nomination for November 19, 2008, and the nomination could be acted upon by the full Senate shortly thereafter.[67]

Table 1. Characteristics of the Financial Stability Oversight Board and the Congressional Oversight Panel in the Emergency Economic Stabilization Act of 2008

	Financial Stability Oversight Board (FSOB) (Section 104)	**Congressional Oversight Panel (COP) (Section 125)**
Placement within the Federal Government	Unclear. Subsection (a) simply says the FSOB is "established".	(a) An "establishment of the legislative branch."
Responsi-bilities	(a) The FSOB is responsible for — (1) reviewing the exercise of auth-ority under a program develop-ped in accordance with this Act, including — (A) policies implemented by the Secretary and the Office of Financial Stability created under Sections 101 and 102, including the appointment of financial ag-ents, the designation of asset classes to be purchased, and plans for the structure of vehi-cles used to purchase troubled assets; and	(b) The COP shall review the current state of the financial markets and the regulatory system, and submit "regular reports" to Congress on — (1) the use by the Secretary of authority under the act, including the use of contracting authority and the administration of the program; (2) the impact of purchases made under the act on financial mar-kets and financial institutions; (3) the extent to which informa-tion made available on transact-

Table 1. (Continued)

	Financial Stability Oversight Board (FSOB) (Section 104)	Congressional Oversight Panel (COP) (Section 125)
	— (B) the effect of such actions in assisting American families in preserving home ownership, stabilizing financial markets, and protecting taxpayers; (2) making recommendations, as appro-priate, to the Secretary regarding use of the authority under this Act; and (3) reporting any suspected fraud, mis-representation, or malfea-sance to the Special Inspector General for the Troubled Assets Relief Pro-gram or the Attorney General of the United States, consistent with Section 535(b) of title 28, United States Code.	transparency; and (4) the effectiveness of foreclo-sure mitigation efforts and the effectiveness of the program from the standpoint of minimize-ing long-term costs to the tax-payers and maximizing the benefits for tax-payers.
Other Authorities and Powers	(e) In addition to the above responsi-bilities, the FSOB has the authority to ensure that the policies implemen-ted by the Secretary are — (1) in accordance with the purpose-es of the Act; (2) in the economic interests of the United States; and (3) consistent with protecting tax-payers, in accordance with Section 113(a) (entitled "Minimization of Long-Term Costs and Maximiza-tion of Benefits for Taxpayers")	(e)(1) In carrying out its responsibi-lities, the COP may hold hearings, "sit and act at times and places," take testi-mony, receive evidence, and administer oaths and affirmations to witnesses. (e)(2) Any member or agent of the COP may, if authorized by the panel, take any action which the COP is authorized to take.
Access to Data	No mention.	(e)(3) The COP may secure directly from any department or agency of the U.S. information needed to carry out its responsibilities. Upon request of the chairperson of the COP, the head of any department or agency shall furnish such information.
Membership	(b) The FSOB is comprised of (1) Chairman of the Board of Governors of the Federal Reserve System, (2) the Secretary of the Treasury; (3) the Director of the Federal Housing Finance Agency; the Chairman of the Securities and Exchange Commission, and the Secretary of Housing and Urban Development.	(c) The COP shall consist of five members, with one member each appointed by (1) the Speaker of the House of Representatives; (2) the minority leader of the House of Representatives; (3) the majority leader of the Senate; (4) the minority leader of the Senate; and (5) the Speaker and the majority leader of the Senate, after consultation with the minority leaders of each house. (c)(6) A vacancy on the COP shall

Table 1. (Continued)

	Financial Stability Oversight Board (FSOB) (Section 104)	Congressional Oversight Panel (COP) (Section 125)
		be filled in the same manner as the original appointment.
Leadership	(c) The chairperson of the FSOB shall be elected by the members of the board (other than the Secretary)	Although Section (c)(7) authorizes a "chairperson" of the COP to call meetings, the act does not indicate how the chairperson is selected.
Pay for Members	No mention	(c)(2) Each member of the COP shall be paid at the daily rate of basic pay for level I of the Executive Schedule ($191,300 in 2008) for each day the member is performing duties in the Commission (3) However, members of the COP who are Members of Congress or full-time federal officers or employ-ees of the U.S. receive no additional pay, allowances, or benefits.
Meetings	(d) The FSOB shall meet two weeks after the first exercise of purchase authority of the Secretary and monthly thereafter.	(c)(7) The COP shall meet at the call of the chairperson or a majority of its members.
Quorum	No mention.	(c)(5) Four members of the COP constitute a quorum, but a lesser number may hold hearings.
Subordinate Bodies	(f) The FSOB may appoint a credit review committee to evaluate the use of the purchase authority provided under the Act and the assets acquired through the use of that authority.	No mention.
Staffing and Consultants	No mention	(d)(1) The COP may appoint and fix the pay of any personnel it deems appropriate. (d)(2) The COP may procure tempo-rary and intermittent services under Section 3109(b) of title 5 (experts and consult-ants for up to one year). (d)(3) Upon request of the COP, the head of any federal department or agency may detail (on a reimburs-able basis) any personnel of that department or agency to the COP.
Reports by the Entity	g) The FSOB shall report to the appropriate committees of Congress and the COP not less than quarterly regarding its responsibilities under subsection (a).	(b)(1)(B) The "regular reports" of the COP (described in subsection (a) above) shall be submitted within 30 days after the first exercise of the Secretary's authority under Section 101(a) or 102, and every 30 days thereafter.

Table 1. (Continued)

	Financial Stability Oversight Board (FSOB) (Section 104)	Congressional Oversight Panel (COP) (Section 125)
		(b)(2) The COP is also to submit a "special report on regulatory reform" not later than Jan. 20, 2009, analyzing the current regulatory system and its effectiveness at overseeing the participants in the financial system and protecting consumers, with recommendations for improvement (including whether other participants in the financial markets should be subject to the regulatory system, the rationale for such a recommendation, and whether there are any gaps in existing consumer protections).
Reports to the Entity	No mention.	Per Section 104(g) of the act, the FSOB is to provide its quarterly reports to Congress to the COP. Per Section 105(d), any report to Congress by the Secretary that is required by section 105 shall also be provided to the COP. Per Section 116(d), any report or audit required under section 116 of the act (including Comptroller General reports) shall also be submitted to the COP. Per Section 117(d), the Comptroller General's report on "margin authority" is also to be provided to the COP. Per Section 121(f)(3), reports by the Special Inspector General for the TARP shall also be submitted to the COP. Per Section 129(e), the report to certain congressional committees on "exercise of loan authority" shall also be provided to the COP.
Funding	No mention.	(g) There is authorized to be appropriated to the COP such sums as may be necessary for any fiscal year, half of which shall be derived from the applicable account of the House of Representatives, and half from the contingent fund of the Senate. (h) An amount equal to the expenses of the COP shall be promptly transferred by the Secretary from time to time upon the presentment of a state-

Table 1. (Continued)

	Financial Stability Oversight Board (FSOB) (Section 104)	Congressional Oversight Panel (COP) (Section 125)
Funding	No mention.	ment of such expenses by the chairperson of the panel. The funds are to be taken from funds provided to the Secretary under the act and sent to the applicable fund of the House of Representatives and the contingent fund of the Senate.
Termination	(h) The FSOB and its authority terminates 15 days after the later of (1) the date that the last troubled asset acquired under Section 101 has been sold or transferred out of the ownership of the federal government, or (2) the date of expiration of the last insurance contract under Section 102.	The COP shall terminate 6 months after the termination date in Section 120 (Dec. 31, 2009, subject to extension)

Table 2. Responsibilities of the Comptroller General and the Special Inspector General for the TARP in the Emergency Economic Stabilization Act of 2008

	Comptroller General (CG) (Section 116)	Special Inspector General (IG) (Section 121)
Placement Within the Federal Government	GAO is a legislative branch agency (per *Bowsher v. Synar,* 478 U.S. 714, at 734 (1986)).	Unclear, although presumably within the Department of the Treasury (since the Secretary is authorized to establish the TARP).
Responsibilities	(a) (1) The CG shall oversee the activities and performance of the TARP and its agents and representatives, including: — (A) the performance of the TARP in meeting the purposes of the Act, particularly foreclosure mitigation, cost reduction, stability of financial markets or banking system, and protection of taxpayers; — (B) the financial condition and internal controls of the TARP and its agents; — (C) the characteristics of transact-tions and commitments entered into, including type, frequence, size, prices paid, terms/conditions, and terms of future commitments;	(c) (1) The Special IG shall conduct, supervise, and coordinate audits and investigations of the purchase, management, and sale of assets under any Section 101 program, and the management of any program under Section 102, including by collecting and summarizing: — (A) a description of the categories of troubled assets purchased or procured by the Secretary; — (B) a listing of the troubled assets in each category; — (C) an explanation of why the Secretary deemed it necessary to purchase each asset; — (D) a listing of each institution selling those assets; — (E) a listing (with detailed biogra-phical information) of each person or entity hired to manage such troubled assets; —

Table 2. (Continued)

	Comptroller General (CG) (Section 116)	Special Inspector General (IG) (Section 121)
	— (D) the characteristics and disposi-tion of acquired assets, including type, acquisition price, market value, sale prices and terms, and use of proceeds); — (E) the efficiency of TARP opera-tions in using appropriated funds; — (F) the compliance of TARP and its agents with applicable laws and regulations; — (G) TARP's efforts to prevent, identify, and minimize conflicts of interest by its agents; — (H) the efficiency of contracting procedures pursuant to Section 107(b) (minority and women contracting). (b)(2) The CG may audit the programs/activities of the TARP, its agents, and any vehicles established.	— (F) a current estimate of the amount of troubled assets on the books, purchased, and sold, and the profit or loss on each sale; and — (G) a listing of the insurance contracts issued. (c)(3) In addition to the above, the Special IG shall also have the autho-rities provided to IGs in section 6 of the Inspector General Act of 1978.
Obligation to Respond to Its Audits	(b)(3) The TARP is required to take action to address deficiencies identi-fied by the CG or other auditor enga-ged by the TARP, or to certify to the appropriate committees of Congress that no action is needed.	No specific provision (although the Inspector General Act requires agencies to furnish requested infor-mation or assistance).
Audit Space and Facilities	(a)(2)(A) The Secretary shall pro-vide appropriate audit space and facilities in the Department of the Treasury.	No specific provision (although the Inspector General Act requires agen-cies to furnish office space and facilities).
Staffing and Contracting	No provision (although GAO will likely use existing staff and contract-ing authority)	(e) The Special IG may (1) select, appoint, and employ such officers and employees as may be necessary, subject to the provisions of title 5 re-garding appointments, classification, and pay; (2) employ experts and consultants at daily rates not to exc-eed GS-15; and (3) enter into contr-acts or other arrangements for audits and studies as may be necessary.
Access to Data and Records	(a)(2)(B) To the extent consistent with law, the CG has access to any information, data, reports, papers, or things belonging to or used by the TARP, and to officers, agents, ad-visors, and employees. The CG shall be given full facilities for verifying	(e)(4) Upon request of the IG, the head of other agencies shall furnish any requested information or assist-ance that is practicable and not in contravention of law. If information or assistance is unreasonably refu-sed, the IG shall report to the appro-

Table 2. (Continued)

	Comptroller General (CG) (Section 116)	Special Inspector General (IG) (Section 121)
Access to Data and Records	transactions, and may make and retain copies of any records.	priate committees of Congress without delay.
Appoint-ment, Removal, and Pay of the Auditor	N/A	(b)(1) The Special IG is to be appointed by the President, with the advice and consent of the Senate. (2) The appointment is to be made on the basis of integrity and demonstrated ability in accounting, auditing, financial analysis, law, management analysis, public administration, or investigation. (3) The nomination is to be made as soon as practicable after the establishment of any program under Sections 101 and 102. (4) The IG may be removed by the President, with communication of the reason to Congress. (6) The IG shall be paid the same as other presidentially-appointed IGs.
Reports	(a)(3) The CG shall submit reports of findings to the appropriate committees of Congress and to the Special IG for the TARP at least every 60 days. The CG may also submit special reports as warranted by GAO's findings. (b)(1) The CG is to annually audit the TARP's financial statements. Also, Section 117 requires the CG to determine the extent to which leverage and sudden deleveraging of financial institutions was a factor behind the crisis, including the roles of the Board of Governors, the SEC, the Secretary, and others.	(f)(1) The Special IG shall submit a report to the appropriate committees of Congress summarizing the IG's activities during the relevant period within 60 days after confirmation and each calendar quarter thereafter. Each report shall include a detailed statement of all purchases, obligations, expenditures, and revenues associated with any program under Sections 101 and 102, as well as information under subsection (c)(1). (f)(2) None of the above authorizes the disclosure of information that is prohibited from disclosure by law or executive order, or part of a criminal investigation. (f)(3) The reports shall also be submitted to the COP.
Funding	(a)(2)(C) Treasury shall reimburse GAO for the full cost of any oversight activities as billed by the CG. (b)(1) Treasury is also to reimburse GAO for the full cost of the audit of the TARP financial statement. In both cases, the reimbursements are credited to GAO's "salaries and exp-enses" appropriation account and available until expended.	Of the funds available to the Secretary of the Treasury under Section 118 (from the sale of securities), $50 million shall be provided to the Special IG until expended.

Table 2. (Continued)

	Comptroller General (CG) (Section 116)	Special Inspector General (IG) (Section 121)
Termination	(e) Any oversight, reporting, or audit requirement terminates on the later of (1) the date that the last troubled asset acquired under Section 101 has been sold or transferred or (2) the date of expiration of the last insurance contract under Section 102. (a)(2) Secretary is to provide the CG with space and facilities until the termination date in Section 120 (Dec. 31, 2009, subject to extension).	(h)The Office of the Special IG shall terminate on the later of (1) the date that the last troubled asset acquired under Section 101 has been sold or transferred or (2) the date of expiration of the last insurance contract under Section 102.

End Notes

[1] For more information on EESA and related issues, see CRS Report RL34730, *The Emergency Economic StabilizationAct and Current Financial Turmoil: Issues and Analysis*, by Baird Webel and Edward V. Murphy.

[2] On October 6, 2008, the Secretary of the Treasury named Assistant Secretary Neel Kashkari as interim Assistant Secretary for the Office of Financial Stability.

[3] On October 28, 2008, the Department of the Treasury transferred the first EESA-related funds to participating institutions. See the remarks of Under Secretary for Domestic Finance Anthony Ryan at [http://www treasury.gov/press/releases/hp 1240. htm]. The department has also published guidelines for the TARP Capital Purchase Program and a list of frequently asked questions. See [http://www.treas.gov/ press/releases/hp1222.htm] for a copy of those documents.

[4] The President has certified to Congress that the additional $100 billion will be needed. See [http://www.whitehouse. gov/news/releas es/2008/ 10/20081014-1.html] for a copy of the President's certification.

[5] GAO's responsibilities in the act are in addition to its existing responsibilities. For example, 31 U.S.C. §712(1) requires the CG to "investigate all matters related to the receipt, disbursement, and use of public money," and 31 U.S.C. §717(b) states that the CG shall "evaluate the results of a program or activity the Government carries out under existing law." For more information on GAO, see CRS Report RL30349, *GAO: Government Accountability Office and General Accounting Office,* by Frederick M. Kaiser.

[6] The act also requires certain reports from the Office of Management and Budget (OMB) and the Congressional Budget Office (CBO). For example, Section 202(a) requires OMB to report to the President and the Congress within 60 days of the first exercise of authority under Section 101(a) (or by December 31, 2008, whichever comes earlier), and semiannually thereafter on how much the troubled asset program is costing, how that cost estimate was derived, and how the estimate changed from the previous report. CBO is required to assess the OMB reports within 45 days of their submission to the Congress. Also, Section 201 of the act authorizes CBO and the Joint Committee on Taxation to receive "all information used by the Secretary in connection with activities authorized under this Act" to assist Congress with its oversight responsibilities.

[7] See, for example, Gibson, Dunn & Crutcher LLP, "Financial Markets in Crisis: Section-bySection Analysis of the Emergency Economic Stabilization Act of 2008," available at [http://blogs law 10/100208-analysis-economics abilizati onact08.pdf]. The authors note that the oversight entities "overlap considerably," and that while Congress may want multiple perspectives, "the potential for these oversight entities to trip over each other in the course of their work is great."

[8] See, for example, CRS Report RL32592, *General Management Laws and the 9/11 Commission's Proposed Office of National Intelligence Director (NID) and National Counterterrorism Center (NCTC),* coordinated by Clinton T. Brass and Curtis W. Copeland. That report indicated that more general management laws would appear to cover the MD and NCTC if they were independent entities in the executive branch than if they were placed within the Executive Office of the President. If the FSOB is considered part of a federal department or agency or an independent agency, then most of these general management laws would appear to apply. For more information about these management statutes, see CRS Report RL30795, *GeneralManagement Laws: A Compendium*, coordinated by Clinton T. Brass.

[9] In contrast, the legislation establishing the Privacy and Civil Liberties Oversight Board (121 Stat. 355) authorizes the Board to request thc Attorney General to subpoena information on its behalf.

[10] As noted earlier in this report, the Department of the Treasury transferred the first EESArelated funds to participating institutions on October 28, 2008.

[11] Amit R. Paley, "N.Y. Prosecutor Picked to Oversee Bailout," *Washington Post,* November 15, 2008, p. Dl. Democratic congressional leaders reportedly selected Richard H. Neiman, superintendent of banks in New York; Elizabeth Warren, a professor at Harvard Law School; and Damon Silvers, associate general counsel of the AFL-CIO.

[12] Amit R. Paley, "Senators Moving Quickly to Install Bailout Watchdog," *Washington Post,* November 20, 2008, p. A10. Those named were Senator Judd Gregg and Representative Jeb Hensarling.

[13] See interim Assistant Secretary Kashkari's remarks before the Institute of International Bankers, at [http://www.cnbc.com/id

[14]Ibid. See [http://www.treasury.govinitiatives/eesa/docs/AmendedBylaws.pdf] for a copy of the bylaws.

[15] Testimony ofNeel Kashkari, interim Assistant Secretary for the Financial Stability Office, U.S. Department of the Treasury, before the Senate Committee on Banking, Housing, and Urban Affairs, October 23, 2008.

[16] See [http://www.treas.govinitiatives/eesa/minutes.shtml] to view those minutes.

[17] Testimony ofNeel Kashkari, interim Assistant Secretary for the Financial Stability Office, U.S. Department of the Treasury, before the Senate Committee on Banking, Housing, and Urban Affairs, October 23, 2008.

[18] Section 3(1) of the act defines the term "appropriate committees of Congress" as the Committee on Banking, Housing, and Urban Affairs, the Committee on Finance, the Committee on the Budget, and the Committee on Appropriations of the Senate; and the Committee on Financial Services, the Committee on Ways and Means, the Committee on the Budget, and the Committee on Appropriations of the House of Representatives.

[19] As noted earlier in this report, the Department of the Treasury transferred the first EES A- related funds to participating institutions on October 28, 2008.

[20] S. 3652, introduced by Senator Maria Cantwell on September 29, 2008, would have established an independent, bipartisan commission to conduct a similar review of the U.S. financial system. The bill also would have established a special inspector general for financial markets oversight.

[21] *Bowsher v. Synar,* 478 U.S. 714, at 734 (1986).

[22] For a detailed comparison of the Special IG for the TARP and other special IGs as well as statutory IGs under the Inspector General Act of 1978, as amended, see CRS Report RS22981, *The Special Inspector General for the Troubled Asset Relief Program (SIG TARP),* by Vanessa K. Burrows.

[23] According to the interim Assistant Secretary for the Office of Financial Stability, in anticipation of the upcoming nomination and confirmation of the Special IG, the Department of the Treasury has already begun meeting with the department's IG.

[24] See U.S. Department of the Treasury, "Tarp Capital Purchase Program; Interim Final Rule," 73 *Federal Register* 62205, October 20, 2008, for a copy of this rule.

[25] See interim Assistant Secretary Kashkari's remarks before the Institute of International Bankers, at [http : //www. cnbc. com/id .

[26] Specifically, Section 121(g) of the act says that "Of the amounts made available to the Secretary of the Treasury under section 118, $50,000,000 shall be available to the Special Inspector General to carry out this section." Section 118 states that the "Secretary may use the proceeds of the sale of any securities issued under chapter 31 of title 31, United States Code." Chapter 31 of Title 31 ("Public Debt") includes savings bonds and savings certificates (Section 3105), retirement and savings bonds (Section 3106), and other vehicles.

[27] See interim Assistant Secretary Kashkari's remarks before the Institute of International Bankers, at [http : //www. cnbc. com/id .

[28] Humberto Sanchez, "Frank Praises GAO for Oversight of Treasury Rescue Plan," *Congress Daily,* October 14, 2008.

[29] GAO has certain data access rights under existing law. For example, 31 U.S.C. §716(a) states that each agency is to "give the Comptroller General information the Comptroller General requires about the duties, powers, activities, organization, and financial transactions of the agency."

[30] For example, 31 U.S.C. §731 permits the Comptroller General to procure the services of up to 20 experts and consultants for up to three years at daily rates of pay for level IV of the Executive Schedule (currently $149,000 per year).

[31] Section 6 of that legislation provides that, after October 1, 2009, if GAO "audits any financial statement or related schedule which is prepared under section 3515 by an executive agency," the agency must reimburse GAO for the cost of the audit if GAO audited the statement for FY2007.

[32] In comparison, the posts of Special Inspector General for Iraq Reconstruction and Special Inspector General for Afghanistan Reconstruction are each to end 180 days after its parent entity's reconstruction funds are less than $250 million.

[33] Andrew Ross Sorkin, "A Bailout Above the Law," New *York Times,* September 23, 2008, P. Cl.

[34] Michael Cooper and Patrick Healey, "McCain, More Critical of Bailout Plan, Faults Oversight," *New York Times,* September 22, 2008, available at [http://www.nytimes.com/ 2008/09/23/us/politics/23campaign.html].

[35] For a complete listing of the reports required by EESA, see CRS Report RL34740, *Reporting Requirements in the Emergency Economic Stabilization Act of 2008,* by Curtis W. Copeland.

[36] For example, the CG is to describe the "characteristics and disposition of acquired assets." The Special IG is to provide a "description of the categories of troubled assets purchased or procured by the Secretary," and a "listing of the troubled assets in each category."

[37] Alan Morrison, "Plugging Leaks in the Bailout,"*Legal Times,* November 10, 2008, p. 46.

[38] For example, in his statement upon the passage of EESA, the Secretary of the Treasury said that the authority provided in the act "gives us the ability to protect and recapitalize our financial system as we work through the stresses in our credit markets." To view a copy of this statement, see [http://www.treasury.gov/press/releases/hp1175.htm].

[39] Aaron Lorenzo and R. Christian Bruce, "Treasury Pulls Back From TARP Purchase of Mortgage-Related Assets, Paulson Says,"*BNA Daily Report for Executives,* November 13, 2008, p. AA-1.

[40] See, for example, Mark Landler, "New Terrain for Arbiters of a Bailout," *New York Times,* November 4, 2008, p. B1, which said "critics from Capitol Hill to Wall Street are lashing out at the program, saying the banks are misusing the capital infusions by hoarding the money rather than lending it, as the Treasury Secretary, Henry M. Paulson Jr., urged in order to unclog the credit markets.... Critics also say that, by not barring banks from paying dividends or hefty bonuses, the Treasury is leading taxpayers to think that their money is being spent frivolously." Also, see Binyamin Appelbaum, `Banks to Continue Paying Dividends; Bailout Money is for Lending, Critics Say," *Washington Post,* October 30, 2008, p. Al; and Charlene Carter, "Leading House Democrats Pressure Treasury on Banks' Use of Federal Funds," *Congress Now,* October 31, 2008, available at [http://congres snow. gallerywatch.com/Article Detail.aspx? articlelD= 7182].

[41] R. Christian Bruce, "Federal Overseer Will Seek Real-Time Data From TARP Asset Mangers and Contractors," *BNA Daily Report for Executives,* November 20, 2008, p. A-20.

[42] Terry Kivian, "Special IG Nominee Pledges Enforcement of TARP Rules," *Congress Daily PM,* November 19, 2008, available at [http://www.nationalj ournal. com/congres s daily/ cdp 20081119 5781.php?related=true&storyl=null&story2=null&story3=null].

[43] Section 116(b) of the act requires TARP to prepare and issue audited financial statements to the appropriate committees of Congress and the public.

[44] For example, the Department of the Treasury posted the first "tranche" report on its public website even though EESA did not require the report to be provided to the public. To view a copy, see [http://www.treas.gov/initiatives/eesa/docs/Tranche-Reportfinal.pdf].

[45] See, for example, Ben Protess, "Bailout Does Still *Redacted,"ProPublica,* November 13, 2008, available at [http ://www.propublica.org/article/bailout-docs-still-redacted-1113%20/]; and Dean Starkman, "Bloomberg Steps Up; Wire Service Sues Fed for Bailout Transparency," *Columbia Journalism Review,* November 7, 2008, available at [http://www.cjr.org/the_audiebloomberg_steps_up.php].

[46] Amit R. Paley, "N.Y. Prosecutor Picked to Oversee Bailout," *Washington Post,* November 15, 2008, p. Dl. Democratic congressional leaders reportedly selected Richard H. Neiman, superintendent of banks in New York; Elizabeth Warren, a professor at Harvard Law School; and Damon Silvers, associate general counsel of the AFL-CIO.

[47] Amit R. Paley, "Senators Moving Quickly to Install Bailout Watchdog," *Washington Post,* November 20, 2008, p. A10. Republican congressional leaders selected Senator Judd Gregg and Representative Jeb Hensarling.

[48] Mike Soraghan, `Bush Picks a Bailout Watchdog," *The Hill,* November 14, 2008. The nominee is Neil M. Barofsky, of New York.

[49] Pursuant to Senate rules, the Senate Homeland Security and Governmental Affairs Committee has the right to hold a hearing on inspectors general, or else 20 days must pass before the nomination proceeds to the full Senate. However, the nomination could be brought to the full Senate by unanimous consent.

[50] R. Christian Bruce and Ralph Lindeman, "Drawdown of Remaining TARP Funds May Be Left for Obama Administration,"BNA *Daily Report for Executives,* p. A-23.

[51] Amit R. Paley, "Bailout Lacks Oversight Despite Billions Pledged," *Washington Post,* November 13, 2008, p. Al.

[52] Ibid.

[53] For example, the legislation was described as having "granted authority to purchase up to $700 billion in troubled mortgage-backed securities from debt-riddled Wall Street firms, a move designed to free up the credit markets." Michael Kranish and Jenny Paul, "Resounding Yes to Bailout," *Boston Globe,* October 4, 2008, p. Al.

[54] For example, several members of the FSOB appear to have been named to the board because of their relationship to the housing industry (e.g., the Director of the Federal Housing Finance Agency and the Secretary of Housing and Urban Development). Section 116(a)(1) of the act states that the CG is to describe the "characteristics of transactions and commitments entered into, including transaction type, frequency, size, prices paid, and all other relevant terms and conditions, and the timing, duration and terms of any future commitments to purchase assets." The CG is also required to describe the "characteristics and disposition of acquired assets, including type, acquisition price, current market value, sale prices and terms, and use of proceeds from sales."

[55] David Cho, Neil Irwin, and Peter Whoriskey, "US Forces Nine Major Banks to Accept Partial Nationalization," *Washington Post,* October 14, 2008, p. A-1; and Neil Irwin and David Cho, "Paulson's Change in Rescue Tactics," *Washington Post,* October 15, 2008, p. D-1.

[56] David Cho, Binyamin Appelbaum, and Zachary A. Goldfarb, "Bailout Expands to Insurers," *Washington Post,* October 25, 2008, p. Al.

[57] Yin Wilczek, "MSRB in Discussions Concerning Possible Bailout of State, Local Governments," *BNA Daily Report for Executives,* October 28, 2008, p. A-21.

[58] Nora Macaluso, "Federal Aid Crucial for Survival of U.S. Automakers, Analysts Say," *BNA Daily Report for Executives,* October 30, 2008, p. AA-1.

[59] Peter Whoriskey, David Cho, and Binyamin Appelbaum, "Treasury Redefines Its Rescue Program; Plan to Buy Distressed Assets is Abandoned in Favor of Aid to Loosen Consumer Credit," *Washington Post,* November 13, 2008, p. Al.

[60] Aaron Lorenzo and R. Christian Bruce, "Treasury Pulls Back From TARP Purchase of Mortgage-Related Assets, Paulson Says," *BNA Daily Report for Executives,* November 13, 2008, p. AA-1.

[61] Stephen Joyce, "New York Governor Pushes for State Representation on TARP Oversight Panel," BNA *Daily Report for Executives,* October 28, 2008, p. A-28.

[62] On October 23, 2008, the interim Assistant Secretary for the Office of Financial Stability testified before the Senate Committee on Banking, Housing, and Urban Affairs that the department was considering implementing a large-scale program to guarantee troubled mortgages, which is authorized under Section 109 of EESA.

[63] Amit R. Paley, "Senators Moving Quickly to Install Bailout Watchdog," *Washington Post,* November 20, 2008, p. A10. Senators Claire McCaskill and Charles E. Grassley reportedly introduced legislation on November 19, 2008, to make clear that the Special IG has authority over all aspects of EESA, and to allow him to hire staff without following the civil service hiring process.

[64] As noted earlier in this report, 31 U. S.C. 712(1) requires the CG to "investigate all matters related to the receipt, disbursement, and use of public money," and 31 U.S.C. §717(b) states that the CG shall "evaluate the results of a program or activity the Government carries out under existing law."

[65] As noted earlier in this report, Section 115(a)(3) of the act states that if the President sends Congress a written report describing the Secretary of the Treasury's plan to spend the second $350 billion, Congress has 15 calendar days to enact a joint resolution of disapproval. For more information about this process, see CRS Report RS22985, *"Fast Track" Parliamentary Procedures of the Emergency Economic Stabilization Act,* by Christopher M. Davis. Although no written report has been submitted, legislation has already been introduced in the 110th Congress (H. J.Res . 101) to invoke this requirement (i.e., to prevent expenditures above $350 billion).

[66] See, for example, S. 3683, S. 3694, S. 3697, and H.R. 7276 in the 110th Congress.

[67] Pursuant to Senate rules, the Senate Homeland Security and Governmental Affairs Committee has the right to hold a hearing on inspectors general, or else 20 days must pass before the nomination proceeds to the full Senate. However, the nomination could be brought to the full Senate by unanimous consent.

In: Government Interventions in Economic Emergencies
Editor: Pablo Sastre
ISBN: 978-1-60741-356-1

Chapter 9

STATEMENT OF PETER R. ORSZAG, FEDERAL RESPONSES TO MARKET TURMOIL, BEFORE THE COMMITTEE ON THE BUDGET U.S. HOUSE OF REPRESENTATIVES

Congressional Budget Office

Chairman Spratt, Ranking Member Ryan, and Members of the Committee, thank you for inviting me to testify this morning on the budgetary and economic implications of the recent turmoil in financial markets and the Administration's proposal to address it.

Since August 2007, the Federal Reserve and the Treasury have been attempting to address a series of severe breakdowns in financial markets that emanated from the bursting of the housing bubble, leading to substantial losses on mortgage-related securities and great difficulty in accurately ascertaining the financial condition of the institutions holding such securities. Those problems generated significant increases in risk spreads (or the interest rates charged on risky assets relative to Treasury securities) but, more important, contributed to a broader collapse of confidence, with the result that financial institutions became increasingly unwilling to lend to one another.

Over the past several weeks, the collapse of confidence in financial markets has become particularly severe. Short-term loans between financial institutions have fallen off sharply. Instead, the Treasury and the Federal Reserve have become the financial intermediaries for them. In other words, rather than financial institutions with excess money lending to institutions needing short-term funding, many institutions with excess short-term money have purchased Treasury securities, the Treasury has placed the proceeds on deposit at the Federal Reserve, and the Federal Reserve has then lent the money out to those institutions needing short- run funding.

Thus far, turmoil in the financial markets has had less impact on macroeconomic activity than may have been expected, and, indeed, economic growth was relatively strong in the second quarter of this year—in part because of the stimulus package enacted earlier this year. A modern economy like the United States', however, depends crucially on the functioning of its financial markets to allocate capital, and history suggests that the real economy typically slows some time after a downturn in financial markets. Moreover, ominous signs about credit difficulties are accumulating. The issuance of corporate debt plummeted in the third quarter, and the short-term commercial paper market has also been hit hard. Bank lending, which has thus far remained relatively strong, will undoubtedly be severely curtailed by the difficulties that banks are facing in raising capital. Such a curtailment of credit means that businesses and individuals will find it increasingly difficult to borrow money to carry out their normal activities. In sum, the problems occurring in financial markets raise the possibility of a severe credit crunch, which could have devastating effects on the U.S. and world economies.

To mitigate the risks, the Department of the Treasury has proposed the Troubled Asset Relief Act of 2008, and similar proposals have also been put forward by the Chairman of the House Financial Services Committee and the Chairman of the Senate Banking Committee. In an analysis of these proposals, it is useful to identify two problems facing financial markets: illiquidity triggered by market panic and the potential insolvency of many financial institutions.

One problem is that the markets for some types of assets and transactions have essentially stopped functioning. To address that problem, the government could conceivably intervene as a "market maker," by offering to purchase assets through a competitive process and thereby provide a price signal to other market participants. (That type of intervention, if designed carefully to keep the government from overpaying, might not involve any significant subsidy from the government to financial institutions.) The second problem, though, involves the potential insolvency of specific financial institutions. By some estimates, global commercial banks and investment banks may need to raise a minimum of roughly $150 billion more to cover their losses. As of mid-September 2008, cumulative recognized losses stood at about $520 billion, while the institutions had raised $370 billion of additional capital.[1] Restoring solvency to insolvent institutions requires additional capital injections, and one possible source of such capital is the federal government.

Those two problems are related in the sense that it is difficult to know which institutions are insolvent without being able to value the assets they hold (which in turn is impeded by illiquid markets). Undisclosed losses are unlikely to be distributed uniformly throughout the financial system, and the inability to identify which institutions are carrying the largest losses has led to a breakdown of trust in the entire financial sector.[2] That loss of trust has sharply increased the cost of raising capital and rolling over debt, which threatens the solvency of all financial institutions. Injecting more capital into financial institutions could help to restore liquidity to some financial markets, because, with larger cushions of capital to protect against default, the institutions would be more willing to lend to one another. Another linkage between these two problems could occur if some institutions are unwilling to sell assets at current market prices if that then triggered the recognition of accounting losses; such reluctance to sell can contribute to illiquid markets. With additional equity, those institutions may be more willing to sell at current market prices even if that required recognizing losses.

Although the problems of illiquidity and insolvency are interrelated, they are at least conceptually distinct. Indeed, some policy proposals appear to be aimed primarily at the illiquidity of particular asset markets, and others appear to be aimed primarily at the potential insolvency of specific financial institutions.

Most of this testimony examines the Troubled Asset Relief Act of 2008. That act appears to be motivated primarily by concerns about illiquid markets. The more the government overpays for assets purchased under that act, however, the more the proposed program would instead provide a subsidy to specific financial institutions, in a manner that seems unlikely to be an efficient approach to addressing concerns about insolvency.

THE TROUBLED ASSET RELIEF ACT OF 2008

The Congressional Budget Office (CBO) has reviewed the Troubled Asset Relief Act of 2008, as proposed by the Administration. The act would authorize the Secretary of the Treasury to purchase, hold, and sell a wide variety of financial instruments, particularly those that are based on or related to residential or commercial mortgages issued prior to September 17, 2008. The authority to enter into agreements to purchase such financial instruments, which the proposal refers to as troubled assets, would expire two years after its enactment.

The legislation would appropriate such sums as are necessary, for as many years as necessary, to enable the Secretary to purchase up to $700 billion of troubled assets at any point during the two-year window of opportunity (though cumulative gross purchases may exceed $700 billion as previously purchased assets are sold) and to cover all administrative expenses of purchasing, holding, and selling those assets. The federal debt limit would be increased by $700 billion.

At this time, given the lack of specificity regarding how the program would be implemented and even what asset classes would be purchased, CBO cannot provide a meaningful estimate of the ultimate net cost of the Administration's proposal. The Secretary would have the authority to purchase virtually any asset, at any price, and sell it at any future date; the lack of specificity regarding how that authority would be implemented makes it impossible at this point to provide a quantitative analysis of the net cost to the federal government.

THE BUDGETARY TREATMENT OF THE PROPOSAL

The federal cost of the proposal could be reflected in the budget either on a cash basis or on a net-expected-cost basis. The proposal would require that the federal budget display the costs of this new activity under the latter approach, using procedures similar to those contained in the Federal Credit Reform Act (but adjusting for market risk in a manner not reflected in that law). In particular, the federal budget would not record the gross cash outlays associated with purchases of troubled assets but, instead, would reflect the estimated net cost to the government of such purchases (broadly speaking, the purchase cost minus the expected value of any estimated future earnings from holding those assets and the proceeds from the eventual sale of them). That approach would be similar to the current budgetary treatment of a broad array of loans and loan guarantees made by the federal government, wherein the best measure of the cost to the government reflects not only initial disbursements but also the resulting cash flows in future years.

In CBO's view, that budgetary treatment best reflects the impact of the purchases of financial assets on the federal government's underlying financial condition. The fundamental idea is that if the government buys a security at the going market price, it has exchanged cash for another asset rather than caused a deterioration in its underlying fiscal position.

CBO expects that the Treasury would probably fully use its $700 billion authority in fiscal year 2009 to purchase various troubled assets. To finance those purchases, the Treasury would have to sell debt to the public. Federal debt held by the public would therefore initially rise by about $700 billion. Nevertheless, CBO expects that, over time, the net cash disbursements under the program would be substantially less than $700 billion, because, ultimately, the government would sell the acquired assets and thus generate income that would offset at least much of the initial cost.

Whether those transactions ultimately resulted in a gain or loss to the government would depend on the types of assets purchased, how they were acquired and managed, and when and under what terms they were sold. In addition to the future evolution of the housing prices, interest rates, and other fundamental drivers of asset values, two key forces would influence the net gain or loss on the assets purchased:

Whether the federal government seeks and is able to succeed in obtaining a fair market price for the assets it purchases and, in particular, whether it can avoid being saddled with the worst credit risks without the purchase price reflecting those risks. Concerns about the government's overpaying are particularly salient when sellers offer assets with varying underlying characteristics that are complicated to evaluate. As discussed further below, such problems are attenuated the more that the government focuses on buying part of a given asset from institutions that all own a share of that asset, rather than buying different assets from different institutions. That is, the government is more likely to pay a fair price when multiple institutions are competing to sell identical assets than when it has to assess competing offers for different assets with hard-to-determine values.

Whether, because of severe market turmoil, market prices are currently lower than the underlying value of the assets. If current prices reflect "fire sale" prices that can result from severe liquidity constraints and the impairment of credit flows, then taxpayers could possibly benefit along with the institutions selling the assets. Under normal circumstances, prices do not long depart from their fundamentals because the incentive to engage in arbitrage and profit from price discrepancies is large. But arbitrage practices work less well when liquidity is restrained, as it is now, and many potential arbitragers cannot get short-term financing.[3] It is therefore at least possible that the prices of some assets are below their fundamental value; in that case, to the extent that the government bought now and held such assets until their market prices recovered to reflect that underlying value, net gains would be possible.

In addition to any net gain or loss on the purchase of $700 billion or more in assets, the government would also incur significant administrative costs for the proposed program. Those costs would depend on what kinds of assets were purchased. On the basis of the costs incurred by private investment firms that acquire, manage, and sell similar assets, CBO expects that the administrative costs of operating the program could amount to a few billion dollars per year, as long as the government held all or most of the purchased assets

The proposed program could affect other federal programs—including, for example, the operations of Fannie Mae, Freddie Mac, federal housing programs, and deposit insurance. The program's impact on the future costs of other federal programs would depend on what kinds of assets were acquired and from what types of institutions and on how successful the program was in restoring liquidity to the nation's financial markets.

Determining a Purchase Price for Troubled Assets

The legislation would authorize the Secretary to purchase almost any conceivable type of asset related to residential or commercial mortgages, from individual loans to complex insurance products, and possibly other assets not directly related to such mortgages. The Treasury Department has indicated that it would conduct reverse auctions for at least some of the purchases. In a reverse auction, many potential sellers would bid on the price to be accepted by the government, and the lowest bidders would win. Using a reverse auction process in which multiple sellers compete to offer the Treasury the lowest price for a set volume of similar troubled assets would help ensure that the government was paying a fair price for those assets.

In the context of financial assets, a reverse auction works best when (1) different sellers are offering to sell their shares in the same asset rather than offering to sell *different* assets and when (2) many sellers participate. When sellers are offering different assets, the lowest bidder may win by offering an asset with particularly risky or poor future prospects, and the price may not reflect the degree to which that specific asset is risky or impaired. Consequently, the federal government could purchase too many risky or impaired assets without enjoying sufficient price discounts. Similarly, if the number of participants in the reverse auction is unduly limited (either because few institutions own the asset that the government wants to purchase or because few owners choose to participate in the auction), the government could overpay relative to a fair price.

One focus of the Treasury program seems likely to be mortgage-backed securities (MBSs), which are ownership shares in large pools of individual mortgages. Financial institutions own hundreds of thousands of such securities, reflecting more than \$7 trillion in pooled mortgage assets; most of the hard-to-value MBS assets are likely to be in the nearly \$3 trillion not owned or insured by Fannie Mae and Freddie Mac. The Treasury Department has indicated that the reverse auctions for MBS assets might be conducted security by security—that is, there would be a separate "mini-auction" for each tranche of the MBSs.[4] If those tranches were widely distributed across financial institutions and if the government offered to purchase only a small share of each tranche, the result should be that the government would obtain a fair price for such purchases.[5]

Reverse auctions may not obtain a fair price for the government for many other types of assets the Treasury may seek to purchase. In particular, determining fair market prices using an auction is difficult for assets that are not clearly the same or very similar in quality—that is, when the seller has more information about the quality of the asset than the buyer does. In such cases, each auction participant will offer up assets with unique attributes known only to the seller, thus increasing the likelihood that the government will pay too much. That type of problem is likely to be particularly severe for assets like individual home mortgages or esoteric derivative products entirely owned by specific financial institutions.[6] Substantial purchases of such assets would make it unlikely that the Treasury could operate the proposed new program at little or no net cost.

In other words, the more that the Treasury program concentrates on assets that are difficult for a buyer to value, the more likely that the government will overpay. The more that occurs, the more the program moves beyond simply reestablishing trading in illiquid financial markets and instead subsidizes the particular financial institutions selling assets to the government, at a cost to taxpayers.

FINANCIAL MARKET AND OTHER EFFECTS OF THE PROPOSAL

The Treasury's proposal is aimed at stabilizing financial markets and the economy by providing liquidity to support credit flows. One reason that credit markets have seized up is the uncertainty about who holds impaired assets and what they are worth, especially those related to mortgages. The underlying losses on those assets reflect the decline in home prices, but the mortgage loans have been repackaged as MBSs and then again into more complex securities such as collateralized debt obligations and credit default swaps that have spread the risk across many financial markets.

The proposal would allow the Treasury to buy up those assets regardless of the form in which they are held. The core problem, though, has moved beyond the mortgage markets and has become a broader collapse of confidence in financial markets. It therefore remains uncertain whether the program will be sufficient to restore trust, especially if the program is limited to the asset classes in which the government is least likely to overpay for its purchases.

At the same time, intervention on a massive scale is not without risks to taxpayers and to the economy.[7] Almost by definition, the intervention cannot solve insolvency problems without shifting costs to the taxpayers. Ironically, the intervention could even trigger additional failures of large institutions, because some institutions may be carrying troubled assets on their books at inflated values. Establishing clearer prices might reveal those institutions to be insolvent. (To the extent such insolvencies were revealed, the net effect might not be deleterious. Providing more transparency about the lack of solvency at specific institutions may be necessary to restore trust in the financial system.)

More broadly, there is an inherent tension between minimizing the costs to taxpayers and pursuing other policy goals. For example, as the manager of troubled mortgage assets, the government would be likely to come under intense pressure to avoid foreclosures or to take other steps to pursue goals for low- and moderate-income housing through activities that would not be subject to the constraints of the normal budget process. Those objectives may benefit specific homeowners, at the expense of taxpayers as a whole.

ALTERNATIVES TO THE TREASURY'S PROPOSAL

Some analysts, in assessing the Treasury's proposal, have pointed out that other recent actions by the Federal Reserve and the Treasury have given taxpayers significantly more upside in the form of equity stakes in the companies that receive assistance. Those actions have been aimed at supporting particular troubled institutions, rather than at enhancing the liquidity of the financial markets. Under some alternative proposals, the government would receive shares in an institution if it ultimately lost money on the sale of assets purchased from the institution. That approach would reduce the risk of overpaying for securities if the seller had more information about the value of those securities than the Treasury did. However, institutions that gave up equity would presumably expect to receive higher prices for their assets, and an equity stake in the firms might not offer any better upside to taxpayers than direct purchases of the assets on a risk- adjusted basis. Furthermore, healthy institutions might be deterred from participating, which could make it more likely that the federal government would overpay for assets by limiting the potential number of sellers—and the potential dilution for existing shareholders if asset prices declined in the future might make it challenging for financial institutions that issued such equity to the government to raise private capital in the future.

An alternative approach that is more directly aimed at addressing insolvency concerns is for the government to invest directly in financial institutions to strengthen their capital positions, without directly purchasing troubled assets. The injections could take the form of preferred stock, which would effectively lower the cost of new capital for the institutions. Such proposals could be modeled along the lines of the Reconstruction Finance Corporation, a Depression-era institution.

A number of twists to that approach have been offered. Some versions require that the institutions match the injection with new private funds in the form of common stock. In addition, some require that the underwriting risk associated with raising new capital be mutualized by the group of participating institutions acting as a syndicate. The syndicate would be responsible for at least half of the underwriting burden, which would give it an incentive to limit membership to solvent institutions only. Participating banks might also be required to suspend dividends, which would increase their retained earnings and thus add directly to capital. (Although institutions can always cut their dividends, doing so usually sends a bad signal to financial markets. A requirement could dilute the effect of that bad signal.)

Such proposals have some advantages:[8]

- They provide some upside to taxpayers in the form of dividends and capital gains on preferred stock. Under some proposals, the payments of dividends to the government would be deferred.
- They avoid the challenge of pricing and then selling individual assets (although they raise the issue of how to price the equity shares the government offers to purchase).
- They avoid rewarding the firms that have made the worst investment decisions.
- They keep the government as a minority shareholder. The firms' managers would continue to run the firms on a profit-maximizing basis, thereby mitigating the risks of the government using its equity positions to pursue a range of public policy goals.
- They could impose losses on shareholders and changes in management.

Such plans have some disadvantages though:

- They fail to address directly the illiquidity problems for some assets and the associated uncertainty.
- The assistance may not be targeted to the institutions most in need of help, and the firms that most need capital may be most reluctant to take it.

The approach could inject additional funds into institutions whose business model is no longer viable. Past experience suggests that extending the operations of insolvent institutions may increase the ultimate cost to taxpayers.

The proposals raise difficult questions about eligibility criteria. For example, would finance companies that are part of large diversified holding companies be eligible?

End Notes

[1] Figures are from Bloomberg as of September 22, 2008. For institutions located in the Americas, recognized losses are about $260 billion, while the amount of additional capital raised to date is $180 billion, which leaves a gap of about $80 billion.

[2] Anil K. Kashyap, Raghuram G. Rajan, and Jeremy C. Stein, "Rethinking Capital Regulation" (paper presented at the Federal Reserve Bank of Kansas City symposium on "Maintaining Stability in a Changing Financial System, Jackson Hole, Wyo., August 21–23, 2008), available at www.kc.frb.org/publicat/sympos/2008/KashyapRajanStein.09.15.08.pdf.

[3] Andrei Shliefer and Robert W. Vishny, "The Limits to Arbitrage," *Journal of Finance,* vol. 52, no. 1 (1997), pp. 35–55.

[4] Rights to the income from the pool of mortgages are divided up into slices, or tranches. The senior tranches will get paid under almost all circumstances; the most junior tranches will take the first risk of loss of income from defaults on the underlying mortgages. Each tranche is identified by a standard CUSIP (Committee on Uniform Security Identification Procedure) number like any other publicly traded security. Pieces of each tranche are likely to be held by many institutions, some troubled, some not.

[5] For further discussion of efficient auction designs, see Lawrence M. Ausubel and Peter Cramton, "Auction Design Matters for Rescue Plan."

[6] Such problems could be attenuated by requiring that private capital pools run by the asset managers hired by the government under the program participate in some share of each purchase made by the government.

[7] Douglas W. Elmendorf, *Concerns About the Treasury Rescue Plan* (September 19, 2008), available at www.brookings.edu/opinion/2008/0919_treasury-plan-elmendorf.aspx.

[8] Ibid.

In: Government Interventions in Economic Emergencies ISBN: 978-1-60741-356-1
Editor: Pablo Sastre

Chapter 10

THE U.S. FINANCIAL CRISIS: LESSONS FROM CHILE

J. F. Hornbeck

SUMMARY

Chile experienced a banking crisis from 1981-84 that in relative terms had a cost comparable in size to that perhaps facing the United States today. The Chilean Central Bank acted quickly and decisively in three ways to restore faith in the credit markets. It restructured firm and household loans, purchased nonperforming loans temporarily, and facilitated the sale or liquidation of insolvent financial institutions. These three measures increased liquidity in the credit markets and restored the balance sheets of the viable financial institutions. The Central Bank required banks to repurchase the nonperforming loans when provision for their loss could be made and prohibited distribution of profits until they had all been retired. Although the private sector remained engaged throughout the resolution of this crisis, the fiscal costs were, nonetheless, very high.

The U.S. Congress is contemplating a $700 billion government assistance package to arrest the financial crisis in the United States. President Bush argued that failure to enact legislation quickly could result in a wholesale failure of the U.S. financial sector. As discussion of the Administration's plan unfolded, however, questions in Congress arose over issues of magnitude and management of the "bailout," the need for oversight, and the possibility that less costly and perhaps more effective alternatives might be available.

In this light, Chile's response to its 1981-84 systemic banking crisis has been held up as one example. The cost was comparable relative to the size of its economy to that facing the U.S. Government today. In 1985, Central Bank losses to rescue financially distressed financial institutions were estimated to be 7.8% of GDP[1] (equivalent to approximately $1 trillion in the United States today). The policy options Chile chose had similarities as well as differences from those contemplated in the United States today. Their relevance is debatable, but they do highlight an approach that succeeded in eventually stabilizing and returning the Chilean banking sector to health, while keeping the credit markets functioning throughout the crisis.

COMPARING FINANCIAL CRISES

The seeds of the Chilean financial crisis were much different than those in the United States. Nonetheless, in both cases, the financial sector became the primary problem, with policy makers concerned over the prospect of a system-wide collapse. Chile's problems originated from large macroeconomic imbalances, deepening balance of payments problems, dubious domestic policies, and the 1981-82 global recession that ultimately led to financial sector distress. Although most of these are not elements of the U.S. crisis, there are a number of similar threads woven throughout both cases.

Broadly speaking, both countries had adopted a strong laissez-faire orientation to their economies and had gone through a period of financial sector deregulation in the years immediately prior to the crisis. A group of scholars characterized Chile's orientation toward the financial sector as the "radical liberalization of the domestic financial markets" and "the belief in the 'automatic adjustment' mechanism, by which the market was expected to produce a quick adjustment to new recessionary conditions without interference by the authorities."[2]

In both cases, given the backdrop of financial sector deregulation, a number of similar economic events occurred that ultimately led to a financial crisis. First, real interest rates were very low, giving rise to a large expansion of short-term domestic credit. With credit expansion came the rise in debt service, all resting on a shaky assumption that short-term rates would not change. In both cases, but for different reasons, rates did rise, causing households and firms to fall behind in payments and, in many cases, to default on the loans.[3] The provision for loan losses was inadequate causing financial institutions to restrict credit. Soon, many found themselves in financial trouble or insolvent, resulting in the financial crisis. Chile's response may prove useful as policy makers evaluate options.

THE CHILEAN BANKING CRISIS OF 1981-84

Following the coup against socialist President Salvador Allende in 1973, General Augusto Pinochet immediately re-privatized the banking system. Banking regulation and supervision were liberalized. Macroeconomic conditions and loose credit gave way to the economic "euphoria of 1980-81." The exuberance included substantial increases in asset prices (reminiscent of a bubble) and strong wealth effects that led to vastly increased borrowing. The banking system readily encouraged such borrowing, using foreign capital, that because of exchange rate controls and other reasons, provided a negative real interest rate. From 1979 to 1981, the stock of bank credit to businesses and households nearly doubled to 45% of GDP. This trend came to a sudden halt with the 1981-82 global recession.[4]

The financial sector found itself suddenly in a highly compromised position. Weak bank regulations had allowed the financial sector to take on tremendous amounts of debt without adequate capitalization. Debt was not evaluated by risk characteristics. Most debt was commercial loans, but banks also carried some portion of consumer and mortgage debt. As firms and households became increasingly financially stressed, and as asset prices plummeted, the solvency of national banks became questionable. Two issues would later be identified: the ability of borrowers to make debt payments, and more importantly, the reluctance of borrowers to do so given there was a broadly-held assumption that the government would intervene. By November 1981, the first national banks and financial institutions that were subsidiaries of conglomerates failed and had to be taken over by regulatory authorities.[5]

Most debt was short term and banks were in no position to restructure because they had no access to long-term funds. Instead, they rolled over short-term loans, capitalized the interest due, and raised interest rates. This plan was described by one economist as an unsustainable "Ponzi" scheme, and indeed was a critical factor in bringing down many banks as their balance sheets rapidly deteriorated. From 1980 to 1983, past-due loans rose from 1.1% to 8.4% of total loans outstanding. The sense of crisis further deepened because many of the financial institutions were subsidiaries of conglomerates that also had control over large pension funds, which were heavily invested in bank time deposits and bank mortgage bonds. In the end, although the roots of the banking crisis were different than those in the United States, the Chilean government faced the possibility of a complete failure of the financial sector as credit markets contracted.[6]

THE GOVERNMENT RESPONSE

The Central Bank of Chile took control of the crisis by enacting three major policies intended to maintain liquidity in the financial system, assist borrowers, and strengthen lender balance sheets. These were: 1) debt restructuring for commercial and household borrowers; 2) purchases of nonperforming loans from financial institutions; and 3) the expeditious sale, merger, or liquidation of distressed institutions.[7]

Debt Restructuring

From the outset of the rescue plan, the Chilean Central Bank considered providing relief to both debtors and lenders. There were two rationales. First, as a matter of equity, there was a sense that households as well as firms should be helped. Second, to maintain a functioning credit market, both borrowers and lenders needed to be involved. The Central Bank decided to restructure commercial, consumer, and mortgage loans. The goal was to extend the loan maturities at a "reasonable" interest rate. The debtor was not forgiven the loan, rather banks were given the means to extend the maturities of the loans to keep the debtor repaying and the credit system functioning. Restrictions were in place. Eligible firms had to produce either a good or service, eliminating investment banks that held stock in such firms. Only viable businesses were eligible, forcing the bankruptcy procedures into play where unavoidable. To keep the program going, the loan conditions of each subsequent iteration of the program became easier: longer maturities; lower interest rates; and limited grace periods.[8]

The program allowed Central Banks to lend firms up to 30% of their outstanding debt to the banking system, with the financing arrangement working in one of two ways. At first, the Central Bank issued money, lent it to debtors, which used it to pay back the bank loans. Later, the Central bank issued money to buy long term bonds from the banks, which used the proceeds to restructure the commercial loans. Variations of this process were applied to consumer and mortgage debtors. In cases where loans were made directly from the Central Bank to the debtor, repayment was expected usually beginning 48 months after the loan was made. The fiscal cost was significant, approximating 1% of GDP in 1984 and 1985.[9]

Restoring Bank Balance Sheets

This program was more controversial and had to be adjusted over time to be effective. The key idea was to postpone recognition of loan losses, not forgive them. It relied on identifying nonperforming loans and giving banks time to provision against them, without risking insolvency. The process has been variously characterized as the Central Bank taking on bad debt through loans, purchases, or swaps. All three concepts play some part of this complex, largely accounting-driven arrangement.

Initially, this program was described as a sale, although there was no exchange of assets. The Central Bank technically offered to "buy" nonperforming loans with noninterest bearing, 10-year promissory notes. Banks were required to use future income to provision against these loans and "buy" them back with the repurchase of the promissory notes. In fact, they were prohibited from making dividend payments until they repaid the Central Bank in full. The banks, though, actually kept the loans and administered them, but did not have to account for them on their balance sheets. This arrangement was intended to encourage banks to stop rolling over non-performing loans, recognize the truly bad ones, and eventually retire them from their portfolios. The banks benefitted by remaining solvent and gaining time to rebuild their loan loss reserves so to address nonperforming loans. The credit market was served by banks being able to continue operating with increased funds from released loan-loss reserves.[10]

This program did not work as hoped at first and had to be adjusted. The Central Bank allowed more time for banks to sell nonperforming loans and also permitted a greater portion of their loan portfolios to qualify. It also began to purchase these loans with an interest-bearing promissory note. The banks, however, actually repaid the interest-bearing note at a rate 2 percentage points below that paid by the Central Bank to the banks. This added differential was sufficient incentive for the banks to sell all their bad loans to the Central Bank, beginning a process of identifying good loans and allowing for the eventual retirement of bad loans from the balance sheets (and the banking system). The cost to the Central Bank increased, but by 1985, the portfolio of non-performing loans at the Central Bank began to decline and was eventually eliminated.[11]

Restructuring Distressed Banks

A major goal of government actions was to ensure that bank owners and creditors were not absolved of responsibility to help resolve the crisis, including using their own resources to absorb some of the costs. The government worked closely with all financial institutions to impose new risk-adjusted loan classifications, capital requirements, and provisioning for loan losses, which would be used to repurchase loans sold to the Central Bank. The banks, through the Central Bank purchase of substandard loans, were given time to return to profitability as the primary way to recapitalize, and became part of the systemic solution by continuing to function as part of the credit market.

A number of banks had liabilities that exceeded assets, were undercapitalized, and unprofitable. Their fate was determined based on new standards and they were either allowed to be acquired by other institutions, including foreign banks, or liquidated. The "too big to fail" rule was apparently a consideration in helping keep some institutions solvent. A total of 14 financial institutions were liquidated, 12 during the 1981-83 period. In most cases, bank creditors were made whole by the government on their deposits with liquidated banks. For three financial institutions that were closed in 1983, depositors had to accept a 30% loss on their assets.[12]

POSSIBLE LESSONS FROM CHILE'S BANK CRISIS

The overriding goal of a strategy to correct systemic crisis in the financial sector is to ensure the continued functioning of credit markets. Chile succeeded in accomplishing this goal and restoring a crisis-ridden banking system to health within four years. The single most important lesson of the Chilean experience was that the Central Bank was able to restore faith in the credit markets by maintaining liquidity and bank capital structures through the extension of household and consumer loan maturities, the temporary purchase of substandard loans from the banks, and the prompt sale and liquidation of insolvent institutions. Substandard loans remained off bank balance sheets until the viable institutions could provision for their loss from future profits. Other losses were covered by the government.

In addition, a number of other insights emerged from the Chilean crisis:

The market could not resolve a system-wide failure, particularly in the case where there was a high expectation of a government bailout.

The expectation of a bailout became self-fulfilling and increased the cost.

Appropriate prudential supervision and regulation were critical for restoring health and confidence to the financial system. Observers lamented the *a priori* lack of attention to proper regulation.

Private institutions that survived shared in the cost and responsibility to resolve the crisis to the apparent long-term benefit of the financial sector.

The fiscal cost of the three policies discussed above was high. Liquidating insolvent institutions had the highest cost followed by the purchase of non-performing loans and rescheduling of domestic debts. The strategy, however, is widely recognized as having allowed the financial system and economy to return to a path of stability and longterm growth.

End Notes

[1] Bosworth, Barry P., Rudiger Dornbusch, and Raúl Labán, eds. *The Chilean Economy: Policy Lessons and Challenges*. Washington, D.C. The Brookings Institution. 1994. p. 41.

[2] Ibid., p. 8 and 339.

[3] In the case of Chile, longer maturities were not widely available so debt had to be rolled over regularly. In the United States, various types of adjustable-rate mortgages given to high-risk borrowers eventually led to massive defaults when interest rates and payments ballooned. The financial problem facing U.S. institutions was compounded by the highly complex and arguably poorly understood securitization of these mortgages.

[4] Ibid., p. 38 and Barandiarán, Edgardo and Leonardo Hernández. *Origins and Resolution of a Banking Crisis: Chile 1982-86*. Santiago: Central Bank of Chile. Working Paper No. 57. December 1999. pp. 13-14.

[5] Barandiarán and Hernández, op. cit., pp. 20-22.

[6] Ibid., pp. 15-18 and 21-23 and Bosworth, Dornbusch, and Labán, op. cit., p. 339.

[7] Barandiarán and Hernández, op. cit., p. 20-23. In addition, because a portion of the debt in Chile was dollar denominated, the government created a preferential exchange rate program to help repay those debts, the value of which had balooned on the balance sheets of corporate and household debtors because of the 1982 peso devaluation. Because this issue is not germane to the U.S. situation, it is not further discussed. The preferential exchange program nonetheless represented a large subsidy that the government of Chile had to absorb.

[8] Ibid., pp. 25-29.

[9] Ibid., pp. 25-26. There was also a cost in expanding the money supply, but the macroeconomic effects proved limited and are not addressed here.

[10] Ibid., pp. 29-30 and Bosworth, Dornbusch, and Labán, op. cit., pp. 41 and 340.

[11] Ibid.

[12] Barandiarán and Hernández, op. cit., pp. 40-46 and Bosworth, Dornbusch, and Labán, op. cit., p. 402.

In: Government Interventions in Economic Emergencies
Editor: Pablo Sastre
ISBN: 978-1-60741-356-1

Chapter 11

THE U.S. FINANCIAL CRISIS: LESSONS FROM JAPAN

Dick K. Nanto

SUMMARY

Japan's five bank bailout packages in the late 1990s may hold some lessons for the United States. Most of the packages were administered by the Deposit Insurance Corporation of Japan (DICJ). The packages had an announced value of $495 billion. The DICJ reports that it provided $399 billion to Japan's troubled financial institutions of which it has recovered $195 billion. Overcoming the crisis in Japan's banks took a combination of capital injections, new laws and regulations, stronger oversight, a reorganization of the banking sector, moderate economic recovery, and several years of banks working off their non-performing loans.

When the U.S. Treasury planned the $700 billion bailout package (Emergency Economic Stabilization Act of 2008, H.R. 3997) to address the U.S. financial crisis, it reportedly examined the experience of Japan as it grappled with its banking crisis in the1990s.[1] This chapter reviews the major actions by the Japanese government in dealing with its crisis and highlights some of the lessons learned from their experience.

Like the current U.S. financial crisis, Japan's began with stock market and real estate bubbles. During the latter half of the 1980s, Japan's monetary authorities flooded the market with liquidity (money) in order to enable businesses to cope with the rising value of the yen. Businesses did invest in new capital equipment to become more competitive in international markets, but the excess liquidity also found its way into speculation in Japan's stock market, in real estate ventures, and in foreign investments. At that time, the market value of both land and equities was rising so fast that investors and speculators could hardly miss. Investors tended to ignore risks. The larger mistake for them was not to borrow and invest and consequently not be positioned to reap the returns from rising markets. Banks considered most loans with real estate as collateral as being unquestionably secure. Then the bubbles burst.

Japan's Nikkei stock market average peaked in 1989 at 40,000 and dropped by 50% in one year and more than two-thirds to about 12,000 by August 2001. Japan's banks are allowed to hold equities as part of their capital base. The value of the unrealized capital gains on such stock holdings dropped from $355 billion in 1989 to $42 billion in 2001. This drastically reduced key capital reserves for many banks. Also, by 2000, commercial land values in the six major metropolitan areas had fallen by 80% from their peak levelin 1991. Residential and industrial land values also had fallen by nearly 20%.[2]

The bursting of this economic bubble caused the value of collateral underlying many bank loans to drop below the value of their loan principal. Also, commercial real estate ventures, especially office buildings, became unprofitable as rents fell. As the economy slowed, companies also faced excess capacity, excess inventories, and lower profits. Also as more and more loans turned sour, more and more of the underlying real estate had to be sold at "bargain" prices. In 1995, Japan's banks reported $280 billion in nonperforming loans,[3] but this figure turned out to be vastly understated.[4] Japanese financial institutions at this time, however, generally did bundle and repackage these loans as collateralized debt obligations or rely extensively on derivatives or other financial instruments. Mortgage defaults tended to be on commercial property, not on private residences.

At first, the Japanese government's strategy was forbearance, a strengthening of deposit protection, provision of emergency liquidity, and some assistance to encourage mergers of failed institutions. The crisis worsened in 1995-1996 following the bankruptcy of several specialized housing loan companies (*jusen*). In 1996, the government made its first injection of capital to purchase assets from ailing housing lenders. This bailout proved to be quite unpopular politically and may have contributed to tentativeness later on the part of government as the downward spiral quickened.

By 1997, Japan's banking sector was in a full systemic crisis. The government responded by making $250 billion (¥30 trillion) available of which $108 billion (¥13 trillion) went to banks and $142 billion (¥17 trillion) to the Deposit Insurance Corporation of Japan. In 1998, the government bought the bankrupt Long-Term Credit Bank[5] and Nippon Credit Bank. These two banks had no consumer deposit system but borrowed funds on financial markets to lend on a long-term basis to businesses. These banks were eventually sold to private investors. The government also took over the management of many financial institutions.

In March 1998, the government injected another $14 billion (¥1.8 trillion) to bolster bank balance sheets and in March 1999 injected another $62.5 billion (¥7.5 trillion). By October 1998, the government had invested $495 billion (¥60 trillion yen), or 12% of gross domestic product, for the financial support of banks.[6]

For much of the 1990s, however, the hope of the government was that if it could keep banks operating, their profits from operations and capital gains from equity holdings could fund the writeoffs of bad loans. The Bank of Japan kept its interest rate for banks low so that they could increase profits from new lending. Between 1995 and 2003, Japan's banks wrote off a cumulative total of $318 billion (¥37.2 trillion) in nonperforming loans, but new ones appeared so fast that the total outstanding amount kept increasing and peaked in March 2002 at $330 billion (¥43.2 trillion) or 8.4% of total lending.[7]

Through a combination of capital injections, new laws and regulations, stronger oversight, a reorganization of the banking sector,[8] moderate economic recovery, and several years of banks working off their non-performing loans, the Japanese banking sector now has recovered. By September 2005, the banks reported 3.5% of their total lending as non-performing, a tolerable amount. By 2008, Japanese banks and brokerage houses had become strong enough that Nomura Holdings had agreed to buy the Europe and Middle East operations of Lehman Brothers as well as Lehman's franchise in Japan and Australia. Mitsubishi UFJ Financial Group has agreed to buy 20% of Morgan Stanley.[9]

NET COST OF BAILOUTS

The various bailout packages in Japan were administered primarily by the Deposit Insurance Corporation of Japan (DICJ). When a financial institution fails, the DICJ may extend assistance to another financial institution that purchases assets or merges with the failed financial institution in order to facilitate the transaction. The DICJ also works to prevent financial institutions from failing. The forms of assistance include a direct money grant, a loan or deposit of funds, purchase of assets, a guarantee or assumption of debts, a subscription of preferred stock, and loss sharing. Not all of the activities of the DICJ, however, are related to the bailout packages. It also has ongoing operations associated with its traditional function of insuring bank deposits. The annual reports of the DICJ, however, provide detail on the disposition of $399 billion of the $495 billion in funds announced in Japan's financial assistance packages.

Table 1. The Deposit Insurance Corporation of Japan's Assistance to Financial Institutions and Funds Recovered as of March 2007

Type	Amount Provided	Amount Recovered
1. Grants	$159 billion (¥18.6 trillion)	None
2. Purchase of Assets	$83 billion (¥9.8 trillion)	$79 billion (¥9.3 trillion)
Of which: Purchase of assets from failed institutions	$54 billion (¥6.3 trillion)	$60 billion (¥7.0 trillion)
Purchase of shares from banks under public management	$25 billion (¥2.9 trillion)	$14 billion (¥1.6 trillion)
3. Capital Injections Under Five Bailout Packages	$106 billion (¥12.4 trillion)	$75 billion (¥8.7 trillion)
4. Other	$51 billion (¥6.0 trillion)	$41 billion (¥4.8 trillion)
Of which: Loans	$36 billion (¥4.2 trillion)	$36 billion (¥4.2 trillion)
Total	$399 billion	$195 billion

Source: Deposit Insurance Corporation of Japan, *Annual Report 2006*, p. 70.

Note: All values converted at the March 2007 exchange rate of 116,26 yen per dollar. Capital injections included purchases of preferred/common stock and subordinated bonds and the extending of subordinated loans.

As shown in **Table 1**, as of March 2007, the DICJ had provided financial assistance in the amount of $399 billion. This included 180 cases with grants of $159 billion, asset purchases of $83 billion, capital injections of $106 billion, and other assistance (mostly loans) of $51 billion.

The grants were funded by $110 billion (¥13 trillion) in DICJ bonds issued (repaid from taxpayer funds) and from premiums from deposit insurance. Of the asset purchases of $83 billion, the DICJ recovered $79 billion. The asset purchases included $54 billion in assets from failed financial institutions (of which $60 billion had been recovered) and $25 billion in shares purchased (of which $14 billion had been recovered).

Capital injections of $106 billion came under five different bailout packages and included subscriptions to preferred or common stock, purchases of subordinated bonds, and the extending of subordinated loans. The DICJ had injected capital into 25 different banks. As of March 2007, $31.3 billion of these assets was still held by the DICJ in the form of preferred shares, common shares, and subordinated loans.

The $51 billion in the "Other" category included loans to banks which were under special public management, taking delivery of assets under warranty for latent defects, compensation for losses, lending to assuming financial institutions, and debt assumption. The last capital injection reported by the DICJ was in March 2003.[10]

The Resolution and Collection Corporation (RCC), a subsidiary of the DICJ, borrows funds from the DICJ to purchase and dispose of assets (within three years) from sound financial institutions and some under special public management. As of March 2007, the RCC had purchased assets with claims of $34.5 billion (¥4.0 trillion) for a discounted price of $3.0 billion (¥355.7 billion). These assets had been sold for $5.2 billion (¥609.4 billion) for a gain of 172% for the RCC. In essence, the RCC paid about 9 cents on a dollar for the troubled assets and was able to dispose of them at a profit. The DICJ consults with the Purchase Price Examination Board (an advisory body to the DICJ) with respect to the price it pays for assets. The RCC made no purchases in FY2006 (ending in March 2007).[11]

Lessons Learned

The following are various lessons and observations that observers have gleaned from the Japanese experience.

- Authorities underestimated the nature and seriousness of the banking problem at first. Most thought the financial problems would resolve themselves through economic growth and by keeping central bank interest rates low in order to increase bank margins and profitability.
- There was a slow recognition of the extent of non-performing loans and the carrying of "zombie" firms that technically were bankrupt but were kept alive by banks. This delayed resolution of the problem.
- Transparency and an updating of definitions and reporting requirements with respect to non-performing loans was important in realizing the true extent of the problems. Many of the rescues of ailing financial firms by a healthier financial institution required a government injection of capital in some form.

There appeared to be a lack of domestic or external constraints and of political leadership that would have urged authorities to take more decisive action earlier.[12]

The government began by creating new institutions to handle emergency financial assistance but later transferred such activities to the Deposit Insurance Corporation of Japan (DICJ), an institution that already was working with troubled financial institutions. The DICJ also was given permanent authority to assist ailing financial institutions when so ordered by the Prime Minister.

The Japanese government injected capital into financial institutions in several ways depending on the situation. In most cases, the DICJ could use its discretion in determining the nature of the assistance.

Troubled assets were bought at a steep discount from their face value from sound financial institutions (to inject capital) and disposed of without unduly disturbing markets — usually within three years. The two banks that were nationalized were later sold to private investors. Capital injections also took the form of subscriptions to stock, grants, and subordinated loans.

Even with the $495 billion financial bailout packages, between 1998 and 2003, Japan's banks wrote off some $318 billion in non-performing loans. The burden was shared.

Government holdings of corporate shares have generated dividend income and capital gains for the DICJ.

Since there are fewer banks in Japan, the authorities could focus recovery efforts on several large banks and fewer than 200 smaller financial institutions (there are about 8,500 banks in the United States) which facilitated information gathering and coordination.

When Japan announced an early financial bailout package, it placed stringent conditions on the assistance that banks were unwilling to accept. The net result was that the banks ignored the package and tried to bolster their balance sheets by not lending. This was seen as worsening the economic conditions for the country.[13] Most of the assistance to failing institutions, however, carried conditions that were enforced by the DICJ.

New technologies, globalization, and the blurring of boundaries between types of financial products and institutions made risk management increasingly difficult for financial regulators.[14]

The bursting of the real estate bubble in Japan caused more difficulty for banks than the bursting of the bubble in stocks because the decline in real estate values effected the value of collateral on much bank lending.[15]

Japan is considered to have acted too slowly with respect to monetary policy, fiscal policy, and the resolution of problems in the banking sector. Once the economy began to recover, fiscal policy is thought to have tightened too soon.[16]

End Notes

1 Faiola, Anthony and David Cho. "Alternative Solutions Diverge From Administration's Approach," *The Washington Post*, September 24, 2008. p. A.1.

2 Bank of Japan. *Financial and Economic Statistics Monthly*, various issues.

3 Japan. Financial Services Agency.

4 For details, see CRS Report RS20994, *Japan's Banking "Crisis,"* by Dick K. Nanto.

[5] Later bought by the New York-based Ripplewood Holdings and other investors.

[6] For the United States, 12% of GDP in 2008 dollars is about $1.7 trillion.

[7] Japan. Financial Services Agency. Quoted in Organization for Economic Cooperation and Development, *OECD Economic Surveys, Japan (Paris, OECD Publishing) Vol. 2006/13, July 2006,* p. 53.

[8] The Industrial Bank of Japan, Daiichi Kangyo, Fuji, and Yasuda Trust Banks merged to form the Mizuho Financial Group (2003). The Bank of Tokyo-Mitsubishi, Mitsubishi Trust Bank, and Nippon Trust Bank merged to form the Mitsubishi Tokyo Financial Group (2001). Sumitomo Bank and Sakura Bank merged to form the Sumitomo Mitsui Financial Group (2002). Sanwa Bank, Tokai Bank, and Toyo Trust & Banking merged to form UFJ Holdings (2001). Asahi Bank merged with Daiwa Bank to form Resona Holdings (2001).

[9] "Bailout Faces Delays as Goldman Gets Boost." *Reuters*, September 23, 2008.

[10] Deposit Insurance Corporation of Japan. *Annual Report 2006*, p. 19, 91. Note: 65% of the outstanding balance of shares was in the Resona Bank. In 2006, the DICJ received $132 million in dividends from these Resona Bank shares but paid $57 million in interest on its bonds floated to finance the purchase of the shares.

[11] Ibid., p. 22, 70, 84.

[12] Kawai, Masahiro. "Reform of the Japanese Banking System." *International Economics and Economic Policy*. Heidelberg: Dec 2005. Vol. 2, Issue 4; p. 307ff.

[13] Slater, Dan. "Economist Draws Parallels Between U.S., Japan Banking Crises, *Business Week*, March 31, 2008. Internet edition.

[14] Nagano, Satoshi. "Lessons Learnt from th mounting Non-performing Loans in Japan after the 1990s," *Journal of Financial Services Marketing*, Vol. 11, 2, pp. 180-89.

[15] Browne, Lynn Elaine. "Does Japan Offer Any Lessons for the United States?" *New England Economic Review*, 2001, 3, p. 3.

[16] Ibid.

In: Government Interventions in Economic Emergencies ISBN: 978-1-60741-356-1
Editor: Pablo Sastre

Chapter 12

THE U.S. FINANCIAL CRISIS: LESSONS FROM SWEDEN

James K. Jackson

SUMMARY

In the early 1990s, Sweden faced a banking and exchange rate crisis that led it to rescue banks that had experienced large losses on their balance sheets and that threatened a collapse of the banking system. Some analysts and others argue that Sweden's experience could provide useful lessons for the execution and implementation of the Emergency Economic Stabilization Act of 2008[1]. The banking crisis facing the United States is unique, so there are no exact parallels from which to draw templates. Sweden's experience, however, represents a case study in how a systemic banking crisis was resolved in a developed country with democratic institutions. The Swedish central bank separated out good assets, which it left to the banks to oversee from bad assets, which it placed in a separate agency with broad authority to work out debt problems or to liquidate assets. Four lessons that emerged form Sweden's experience are: 1) the process must be transparent; 2) the resolution agency must be politically and financially independent; 3) market discipline must be maintained; and 4) there must be a plan to jump-start credit flows in the financial system. This chapter provides an overview of the Swedish banking crisis and an explanation of the measures Sweden used to restore its banking system to health.

BACKGROUND

Sweden's banking crisis grew slowly over time and was the result of a number of policy decisions[2]. In particular, the crisis arose from a set of economic policies that attempted to: 1) support Sweden's fixed exchange rate policy, 2) deregulate the financial sector, 3) expand credit, and 4) provide low-cost loans for residential purchases and for university students. Eventually, a drop in asset values weakened the balance sheets of banks and reduced liquidity in the economy. One key factor in Sweden's financial crisis was a set of policy measures the country adopted in the mid-1980s to liberalize the highly regulated financial sector. Prior to this liberalization, banks, insurance companies, and other institutions were subjected to lending ceilings and were required to invest in bonds issued by the government and mortgage institutions.

Large central government deficits and a national policy that favored residential investment led to requirements that banks hold more than 50% of their assets in such bonds, typically with long maturities and low interest rates. In addition, the banks were carefully scrutinized and monitored by Riksbank, Sweden's central bank. This close supervision meant, however, that the banks themselves were unaccustomed to performing risk analysis, and were ill-prepared to perform risk analysis on commercial paper associated with real estate loans. This lack of experience led to unhealthy risk taking when the nation began to deregulate its financial sector and allow banks to participate in a broader array of financial instruments. Indeed, some analysts argue that it was this inexperience, rather than the deregulation effort itself, that played a role in the banking crisis. Sweden also favored housing and college education by operating a system that provided loans with highly favorable terms with little or no credit evaluation. Other economic problems compounded Sweden's efforts to gain control over the macroeconomic conditions within the country and place the economy on a well-balanced positive growth track[3].

Deregulation

In the early to mid-1980s, Sweden began deregulating its financial markets at such a rapid pace that it took most observers by surprise[4]. In part the deregulation was spurred by the rapid development that had occurred in the growth of money market accounts, certificates of deposit, and government securities that arose from growing central government budget deficits. These actions shifted Sweden's monetary policy to an expansive posture and allowed banks, mortgage institutions, finance companies, and others to compete in the domestic credit market. The expansion in credit helped stimulate economic growth, but it also fed inflation and added to general expectations of inflation in the economy. In addition, Sweden's tax system stimulated consumer borrowing by allowing taxpayers to fully deduct interest payments and exchange controls stimulated corporate borrowing by favoring domestic investment over foreign investment.

These activities combined with an expansionary fiscal policy to increase credit in the economy added to the stock, or the overall amount, of debt. This credit boom pushed up the prices of corporate stocks and real estate — both commercial real estate and residential housing. As the pace of economic growth accelerated, the rate of price inflation also increased, which led to the Swedish Krona being overvalued. By the late 1980s, Sweden removed a broad range of foreign exchange controls, but it maintained its fixed exchange rate system. During this time, Sweden experienced current account deficits and large outflows of direct investment and other long-term capital, which led to a growing stock of private sector short-term debt in foreign currency[5]. In essence, Swedish households and businesses were borrowing in foreign currency at interest rates that were below those that were charged for loans denominated in Swedish Krona. The result of this borrowing was a substantial amount of exchange rate risk in the balance sheets of the private sector.

By the early 1990s, a combination of reforms in the tax system and periods of high interest rates caused asset prices to fall. As the pace of economic growth cooled, the rate of unemployment began to rise, public sector debt rose, bankruptcies surged, and the banking system was shocked as the rising bankruptcies forced banks to curtail their lending activities in order to build up their loan loss reserves. A further setback for the economy occurred with German reunification in 1990, which resulted in higher German interest rates and an appreciating currency. Sweden's fixed exchange rate policy obligated Sweden to import the higher German interest rates, pushing its own interest rates higher and busting a property market bubble. When Sweden was forced to abandon its exchange rate peg in November 1992, the real exchange rate fell substantially, while real interest rates remained high, which caused a large number of private sector loans to become non-performing.

THE FINANCIAL CRISIS

In early 1990, Sweden's economy appeared to be doing well. The unemployment rate was at an all-time low and the stock market was booming. At the same time, the rate of price inflation was rising, the real effective exchange rate was appreciating, and there was a general consensus that the economy was growing at an unsustainable rate. In addition, rising stock market prices reinforced the continued expansion in real estate, especially in the commercial property market. By mid-1990, however, commercial occupancy rates had fallen, pushing down the price of stocks for both the real estate and construction sectors[6].

The first financial firm to feel the effects of the drop in real estate prices was Nyckeln, one of Sweden's fastest growing financial firms. Nyckeln, like other financial firms, was owned by several of Sweden's largest banks. Nyckeln had achieved its rapid growth by specializing in commercial real estate financing and financing its operations through a new type of commercial paper called *marknadsbevis*, which the banks had guaranteed. At this time, Sweden's commercial paper market had become the third largest commercial paper market in Europe. In 1991, the value of commercial paper dropped sharply when interest rates in Sweden began rising as a result of rising international rates that were pushed up by German reunification. With the fall of Nyckeln, two of Sweden's six largest banks were heavily affected and announced that they could not meet their regulatory capital requirements.

Concern quickly spread through all of Sweden's commercial paper market, which essentially shut down. By the end of the year, three of Sweden's major financial firms had defaulted. Two of the major banks faced actual insolvency problems and the government of Sweden, the major shareholder in the two banks, injected equity into one of the banks and issued guarantees to the other bank for loans that enabled the banks to fulfill their capital requirements. By the spring of 1992, yet another Swedish bank went bankrupt. At this point, the Swedish government took ownership of the third bank and began to treat the defaults and bankruptcy as a crisis. The government refused to offer complete forbearance of the non-performing loans and did not offer unlimited liquidity support, but opted to guarantee the bank's debts, an action it would extend to all of Sweden's banks within a few weeks.

As a major step in resolving the banking crisis, the central bank divided each bank into two separate entities, one with its good assets, the other with its bad assets. The entities holding the good assets continued to operate under their old names and were later merged under a new name. The bad assets were transferred to two asset management companies. The asset management companies were owned by the government, but had a high degree of independence and were free of many of the regulations that applied to banks. The management companies attempted to assess the value of the non-performing loans they had inherited and then moved to rescue whatever economic value they could. As a result, the companies injected equity into troubled borrowers to maintain and restore their values and, at times, took over defaulting companies, which they ran as a private owner until the companies could be liquidated. Assets were sold in three ways: initial public offerings on the Stockholm stock exchange; corporate transaction outside the stock exchange; and transactions involving individual properties. A quick rebound in the Swedish economy that stemmed from an increase in economic growth in Europe and elsewhere allowed all of the managed assets to be liquidated by 1997, ultimately at a lower cost to the Swedish taxpayers than had initially been projected.

LESSONS LEARNED FROM SWEDEN'S EXPERIENCE

Each financial crisis is unique and largely dependent on the specific combination of national and international factors that exist at the time. In addition, the resolution of the crisis is intricately interwoven with a broad set of laws and national characteristics that are unique to each crisis and each national setting. A number of differences between the Swedish and U.S. experiences are readily apparent.

Unlike the situation in the United States, the Swedish government had a financial stake in the largest banks prior to the crisis. This made the Swedish government a direct stakeholder in the institutions and provided an impetus for it to act.

Sweden's real estate loans and commercial paper were nearly all domestically held, so that it did not face both a domestic and international financial issue.

Many nonperforming loans in Sweden were a result of unhedged private sector exchange rate risk when the currency peg collapsed.

In the United States, the financial sector problems are linked to the securitization of mortgages, which led to credit exposures that extended well beyond the retail banking sector.

Sweden's economy is small and open, which enables it to rely on an export-led recovery strategy. The U.S. economy is larger relative to the global economy and it has a strong influence on the pace of global economic growth. As a result, the United States is more likely to rely on a recovery strategy that is based on domestic demand.

An analysis of the Swedish banking crisis of the 1990s reveals that there are a number of factors that were inherently responsible for the resolution of the crisis that apply specifically to the Swedish case. Despite these caveats, the Swedish experience may offer some insight into one possible way of resolving a domestic financial crisis. One factor that helped Sweden quickly resolve its financial crisis was a strong international economic recovery that pushed up real estate values in Sweden and improved the balance sheets of banks. Others argue that a number of procedural factors, in addition to the economic recovery, helped bring the financial crisis to a resolution. In particular, they argue that four factors played an important role in this process in Sweden and could prove beneficial in resolving other financial crises:[7]

First, transparency of the process is important. In Sweden, expected losses were recognized early on and helped to preserve the confidence of the market.

Second, the process seems to work best with a politically and financially independent agency. This type of structure shields decision makers from political pressures, especially as banks are closed and assets are liquidated. Financial independence of the agency gives credibility to the notion of political independence. In addition, financial independence allows for a rapid response when funding needs emerge suddenly and waiting for a government appropriation is impractical.

Third, is the importance of maintenance of market discipline and avoiding blanket guarantees. According to this concept, extending blanket guarantees increases the risk of future financial crisis because it weakens market discipline exerted by uninsured creditors. Blanket guarantees of all the liabilities of problem institutions in the throes of a crisis reduces the credibility of claims that such guarantees will not be extended in future bank failures. Although the guarantees were intended to calm the markets, some analysts argue they likely reduced incentives to monitor bank risk by creditors. Some analysts argue that a better solution would be a bank holiday that would allow bank examiners enough time to assess the extent of non-performing loans while it would allow insured depositors access to their funds. In addition, uninsured depositors would be allowed to move their funds out, but would be forced to assume some of the losses. Also non-viable banks would not be eligible to receive financial support from the government and public funds would not be used to support a non-viable institution.

Fourth, is a plan to jump-start credit flows in the financial system by repairing the damaged creditworthiness of the broader economy. Even if banks can be completely restored to financial health through recapitalization, borrowers may be in no position to repay any new loans they may get. Such a plan may include such items as a fiscal stimulus to aid borrowers.

End Notes

[1] Dougherty, Carter, Stopping a Financial Crisis, The Swedish Way, *The New York Times*, September 23, 2008; Purvis, Andrew, Sweden's Model Approach to Financial Disaster, *Time*, September 24, 2008.

[2] Englund, Peter, The Swedish Banking Crisis: Roots and Consequences, *Oxford Review of Economic Policy,* Autumn 1999. P. 80-97.

[3] Ibid, p. 83-84.

[4] Ingves, Stefan, *The Nordic Banking Crisis From an International Perspective*, International Monetary Fund, September 11, 2002.

[5] Backstrom, Urban, *What Lessons Can be Learned From Recent Financial Crises? The Swedish Experience.* Federal Reserve Symposium "Maintaining Financial Stability in a global Economy," August 29, 1997.

[6] Englund, The Swedish Banking Crisis, p. 84-89.

[7] Ergungor, O. Emre, *On the Resolution of Financial Crises: The Swedish Experience,* Federal Reserve Bank of Cleveland Policy Discussion Paper, June 2007, p. 1-12.

In: Government Interventions in Economic Emergencies
Editor: Pablo Sastre
ISBN: 978-1-60741-356-1

Chapter 13

FINANCIAL MARKET INTERVENTION

Edward V. Murphy

SUMMARY

Financial markets continue to experience significant disturbance and the banking sector remains fragile. Efforts to restore confidence have been met with mixed success thus far. After attempting to deal with troubled institutions on a case-by-case basis, Treasury has proposed a plan to purchase mortgage-related assets to alleviate stress in financial markets and in the banking system. This chapter provides answers to some frequently asked questions concerning the financial disruptions of September 2008 and the Troubled Asset Relief Program (TARP) in H.R. 3997.

CURRENT CONCERNS

What, If Anything, Is Wrong with the Financial System?

Banks and other financial institutions have been reluctant to lend or otherwise engage with other institutions for fear of exposure to the bad assets of troubled counterparties. That is, a relatively healthy bank is afraid to sign a contract with other institutions because of the fear that the other institution will not be able to fulfil its obligations. For similar reasons, banks that need to raise capital have had trouble doing so because potential investors are afraid that the full extent of damage to banks' assets has not yet been revealed. Under these conditions it is difficult for people who depend on regularly accessing credit markets to get loans, which in turn can affect the broader economy. Often, this lack of confidence in other financial institutions expresses itself in wide spreads between market interest rates and the yield on Treasury securities. These spreads have been relatively wide for the past year. They spiked following recent interventions intended to prevent disorderly bankruptcies, an indication of significant loss of confidence.[1]

When Did Trouble in the Financial Markets Start?

Loss of market confidence can be proxied by spreads in interest rates between Treasury securities and riskier assets of similar maturities. These spreads first spiked in August 2007.[2] Although spreads declined following policy responses by the Federal Reserve, the Treasury, and the passage of the stimulus package, the spreads did not return to their pre-August 2007 level. The persistence of historically wide spreads during 2007-2008 suggests that full confidence has not been restored.

What Caused Financial Market Turmoil?

Although there are several contributing elements, most observers agree that rising defaults among residential mortgage borrowers sparked the initial loss in financial market confidence.[3] Various observers place different emphasis on low interest rates that caused a housing bubble that in this view was bound to eventually burst, insufficient regulation of subprime mortgage lending practices, and insufficient monitoring of complex financial products and services, especially rating agencies and derivatives markets.[4]

If 97% of Borrowers Are Still Current on Their Mortgage, Why Is the Financial Turmoil So Large?

Several factors magnify the effects of loan defaults on the financial system. First, banks are leveraged, which means that for a given dollar reduction in the value of their assets they must either raise additional capital or reduce their lending by a multiple of the loss.[5] Second, banks have become less transparent because of changes in accounting and risk management. This lack of transparency has made it more difficult for banks to raise additional capital as an alternative to reducing lending or selling assets. Third, the use of financial derivatives that should have reduced risk in the banking system may have had the effect of increasing leverage and making it even harder to identify sound counterparties.

Where Are the Problem Loans Located?

Two of the problem loan categories, subprime and Alt-A, are disproportionately located in areas that had previously experienced rapid price appreciation. This includes Florida, California, Arizona, and Nevada. In addition, subprime loans are disproportionately located in relatively low income and minority neighborhoods across the country.[6]

Why Did the Financial Shocks Happen?

Reasonable people will continue to disagree as to the root cause of the turmoil. The following factors are not mutually exclusive. Some believe that low interest rates and loose monetary policy caused a housing bubble that was bound to burst when interest rates rose.[7] Others place more emphasis on loose lending standards that may have been fostered by a lack of regulation of non-bank lenders and a lack of market discipline by mortgage-backed securities issuers who sold the loans to other investors.[8] Another group places the blame on the failure of officials to regulate relatively recent innovations in finance. Still others emphasize potentially irresponsible marketing practices or fraud by subprime lenders. Some observers blame investors and borrowers who did not adequately investigate the risks of their decisions.

Who Is Affected by the Financial Turmoil?

The financial turmoil also affects anyone seeking credit, including troubled home owners who wish to refinance out of a troubled mortgage. Restrictions in credit have contributed to a downward spiral in home prices. The people most directly affected by financial market turmoil are investment bankers and investors. These people may lose their jobs and livelihood. Business firms are also affected because their cost of financing possible projects has risen, which in turn can hurt the broader economy.

How Have Policymakers Responded to Financial Turmoil?

Many modern macroeconomists believe that there are two basic policy responses to avoid an economic slowdown.[9] First, the Federal Reserve can provide expansionary monetary policy by lowering interest rates, as it did starting in the fall of 2007.[10] Second, the government can provide expansionary fiscal policy by spending more than it collects in taxes, as it did with the stimulus package.[11] In addition to pursuing both of these responses, policymakers have also sought to prevent the financial sector from ceasing to function. Liquidity was increased by expanding the range of collateral accepted at the Federal Reserve's discount window and by holding regular liquidity auctions.[12] Policymakers at the Federal Reserve and the Treasury have also tried to overcome collective action problems among private investors to help arrange buyers of distressed firms, as it did for Bear Stearns and Lehman Brothers (even though the government was unwilling to also provide funding to facilitate a purchase of Lehman Brothers).[13]

Policymakers have also sought to help stabilize mortgage markets. In addition to Treasury, the Department of Housing and Urban Development (HUD), and the Federal Deposit Insurance Corporation (FDIC) efforts to help organize loan servicers through the HOPE Now program, the Securities and Exchange Commission (SEC) and Internal Revenue Service (IRS) have issued rules clarifying the ability of loan servicers to modify loans held in securitized trusts.[14] The government also enacted (P.L. 110-289) a voluntary plan to allow banks to write down the balance of existing loans so that borrowers can refinance into FHA to avoid foreclosure.[15] The act also provided some Community Development Block Grant (CDBG) funds to allow local communities to acquire and redevelop vacant and foreclosed properties.[16] The act also created a new regulator for the government-sponsored enterprises (GSEs), Fannie Mae, Freddie Mac, and the Federal Home Loan Banks.[17] The act gave Treasury the temporary authority to purchase debt and equity securities of the GSEs.

September 2008 saw a series of financial market interventions. First, the newly reorganized Federal Housing Finance Agency (FHFA) placed the GSEs in a conservatorship with agreements by the Federal Reserve Bank of New York to assure liquidity and by the Treasury to purchase enough preferred stock and securities to ensure adequate capitalization.[18] On a single weekend, policymakers helped broker a deal to sell investment bank Merrill Lynch to Bank of America and failed to broker a similar deal for Lehman Brothers, reportedly because the government declined to provide financial support. Lehman Brothers subsequently declared bankruptcy. A policy of no financial support did not survive the week, as insurer AIG was granted a bridge loan three days later.[19] The next day financial markets froze up and Treasury announced a proposal to buy mortgage-related assets from financial institutions.

Why Has the Federal Reserve Not Restored Order in Financial Markets?

The Federal Reserve's primary tools help provide liquidity but do not restore capital levels. Liquidity generally refers to the ability to access markets, either as a firm issuing bonds or as a person selling a good, without suffering "fire-sale" prices. An adequate capital level is generally determined as a relation between assets and liabilities. All of a firm's assets can be completely liquid (cash) but the firm can remain undercapitalized if small losses can reduce its capital to near insolvency. These concepts are related. Even if a firm has liquid assets, it may have difficulty accessing credit markets to borrow more funds because it is too close to insolvency to be perceived as a good credit risk. Complexities of mortgage-related securities have made it difficult to ascertain their value, thus those assets have become less liquid. Furthermore, investors know that some banks have suffered loan losses that reduced their capital, but the complexities of the mortgagerelated assets have made it difficult to identify which banks are undercapitalized. As a result, the liquidity of mortgage-related assets has been reduced, and the liquidity of financial firms has been reduced. The Federal Reserve has taken steps to increase the liquidity of particular assets, for example, by expanding the categories of assets that it will accept as collateral for loans, but the Federal Reserve has not restored bank capital.

What Does Treasury Propose to Do?

The Department of the Treasury proposed replacing the case-by-case approach to interventions in the financial markets that had prevailed from summer 2007 through summer 2008 with a systemic program.[20] Some believe that intervening on behalf of some ailing financial institutions but not others contributes to investor uncertainty. Treasury proposed a program similar to the Resolution Trust Corporation (RTC) that could acquire $700 billion of mortgage-related assets from the banking system. The original proposal gave the Secretary of the Treasury broad discretion to determine the terms of asset acquisition and the operations of the program. Some policymakers have suggested that any program provide greater management oversight, limits on the executive pay of participating financial institutions, and other conditions to monitor the use of taxpayer funds. Some policymakers have also suggested that bankruptcy judges be granted the authority to modify loans of troubled borrowers under some circumstances. Another possibility is providing a government guarantee of payment on the assets rather than government acquisition.

What Were Some of the Additions and Deletions to the Proposal Offered in H.R. 3997?

The expressed purpose of the Emergency Economic Stabilization Act of 2008, H.R. 3997, was to "...provide authority and facilities that the Secretary of the Treasury can use to restore liquidity and stability to the financial system."[21] This measure, voted down on September 29, 2008, addressed some of the concerns that some policymakers may have had regarding the three-page Treasury plan. A short description of some of the provisions of the Troubled Asset Relief Program (TARP) follows.

It excludes foreign central banks from the definition of eligible financial institutions but includes institutions in U.S. territories, such as Guam and the Virgin Islands.

It provides for insurance of some troubled assets as an alternative to, or in addition to, purchasing troubled assets.

It creates a Financial Stability Oversight Board to review the exercise of authority under the program. The board will be made up of the Chairman of the Federal Reserve, the Secretary of the Treasury, the Secretary of the Department of Housing and Urban Development, the Director of the Federal Housing Finance Agency, and the Chairman of the Securities and Exchange Commission.

The Treasury will manage the acquisition and sale of assets with any proceeds accruing to the general fund for reduction of the public debt.

The measure instructs the Secretary of Treasury to implement a plan to maximize assistance for homeowners and to encourage loan servicers to participate in the Hope for Homeowners program. Assistance to homeowners includes consent to reasonable loan modification requests.

The measure puts limits on executive compensation of institutions that participate. Under certain circumstances, these limits include limits on incentive compensation for risk-taking during the period that the program has an equity or debt position in the firm, recovery of incentive bonuses paid to senior executives based on financial statements that are later shown to be false, and a prohibition of golden parachutes.

The Comptroller General has ongoing oversight of TARP management and activities.

There is to be a study of excessive leverage in financial institutions.

The President will appoint a special inspector for TARP, with Senate confirmation.

The debt limit is raised to $11.3 trillion.

A Congressional Oversight Panel is created in the legislative branch to monitor financial markets and make regular reports to Congress, and to provide a report on financial market regulatory reform by January 20, 2009.

There is no provision for allowing bankruptcy judges to reduce mortgage debt.

End Notes

[1] CRS Report RS22956, *The Cost of Government Financial Interventions, Past and Present,* by Baird Webel, N. Eric Weiss, and Marc Labonte.

[2] CRS Report RL34182, *Financial Crisis? The Liquidity Crunch of August 2007*, by Darryl E. Getter, Edward V. Murphy, Marc Labonte, and Mark Jickling.

[3] CRS Report RL33775, *Alternative Mortgages: Causes and Policy Implications of Troubled Mortgage Resets in the Subprime and Alt-A Markets,* by Edward V. Murphy.

[4] CRS Report RS22932, *Credit Default Swaps: Frequently Asked Questions,* by Edward V. Murphy.

[5] CRS Report RL34412, *Averting Financial Crisis,* by Mark Jickling.

[6] CRS Report RL34232, *Understanding Mortgage Foreclosure: Recent Events, the Process, and Costs,* by Darryl E. Getter.

[7] CRS Report RL33666, *Asset Bubbles: Economic Effects and Policy Options for the Federal Reserve,* by Marc Labonte.

[8] CRS Report RS22722, *Securitization and Federal Regulation of Mortgages for Safety and Soundness*, Edward V. Murphy.

[9] CRS Report RL34349, *Economic Slowdown: Issues and Policies*, by Jane G. Gravelle, Thomas L. Hungerford, Marc Labonte, N. Eric Weiss, and Julie M. Whittaker.

[10] CRS Report RS22371, *The Pattern of Interest Rates: Does It Signal an Impending Recession?* by Marc Labonte and Gail E. Makinen.

[11] CRS Report RS22850, *Tax Provisions of the Economic Stimulus Package*, by Jane G. Gravelle.

[12] CRS Report RL34427, *Financial Turmoil: Federal Reserve Policy Responses*, by Marc Labonte.

[13] CRS Report RL34420, *Bear Stearns: Crisis and 'Rescue' for a Major Provider of Mortgage-Related Products*, by Gary Shorter.

[14] CRS Report RL34372, *The HOPE NOW Alliance/American Securitization Forum (ASF) Plan to Freeze Certain Mortgage Interest Rates*, by David H. Carpenter and Edward V. Murphy.

[15] CRS Report RL34623, *Housing and Economic Recovery Act of 2008*, by N. Eric Weiss, Darryl E. Getter, Mark Jickling, Mark P. Keightley, Edward V. Murphy, and Bruce E. Foote.

[16] CRS Report RS22919, *Community Development Block Grants: Legislative Proposals to Assist Communities Affected by Home Foreclosures*, by Eugene Boyd and Oscar R. Gonzales.

[17] CRS Report RL33940, *Reforming the Regulation of Government-Sponsored Enterprises in the 110th Congress*, by Mark Jickling, Edward V. Murphy, and N. Eric Weiss.

[18] CRS Report RS22950, *Fannie Mae and Freddie Mac in Conservatorship*, by Mark Jickling.

[19] CRS Report RS22956, *The Cost of Government Financial Interventions, Past and Present* Baird Webel, N. Eric Weiss, and Marc Labonte.

[20] CRS Report RS22957, *Proposal to Allow Treasury to Buy Mortgage-Related Assets to Address Financial Instability*, by Edward V. Murphy and Baird Webel.

[21] H.R. 3997 was originally introduced as a tax relief measure to assist service members. The present discussion is based on a draft (as of 9:10 p.m., Sep. 28, 2008) offered by the House in the nature of a substitute.

In: Government Interventions in Economic Emergencies ISBN: 978-1-60741-356-1
Editor: Pablo Sastre

Chapter 14

FUTURE OF FINANCIAL SERVICES HEARING

Ben S. Bernanke

Chairman Frank, Ranking Member Bachus, and members of the Committee, I appreciate this opportunity to discuss recent developments in financial markets and the economy. As you know, the U.S. economy continues to confront substantial challenges, including a weakening labor market and elevated inflation. Notably, stresses in financial markets have been high and have recently intensified significantly. If financial conditions fail to improve for a protracted period, the implications for the broader economy could be quite adverse.

The downturn in the housing market has been a key factor underlying both the strained condition of financial markets and the slowdown of the broader economy. In the financial sphere, falling home prices and rising mortgage delinquencies have led to major losses at many financial institutions, losses only partially replaced by the raising of new capital. Investor concerns about financial institutions increased over the summer, as mortgage-related assets deteriorated further and economic activity weakened. Among the firms under the greatest pressure were Fannie Mae and Freddie Mac, Lehman Brothers, and, more recently, American International Group (AIG). As investors lost confidence in them, these companies saw their access to liquidity and capital markets increasingly impaired and their stock prices drop sharply.

The Federal Reserve believes that, whenever possible, such difficulties should be addressed through private-sector arrangements—for example, by raising new equity capital, by negotiations leading to a merger or acquisition, or by an orderly wind-down. Government assistance should be given with the greatest of reluctance and only when the stability of the financial system, and, consequently, the health of the broader economy, is at risk. In the cases of Fannie Mae and Freddie Mac, however, capital raises of sufficient size appeared infeasible and the size and government-sponsored status of the two companies precluded a merger with or acquisition by another company. To avoid unacceptably large dislocations in the financial sector, the housing market, and the economy as a whole, the Federal Housing Finance Agency (FHFA) placed Fannie Mae and Freddie Mac into conservatorship, and the Treasury used its authority, granted by the Congress in July, to make available financial support to the two firms. The Federal Reserve, with which FHFA consulted on the conservatorship decision as specified in the July legislation, supported these steps as necessary and appropriate. We have seen benefits of this action in the form of lower mortgage rates, which should help the housing market.

The Federal Reserve and the Treasury attempted to identify private-sector approaches to avoid the imminent failures of AIG and Lehman Brothers, but none was forthcoming. In the case of AIG, the Federal Reserve, with the support of the Treasury, provided an emergency credit line to facilitate an orderly resolution. The Federal Reserve took this action because it judged that, in light of the prevailing market conditions and the size and composition of AIG's obligations, a disorderly failure of AIG would have severely threatened global financial stability and, consequently, the performance of the U.S. economy. To mitigate concerns that this action would exacerbate moral hazard and encourage inappropriate risk-taking in the future, the Federal Reserve ensured that the terms of the credit extended to AIG imposed significant costs and constraints on the firm's owners, managers, and creditors. The chief executive officer has been replaced. The collateral for the loan is the company itself, together with its subsidiaries.[1] (Insurance policyholders and holders of AIG investment products are, however, fully protected.) Interest will accrue on the outstanding balance of the loan at a rate of three-month Libor plus 850 basis points, implying a current interest rate over 11 percent. In addition, the U.S. government will receive equity participation rights corresponding to a 79.9 percent equity interest in AIG and has the right to veto the payment of dividends to common and preferred shareholders, among other things.

In the case of Lehman Brothers, a major investment bank, the Federal Reserve and the Treasury declined to commit public funds to support the institution. The failure of Lehman posed risks. But the troubles at Lehman had been well known for some time, and investors clearly recognized--as evidenced, for example, by the high cost of insuring Lehman's debt in the market for credit default swaps--that the failure of the firm was a significant possibility. Thus, we judged that investors and counterparties had had time to take precautionary measures.

While perhaps manageable in itself, Lehman's default was combined with the unexpectedly rapid collapse of AIG, which together contributed to the development last week of extraordinarily turbulent conditions in global financial markets. These conditions caused equity prices to fall sharply, the cost of short-term credit--where available--to spike upward, and liquidity to dry up in many markets. Losses at a large money market mutual fund sparked extensive withdrawals from a number of such funds. A marked increase in the demand for safe assets—a flight to quality—sent the yield on Treasury bills down to a few hundredths of a percent. By further reducing asset values and potentially restricting the flow of credit to households and businesses, these developments pose a direct threat to economic growth.

The Federal Reserve took a number of actions to increase liquidity and stabilize markets. Notably, to address dollar funding pressures worldwide, we announced a significant expansion of reciprocal currency arrangements with foreign central banks, including an approximate doubling of the existing swap lines with the European Central Bank and the Swiss National Bank and the authorization of new swap facilities with the Bank of Japan, the Bank of England, and the Bank of Canada. We will continue to work closely with colleagues at other central banks to address ongoing liquidity pressures. The Federal Reserve also announced initiatives to assist money market mutual funds facing heavy redemptions and to increase liquidity in short-term credit markets.

Despite the efforts of the Federal Reserve, the Treasury, and other agencies, global financial markets remain under extraordinary stress. Action by the Congress is urgently required to stabilize the situation and avert what otherwise could be very serious consequences for our financial markets and for our economy. In this regard, the Federal Reserve supports the Treasury's proposal to buy illiquid assets from financial institutions. Purchasing impaired assets will create liquidity and promote price discovery in the markets for these assets, while reducing investor uncertainty about the current value and prospects of financial institutions. More generally, removing these assets from institutions' balance sheets will help to restore confidence in our financial markets and enable banks and other institutions to raise capital and to expand credit to support economic growth.

At this juncture, in light of the fast-moving developments in financial markets, it is essential to deal with the crisis at hand. Certainly, the shortcomings and weaknesses of our financial markets and regulatory system must be addressed if we are to avoid a repetition of what has transpired in our financial markets over the past year. However, the development of a comprehensive proposal for reform would require careful and extensive analysis that would be difficult to compress into a short legislative timeframe now available. Looking forward, the Federal Reserve is committed to working closely with the Congress, the Administration, other federal regulators, and other stakeholders in developing a stronger, more resilient, and better regulated financial system.

End Notes

[1] Specifically, the loan is collateralized by all of the assets of the company and its primary non-regulated subsidiaries. These assets include the equity of substantially all of AIG's regulated subsidiaries.

In: Government Interventions in Economic Emergencies
Editor: Pablo Sastre
ISBN: 978-1-60741-356-1

Chapter 15

TESTIMONY BY SECRETARY HENRY M. PAULSON, JR. BBEFORE THE HOUSE COMMITTEE ON FINANCIAL SERVICES HEARING ON TURMOIL IN U.S. CREDIT MARKETS: RECENT ACTIONS REGARDING GOVERNMENT SPONSORED ENTITIES, INVESTMENT BANKS AND OTHER FINANCIAL INSTITUTIONS

U.S. Treasury Department, Office Of Public Affairs

Washington, DC— Chairman Frank, Congressman Bachus, members of the committee, thank you for the opportunity to appear before you today. I appreciate that we are here to discuss an unprecedented program, but these are unprecedented times for the American people and our economy. I also appreciate that Congress and the Administration are working closely together so that we can help the American people by quickly enacting a program to stabilize our financial system.

We must do so in order to avoid a continuing series of financial institution failures and frozen credit markets that threaten American families' financial well-being, the viability of businesses both small and large, and the very health of our economy.

The events leading us here began many years ago, starting with bad lending practices by banks and financial institutions, and by borrowers taking out mortgages they couldn't afford. We've seen the results on homeowners – higher foreclosure rates affecting individuals and neighborhoods. And now we are seeing the impact on financial institutions.

These bad loans have created a chain reaction and last week our credit markets froze up – even some Main Street non-financial companies had trouble financing their normal business operations. If that situation were to persist, it would threaten all parts of our economy.

Every business in America relies on money flowing through the financial system smoothly every day – not only to borrow, expand and create jobs, but to finance their normal business operations and preserve existing jobs.

Since the housing correction began last summer, Treasury has examined many proposals as potential remedies for the turmoil that the correction has caused in our banking system.

With the Federal Reserve, we have sought to address financial market stresses with as minimal exposure for the US taxpayer as possible. The Federal Reserve took bold steps to increase liquidity in the markets. And we worked together on a case-by-case basis – addressing problems at Fannie Mae and Freddie Mac, working with market participants to prepare for the failure of Lehman Brothers, and lending to AIG so it can sell some of its assets in an orderly manner.

We have also taken a number of powerful tactical steps to increase confidence in the system, including a temporary guaranty program for the U.S. money market mutual fund industry. These steps have been necessary but not sufficient. More is needed. We saw financial market turmoil reach a new level last week, and spill over into the rest of the economy. We must now take further, decisive action to fundamentally and comprehensively address the root cause of this turmoil.

And that root cause is the housing correction which has resulted in illiquid mortgage-related assets that are choking off the flow of credit which is so vitally important to our economy. We must address this underlying problem, and restore confidence in our financial markets and financial institutions so they can perform their mission of supporting future prosperity and growth.

We have proposed a program to remove troubled assets from the system – a program we analyzed internally for months, and had hoped would never be necessary. Under our proposal, we would use market mechanisms available to small banks, credit unions, and thrifts, across the country – not just big banks. These mechanisms will help set values of complex, illiquid mortgage and mortgage-related securities to unclog our credit and capital markets, and make it easier for private investors to purchase these securities and for financial institutions to raise more capital.

This troubled asset purchase program has to be properly designed for immediate implementation and be sufficiently large to have maximum impact and restore market confidence. It must also protect the taxpayer to the maximum extent possible, and include provisions that ensure transparency and oversight while ensuring the program can be implemented quickly and run effectively, as it needs to get the job done.

I understand the view that I have heard from many of you on both sides of the aisle, urging that the taxpayer should share in the benefits of this plan to our financial system. Let me make clear – this entire proposal is about benefiting the American people, because today's fragile financial system puts their economic well-being at risk. When local banks and thrifts aren't able to function as they should, Americans' personal savings, and the ability of consumers and businesses to finance spending, investment and job creation are threatened.

The ultimate taxpayer protection will be stabilizing our system, so that all Americans can turn to financial institutions to meet their needs – financing a home improvement or a car or a college education, building retirement savings or starting a new business. The $700 billion program we have proposed is not a spending program. It is an asset purchase program, and the assets which are bought and held will ultimately be resold with the proceeds coming back to the government. Depending on the rate at which our housing market and economy recover, the loss to the taxpayers should be much less than the purchase price of the assets. And those purchases will be spread out over time, occurring as warranted by market conditions.

I am convinced that this bold approach will cost American families far less than the alternative – a continuing series of financial institution failures and frozen credit markets unable to fund everyday needs and economic expansion.

I understand that this is an extraordinary ask, but these are extraordinary times. I'm encouraged by the bipartisan consensus for an urgent legislative solution. We need to enact this bill quickly and cleanly, and avoid slowing it down with unrelated provisions or provisions that don't have broad support. This troubled asset purchase program on its own is the single most effective thing we can do to help homeowners, the American people and stimulate our economy.

Earlier this year, Congress and the Administration came together quickly and effectively to enact a stimulus package that has helped hard-working Americans and boosted our economy. We acted cooperatively and faster than anyone thought possible. Today we face a much more challenging situation that requires bipartisan discipline and urgency.

When we get through this difficult period, which we will, our next task must be to address the problems in our financial system through a reform program that fixes our outdated financial regulatory structure, and provides strong measures to address other flaws and excesses. I have already put forward my recommendations on this subject. Many of you also have strong views, and we must have that critical debate, but we must get through this period first.

Right now, all of us are focused on the immediate need to stabilize our financial system, and I believe we share the conviction that this is in the best interest of all Americans.

Now let's work together to get it done. Thank you.

In: Government Interventions in Economic Emergencies
Editor: Pablo Sastre
ISBN: 978-1-60741-356-1

Chapter 16

GOVERNMENT INTERVENTIONS IN FINANCIAL MARKETS: ECONOMIC AND HISTORIC ANALYSIS OF SUBPRIME MORTGAGE OPTIONS

N. Eric Weiss

SUMMARY

This chapter summarizes and analyzes four previous government market interventions (Home Owners Loan Corporation in 1933, Continental Illinois in 1984, the savings and loan insurance fund shortfall in 1989, and the Latin American debt crisis in 1989), in light of current mortgage market conditions. Current proposals to help delinquent homeowners share many features in common with all of these actions.

The Home Owners Loan Corporation (HOLC) purchased delinquent mortgages at a discount and worked with homeowners to restructure the mortgages into more manageable terms. HOLC accepted slightly more than one million applications from homeowners to refinance their homes between June 1933 and June 1935. It rejected 488,000 applications, most for "inadequate security" and "lack of distress." HOLC foreclosed on 194,000 of those it was attempting to assist. At the time, many had serious concern that HOLC could be a costly undertaking, but when it disbanded in the early 1 950s, HOLC returned a small profit to the government. HOLC successfully conceived and implemented new ways to contact delinquent homeowners and, in some cases, help homeowners find new jobs.

In 1984, Continental Illinois National Bank suffered a run after loans that it had not properly underwritten failed. The Federal Reserve and the Federal Deposit Insurance Corporation led intervention efforts. There were concerns that allowing the bank to fail could have serious repercussions throughout the financial system. This led to the FDIC Improvement Act of 1991.

In the 1980s, the Federal Savings and Loan Insurance Corporation approached insolvency because of the failure of member savings and loan institutions, also known as thrifts. Working together, Congress and the George H. W. Bush administration established the Resolution Trust Corporation (RTC), which was funded by the Resolution Funding Corporation

(REFCORP). The thrift industry is still paying off the intervention operation, which is estimated to have cost $152.9 billion.

In 1989, Brady bonds helped less developed countries, mostly in Latin America, restructure their debt by renegotiating terms and writing down some of the loans. The plan, proposed by then-U.S. Treasury Secretary Nicholas F. Brady, overcame coordination problems in previous restructuring efforts. In addition to writing down some loans, the plan included some interest rate reductions, and having debtor nations post U.S. Treasury bonds as collateral with the Federal Reserve. Approximately $91.8 billion was refinanced under the plan. Repayment continues today.

H.R. 5818 and H.R. 5830 are among the bills before Congress that would intervene in economic (housing) markets.

INTRODUCTION

Increasing delinquency and default rates on subprime mortgages in 2007 and 2008, along with liquidity problems in other financial sectors, have led some to call on the federal government to intervene in the mortgage market. The Administration and the mortgage industry have developed an approach called HOPE NOW that works with borrowers with subprime mortgages facing interest rate increases and increasing payments who could be helped with a combination of counseling and either an interest rate freeze or a new mortgage.[1] Critics of the plan believe that HOPE NOW is doing too little, too slowly to help those in need today and those who will face interest rate increases over the next few years.[2]

Foreclosure is costly for the lender, the borrower, and owners of neighboring property. Efforts to reduce foreclosures could very well be in the interest of all three affected parties. In foreclosure the lender is unlikely to recover the outstanding balance on the mortgage and the cost of foreclosure. The borrower is likely to lose any equity in the home, incur additional costs, and suffer credit impairment. A large number of vacant homes in a neighborhood can reduce the value of occupied homes. This spillover from the borrower and mortgage holder of the vacant homes to the neighbors is an example of what economists term an externality and provides a possible economic rationale for government intervention.

Some analysts and journalists have drawn a parallel between the delinquency and default problems facing homeowners with subprime mortgages and distressed homeowners during the Great Depression.[3] The Home Owners' Loan Corporation (HOLC) was created in 1933 to refinance homeowners' mortgages. This chapter analyzes HOLC, the Continental Illinois failure and government reaction in 1984, the savings and loan crisis of the 1 980s, and the 1989 Brady Plan for bonds from developing countries.

POLICY ISSUES

One of the first issues that Congress may choose to consider when contemplating an intervention is which home owners should be included in the plan. When there is a limited amount of aid, how should it be divided? At the one extreme, if assistance goes to only a few, those who obtain it may receive more assistance than is necessary or some in identical situations could be excluded. At the other extreme, if the assistance goes to a large number, there is a risk of spreading the help too thinly to be of assistance, or those who do not need help may receive it.

In short, who "deserves" to be helped? For example, should owners of rental property be assisted or only present owners? Should vacation and other second homes be included? Should persons with two homes who are trying to sell one be aided? Should owners of any type of housing be helped or just owners of single- family housing?[4]

If only one group, such as owners with subprime mortgages, is to be helped, should this group be further divided? For example, should those current on their mortgages be assisted? Should those who are behind on their payments be aided? What about those whose mortgage interest rates will reset in the future?

Should borrowers with certain types of mortgages be excluded? For example, should those with no- or low-documentation loans be excluded? Should an owner who made false or fraudulent statements to obtain the mortgage be aided?

Does it matter if the mortgage was obtained to purchase a home as opposed to refinancing the home? If refinancings are to be included, should there be a limit to the amount of cash equity that the borrower extracted from the house?

Finally, should there be a cutoff date? If there should, should it be a "date certain" or when a certain objective measure is reached?

One response is the HOPE NOW, which is available to homeowners through free telephone consultations with a HUD-approved credit counselor.[5] Its financial assistance is offered only to owner-occupied housing financed by subprime mortgages where the owners are current in their payments, but are not likely to be able to make payments after the mortgage resets. Some of the homeowners accepted by the program will have their mortgage interest rates frozen. Others will be helped to refinance with the Federal Housing Administration (FHA). Homeowners who are delinquent on their mortgage payments may be eligible to refinance in the FHASecure program.[6]

Economists and others worry that any government intervention in market outcomes could lead to the expectation of future intervention. This expectation, called moral hazard, could lead to riskier decisions in the future as home buyers (both those helped and those who did not require aid in the current case) take more risk than they might otherwise do in the expectation that the government will assist them in the future. In turn, this could lead to resources being used in a riskier way than would have occurred without the intervention. Insurance policies usually include deductibles and co-pays to limit moral hazard and to discourage excessive use. The rationale for such standard practices is that because the policy holder would bear part of the financial loss, he or she will exert greater prudence.

A Brief Overview of Subprime Delinquency and Default

In mortgage finance, delinquency occurs when a payment on a loan is overdue. Default occurs when a borrower has failed to meet any of the terms of a mortgage contract, including timely payment. Foreclosure occurs when the lender files to seize the house (collateral) because the borrower is in default. Foreclosure procedures vary from state to state.

Foreclosure is a costly process: one widely cited study estimates that the total cost to a lender of foreclosure, including lost interest, legal fees, and the cost of disposing of the house, is $58,759, and takes an average of 18 months.[7] A more recent report by the staff of the Joint Economic Committee (JEC) estimated the direct loss of property value at $53,493, and the loss of neighborhood property value at an additional $24,163.[8] The JEC estimated that each foreclosure would reduce property tax collections by $692. The JEC estimate did not include legal costs and interest foregone during foreclosure. A Federal Reserve Bank of Chicago report cited an estimate that a lender loses more than $50,000 per foreclosure.[9]

The Nature of the Subprime Reset Problem

As long as home prices were rising, lenders and borrowers had less need to worry about the ability of the borrower to make payments after a mortgage reset because the mortgage would be refinanced before the reset, and the borrower would profit from the price appreciation.[10] If a borrower could not make the mortgage payments, house price appreciation made certain that the lender was paid and the borrower might also make a profit. One reaction to this was the popularity of no- documentation or low-documentation mortgages in which borrowers supplied little or no information about their financial situations. Another response was the extension of subprime mortgages to borrowers with impaired credit histories. All of these mortgages depended heavily upon home price appreciation to provide repayment in case of foreclosure. Where home prices stop appreciating rapidly, the collateral represented by the home can be insufficient to liquidate the debt without a loss to the lender.

Selected Previous Government Interventions

The federal government has intervened in the past to modify market outcomes. In keeping with the current debate on the subprime mortgage actions, this section analyzes in greater detail those previous government actions that directly affected individuals and those that are most relevant to the current discussion on assisting homeowners.

This chapter examines four government market interventions: (1) the Home Owner Loan Corporation (HOLC) of 1933; (2) Continental Illinois in 1994; (3) the savings and loan crisis of the 1 980s; and (4) Brady bonds in 1989. HOLC is included because it has been widely mentioned as a possible model for government action. Continental Illinois, in 1984, is included because the bank failed to properly underwrite loans, and because the Federal Reserve and the Federal Deposit Insurance Corporation led assistance efforts. The savings and loan crisis of the 1980s is included because the problems were closely connected to the financing of homes. Brady bonds are discussed in part because previous attempts to solve the international financial distress failed and also because the comparison between earlier attempts and then-U.S. Treasury Secretary Nicholas F. Brady's proposal might be useful.

Home Owners' Loan Corporation

HOLC was established in 1933 to prevent mortgage foreclosures.[11] Mortgages at that time usually were for three to five years, were generally expected to be renewed, and did not amortize (i.e., were not designed to be paid in full by a series of monthly payments). HOLC exchanged its bonds for mortgages that were in default and mortgages held by financial institutions that were in distress. In HOLC's first year, the federal guarantee increased from interest only to interest and principal. Mortgages were limited to one- to four-unit structures, with an HOLC-appraised value of $20,000 or less ($321,791 in 2008 dollars), could be for no more than the lesser of $14,000 ($225,254 in 2008 dollars) or 80% of HOLC appraised value, carried a maximum interest rate of 5%, and required monthly amortizing payments for not more than 15 years.[12] The $14,000 maximum mortgage meant that a house worth the maximum value of $20,000 could not have a mortgage for the maximum 80% loan-to-value (LTV) ratio.

HOLC was authorized to issue up to $4.75 billion ($76 billion in 2008 dollars) in bonds that could either be exchanged for defaulted mortgages or for cash. The cash could be used to purchase mortgages from lenders who did not want to take the HOLC bonds. The bonds carried a maximum interest rate of 4% for a maximum of 18 years and were exempt from all state, local, and federal taxes.13 HOLC lent homeowners money to pay taxes and insurance.

Contemporary Issues

At the time that HOLC was created, some were concerned that lenders would not accept the HOLC bonds. This was addressed by allowing the defaulted mortgages to be purchased for cash and increasing the government guarantee on interest to a federal guarantee on both principal and interest. Today, both private and FHA mortgage insurance guarantee payment of principal and interest.

Results

Not all of those eligible applied, and not all those who applied were eligible. Approximately 40% of those eligible for HOLC mortgages applied and half of these were rejected or withdrawn. Of this 50%, 16% were withdrawn, 18% were rejected because of inadequate house value, and 13% were rejected for lack of distress.[14]

HOLC employees were not civil servants, and the corporation did not follow federal procurement regulations. Although some forecast that HOLC would lose money, it ended up making a relatively small profit when it was liquidated in 1951, in part because declining interest rates and the government guarantee allowed it to borrow inexpensively.[15] HOLC developed its own mortgage processing and servicing system. It supervised and trained appraisers.

HOLC negotiated flexible repayment terms, but it sought eventual full repayment of the mortgages. It developed new methods of working with borrowers who became delinquent, including personal contact with the borrowers. HOLC would try to find jobs for unemployed homeowners and suggested renting out spare bedrooms. Beginning in 1937, it rewrote loans to make them more affordable. Of the one million loans HOLC issued, it acquired 200,000 homes from borrowers who were unable to pay their mortgages; the national foreclosure rate was 19.4%, but there was wide variation in different states.[16] New York and Massachusetts had foreclosure rates of more than 40%, but foreclosure rates in Michigan, West Virginia, Florida, Montana, Idaho, Wyoming, New Mexico, Nevada, and Oregon were less than 10%.[17] HOLC set the price on the foreclosed homes, included financing, and worked with local real estate agents. At its peak, HOLC had 20,000 employees in 458 offices where applications were accepted.[18]

Although there were provisions to purchase mortgages held at troubled banks, HOLC was designed to work with homeowners.[19] Based on the appraised value, the amount of the new mortgage could be less than the original mortgage, and the lender could take a loss on the mortgage. From an economic point of view, this was providing the lender with financial incentives to mark the mortgage to the current (market) value and to recognize the loss.

Application to Subprime Mortgage Restructuring

A program similar to HOLC could be adopted by Congress. Several questions would need to be answered in applying the lessons from the HOLC to the current situation:

What is the maximum house value that could participate in the program?
What should the maximum loan-to-value ratio be?
What should the maximum term of the loans be?
Should there be any restrictions on the interest rate?
Should the government or the private sector run the program?
How should delinquencies and default by those being assisted be treated?
Should the new organization follow HOLC's experience and help delinquent homeowners find better jobs and rent out spare bedrooms?
Should there be a predetermined ending date for the program? If so, should this be a fixed date or one at which some measurable criterion is met?

Continental Illinois

In the first quarter of 1984, Continental Illinois, a major United States money center bank, lost $140 million ($291 million in 2008 dollars) triggering a run by uninsured depositors.[20] The Federal Reserve made secret loans to Continental to provide liquidity and to prop it up. In May 1984, the Federal Deposit Insurance Corporation, the Federal Reserve, and 16 money center banks announced that they would support the uninsured deposits. Additional assistance was required in July 1984. Government assistance totaled $4.5 billion ($9.3 billion in 2008 dollars). The FDIC purchased problem loans at a discount and invested $1 billion ($2 billion in 2008 dollars) in Continental. Continental was re-capitalized giving the federal government 80% of its shares; most of the equity of the shareholders was eliminated.

Contemporary Issues

There was little congressional debate in the Continental case because there was no congressional action required. Observers expressed concern that, by giving a de facto guarantee on uninsured deposits, market discipline was being weakened. Some argued that a bank of Continental's size could not be allowed to fail because failure would impact other

U.S. and foreign banks. Some questioned the effectiveness of government bank regulation that allowed Continental to engage in risky lending and incur what were then record losses.

Results

The intervention led to management changes. Bank of America purchased Continental in 1994. Congress passed the FDIC Improvement Act of 1991 to strengthen large bank regulation.[21]

Application to Subprime Mortgage Restructuring

In this case, the Federal Reserve, FDIC, and other banks engaged in the immediate intervention. This appears to be similar to the actions of the Federal Reserve and JP Morgan Chase in the recent intervention leading to the JP Morgan's purchase of Bear Stearns.[22] Continental had grown rapidly and raised funds by borrowing from other banks (federal funds) and with large, wholesale certificates of deposit (CDs). Continental participated heavily with Penn Square Bank in loans to gas and oil projects. After Penn Square was closed because of defaults on these loans, other banks and CD holders became concerned that Continental might not be able to pay them back. The banks and CD holders refused to roll over their investments.

An analysis by the FDIC concluded that Continental had failed to properly underwrite oil and gas loans made with Penn Square Bank. Many analysts say that subprime lenders also failed to properly underwrite loans, but in this case the loans were to homeowners.

Savings and Loans

In the 1980s, many U.S. savings and loan associations (S&Ls) expanded beyond their traditional business of making mortgages to local home buyers. At the same time, S&L profitability declined because of rising interest rates and a mismatch between maturing of S&L assets and liabilities, resulting in 563 S&L failures between 1980 and 1988.[23] In some cases, fraud, including land "flips," was a factor in S&L failures. The Federal Savings and Loan Insurance Corporation (FSLIC), a federal agency that insured most S&L deposits, became insolvent. Some S&Ls were chartered and guaranteed by states including Ohio and Maryland; these state- sponsored insurers also failed as depositors withdrew their money out of concern for the institutions' financial safety.

Contemporary Issues

Debate centered on estimates of the cost of restructuring the S&L industry and how to pay the cost. There was some concern over forcing high-risk S&Ls out of business.

Results

Congress passed the Financial Institutions Reform, Recovery, and Enforcement Act of 1989 (FIRREA) to "reform, recapitalize, and consolidate" the federal deposit insurance system, but not bail out individuals or lenders.[24] Borrowers were still required to pay their loans. To the extent that federal intervention led to general confidence in financial markets, consumers benefitted. Congress provided $91.3 billion ($158.7 billion in 2008 dollars) to the

Resolution Trust Corporation to pay for the restructuring. One estimate of the direct and indirect costs to the private and public sectors was $152.9 billion ($191.4 billion in 2008 dollars).[25]

Application to Subprime Mortgage Restructuring

The S&L intervention is included because the problems in the thrift industry were in part due to mortgage lending. However, the purpose of the savings and loan intervention was to minimize the cost to the government of honoring the federal insurance of deposits at illiquid and insolvent savings and loans. Most depositors were not at risk unless the federal government failed to honor its guarantee, and this was not considered. A few depositors were at risk for the amount above $100,000.[26] The intervention was important to the viability of the financial system; the same could be argued for much of the Federal Reserve's recent actions.

Brady Bonds

In 1982, a variety of factors combined to result in problems for Latin American nations trying to repay loans, mostly to U.S. commercial banks. Most observers blame relaxed lending standards, poor debt management by borrower countries, and a changing international economy for the inability of debtor nations to repay their debts.[27] U.S. banks accounted for $91.8 billion ($205.1 billion in 2008 dollars) of $219.4 billion ($490.2 billion in 2008 dollars) lent worldwide to 17 highly indebted countries. Initial attempts by then-U.S. Treasury Secretary James Baker to combine structural economic changes of debtor nations, and debt rescheduling including lengthening maturities did not succeed because of difficulties in coordinating action among lenders.[28] In 1989, then-U.S. Treasury Secretary Nicholas F. Brady proposed what became known as the Brady Plan — a combination of bank loan forgiveness and repackaging remaining debt into bonds that could be traded on securities markets. One key feature of the Brady Plan was for lenders to recognize that doubt over the timely repayment of the existing debt had reduced its value and to agree to allow borrowers to buy back debt at a discount.

After the buyback, the remaining loan principal was restructured using three types of bonds:

In the first case, dollar-denominated discount bonds paying market interest rates were exchanged for outstanding commercial bank loans. These bonds were interest only; principal was repaid at maturity.

In the second case, dollar-denominated, below market interest rate bonds were exchanged at face (par) value for outstanding commercial bank loans. These bonds, also, were interest only with the principal repaid at maturity.

In the third case, dollar-denominated bonds were exchanged for outstanding loans at face value and paid market interest rates.

In addition, banks provided new money to maintain liquidity of the borrower nations.

Borrower nations were required to purchase U.S. Treasury zero coupon bonds that were held in escrow at the Federal Reserve Bank of New York to partially collateralize the principal of discount and par bonds.[29] Debtor countries, also, collateralized 12-18 months of interest by making a deposit at the Federal Reserve Bank of New York or by purchasing U.S. Treasury bills. The World Bank and the International Monetary Fund (IMF) made structural adjustment loans to debtor nations.

Contemporary Issues

Discussions at the time centered over what countries would be eligible for debt restructuring and the terms of the restructuring. The analogy for aiding homeowners delinquent on mortgage payments would be the question of who should be eligible and how the mortgages should be recast.

Results

The Brady Plan is widely credited with accelerating the creation of new international financing mechanisms. By shifting much lending from bank loans to bonds, liquidity was added to the international financial system, which has grown in the intervening years, benefitting many nations. Liquidity and the multiple types of bond exchanges meant that lenders did not have to agree on a single solution.

Application to Subprime Mortgage Restructuring

On the one hand, the Brady Plan restored financial stability to U.S. commercial banks and international lending grew. More affordable terms and the assurance of long-term financing were benefits to both borrowers and lenders. Brady bonds allowed the federal government to facilitate the restructuring of debt into more affordable payments without any federal guarantee.

On the other hand, shifting the denomination debt from the borrower's currency to dollars shifted exchange rate risk from lenders to borrowers. New collateral shifted more risk from the U.S. banks to the debtor nations. Not every debtor nation was willing and able to renegotiate its loans. Banks negotiated custom agreements with some debtor nations. This was practical because of the size of the loans. Mexico, for example, had $17 billion ($40 billion in 2008 dollars) in short term debt.[30] This renegotiation might be more difficult in the case of two million mortgages that could default in 2008 and 2009, most valued in the hundreds of thousands of dollars.[31]

Lenders recognized losses on existing loans, but had more assurance that renegotiated loans would be repaid in full and on time. Borrowers had more manageable repayment schedules.

A similar approach could be used to restructure subprime loans. Some mortgages could have their principal and/or interest rates reduced. This could be viewed as an acknowledgment of the economic reality that the value of the subprime mortgage is less than its face value because of the weakened value of the home as collateral and the increased probability of default. Lenders might be willing to advance additional funds to some subprime borrowers if these funds were placed in escrow as collateral for a new loan. HOLC used a similar recognition of the reduced value of the mortgages it purchased.

It is likely that not every subprime borrower facing an interest rate reset would be willing or able to renegotiate their loans. Lenders would be unlikely to agree to renegotiate terms that would leave them worse off than foreclosure. For example, if a homeowner cannot afford to make payments on a fixed rate mortgage based on the current value of the home, the lender is likely to decide that foreclosure is the more profitable option. If this inability to make payments is temporary, such as would be the case if someone is unemployed but likely to find a new job shortly, the longer run interests of the lender might be to negotiate a new mortgage. If, however, the inability to make payments is seen as permanent, then lenders are more likely to be unwilling to negotiate.

It is not likely that a domestic private sector, third party would make additional loans to subprime borrowers in a manner such as the IMF and World Bank did for debtor nations. This might be a role for FHA or the Veterans Administration.

CONCLUSION

If Congress were to consider some intervention to aid homeowners, there are a number of questions for its consideration:

Who should be helped? Should there be an income limit? Should it be limited to owner-occupied housing?

What should be the tax treatment of the assistance?

Who should administer the program? What should happen if foreclosure becomes necessary?

What should be the government's continuing role? Should the program have a fixed life?

What restrictions, if any, should be placed on the ability of homeowners that receive assistance to sell their homes in the future? What if the sale is at a profit? What if the sale is at a loss?

If the government makes a financial contribution, how much should it be and how should it be financed?

One of the lessons from these four instances of government intervention is that those in financial difficulty are frequently reluctant to acknowledge the existence or severity of the problem. On the other hand, in these four cases, recognition that substantial losses had occurred was a key to beginning the recovery process. The question remaining was how the losses could be paid for at the least cost.

Most government market interventions have used the emergency medicine principal of triage to divide those into distress into three groups: those who cannot be helped with the resources available, those who will recover (or at least survive) without any help, and those who will recover only with immediate assistance. The difficulty is in determining to which category the affected persons or institutions should be assigned.

HOLC and Brady bonds involved negotiations between the borrower and the organizations involved in the refinancing. Not every distressed borrower was willing or able to meet the terms of the assistance effort. It is probably unrealistic to expect that any plan could keep all subprime borrowers in their homes. For example, some borrowers will become unemployed and not have the income to make even reduced mortgage payments. Even a moratorium on foreclosures would prevent loss of homes only while the moratorium lasts.

The HOLC experience was that some of those who could be helped would not contact the HOLC. It was necessary for HOLC to reach out to borrowers who became delinquent and to develop personalized plans to modify the mortgage so that it could be repaid eventually. Many of the largest mortgage lenders and associations such as those represented by HOPE NOW are urging delinquent homeowners to talk with their lenders and credit counselors.[32] HOPE NOW, also, is dividing callers into three categories trying to work quickly with the easiest situations first so that those who require more extensive help can get the resources needed.

Economists use the phrase "moral hazard" to represent the change in behavior due to insuring risks. Purchasing insurance probably makes some individuals more likely to take risks than would be prudent without the financial safety net. Economists who worry about moral hazard are concerned that a government intervention in a market outcome also encourages individuals and companies to pay less attention to risk in the future in the expectation that the government will intervene again. They worry that in the case of a government intervention to help homeowners, the possibility of a repeat of the intervention could encourage some lenders to lend more than they would, absent the history of government action. It is possible that homeowners who are helped and others who see the intervention occur also could react this way.

End Notes

[1] See [http://www.hopenow.com/].

[2] See, for example, Mary Umberger, "Rate freeze called too little, too much; Critics say it delays inevitable; others oppose intervention," *Chicago Tribune,* December 7, 2007, p. 1.

[3] Damian Paletta, "Democrat Floats Plan to Refinance Home Loans With U.S. Help," *Wall Street Journal,* February 27, 2008, p. A14.

[4] Single-family includes structures with one to four units. It excludes condominiums and cooperatives. In 2005, there were 84.5 million owner-occupied single-family buildings, while an additional 7.6 million were vacant. Of those occupied, 67.2 million were occupied by owners and 17.3 million were rentals. Source: U.S. Census Bureau, *American Housing Survey 2005,* Table 1A1, available at [http://www.census.gov/hhes/www/housing/ahs/ahs05/ ahs05 .html].

[5] For details, see CRS Report RL34372, *The HOPE NOW Alliance/American Securitization Forum (ASF) Plan to Freeze Certain Mortgage Interest Rates,* by David H. Carpenter and Edward Vincent Murphy.

[6] For more details, see the FHA Web page at [http://portal.hud.gov/portal/ page?_pageid=33,7 1 7446 &_dad=portal&_schema=PORTAL].

[7] CRS Report RL34232, *Understanding Mortgage Foreclosure: Recent Events, the Process, and Costs,* by Darryl E. Getter. See, also, Amy Crews Cutts and Richard K. Green, *Innovative Service Technology: Smart Enough to Keep People in Their Homes,* Freddie Mac Working Paper #04-03, July 2004, p. 5, available at [http://www.freddiemac.com/news/ pdf/fmwp_0403_servicing.pdf]. (The paper cites a study by Craig Focardi, Servicing Default Management: An Overview of the Process and Underlying Technology," *TowerGroup Research Note,* No. 033-1 3C, November 15, 2002).

[8] U.S . Congress, Joint Economic Committee, *The Subprime Lending Crisis: The Economic Impact on Wealth, Property Values and Tax Revenues, and How We Got Here,* October 2007, p. 13 and CRS calculations.

[9] This estimate by GMAC-RFC (Residential Funding Corporation) is cited by Desire Hatcher, "Foreclosure Alternatives: A Case for Preserving Homeownership," *Profitwise News and Views,* February 2006, p. 1, at [http://www.chicagofed.org/community _development/files/02_2006_foreclosure_alt.pdf].

[10] CRS Report RL33930, *Subprime Mortgages: Primer on Current Lending and Foreclosure Issues,* by Edward Vincent Murphy.

[11] C. Lowell Harriss, *History and Policies of the Home Owners' Loan Corporation* (New York: National Bureau of Economic Research, 1951). 48 Stat. 128 et seq. created the HOLC.

[12] Interest-only payments were later allowed for the first three years. All historic dollar amounts in this report are update to 2008 dollars using the Consumer Price Index and the calculator available from the Federal Reserve Bank of Minneapolis at [http://woodrow.mpls.frb.fed.us/research/data/us/calc/].

[13] This exclusion included estate, inheritance, and gift taxes, but not a progressive surtax.

[14] Harriss, p. 24.

[15] Harriss, p. 6.

[16] Harriss, p. 75.

[17] Harriss, p. 75.

[18] Harriss, p. 140.

[19] In a time when all records were kept on paper, a bank failure could prevent homeowners from making mortgage payments resulting in their delinquency.

[20] Federal Deposit Insurance Corporation, "Continental Illinois and Too Big To Fail" and "Continental Illinois National Bank and Trust Company," *History of the Eighties — Lessons for the Future,* at [http://www.fdic.gov/bank/historical/history/235_258.pdf#search=' Continental%20Illinois'] and [http : //www.fdic . gov/bank/historical/managing/ history2-04.pdf], respectively. A "money center bank" is one of the nation's largest and usually does business internationally with governments, businesses, and other banks.

[21] P.L. 102-242, 105 Stat. 2236 et seq.

[22] See CRS Report RL34420, *Bear Stearns: Crisis and 'Rescue' for a Major Provider of Mortgage-Related Products*, by Gary Shorter.

[23] In short, the S&Ls financed long term loans by taking in short term deposits. When interest rates increased, to keep and to attract deposits the S&Ls had to pay higher interest rates than they were earning on their loans.

[24] P.L. 101-73, 103 Stat. 183 et seq.

[25] Timothy Curry and Lynn Shibut, "The Cost of the Savings and Loan Crisis: Truth and Consequences," *FDIC Banking Review, December 2000*, p. 31, available at [http://www.fdic.gov/bank/analytical/banking/2000dec/brv1 3n2_2.pdf].

[26] P.L. 96-22 1, 94 Stat. 132 et seq., Depository Institutions Deregulation and Monetary Control Act of 1980.

[27] This section is based on CRS Report RL30348, *Ecuador's Brady Bond Default: Background and Implications*, by J. F. Hornbeck, and also Patricia A. Wertman, "The 'Brady Plan': A New Director in Third World Debt Strategy," CRS Review, October 1989, pp. 22-23.

[28] Mark Spiegel, "Collective Action Difficulties in Foreign Lending: Banks and Bonds," Federal Reserve Bank of San Francisco Economic Letter, August 23, 1996, available at [http://www.frbsf.org/econrsrch/wklyltr/el9 6-24.html].

[29] The issuer of a zero coupon bond pays all interest and principal at maturity. The bond is sold for less than this single payment. A zero coupon bond pays compound interest — interest on interest like a saving account does — while a coupon bond pays simple interest.

[30] "Companies and Markets: Focus on Precise Terms of Mexican Debt Moratorium," *Financial Times,* August 31, 1982, p. 19.

[31] Mark Zandi, "Testimony of Mark Zandi before U.S. House Judiciary Committee," October 30, 2007, at [http://judiciary.house.gov/OversightTestimony.aspx?ID=1 188].

[32] Members of HOPE NOW include Fannie Mae, Freddie Mac, Bank of America, Countrywide, JPMorgan Chase, Washington Mutual, and Wells Fargo. A complete list is available at [http://www.hopenow.com/]. In addition, FHA is urging borrowers experiencing financial difficulty to contact their lenders. FHA has information available at [http://portal.hud.gov/portal/page?_pageid=33,7 1 7348&_dad=portal&_schema=PORTAL].

In: Government Interventions in Economic Emergencies ISBN: 978-1-60741-356-1
Editor: Pablo Sastre

Chapter 17

STATEMENT BY SECRETARY HENRY M. PAULSON, JR. ON COMPREHENSIVE APPROACH TO MARKET DEVELOPMENTS

U. S. Department of the Treasury

Washington, DC—Last night, Federal Reserve Chairman Ben Bernanke, SEC Chairman Chris Cox and I had a lengthy and productive working session with Congressional leaders. We began a substantive discussion on the need for a comprehensive approach to relieving the stresses on our financial institutions and markets.

We have acted on a case-by-case basis in recent weeks, addressing problems at Fannie Mae and Freddie Mac, working with market participants to prepare for the failure of Lehman Brothers, and lending to AIG so it can sell some of its assets in an orderly manner. And this morning we've taken a number of powerful tactical steps to increase confidence in the system, including the establishment of a temporary guaranty program for the U.S. money market mutual fund industry.

Despite these steps, more is needed. We must now take further, decisive action to fundamentally and comprehensively address the root cause of our financial system's stresses.

The underlying weakness in our financial system today is the illiquid mortgage assets that have lost value as the housing correction has proceeded. These illiquid assets are choking off the flow of credit that is so vitally important to our economy. When the financial system works as it should, money and capital flow to and from households and businesses to pay for home loans, school loans and investments that create jobs. As illiquid mortgage assets block the system, the clogging of our financial markets has the potential to have significant effects on our financial system and our economy.

As we all know, lax lending practices earlier this decade led to irresponsible lending and irresponsible borrowing. This simply put too many families into mortgages they could not afford. We are seeing the impact on homeowners and neighborhoods, with 5 million homeowners now delinquent or in foreclosure. What began as a sub-prime lending problem has spread to other, less-risky mortgages, and contributed to excess home inventories that have pushed down home prices for responsible homeowners.

A similar scenario is playing out among the lenders who made those mortgages, the securitizers who bought, repackaged and resold them, and the investors who bought them. These troubled loans are now parked, or frozen, on the balance sheets of banks and other financial institutions, preventing them from financing productive loans. The inability to determine their worth has fostered uncertainty about mortgage assets, and even about the financial condition of the institutions that own them. The normal buying and selling of nearly all types of mortgage assets has become challenged.

These illiquid assets are clogging up our financial system, and undermining the strength of our otherwise sound financial institutions. As a result, Americans' personal savings are threatened, and the ability of consumers and businesses to borrow and finance spending, investment, and job creation has been disrupted.

To restore confidence in our markets and our financial institutions, so they can fuel continued growth and prosperity, we must address the underlying problem.

The federal government must implement a program to remove these illiquid assets that are weighing down our financial institutions and threatening our economy. This troubled asset relief program must be properly designed and sufficiently large to have maximum impact, while including features that protect the taxpayer to the maximum extent possible. The ultimate taxpayer protection will be the stability this troubled asset relief program provides to our financial system, even as it will involve a significant investment of taxpayer dollars. I am convinced that this bold approach will cost American families far less than the alternative – a continuing series of financial institution failures and frozen credit markets unable to fund economic expansion.

I believe many Members of Congress share my conviction. I will spend the weekend working with members of Congress of both parties to examine approaches to alleviate the pressure of these bad loans on our system, so credit can flow once again to American consumers and companies. Our economic health requires that we work together for prompt, bipartisan action.

As we work with the Congress to pass this legislation over the next week, other immediate actions will provide relief.

First, to provide critical additional funding to our mortgage markets, the GSEs Fannie Mae and Freddie Mac will increase their purchases of mortgage-backed securities (MBS). These two enterprises must carry out their mission to support the mortgage market.

Second, to increase the availability of capital for new home loans, Treasury will expand the MBS purchase program we announced earlier this month. This will complement the capital provided by the GSEs and will help facilitate mortgage availability and affordability.

These two steps will provide some initial support to mortgage assets, but they are not enough. Many of the illiquid assets clogging our system today do not meet the regulatory requirements to be eligible for purchase by the GSEs or by the Treasury program.

I look forward to working with Congress to pass necessary legislation to remove these troubled assets from our financial system. When we get through this difficult period, which we will, our next task must be to improve the financial regulatory structure so that these past excesses do not recur. This crisis demonstrates in vivid terms that our financial regulatory structure is sub-optimal, duplicative and outdated. I have put forward my ideas for a modernized financial oversight structure that matches our modern economy, and more closely links the regulatory structure to the reasons why we regulate. That is a critical debate for another day.

Right now, our focus is restoring the strength of our financial system so it can again finance economic growth. The financial security of all Americans – their retirement savings, their home values, their ability to borrow for college, and the opportunities for more and higher-paying jobs – depends on our ability to restore our financial institutions to a sound footing.

In: Government Interventions in Economic Emergencies ISBN: 978-1-60741-356-1
Editor: Pablo Sastre

Chapter 18

REMARKS BY SECRETARY HENRY M. PAULSON, JR. ON FINANCIAL RESCUE PACKAGE AND ECONOMIC UPDATE

U. S. Department of the Treasury

Washington - Good morning. I will provide an update on the state of the financial system, our economy, and our strategy for continued implementation of the financial rescue package.

CURRENT STATE OF GLOBAL FINANCIAL SYSTEM

The actions taken by Treasury, the Federal Reserve and the FDIC in October have clearly helped stabilize our financial system. Before we acted, we were at a tipping point. Credit markets were largely frozen, denying financial institutions, businesses and consumers access to vital funding and credit. U.S. and European financial institutions were under extreme pressure, and investor confidence in our system was dangerously low.

We also acted quickly and in coordination with colleagues around the world to stabilize the global financial system. Going into the Annual IMF/World Bank meetings in early October, I made clear that we would use the financial rescue package granted by Congress to purchase equity directly from financial institutions – the fastest and most productive means of using our new authorities to stabilize our financial system. We launched our capital purchase program the following week when we announced that nine of the largest U.S. financial institutions, holding approximately 55 percent of U.S. banking assets would sell $125 billion in preferred stock to the Treasury. At the same time, the FDIC announced it would temporarily guarantee all newly issued senior unsecured debt of participating organizations for up to three years. In addition, the FDIC provided an unlimited guarantee on non-interest bearing transaction accounts that expires at the end of next year.

As I assess where we are today, I believe we have taken the necessary steps to prevent a broad systemic event. Both at home and around the world we have already seen signs of improvement. Our system is stronger and more stable than just a few weeks ago. Although this is a major accomplishment, we have many challenges ahead of us. Our financial system remains fragile in the face of an economic downturn here and abroad, and financial institutions' balance sheets still hold significant illiquid assets. Market turmoil will not abate until the biggest part of the housing correction is behind us. Our primary focus must be recovery and repair.

HOUSING AND MORTGAGE FINANCE

Overall, we are in a better position than we were, but we must address the continued challenges of a weak economy, especially the housing correction and lending contraction.

On housing, we have worked aggressively to avoid preventable foreclosures and keep mortgage financing available. In October 2007, we helped establish the HOPE NOW Alliance, a coalition of mortgage servicers, investors and counselors, to help struggling homeowners avoid preventable foreclosures. HOPE NOW created a streamlined protocol to assist struggling borrowers who could afford their homes with a loan modification. The industry is now helping 200,000 homeowners a month avoid foreclosure. In addition, HUD has created new programs to complement existing FHA options, and to refinance a larger number of struggling borrowers into affordable FHA mortgages.

Most significantly, we acted earlier this year to prevent the failure of Fannie Mae and Freddie Mac, the housing GSEs that now touch over 70 percent of mortgage originations. I clearly stated at that time three critical objectives: providing stability to financial markets, supporting the availability of mortgage finance, and protecting taxpayers – both by minimizing the near term costs to the taxpayer and by setting policymakers on a course to resolve the systemic risk created by the inherent conflict in the GSE structure.

Fortunately we acted, citing concerns about both the quality and quantity of GSE capital. Unfortunately, our actions proved all too necessary. The GSEs were failing, and if they did fail, it would have materially exacerbated the recent market turmoil and more profoundly impacted household wealth: from family budgets, to home values, to savings for college and retirement.

Earlier this week, Fannie Mae reported a record loss, including write-downs of its deferred tax assets that make up a significant portion of its capital. We monitor closely the performance of both Fannie Mae and Freddie Mac, and both are performing within the range of our expectations. The magnitude of the losses at Fannie Mae were within the range of what we expected, and further confirms the need for our strong actions.

Eight weeks ago, Treasury took responsibility for supporting the agency debt securities and the agency MBS through a preferred stock purchase agreement that guarantees a positive net worth in each enterprise – effectively, a guarantee on GSE debt and agency MBS. We also established a credit facility to provide the GSEs the strongest possible liquidity backstop. As the enterprises go through this difficult housing correction we will, as needed and promised, purchase preferred shares under the terms of that agreement. The U.S. government honors its commitments, and investors can bank on it.

When we took action in September, I said that we would be entering a "time out" – a period where the new President and Congress must decide what role government in general, and the GSEs in particular, should play in the housing market. In my view, government support needs to be either explicit or non-existent, and structured to resolve the conflict between public and private purposes. And policymakers must address the issue of systemic risk. In the weeks ahead, I will share some thoughts outlining my views on long term reform.

In the meantime, the GSEs now operate on stable footing. They have strong government support backing both future capital and liquidity needs. We have stabilized the GSEs and limited systemic risk, and our authorities provide us with additional flexibility to use as necessary to accomplish our objectives.

IMPLEMENTING THE FINANCIAL RESCUE PACKAGE

More recently, we have also taken extraordinary steps to support our financial markets and financial institutions. As credit markets froze in mid-September, the Administration asked Congress for broad tools and flexibility to rescue the financial system. We asked for \$700 billion to purchase troubled assets from financial institutions. At the time, we believed that would be the most effective means of getting credit flowing again.

During the two weeks that Congress considered the legislation, market conditions worsened considerably. It was clear to me by the time the bill was signed on October 3rd that we needed to act quickly and forcefully, and that purchasing troubled assets – our initial focus – would take time to implement and would not be sufficient given the severity of the problem. In consultation with the Federal Reserve, I determined that the most timely, effective step to improve credit market conditions was to strengthen bank balance sheets quickly through direct purchases of equity in banks.

Of course, before that time, the only instances in which Treasury had taken equity positions was in rescuing a failing institution. Both the preferred stock purchase agreement for Fannie Mae and Freddie Mac, and the Federal Reserve's secured lending facility for AIG came with significant taxpayer protections and conditions. As we planned a capital purchase plan to support the overall financial system by strengthening balance sheets of a broad array of healthy banks, the terms had to be designed to encourage broad participation, balanced to ensure appropriate taxpayer protection and not impede the flow of private capital.

CAPITAL PURCHASE PLAN

We announced a plan on October 14th to purchase up to \$250 billion in preferred stock in federally regulated banks and thrifts. By October 26th we had \$115 billion out the door to eight large institutions. In Washington that is a land-speed record from announcing a program to getting funds out the door. We now have approved dozens of additional applications, and investments are being made in approved institutions. Although we are moving very quickly it will take time to complete legal contracts and execute investments in the significant number of institutions who meet the eligibility requirements and are approved, but we are on the path to getting this done.

Although this program's primary purpose is stabilizing our financial system, banks must also continue lending. During times like these with a slowing economy and some deterioration in credit conditions, even the healthiest banks tend to become more risk-averse and restrain lending, and regulators' actions have reinforced this lending restraint in the past. With a stronger capital base, our banks will be more confident and better positioned to play their necessary role to support economic activity. Today banking regulators issued a statement emphasizing that the extraordinary government actions taken by the Fed, Treasury and FDIC to stabilize and strengthen the banking system are not merely one-sided; all banks – not just those participating in the Capital Purchase Program – have benefited, so they all also have responsibilities in the areas of lending, dividend and compensation policies, and foreclosure mitigation. I commend this action and I am particularly focused on the importance of prudent bank lending to restore our economic growth.

Since announcing the Capital Purchase Program, we have been examining a wide range of ideas that can further strengthen the financial system and get lending going again to support the broader economy. First and foremost, because the system remains fragile, we must continue to stand ready to prevent systemic failures. That is the basis for Monday's action to purchase preferred shares in AIG. The stability of our system remains the highest priority.

We must also allow markets and institutions to absorb the extensive array of new policies put in place in a very short period of time. The injection of up to $250 billion of capital into individual banks, the FDIC's temporary guarantee of bank debt and the Federal Reserve's multiple liquidity facilities for banks, money funds and commercial paper issuers have all significantly enhanced liquidity and helped improve market conditions.

Priorities for Remaining TARP Funds

We have evaluated options for most effectively deploying the remaining TARP funds, and have identified three critical priorities. First, we must continue to reinforce the stability of the financial system, so that banks and other institutions critical to the provision of credit are able to support economic recovery and growth. Although the financial system has stabilized, both banks and non-banks may well need more capital given their troubled asset holdings, projections for continued high rates of foreclosures and stagnant U.S. and world economic conditions. Second, the important markets for securitizing credit outside of the banking system also need support. Approximately 40 percent of U.S. consumer credit is provided through securitization of credit card receivables, auto loans and student loans and similar products. This market, which is vital for lending and growth, has for all practical purposes ground to a halt. Addressing these two priorities will have powerful impacts on the overall financial system, the strength of our financial institutions and the availability of consumer credit. Third, we continue to explore ways to reduce the risk of foreclosure.

Over these past weeks we have continued to examine the relative benefits of purchasing illiquid mortgage-related assets. Our assessment at this time is that this is not the most effective way to use TARP funds, but we will continue to examine whether targeted forms of asset purchase can play a useful role, relative to other potential uses of TARP resources, in helping to strengthen our financial system and support lending. But other strategies I will outline will help to alleviate the pressure of illiquid assets.

FURTHER STRATEGIES

First, we are designing further strategies for building capital in financial institutions. Stronger capital positions will enable financial institutions to better manage the illiquid assets on their books and better ensure that they remain healthy. Any future program should maintain our principle of encouraging participation of healthy institutions while protecting taxpayers. We are carefully evaluating programs which would further leverage the impact of a TARP investment by attracting private capital, potentially through matching investments. In developing a potential matching program, we will also consider capital needs of non-bank financial institutions not eligible for the current capital program; broadening access in this way would bring both benefits and challenges. Non-bank financial institutions provide credit that is essential to U.S. businesses and consumers. However, many are not directly regulated and are active in a wide range of businesses, and taxpayer protections in a program of this sort would be more difficult to achieve. Also before embarking on a second capital purchase program, the first one must be completed, and we have to assess its impact and use this information to evaluate the size and focus of an additional program in light of existing economic and market conditions.

Second, we are examining strategies to support consumer access to credit outside the banking system. To date, Fed, FDIC and Treasury programs have been targeted at our banking system, and the non-bank consumer finance sector continues to face difficult funding issues. Specifically, the asset-backed securitization market has played a critical role for many years in lowering the cost and increasing the availability of consumer finance. This market is currently in distress, costs of funding have skyrocketed and new issue activity has come to a halt. Today, the illiquidity in this sector is raising the cost and reducing the availability of car loans, student loans and credit cards. This is creating a heavy burden on the American people and reducing the number of jobs in our economy. With the Federal Reserve we are exploring the development of a potential liquidity facility for highly-rated AAA asset-backed securities. We are looking at ways to possibly use the TARP to encourage private investors to come back to this troubled market, by providing them access to federal financing while protecting the taxpayers' investment. By doing so, we can lower costs and increase credit availability for consumers. Addressing the needs of the securitization sector will help get lending going again, helping consumers and supporting the U.S. economy. While this securitization effort is targeted at consumer financing, the program we are evaluating may also be used to support new commercial and residential mortgage-backed securities lending.

Third, we are examining strategies to mitigate mortgage foreclosures. In crafting the financial rescue package, we and the Congress agreed that Treasury would use its leverage as a major purchaser of troubled mortgages to work with servicers and achieve more aggressive mortgage modification standards. Now that we are not planning to purchase illiquid mortgage assets, we must find another way to meet that commitment.

FDIC Chairman Bair has given us a model, in the mortgage modification protocol she developed with IndyMac Bank. Through the end of October, the FDIC has completed loan modifications for 3,500 borrowers, with several thousand more modifications currently being processed. These modifications have reduced payments for participating homeowners by an average of $380 month, or about 23 percent. We have worked with the FHFA, the GSEs, HUD and the Hope Now alliance who yesterday announced a streamlined industry-wide modification program that for the first time adopts an explicit affordability target similar to the model pioneered at IndyMac. With this commitment, the GSEs and large portfolio investors are setting a new industry standard for foreclosure mitigation. Potentially hundreds of thousands more struggling borrowers will be enabled to stay in their homes at an affordable monthly mortgage payment.

Beyond these efforts, there has been significant work to design and evaluate a number of proposals to induce further modifications. Each of these would, however, require substantial government subsidies. The FDIC, for example, has developed a proposal that Treasury and others in the Administration continue to discuss. I believe it is an important idea. As we evaluate the merits of any new proposal, we also will have to identify and justify the means to finance it. We must be careful to distinguish this type of assistance, which essentially involves direct spending, from the type of investments that are intended to promote financial stability, protect the taxpayer, and be recovered under the TARP legislation. Maximizing loan modifications, nonetheless, is a key part of working through the housing correction and maintaining the quality of communities across the nation, and we will continue working hard to make progress here.

We will continue to pursue the three strategies I have just outlined: how best to strengthen the capital base of our financial system; how best to support the asset-backed securitization market that is critical to consumer finance, and how to increase foreclosure mitigation efforts. All of these strategies are important, but ensuring the financial system has sufficient capital is essential to getting credit flowing to consumers and businesses and that is where the bulk of the remaining TARP funds should be deployed --- in a program to support the system and as a contingency reserve for addressing any unforeseen systemic events.

We are focused on developing and preparing programs which can be implemented for each of these strategies. We will continue to brief President-elect Obama's transition team on all of these issues.

Global Challenge

Of course managing through this market turmoil while mitigating the impact of the credit crisis is a global as well as a national issue. We in the U.S. are well aware and humbled by our own failings and recognize our special responsibility to the global economy. The U.S. housing correction exposed gaping shortcomings in the outdated U.S. regulatory system, shortcomings in other regulatory regimes and excesses in U.S. and European financial institutions. These institutions found themselves with large holdings of structured products, including complex and opaque mortgage-backed securities. Some European institutions were characterized by high leverage, exposure to their own housing markets, exposure to Central European institutions, weak business models or overly aggressive expansion, while others faced weaknesses because of inadequate depositor protection systems. It should not be surprising that after 13 months of stress in the global capital markets, banks from the U.S. to the U.K., from Germany to Iceland, from Russia to France, had difficulties that exposed some of these weaknesses for the first time. For some of these banks, this proved to be a hurdle too high and government action was necessary to support financial stability.

In that regard the G7 Finance Ministers meeting last month represented a major turning point in stabilizing the global financial system as the ministers came together to support a number of powerful strategies that were soon turned into effective actions in the United States and Europe. It is also clear that our first priority must be recovery and repair. And of course we must take strong actions to fix our system so that the world does not have to suffer something like this ever again. The Leaders summit President Bush will be hosting this weekend marks a very important step in what will be an ongoing process of recovery and reform.

And to adequately reform our system, we must make sure we fully understand the nature of the problem which will not be possible until we are confident it is behind us. Of course, it is already clear that we must address a number of significant issues, such as improving risk management practices, compensation practices, oversight of mortgage origination and the securitization process, credit rating agencies, OTC derivative market infrastructure and regulatory policies, practices and regimes in our respective countries. And we recognize that our financial institutions and our markets are global, but our regulatory regimes are national, so we will examine how best to improve cooperation and information sharing to foster global financial system stability.

But let us not forget one fundamental issue which lies at the heart of our problems. Over a period of years, persistent and growing global imbalances fueled a dramatic increase in capital flows, low interest rates, excessive risk taking and a global search for return. Those excesses cannot be attributed to any single nation. There is no doubt that low U.S. savings are a significant factor, but the lack of consumption and accumulation of reserves in Asia and oil-exporting countries and structural issues in Europe have also fed the imbalances.

If we only address particular regulatory issues – as critical as they are – without addressing the global imbalances that fueled recent excesses, we will have missed an opportunity to dramatically improve the foundation for global markets and economic vitality going forward. The pressure from global imbalances will simply build up again until it finds another outlet.

The nations attending this weekend's summit represent the 20 largest economies in the world – over 77 percent of global GDP. President Bush is convening this group of countries to discuss and address problems such as global imbalances, making regulatory regimes more effective, fostering cooperation among regulators, and reforming international institutions to better address today's global economy. We can't simply task the IMF, the FSF or other International Financial Institutions to solve the problems, unless member nations all see that they have a shared interest in a solution. There are no easy answers, because until we reach a consensus on a broad-based reform agenda, we will not reach a solution. This weekend provides an opportunity for nations to take an important step, but only one step, on the necessary path to reform.

CONCLUSION

The road ahead, for the U.S. economy and the global economy, is full of challenges. And it will take strong leadership to address them. I am confident the United States, under this and the next Administration, will rise to these challenges. I will do everything I can to put us on the right path, both by working diligently through the end of my term and by working closely to ensure the smoothest possible transition.

In: Government Interventions in Economic Emergencies ISBN: 978-1-60741-356-1
Editor: Pablo Sastre

Chapter 19

PROPOSAL TO ALLOW TREASURY TO BUY MORTGAGE-RELATED ASSETS TO ADDRESS FINANCIAL INSTABILITY

Edward V. Murphy and Baird Webel

SUMMARY

Financial markets underwent severe stress during the week of September 15-22, 2008. After Lehman Brothers declared bankruptcy and AIG received a bridge loan from the Federal Reserve, policymakers reassessed their case-by-case approach to resolving financial problems. Secretary of the Treasury Paulson announced a plan to allow Treasury to purchase mortgage-related assets from U.S. financial institutions. The announced intent of the plan is to unclog financial markets, increase the health of the banking sector, and reduce ongoing risks to the economy. This chapter discusses a draft of the proposal as it stood on September 21, 2008, and analyzes frequently asked questions.

Following a week of severe stress in financial markets, the Secretary of the Treasury and the Chairman of the Federal Reserve met with congressional leaders on September 19, 2008, to ask for legislation to authorize direct intervention in the economy. An unofficial three-page draft of a specific proposal circulated over the weekend of September 20, 2008.[1] A revised draft circulated September 21. Both draft proposals allow Treasury to purchase up to $700 billion in mortgage-related assets in an attempt to reduce disruptions in the financial system. This chapter describes the provisions of the draft legislative proposals that were circulated and provides an analysis of several questions that the proposals raise.

THE DRAFT PROPOSALS

Purchase of Mortgage-Related Assets

The proposal grants Treasury the authority to purchase mortgage-related assets for two years. The proposal would limit the amount of assets purchased to $700 billion outstanding at any one time. Funding for the purchases comes from selling Treasury securities. The Secretary of the Treasury is granted discretion to administer the program, and decisions by the Secretary would not be reviewable in court or by any administrative agency.

Debt Limit

Both draft proposals increase the debt limit of the federal government. The new debt limit in each draft is $11,315,000,000,000. This $11.3 trillion new limit compares to the current debt limit of $10.6 trillion. The total current debt is $9.6 trillion. If the full authority of the program were immediately exercised and funded exclusively with new debt, and there were no additional new debt from existing government operations, the current debt would rise to $10.3 trillion.

Definition of Troubled Asset

The September 20 draft defines mortgage-related assets as "residential or commercial mortgages and any securities, obligations, or other instruments that are based on or related to such mortgages, that in each case was issued on or before September 17, 2008."

The September 21 draft defines troubled assets in the same way but adds a clause allowing the Secretary of the Treasury in consultation with the Chairman of the Federal Reserve to add any other financial instrument, "the purchase of which the Secretary determines necessary to promote financial market stability."

These definitions could encompass whole mortgage loans, mortgage-backed securities (MBS), and subordinated mortgage securities such as collateralized debt obligations (CDOs) or collateralized mortgage obligations (CMOs). It is unclear whether the September 20 definition also encompasses derivatives that reference the defaults of underlying mortgages in MBS such as certain credit default swaps (CD S). The September 21 draft would allow the purchase of credit default swaps if the Chairman of the Federal Reserve agreed. It is unclear whether the Secretary of the Treasury could purchase CDS without Federal Reserve consultation under the September 21 language.

Authority to Take Action

Using the term "necessary actions," the draft proposals grant authority to administer the program and place certain limits on participation. Treasury may employ personnel, contract for services, and issue appropriate definitions, regulations, and guidances. Treasury may designate financial institutions as financial agents of the government. Treasury may also establish vehicles authorized to purchase mortgage-related assets and issue obligations. The administrative vehicles could encompass trusts or corporations to administer the assets. The September 21 draft also includes a provision to apply Federal Acquisition Regulation when awarding contracts to asset managers and requires the asset managers to acknowledge a fiduciary duty to the United States.

Restrictions

The draft proposals include two significant restrictions. First, purchased assets must have been originated or issued before September 17, 2008. Furthermore, the seller of the asset to the Treasury is limited to "any financial institution having its headquarters in the United States." Under the September 20 draft proposal, it is unclear whether U.S. affiliates of foreign institutions would be included. Similarly, it is unclear whether there are restrictions on the ability of U.S. institutions to serve as intermediaries, buying mortgage assets from foreign institutions and then selling them to Treasury.

Under the September 21 draft proposal, foreign central banks and institutions owned by foreign governments are specifically excluded. This draft directs the Treasury to coordinate with foreign financial authorities to work to establish similar authorities overseas and to coordinate activities.

Factors to Guide Intervention

The draft proposals listed two factors for Treasury to consider when exercising authority under the program. First, Treasury shall consider means for "providing stability or preventing disruption to the financial markets or banking system." The proposal does not provide a definition for the terms stability, disruption, financial market, or banking system. Second, Treasury shall consider means for "protecting the taxpayer." Protection is not defined.

Management of Mortgage-Related Assets

Treasury is given authority to manage the mortgage-related assets acquired through the program. Management includes exercising any rights acquired through purchase (presumably including any rights regarding foreclosure in the case of whole loans). Rights of management of assets acquired before the termination of the program extends beyond the termination date; that is, Treasury can continue to hold acquired mortgage assets after the expiration of authority to acquire new mortgage-related assets. Treasury may also manage the mortgage revenues and any portfolio risk of the program.

Loss Mitigation and Loan Modification

The September 20 draft did not contain any provisions for loss mitigation or loan modification of mortgage loans. The September 21 draft contains two provisions to address troubled borrowers. First, for whole mortgage loans acquired by Treasury, loan servicers must follow industry best practices for loan modifications. Best practices are identified by the Secretary in consultation with the Hope for Homeowners Oversight Board. Second, if the program acquires MBS or similar assets that put the government in the position of one of the investors with an interest in an underlying mortgage, then the government will consent to reasonable loan modifications.

Sunset

Authority to purchase mortgage-related assets under the program expires two years from the date of enactment. Recall that authority to manage already acquired mortgage-related assets continues after the sunset provision.

Reports to Congress

The Secretary of the Treasury must report to congressional committees with respect to authority exercised under the program. The first report is required within three months of first exercise of authority, and reports continue semiannually thereafter. The committees to report to include the Committee on the Budget, Financial Services, and Ways and Means of the House of Representatives and the Committees on the Budget, Finance, and Banking, Housing, and Urban Affairs of the Senate. The September 21 draft also requires a GAO study on the impact of troubled asset purchases.

Frequently Asked Questions

Does the Proposal Include Provisions to Help Home Owners Facing Foreclosure?

The September 20 draft proposal did not include any provisions specifically designed to help home owners facing foreclosure. The September 21 draft requires loan servicers to follow industry best practices and to modify loans in accordance with the Hope for Homeowners Oversight Board.

Proponents of such measures might argue that actions to unfreeze mortgage markets will help liquidity flow back into mortgage markets, which in turn might make it easier for borrowers to refinance out of troubled mortgages or sell their homes to avoid foreclosure. Critics might counter that this is a relatively expensive and indirect way to aid troubled mortgage borrowers.

Is the Program Limited to Home Mortgages?

No. The program also includes securities based on residential mortgages. It is unclear whether the program applies to derivatives that reference mortgage-related securities. In addition to residential mortgages, the draft proposals also include commercial mortgages and related assets.

What Price Will Treasury Pay for the Assets It Purchases?

The proposal leaves the price to the discretion of the Secretary of the Treasury. A press release states that the price of assets purchased will be established through market mechanisms where possible, such as through reverse auctions.[2]

What Happens to Funds the Treasury Receives from Disposing of the Assets?

Treasury's press release reports that returns from the sale of assets will be returned to Treasury's general fund for the benefit of taxpayers.

What Is the Potential Cost of Bad Mortgage-Related Debt?

The answer to this question depends in large part on real estate markets. On the residential side, if house prices continue to decline, then the number of home owners who cannot sell or refinance to avoid foreclosure will continue to rise. The performance of commercial mortgages going forward will be affected by developments in the broader economy. If a deep recession is avoided, then commercial mortgage defaults may be minimized.

The program appears to be targeted at the troubled mortgage-related assets that are burdening bank balance sheets. If this is the case, then certain categories of securities may be more likely to be acquired than others. For example, because of the explicit Treasury guarantees associated with the conservatorship of Fannie Mae and Freddie Mac, their securities (called agency debt and agency MBS) should be of less immediate concern. This suggests that the problem assets are more likely to be in the non-agency sector. According to one industry source,[3] the estimate of outstanding non-agency MBS was $1.3 trillion at the end of 2007, with another $25 billion issued in 2008. There was also another $1.3 trillion in outstanding collateralized mortgage obligations. Thus, the total amount of mortgage-related assets that might be acquired by the program would be nearly four times the $700 billion limit in the proposal.

The above estimate does not include any direct purchases of whole mortgage loans or derivatives that reference the mortgage-related assets. However, it might be double counting to include both the mortgage-related securities and the underlying mortgages or referenced derivatives. If issues with the underlying mortgages are resolved, then any mortgage-backed security or derivative that references those mortgages would not be in default.

What Role Did Housing Play in Financial Turmoil?

Several factors have contributed to financial instability, but most observers agree that a major component of the financial stress has been the boom and bust in housing that coincided with low short- term interest rates. It has been argued that rapid house price appreciation in some areas and low interest rates led to overconfidence by investors, lenders, borrowers, and regulators. Builders responded to higher prices with increased construction, and the pace of home price increases could not be sustained. Inventories of unsold homes began climbing and prices stagnated at the same time as short-term interest rates began rising. Any borrowers, including in the subprime market, who had depended on being able to refinance at low interest rates or depended on rapid home price appreciation found their plans frustrated and defaults occurred at increasing rates. The value of financial assets that depended on home owners making their payments, such as mortgage-backed securities (MBS), declined significantly.

How Did Financial Markets Magnify the Effects of Mortgage Defaults?

Three factors in the financial system magnified the effects of defaults by reducing confidence, particularly in bank balance sheets.

(1) Lack of transparency — The financial structures used to fund mortgages had become very complex, making it harder for firms to assess the value of assets or the condition of potential counterparties.

(2) Leverage — Because financial firms had very little capital relative to their commitments, even small percentage declines in the value of their mortgage assets could significantly impair their solvency. Combined with poor transparency, this further contributed to caution on the part of counterparties in financial transactions.

(3) Derivatives — Increased use of complex derivatives, such as credit default swaps, made it very difficult to project how the failure of a financial firm would affect other firms. Would counterparties to derivatives contracts have the reserves to fulfill their obligations? If not, would the marking down of derivative values cause a new round of de-leveraging?

How, If At All, Could Financial Turmoil Affect the Wider Economy If Nothing Is Done?

There are several sectors of the economy that depend on regular financing to operate. Also, consumers frequently depend on financing to purchase expensive items. Therefore, disruptions to the financial system can cause problems for business investment and consumer expenditures on durable goods. In addition, declines in the value of assets linked to finance, such as houses and retirement accounts, cause consumers to feel poorer and to cut back spending.

How, If At All, Could Intervention in Mortgage-Related Securities Markets Calm Financial Markets?

An intervention in financial markets could restore financial stability if it restores confidence. Removing bad debt from bank balance sheets directly addresses several problems. Shortcomings in transparency become a less pressing concern for institutions that can participate because counterparties would know that the institution has the opportunity to clean up its balance sheet. Similarly, the program may provide an orderly way to resolve derivatives contracts.

What Is the Rationale for Acting Now?

According to a press release from the Treasury, illiquid mortgage-related assets had clogged the financial system.[4] The juxtaposition of the refusal to intervene on behalf of Lehman Brothers the same week that a bridge loan was extended to AIG has convinced some that the case-by-case approach of recent weeks should be replaced by a more broadly based intervention. In addition, the sudden spike in interest rate spreads and declines in financial activity following the AIG intervention convinced some policymakers that financial fragilities could worsen if they are not addressed.

How Did Interest Rate Spreads Indicate A Sudden Loss of Confidence?

"Spreads" often refers to the difference between a particular interest rate and the yield of a Treasury security of comparable maturity (although there are other spreads). So defined, high spreads are often an indicator that people believe the Treasury security to be less risky than the other asset (although there can be other reasons for widening spreads.) Although the Federal Reserve had lowered policy interest rates to 2% by April 2008, other interest rates remained relatively high. Examples include the interest rate that banks charge each other, the interest rate on asset-backed commercial paper, and mortgage rates. The Federal Housing Finance Agency (FHFA) indicated that the high spreads on Fannie and Freddie securities were a significant factor in the decision to put the companies into conservatorship. Then, during the week of September 15-20, following the Lehman Brothers bankruptcy and the loan to AIG, the spread on commercial paper almost tripled in a single day, and prompting concern that the entire financial system could shut down.

Couldn't the Same Assets Be Purchased through Fannie Mae and Freddie Mac Now That They Are in a Conservatorship Backed by the Treasury?

Only parts of the proposal could be implemented through Fannie Mae and Freddie Mac. First, the charters of Fannie Mae and Freddie Mac do not allow them to acquire commercial mortgages. Second, some of the delinquent mortgages that contribute to the problem are jumbo loans in California (jumbo refers to mortgages too large to be purchased by Fannie

Mae and Freddie Mac). However, Fannie Mae and Freddie Mac could acquire residential MBS that conform to their new higher loan limits. Operating a troubled MBS and mortgage purchase program through Fannie Mae and Freddie Mac would have a similar result as under the new proposal because Treasury is already committed to purchase preferred stock to maintain the solvency of the institutions.

End Notes

[1] This report is based on a draft acquired via email from CongressNow Alert. "Alert: Bush Administration Financial Plan," *CongressNow*, September 20, 2008, 10:21 a.m. CongressNow is a Roll Call Group Business and distributed the alert through emails@congressnow.com.

[2] "Statement by Secretary Henry M. Paulson, Jr. on Comprehensive Approach to Market Developments," Press Release, Department of Treasury, September 19, 2008, available at [http://www.treas.gov/press 11 49.htm].

[3] Statistics from the Securities Industry and Financial Markets Association (SIFMA), available at [http://www.sifma.org/research/statistic s/market-sector-statistics.shtml#mbs].

[4] "Statement by Secretary Henry M. Paulson, Jr. on Comprehensive Approach to Market Developments," Press Release, Department of Treasury, September 19, 2008, available at [http://www.treas.gov/press 11 49.htm].

In: Government Interventions in Economic Emergencies
Editor: Pablo Sastre
ISBN: 978-1-60741-356-1

Chapter 20

The Resolution Trust Corporation: Historical Analysis

Gary Shorter

Summary

In a 1989 legislative response to financial troubles in the thrift industry, the Financial Institutions Reform, Recovery, and Enforcement Act of 1989 (FIRREA, P.L. 101-73) was enacted: FIRREA's principal mission was to conduct a partially tax-payer funded program to address the troubles of the nation's many insolvent thrifts. To do so, it established a new entity, the Resolution Trust Corporation (RTC), whose mission was to address troubled thrifts by arranging their sale to other institutions or shuttering them and disposing of their assets. The RTC would eventually obtain \$105 billion in funding but a major part of its principal funding came from an off-budget entity, the Resolution Funding Corporation (REFCORP). REFCORP was created by FIRREA as a publicprivate partnership, which acquired the funds that it would provide to the RTC through proceeds from its sale of U.S. Treasury bonds. During its years of operation, 1989 to 1995, the RTC was alternately criticized for dumping thrift assets and for taking too much time to dispose of them. It subsequently began selling block assets, it partnered with private entities in the joint ownership of some assets, and it issued securities backed by commercial mortgages. When shut down in 1995, the RTC had closed 747 insolvent thrifts and recovered about 85% of the value of the assets it had seized. Estimates vary but several observers cite direct and indirect governmental costs totaling about \$150 billion for the undertaking.

Introduction

Between the late 1970s and the mid-1980s, savings and loan institutions (thrifts) faced a constellation of developments that would challenge their financial viability. The developments included (1) high and volatile interest rates in the late 1970s and early 1980s, which increased the thrifts' interest rate risk;[1] (2) the phase out and elimination of the Federal

Reserve's Regulation Q (a regulation that had placed limits on the interest rates that banks and thrifts could pay), which encouraged the emergence of new instruments such as money market funds that hurt thrift industry profitability; (3) state and federal deregulation of depository institutions, which enabled thrifts to get involved in new but potentially riskier markets; and (4) reductions in regulatory capital requirements, which allowed thrifts to use alternative accounting procedures that increased their reported levels of capital.

Collectively, the developments had negative impact on the thrift industry: by 1986, 441 thrifts with $113 billion in assets were found to be insolvent.[2]

The Enactment of FIRREA and the Beginnings of the RTC

To help remedy the thrift industry's problems and restore the public's flagging confidence, Congress passed the Financial Institutions Reform, Recovery, and Enforcement Act of 1989 (FIRREA, P.L. 101-73). Enacted in August 1989, FIRREA's principal thrust was the creation of a program to close and clean up insolvent thrifts who collectively held billions of dollars in deposits insured at the time by the Federal Savings and Loan Insurance Corporation (FSLIC).[3]

The vehicle created by FIRREA to conduct the cleanup was the Resolution Trust Corporation (RTC). Principal funding for the RTC came from an off-budget entity, the Resolution Funding Corporation (REFCORP), a FIRREA-created public-private partnership, which was apart from but was operated by the Federal Home Loan Bank (FHLB) System, a federal entity that supplies credit reserves to thrift institutions (similar to what the Federal Reserve does for commercial banks). REFCORP issued about $30 billion in noncallable, zero coupon, 30 and 40 year U.S. Treasury bonds to fund the RTC, The interest payments on those bonds were largely funded by a FIRREA-directed annual payment of $300 million from the member banks of the FHLB and taxpayer dollars.[4]

In addition to the $30 billion from REFCORP, the RTC received $18.8 billion from the U.S. Treasury, and $1.2 billion from Federal Home Loan member banks, giving it a total of about $50 billion in initial funding. Subsequent legislation increased RTC's funding, which would eventually total about $105.1 billion.[5]

The Structure of the RTC

As directed by FIRREA, the board of directors of the Federal Deposit Insurance Corporation (FDIC) also assumed the role of the RTC's board. FIRREA also established an RTC Oversight Board whose mandate was to oversee the development of RTC policy. The Oversight Board also oversaw the RTC's budget, and monitored its use of taxpayer funds. The board, however, was not to be involved in detailed RTC operational issues, such as matters pertaining to individual transactions.

As specified by FIRREA, the Oversight Board had five members, three of whom were federal officials: the Secretary of the Treasury (who served as the board's chairman), the Chairman of the Federal Reserve Board, and the Secretary of Housing and Urban

Development. The two remaining members were nominated by the President and confirmed by the Senate.

In 1991, motivated by a number of issues, including the RTC's need for interim funding and concerns that its dual board structure was cumbersome and inefficient (for example, the Oversight Board had to approve policies recommended by the RTC/FDIC board), Congress passed the RTC Refinancing, Restructuring, and Improvement Act of 1991 (P.L. 102-233). Among other things, the law replaced the Oversight Board with what has been described as a more limited and less intrusive Thrift Depositor Protection Oversight Board (TDPO), which included the Secretary of the Treasury and the Chairman of the Federal Reserve Board but not the Secretary of Housing and Urban Development. The law also removed the FDIC's board from it role as the RTC's board; and it replaced the FDIC as the RTC's manager with the RTC's Chief Executive Officer (also was also a member of the TDPO).[6]

The process of closing or resolving individual thrifts involved one of three alternatives: (1) some thrifts were sold to a healthy acquirer, which involved the RTC paying another institution to buy the insolvent thrift, with most of its assets intact; (2) some thrifts were to be shut down with their depositors being paid off and with the RTC retaining all of its assets for later sale; and (3) some thrifts were shut down with their deposits being transferred to another institution. Because deposits are liabilities (they represent claims on the institution by depositors), the RTC was required to pay the institution receiving the deposits. But because the expected value to the new firms of the customers who owned the deposits often exceeded the face value of the deposits, the RTC frequently paid less than face value for the depository accounts.

The assets that the RTC controlled for thrifts in conservatorship or for thrifts in the later receivership phase took a variety of forms, including cash, mortgages, loans, securities (including some below-investment grade securities known as junk bonds), land, commercial properties, and houses. FIRREA required the RTC to utilize the services of private-sector companies in managing and disposing of assets whenever possible.

Initially, the agency faced significant criticism that it was not resolving failed thrifts at a rate that kept pace with the growing number of thrifts in conservatorship. The RTC responded to the criticism with a concerted effort to resolve troubled thrifts at a faster rate. That effort, however, added greatly to the agency's collection of assets, especially problem assets. Soon, concerns over the pitfalls of dumping assets with often little regard for the low values they fetched were superseded by concerns, including some from members of Congress, that a faster approach to asset disposal was needed if the agency was going to complete its mission.[7]

In mid-1990, the agency began conducting bulk sales of packaged assets, a contrast to its initial approach of selling assets one by one. Although the bulk sale strategy was criticized for fostering a lack of competition among bidders (including the provision of "sweetheart deals" to some large investors), possibly lowering asset sale prices due to discounts and thus undermining some real estate markets, the criticism was overshadowed by the agency's need to rid itself of assets.[8]

In some of its auctions[9] of non-performing loans, the RTC packaged assets by product, geographic location and collateral type, some packages being as small as a few thousand dollars, others in the tens of millions, with average packages running between $3 million and $4 million.[10] Other bulk packages were less diversified and very asset-specific, consisting of single-property types such as hotels or motels.[11]

Equity Partnerships

At times, however, the bulk asset sales faced market pricing that was considerably less than the agency desired. To help address such shortcomings, the agency pioneered "equity partnerships" to help liquidate some of the packages of its real estate and financial assets. While the strategy employed a number of different structures, all of the equity partnerships involved a private sector partner acquiring a partial interest in a pool of assets, controlling the management and sale of the assets in the pool, and making distributions to the RTC based on the RTC's retained equity interest.[12]

Commercial Mortgages and Securitization

The RTC is widely regarded as a pioneer in the securitization of complex securitized instruments backed by commercial and multi-family loans, commercial mortgage-backed securities (CMBS), which constituted a significant share of the agency's assets. Initially, the CMBS were reportedly difficult to sell due in part to the fact that the huge losses that had occurred in the value of commercial mortgages was a major factor in the thrifts' troubles. Eventually, however, sales of the CMBS reportedly became quite healthy, and the innovative approach to asset disposal would later earn the RTC praise.[13]

CONCLUSION

The RTC Completion Act of 1993 (P.L. 103-204) terminated the RTC as of December 31, 1995. All of its remaining assets, liabilities, and duties were transferred to the FDIC.

In the end, the RTC orchestrated the closing of 747 thrifts, more than 25% of the industry. It was also responsible for selling more than $450 billion of their real estate and disposing of 95% of their overall assets with a recovery rate of more than 85%.[14]

Estimates of the direct and indirect cost of the entire RTC thrift resolution process have ranged from $100 billion to as high as $500 billion, with the most widely and recently reported estimate in the area of $150 billion (the majority being taxpayer financed),[15] an amount said to be below original estimates.[16]

End Notes

[1] Interest rate risk is the risk that an investment's value will change due to a change in the absolute level of the interest rates.

[2] Timothy Curry and Lynn Shibut, "The Cost of the Savings and Loan Crisis: Truth and Consequences," *FDIC Banking Review*, December 2000, pp. 26-28.

[3] Abolished by FIRREA, the Federal Savings and Loan Insurance Corporation formerly administered deposit insurance for savings and loan institutions, which FIRREA transferred to the Federal Deposit Insurance Corporation.

[4] "Proposed Rule," *Federal Register*, vol. 65, no. 24, February 4, 2000, p. 5448; and Carl Horowitz, "The Continuing Thrift Bailout," *Investor's Business Daily*, February 1, 1996.

[5] For example, the RTC Completion Act of 1993 (P.L. 103-204) enabled the RTC to continue to fund its operations. In its first few years, a number of members of Congress grew disenchanted with the RTC's performance and

recommended that it be significantly overhauled. For example, in 1991, the Hon. Frank Annunzio recommended completely eliminating the RTC and replacing it with a private sector program. Lee Davison, "The Resolution Trust Corporation and Congress: 1989-1993, Part II," *Federal Deposit Insurance Corporation's Banking Review*, vol. 18, no. 3, 2006.

[6] David S. Holland, *When Regulation was Too Successful — the Sixth Decade of Deposit Insurance: A History of the Troubles of the U.S. Banking Industry in the 1980s and Early 1990s*, New York: Greenwood Publishing Group, 1998, p. 81.

[7] Lee Davison, "The Resolution Trust Corporation and Congress, 1989-1993 Part I: 1989-1990," *FDIC Banking Review*, vol. 18, no, 2, 2006, pp. 38-42.

[8] Ibid., pp. 38-39.

[9] The RTC made widespread use of auctions, both sealed-bid auctions, in which bidders proffer bids sealed in an envelope and "open-outcry" auctions using auctioneers who set up auction sites that were often near the location of the assets. Some observers suggest that the agency lent groundbreaking legitimacy to the notion of asset auctions.

[10] Jeffrey Marshall, "Learning from the RTC," *United States Banker,* vol. 103, iss. 9, pp. 28-32.

[11] Ibid, pp. 29-30.

[12] An example was the RTC's partnership with Colony Capital of Los Angeles, which invested in the RTC's National Land Fund and became a joint-venture partner. The Colony pool had 119 assets with a book value of $480 million largely in finished residential lots. Colony put up 25% of the purchase price and became the managing general partner; the RTC was a passive limited partner getting 75% of the cash flow as the assets were sold to a point when the total reached the agency's "original imputed contribution." After that point, Colony's equity share rose to 50%.

[13] George Alexander and Tom Rayburn, "FDIC Closes the Books on RTC Securitization Program," *CMBS World*, Winter 2005, pp. 50-52.

[14] Frederick Mishkin and Stanley Eakins, *Financial Markets and Institutions*, Addison Wesley Longman, 2000, p. 498.

[15] For example, see Curry and Shibut, "The Cost of the Savings and Loan Crisis: Truth and Consequences," p. 26, and Mishkin and Stanley Eakins, *Financial Markets and Institutions*, p. 498.

[16] Jerry W. Markham, *A Financial History of the United States*, M.E. Sharpe, 2002, p. 173.

In: Government Interventions in Economic Emergencies ISBN: 978-1-60741-356-1
Editor: Pablo Sastre

Chapter 21

ECONOMIC SLOWDOWN: ISSUES AND POLICIES

Jane G. Gravelle, Thomas L. Hungerford, Marc Labonte, N. Eric Weiss and Julie M. Whittaker

SUMMARY

Recent policies have sought to contain damages spilling over from housing and financial markets to the broader economy, including monetary policy, the responsibility of the Federal Reserve, and fiscal policy. Legislators and the President adopted an economic stimulus package (P.L. 110-185) on February 13. Another stimulus package, H.R. 7110, has passed the House. Over the past few months, the government has also intervened in specific financial markets, including financial assistance to troubled firms. Legislation authorizing a massive intervention in financial markets was adopted on October 3 (P.L. 110-343); it includes authority to purchase $700 billion in troubled assets. In addition, the Fed has lent directly to financial institutions through an array of new facilities, and the amounts of loans outstanding have risen into the hundreds of billions of dollars. President-Elect Obama has proposed a much larger stimulus package than that in H.R. 7110.

The estimated budget cost of the stimulus enacted in February was about $150 billion for FY2008. The largest provision (in terms of budgetary cost) was a tax rebate for individuals. The Senate committee bill also included an extension in unemployment compensation benefits; the Iraq/Afghanistan supplemental appropriations completed June 26 included a 13-week extension, signed on June 30. The current stimulus proposal would increase spending on infrastructure, unemployment benefits, Medicaid, and food stamps by $50 to $60 billion; unemployment was extended by an additional seven weeks on November 21, 2008.

The need for additional fiscal stimulus depends on the state of the economy. The National Bureau of Economic Research (NBER) has declared the economy in recession since December 2007. Growth rates, after two strong quarters, were negative in the fourth quarter of 2007, positive in the first and second quarters of 2008, and a negative 0.5% in the third quarter. According to one data series, employment fell in every month of 2008. The unemployment rate, which rose slightly in the last half of 2007, declined in January and February of 2008, but began rising in March and in November stood at 6.7%. Some forecasters believe that the ongoing financial turmoil will result in a recession that is deeper and longer than average.

Fiscal policy temporarily stimulates the economy through an increase in the budget deficit. There is a consensus that proposals that result in more spending, can be implemented quickly, and leave no long-term effect on the budget deficit would increase the benefits and reduce the costs of fiscal stimulus. Economists generally agree that spending proposals are somewhat more stimulative than tax cuts since part of a tax cut will be saved by the recipients. The most important determinant of the effect on the economy is its size. The recent stimulus package increased the deficit by about 1% of GDP.

The broad intervention into the financial markets has been passed to avoid the spread of financial instability into the broader market but there are disadvantages, including leaving the government holding large amounts of mortgage debt.

The National Bureau of Economic Research (NBER) has declared the U.S. economy in recession since December of 2007. Numerous actions have already been taken and continue to be considered to contain damages spilling over from housing and financial markets to the broader economy. These policies include traditional monetary and fiscal policy, as well as broader interventions into the financial sector.

Earlier in the year, in response to weaker economic growth, legislators and the Administration proposed economic stimulus packages. After negotiations with the Administration, the Recovery Rebates and Economic Stimulus for the American People Act of 2008 (H.R. 5140) was introduced by Speaker Pelosi and passed by the House on January 29. On January 30, the Senate Committee on Finance reported the Economic Stimulus Act of 2008, which contained provisions not included in the House bill. On February 7, the Senate adopted the House bill with added rebates for retirees and the House adopted the revised bill. On February 13, the bill was signed into law as P.L. 110-185.

Some proposals discussed but not adopted in that package might be considered in a second stimulus bill. At this point the scope of a second proposal remains uncertain. A provision that was considered (but not enacted) in the February stimulus bill and that might be considered in a second was a 26-week extension of unemployment benefits. The Iraq/Afghanistan supplemental appropriations, adopted by Congress on June 26 and signed by the President on June 30 as P.L. 110-252, extended benefits for 13 weeks. A second stimulus plan (H.R. 7110) passed the House on September 26 and included \$36.9 billion on infrastructure (\$12.8 billion highway and bridge, \$7.5 billion water and sewer, \$5 billion Corps of Engineers); \$6.5 billion in extended unemployment compensation, and \$14.5 billion in Medicaid, and \$2.7 billion in food stamp and nutrition programs. On October 3, the House passed the Unemployment Compensation Extension Act of 2008 (H.R. 6867), which would provide extended unemployment benefits. Congress adopted an extension of unemployment compensation in a lame-duck session in November but did not adopt a general stimulus.

Financial market conditions worsened significantly in September 2008. Although the real production of goods and services has so far showed unexpected resilience since financial turmoil began in August of 2007, the ability of private borrowers to access credit markets remained restricted throughout the year. Evidence of a credit crunch was seen in the persistence of wide spreads between the interest rates that private borrowers paid for credit and the yields on Treasury securities of comparable maturity. One indication of restricted credit despite stimulative Federal Reserve monetary policy was the failure of mortgage rates to fall significantly. Instead, the spread between Treasuries and Government Sponsored

Enterprise (GSE) bonds remained elevated over the summer. The newly created Federal Housing Finance Agency (FHFA) cited the persistence of this wide spread as a major factor in its decision to place the GSEs in conservatorship in September. During the week of September 15-19, financial markets were further disturbed by the bankruptcy of investment bank Lehman Brothers and Federal Reserve intervention on behalf of the insurer AIG. These actions eroded market confidence further, resulting in a sudden spike of the commercial paper rate spread from just under 90 basis points to 280 basis points, a spike that in times past might have been called a panic. If financial market confidence is not restored and private market spreads remain elevated, the broader economy could slow due to difficulties in financing consumer durables, business investment, college education, and other big ticket items.

On September 18, Administration and Federal Reserve officials with the bipartisan support of the Congressional leadership, announced a massive intervention in the financial markets, requesting authority to purchase up to $700 billion in assets over the next two years. The Treasury has also provided insurance for money market funds, where withdrawals have been significant. Congressional leaders and other Members raised a number of issues and made some additional proposals, which included setting up an oversight mechanism, restrictions on executive compensation of firms from which assets are purchased, acquiring equity stakes in the participating firms, and allowing judges to reduce mortgage debt in bankruptcies (not included in the final Act).

A tentative agreement announced September 26 by the Senate Banking Committee and the House Financial Services Committee would allow an initial $250 billion of financing with an additional $100 billion upon certification of need, with Congress allowed 30 days to object to the final $350 billion. The plan would have oversight by an Inspector General, audit by the Governmental Accountability Office, setting standards of appropriate compensation, and providing for equity positions in all participating companies. A final proposal, H.R. 3997, which termed the program the Troubled Asset Relief Program (TARP) also included an oversight board and options for firms to purchase insurance, failed to pass in the House. A second bill (H.R. 1424) that preserved the central elements of the failed proposal but added an expansion of deposit insurance coverage was passed by the Senate on October 1, by the House on October 3, and signed into law as P.L. 110-343. There are, however, concerns about how to price acquired assets in a way that balances protection of taxpayers with providing adequate assistance to firms. The Treasury had indicated use of a reverse auction mechanism to purchase mortgage backed securities, where companies will bid to sell their assets. It is not clear how well such an auction would work with heterogeneous assets.[1]

The Treasury subsequently announced that it will use the first $250 billion authorized to purchase preferred stock in financial institutions and has now indicated it will use the funds for capital injections, consumer credit (such as auto loans, student loans and credit cards) and mortgage assistance.[2] Congressional leaders have urged Treasury to provide $25 billion in aid to U.S. auto manufacturers but according to news reports opposition by the administration and congressional Republicans make that unlikely.[3] On November 10 a restructuring of government assistance to AIG was announced which increased the amount at risk from $143.7 billion to $173.[4] billion, extended the loan length and reduced the interest rate. The Federal Reserve also announced on October 14 that it would begin purchasing commercial paper.[4] News reports also indicate the Federal Deposit Insurance Corporations (FDIC) has a plan, supported by congressional Democrats, to offer financial incentives to companies that agree to reduce monthly mortgage payments, but that this plan is opposed by the Bush administration.[5] On November 23, the government announced a plan to assist Citicorp, and on November 25 the Federal Reserve indicated plans to purchase $200 billion in asset backed securities through the Term Asset-Backed Securities Loan Facility (TALF); these securities are based on auto, credit card, student and small business loans. The Federal Reserve also announced a plan to purchase $600 billion of mortgage related securities owned or guaranteed by the housing GSEs.

Much of the intervention up to this point has been in the financial markets. However, the big three U.S. automakers (GM, Ford, and Chrysler) have asked for $34 billion in loans to forestall bankruptcy. The rise in gasoline prices reduced demand for profitable SUVs and the credit crunch and recession have further decreased consumer demand. Congressional leaders proposed using some of the TARP funds, but the Treasury did not agree with that position, so such a loan would require legislation or need to be considered in 2009. Some analysts believe a failure of the auto industry could be disastrous for the Midwest and some also believe a much larger amount will be needed. Others believe bankruptcy of the firms, which would be accompanied with adjustments in payroll as in other bankruptcy cases, would be a better alternative.[6] After Congress did not adopt an emergency loan of $14 billion in a special post-election session in December, 2008, the Administration is considering providing funds from TARP.

This chapter first discusses the current state of the economy, including measures that have already been taken by the monetary authorities, and assesses the need for and potential consequences of fiscal stimulus. The second part of the report reviews the proposals discussed during debate on the recently enacted fiscal stimulus, both those adopted and those considered but not adopted. The various stimulus packages differed somewhat, and the report briefly describes those differences. This section also includes a discussion of the potential elements of a second stimulus proposal, and concludes with a discussion of the macroeconomic effects of the proposals. The final section of the paper discusses recent and proposed financial interventions.

The Current State of the Economy[7]

The need for fiscal stimulus depends, by definition, on the state of the economy. According to the National Bureau of Economic Research (NBER), the official arbiter of the business cycle, the economy has been in recession since December 2007. It defines a recession as a "significant decline in economic activity spread across the economy, lasting more than a few months" based on a number of economic indicators, with an emphasis on trends in employment and income.[8] But because a recession is defined as a lasting decline, the NBER typically does not declare a recession until it is well under way. For example, the recession that began in March 2001 was not declared by the NBER until November 2001, the same month in which the NBER later declared the recession to have ended. The current recession was declared in late November of 2008.

In October 2008, a consensus among forecasters developed that the economy was in, or was about to enter, in a recession and in November and December the forecast worsened.[9] After two strong quarters, economic growth fell by 0.2% in the fourth quarter of 2007 and increased by 0.9% in the first quarter of 2008. Revised figures show a 2.8% growth rate in the second quarter of 2008. The Bureau of Economic Analysis's estimate, however, indicates that real GDP decreased by 0.5% in the third quarter. (Although negative growth is not an official prerequisite for a recession, all historical recessions have featured it.)

After a long and unprecedented housing boom, the median house price of existing homes fell by 1.8% in 2007—possibly the first year of falling prices since the Great Depression, according to the organization which compiles the data.[10] And the decline continued in 2008 and appears to be worsening over time. Other housing data fell even further—existing home sales fell by 22% in the twelve months through December 2007, and residential investment (house building) fell by 18% in the four quarters ending in the fourth quarter of 2007. The decline in residential investment has acted as a drag on overall GDP growth, while the other components of GDP have grown at more healthy rates. Many economists argued that the housing boom was not fully caused by improvements in economic fundamentals (such as rising incomes and lower mortgage rates), and instead represented a housing *bubble*—a situation where prices were being pushed up by "irrational exuberance."[11]

Most economists believe that a housing downturn alone would not be enough to singlehandedly cause a recession.[12] But in August 2007, the housing downturn spilled over to widespread financial turmoil.[13] Triggered by a dramatic decline in the price of subprime mortgage-backed securities and collateralized debt obligations, large losses and a decline in liquidity spread throughout the financial system. The Federal Reserve (Fed) was forced to create unusually large amounts of liquidity to keep short-term interest rates from rising in August 2007, and has since reduced interest rates significantly. Recent cuts in interest rates by the Federal Reserve included a cut the federal funds rate by three-quarters of a percentage point on March 18 and an additional cut of a quarter of a percentage point on April 30, a one half of a percentage point cut on October 8, a cut of one half of a percentage point on October 29, and a cut of ¾ to 1 percentage point on December 16. In addition, the Fed has lent directly to financial institutions through an array of new facilities, and the amounts of loans outstanding have risen into the hundreds of billions of dollars.[14] A reduction in lending by financial institutions in response to uncertainty or financial losses is another channel through which the economy could enter a recession.

To date, financial markets remain volatile, new losses have been announced at major financial institutions, and responses outside traditional monetary policy have been undertaken. In March, the financial firm Bear Stearns encountered liquidity problems, was provided emergency financing by JPMorgan Chase and the Federal Reserve Bank of New York, and was purchased, after a plummet in stock value, by JPMorgan Chase. Then in July, the government sponsored enterprises (GSEs) Fannie Mae and Freddie Mac experienced rapidly falling equity prices in response to concerns about the value of their mortgage backed securities assets. In July, Congress authorized Treasury to extend the GSEs an unlimited credit line (which has not been utilized to date) in H.R. 3221 because of concern that the failure of a GSE would cause a systemic financial crises. The federal government took control of Fannie Mae and Freddie Mac in early September. According to news reports, government officials decided not to intervene on behalf of Lehman Brothers and Merrill Lynch;[15] on September 14 Bank of America took over Merrill Lynch without federal intervention, and on September 15, Lehman Brothers filed for bankruptcy. The Treasury and Federal Reserve were trying to engineer a private bailout of the nations largest insurance company, AIG, but on September 16 seized control with an $85 billion emergency loan.[16]

On September 18, Administration and Federal Reserve officials with the bipartisan support of the Congressional leadership, announced a massive intervention in the financial markets.[17] The proposal asked for authority to purchase up to $700 billion in assets over the next two years. The Treasury has also provided insurance for money market funds, where withdrawals have been significant. These proposals suggest that government economists see problems with the transmission of traditional monetary stimulus into the financial sector and ultimately into the broader economy, where a significant contraction of credit could significantly reduce aggregate demand. Although the legislation passed with some delay, the stock market has fallen significantly. The original proposal had discussed buying mortgage related assets, particularly mortgage-backed securities, but the Treasury has indicated it will spend the initial $250 billion on preferred stock in financial institutions. The Federal Reserve has also announced purchases of commercial paper, $200 billion of asset backed securities, and $600 billion of mortgage related securities; the government has also announced a plan to assist Citigroup.

At the same time as the economy and financial sector has been grappling with the housing downturn, energy prices had risen significantly, from $48 per barrel in January 2007 to $115 dollars on April 30, 2008 and $144 as of July 2, 2008. After that, oil prices began a downward trend, and had fallen below $70 by October and $60 by the end of November. On December 10, the price was $43. Most recessions since World War II, including the most recent, have been preceded by an increase in energy prices.[18] Energy prices had gone up almost continuously in the current expansion, however, without causing a recession, which may point to the relative decline in importance of energy consumption to production. Although a housing downturn (and associated financial turmoil) or an energy shock might not be enough to cause a recession in isolation, the combination could be sufficient. Unless energy prices begin to rise again, there is little reason to believe they will place any further downward pressure on economic growth going forward.

In sum, there are some indications that a slowdown has occurred and that there are problems in several sectors. Growth rates, after two strong quarters, were negative in the fourth quarter of 2007, were positive in the first and second quarters of 2008, and negative in the third quarter of 2008. According to one data series, employment fell in the first 10 months of 2008. The unemployment rate, which was 4.8% in February 2008, rose to 6.1% in August 2008, remained there in September 2008, and rose again to 6.5% in October 2008 and to 6.6% in November. Forecasters project slower growth for 2008, and appear to have reached a consensus that the U.S. is in a recession. Problems exist in several different sectors of the economy: housing, energy, and financial markets. The continuing turmoil in financial markets could result in a credit crunch and result in contractions in the interest sensitive sectors of the economy.

Is Additional Fiscal Stimulus Needed?

The economy naturally experiences a boom and bust pattern called the business cycle. A recession can be characterized as a situation where total spending in the economy (*aggregate demand*) is too low to match the economy's potential output (*aggregate supply*). As a result, some of the economy's labor and capital resources lay idle, causing unemployment and a low capacity utilization rate, respectively. Recessions are short-term in nature—eventually, markets adjust and bring spending and output back in line, even in the absence of policy intervention.[19]

Policymakers may prefer to use stimulative policy to attempt to hasten that adjustment process, in order to avoid the detrimental effects of cyclical unemployment. By definition, a stimulus proposal can be judged by its effectiveness at boosting total spending in the economy. Total spending includes personal consumption, business investment in plant and equipment, residential investment, net exports (exports less imports), and government spending. Effective stimulus could boost spending in any of these categories.

Fiscal stimulus can take the form of higher government spending (direct spending or transfer payments) or tax reductions, but generally it can boost spending only through a larger budget deficit. A deficit-financed increase in government spending directly boosts spending by borrowing to finance higher government spending or transfer payments to households. A deficitfinanced tax cut indirectly boosts spending if the recipient uses the tax cut to increase his spending. If an increase in spending or a tax cut is financed through a decrease in other spending or increase in other taxes, the economy would not be stimulated since the deficit-increasing and deficit-decreasing provisions would cancel each other out.

How much a larger deficit can stimulate economic activity depends on the state of the economy at that time. When the economy is in a recession, fiscal stimulus could mitigate the decline in GDP growth by bringing idle labor and capital resources back into use. When the economy is already robust, a boost in spending could be largely inflationary—since there would be no idle resources to bring back into production when spending is boosted, the boost would instead bid up the prices of those resources, eventually causing all prices to rise.

Because total spending can be boosted only temporarily, stimulus has no long-term benefits, and may have long-term costs. Most notably, the increase in the budget deficit "crowds out" private investment spending because both must be financed out of the same finite pool of national saving, with the greater demand for saving pushing up interest rates.[20] To the extent that private investment is crowded out by a larger deficit, it would reduce the future size of the economy since the economy would operate with a smaller capital stock in the long run. In recent years, the U.S. economy has become highly dependent on foreign capital to finance business investment and budget deficits.[21] Since foreign capital can come to the United States only in the form of a trade deficit, a higher budget deficit could result in a higher trade deficit, in which case the higher trade deficit could dissipated the boost in spending. Indeed, conventional economic theory predicts that fiscal policy has no stimulative effect in an economy with perfectly mobile capital flows.[22] Some economists argue that these costs outweigh the benefits of fiscal stimulus.

The most important determinant of a stimulus' macroeconomic effect is its size. The recently adopted stimulus package (P.L. 110-185) increased the budget deficit by about 1% of gross domestic product (GDP). In a healthy year, GDP grows about 3%. In the moderate recessions that the U.S. experienced in 1990-1991 and 2001, GDP contracted in some quarters by 0.5% to 3%. (The U.S. economy has not experienced contraction in a full calendar year since 1991.) Thus, a swing from expansion to recession would result in a change in GDP growth equal to at least 3.5 percentage points. A stimulus package of 1% of GDP could be expected to increase total spending by about 1%.[23] To the extent that spending begets new spending, there could be a multiplier effect that makes the total increase in spending larger than the increase in the deficit. Offsetting the multiplier effect, the increase in spending could be neutralized if it results in crowding out of investment spending, a larger trade deficit, or higher inflation. The extent to which the increase in spending would be offset by these three factors depends on how quickly the economy is growing at the time of the stimulus—an increase in the budget deficit would lead to less of an increase in spending if the economy were growing faster.

Thus, if the slowdown proved to be short and mild, additional stimulus may not be necessary for the economy to revive relatively quickly. If, on the other hand, the economy entered a deeper, prolonged recession, as some economists believe to be likely, then fiscal stimulus may not be powerful enough to avoid it. Economic forecasts are notoriously inaccurate due to the highly complex nature of the economy, so it is difficult to accurately assess how deep the downturn will be, and how much fiscal stimulus would be an appropriate response.

The main obstacle to another round of fiscal stimulus may be the size of the current budget deficit. Although the stimulus measures proposed are not that large in isolation, some observers believe the deficit will already exceed $1 trillion in 2009. While there have been larger deficits in the past relative to GDP and current government borrowing rates are extremely low (because of the financial turmoil), there is a fear that a deficit of this size could become burdensome to service when interest rates return to normal. A larger deficit could crowd out private investment, act as a drag on economic growth, and increase reliance on foreign borrowing (which would result in a larger trade deficit). By doing so, the deficit places a burden on future generations, and could further complicate the task of coping with long-term budgetary pressures caused by the aging of the population.[24] In the highly unlikely, worst case scenario, if too much pressure is placed on the deficit through competing policy priorities, then investors could lose faith in the government's ability to service the debt, and borrowing rates could spike. Many of these issues could be avoided if the elements of the stimulus package are temporary, although there is often later pressure to extend policies beyond their original expiration date.

In judging the need for an additional stimulus package, policymakers might also consider that stimulus is already being delivered, in addition to the stimulus package passed in February, from two other sources. First, the federal budget has *automatic stabilizers* that cause the budget deficit to automatically increase (and thereby stimulate the economy) during a downturn in the absence of policy changes. When the economy slows, entitlement spending on programs such as unemployment compensation benefits automatically increases as program participation rates rise and the growth in tax revenues automatically declines as the recession causes the growth in taxable income to decline. In January, the Congressional Budget Office projected that under current policy, which excluded the February stimulus package, the budget deficit would increase by $56 billion in 2008 compared to 2007. This amount is significant, although smaller than, the approximately $150 billion deficit increase due to the recent stimulus package.[25]

Second, the Federal Reserve has already delivered a large monetary stimulus. By the end of April 2008, the Fed had reduced overnight interest rates to 2% from 5.25% in September 2007.[26] On October 8, the interest rate was lowered to 1.5%, and to 1.0% on October 29. Lower interest rates stimulate the economy by increasing the demand for interest-sensitive spending, which includes investment spending, residential housing, and consumer durables. In addition, lower interest rates would stimulate the economy by reducing the value of the dollar, all else equal, which would lead to higher exports and lower imports.[27]

One might take the view that the Federal Reserve has chosen a monetary policy that it believes will best avoid a recession given the actions already taken. If it has chosen that policy correctly, an argument can be made that an additional fiscal stimulus is unnecessary since the economy is already receiving the correct boost in spending through lower interest rates and through the first stimulus package. In this light, additional fiscal policy would be useful only if monetary policy is unable to adequately boost spending—either because the Fed has chosen an incorrect policy or because the Fed cannot boost spending enough through lower interest rates to avoid a recession, and direct intervention in financial markets is not adequate.[28]

Finally, some economists argue that if the root of the problem is concentrated in the housing and financial sectors, the economy is unlikely to return to sustainable expansion until those problems are solved. If so, fiscal stimulus may, at most, provide a temporary boost as long as those problems are outstanding, but cannot singlehandedly shift the economy to a sustainable path of expansion. For example, the first stimulus package did not prevent the economy from deteriorating in the third quarter of 2008. These problems were addressed in major housing and financial legislation in 2008, as described above, but it remains to be seen whether they have been solved.

STIMULUS PROPOSALS ENACTED AND CONSIDERED

Congress enacted and the President signed a stimulus package in February of 2008, although a second package may still be considered. During discussion of the stimulus package, a variety of proposals were advanced. The administration proposed initially to largely limit the stimulus to a tax reduction, but there was also discussion in Congress of spending programs such as extending unemployment benefits and food stamps. The House leadership initially negotiated a proposal with the administration which included refundable rebates to low income workers; the Senate added rebates for low income retirees and unemployment benefit extensions, with the former eventually adopted and the latter not adopted.

The House, Senate Finance Committee, and final versions of the economic stimulus package are briefly described below. The House version is the Recovery Rebate and Economic Stimulus for the American People Act of 2008 (H.R. 5140). The estimated budget cost of H.R. 5140 is $145.9 billion for FY2008 and $14.8 billion for FY2009 (see **Table 1**). The 10-year cost is estimated to be $117.2 billion.

The bill reported by the Senate Committee on Finance, the Economic Stimulus Act of 2008, includes additional provisions, such as energy provisions and extended unemployment compensation benefits, but excludes changes to the conforming loan limits for mortgages. There are some differences in the provisions that both bills share as well, which will be discussed below. Its estimated budget cost for FY2008 is $158.1 billion—about 8% higher than H.R. 5140 (see **Table 2**). The 10-year budget cost is estimated to be $155.7 billion.

Table 1. Estimated Budget Cost of Original House Bill (H.R. 5140) (Billions of Dollars)

Provision	FY2008	FY2009	FY2008 -2018
Rebates for Individuals	-101.1	-8.6	-109.7
Increase Sec. 179 Expensing and Phaseout Amounts for 2008	-0.9	-0.6	-0.1
50% Bonus Depreciation	-43.9	-5.6	-7.4
Total	**-145.9**	**-14.8**	**-117.2**

Source: Joint Committee on Taxation, JCX-6-08, Jan. 28, 2008.

The final bill followed the House proposal in all respects except for modifications to the rebate. The Senate's proposal to extend the House proposal's rebates to Social Security recipients and disabled veterans, and to prohibit them for illegal immigrants was included in the final bill, increasing the first year cost by $6 billion. The legislation also included appropriations to carry out rebates.

Table 2. Estimated Budget Cost for the Economic Stimulus Act of 2008 As Reported by the Senate Committee on Finance (Billions of Dollars)

Provision	FY2008	FY2009	FY2008-2018
Stimulus Rebate	-115.1	-11.2	-126.4
Business Stimulus Incentives	-32.3	-28.9	-11.9
Extensions of Energy Provisions	-0.7	-1.1	-5.7
Expansion of Qualified Mortgage Bonds	—	-0.1	-1.7
Extension of Unemployment Compensation	-10.1	-4.4	-9.9
Total	**-158.1**	**-45.7**	**-155.7**

Source: Joint Committee on Taxation, JCX-13-08, Jan. 30, 2008.

Table 3. Estimated Budgetary Cost of the Final Bill, H.R. 5140 (Billions of Dollars)

Provision	FY2008	FY2009	FY2008-2018
Rebates for Individuals	-106.7	-10	-116.7
Appropriations to Carry Out Rebates	-0.2	-0.1	-0.3
Increase Sec. 179 Expensing and Phaseout Amounts for 2008	-0.9	-0.6	-0.1
50% Bonus Depreciation	-43.9	-5.6	-7.4
Total	**-151.7**	**-16.3**	**-124.5**

Source: Joint Committee on Taxation, JCX-17-08, Feb. 8, 2008.

TAX REBATES[29]

The centerpiece of both the original House bill (H.R. 5140), the Senate committee proposal, and the final legislation is the tax rebate for individuals. Unlike the 2001 rebate, the rebates have elements of refundability, although the Senate committee proposal's and the final bill's refundability is greater than in the initial House proposal. The House proposal, H.R. 5140, would provide $109.7 billion in rebates, while the Senate committee proposal would provide $126.3 billion.[30] The final proposal adds $6 billion in the first year to the original House plan. The rebate is technically a credit for 2008, but payments would be mailed in 2008 based on 2007 returns. Iftaxpayers qualify for a higher credit based on their 2008 circumstances, they could claim the excess on their 2008 returns.

There are five elements of the rebate proposals that are outlined in **Table 4**. The first is the basic nature of the rebate. The House proposal effectively suspended part of the 10% income tax bracket, allowing a reduction in tax liability of 10% of the first $6,000 of taxable income for single individuals and 10% of the first $12,000 of taxable income for married couples. Absent any other provisions, the benefit would increase gradually until a maximum benefit was reached at $600 for single individuals and $1,200 for married couples. The Senate committee plan allowed a flat rebate of $500 for single individuals and $1,000 for couples. The basic rebate follows the House plan.

Table 4. Comparative Provisions of the Rebate

Provision	House Bill	Senate Committee Bill	Final Bill
General Rebate Proposal	10% of the first $6,000 of taxable income ($12,000 for couples), to extent of tax liability (maximum $600/$1,200)	Flat rebate of $500, $1,000 for couples	Same as House
Refundability Provisions	$300 rebate ($600 for couples) available if earned income is at least $3,000	Full $500 rebate allowed if earned income plus Social Security benefits are at least $3,000 or taxable income is at least $1.	Same as Senate, but with House rebate level of $300.
High Income Phase-out Provisions	Phased out at 5% of income over $75,000 for single individuals, $150,000 for couples	Phased out at 5% of income over $150,000 for single individuals, $300,000 for couples.	Same as House
Child Provisions	$300 per qualifying child if eligible for any other rebate	$300 per qualifying child if eligible for any other rebate	Identical Provisions
Other Features	None	Expands rebates to veterans receiving disability; disallows the rebate to illegal immigrants.	Same as Senate, with House rebate level of $300.

Source: CRS.

The second element is the basic refundability feature, which extends benefits to lower income households without tax liability. In the House bill, individuals without tax liability but with earnings of at least $3,000 can receive a minimum rebate of $300 for singles and $600 for married couples. (Households with earnings under $3,000 would not receive a rebate.) In the Senate committee proposal, the full flat amount can be received for households with at least $3,000 in combined earnings and Social Security benefits. This inclusion of Social Security benefits would extend the rebate to a large group of retired individuals who do not have taxable income. The final bill allows the refundability for Social Security, but at the lower House rebate level.

The third element is the treatment of high income taxpayers. In both bills, the benefit is phased out at higher incomes; the phaseout points are higher in the Senate committee proposal. The final bill follows the House provisions.

The fourth element is the child rebate, which in all plans is set at $300 per child and allowed if a basic or refundable rebate is received.

The fifth element, present initially only in the Senate committee proposal, limits and expands the scope of the rebates by extending them to veterans on disability and denying them to illegal immigrants by requiring the taxpayer identification number to be a social security number. These provisions were included in the final bill.

Compared to the experience with a rebate in 2001, the proposed rebates are more favorable to lower income individuals because of their refundability provisions. For a non-refundable credit, about 37% of taxpayers would not receive a credit because of lower incomes; in the original House bill, 20% would not receive a credit and in the Senate committee proposal and final legislation, 6.5% would not.[31] The increase in coverage in the Senate committee proposal and final bill is due to coverage of the elderly. The original House bill is more progressive (i.e., relatively more favorable to lower income households) than a non-refundable rebate, and the Senate committee bill is more progressive than the House bill (except at the top of the income distribution).

Although some rebates in the past appeared to be relatively ineffective in increasing spending, there is some evidence the 2001 rebate was spent.[32] In general, economic analysis suggests that benefits that go more heavily to low income individuals are likely to be more effective, per dollar of payment, than those with smaller benefits because lower income households are more likely to spend the rebate, and spending is necessary to produce a stimulus. The extension of rebates to those with Social Security payments could be quite complex administratively, since it would require filing and processing up to an additional 18 million tax returns.[33]

Preliminary Evidence on the Rebates' Economic Effects

Mainstream economic theory states that overall spending in the economy is stimulated only if the rebates lead to higher consumption. But households may decide to consume or save the rebates. There are now data available on disposable income and personal consumption expenditures through September 2008 to begin to judge whether the rebates have led to higher consumer spending. **Table 5** shows the breakdown of rebate checks sent by month. Through the end of June, $79.8 billion (or three quarters of the rebates) were received.[34]

Households may choose to increase consumption before, when, or after the rebates are received. (Households might decide to increase consumption beforehand in anticipation of receiving the rebate, assuming they are not liquidity constrained, meaning they had access to credit or savings.) Thus, to evaluate the full effects of the rebate on consumption would require data for all three periods, as well as assumptions about how quickly the rebate will be spent. At this point, only prior and contemporaneous consumption data are available; some of the stimulative effects will come in future months, making this analysis incomplete at present.

Furthermore, the dataavailable at this time are preliminary, and future revisions to the data could potentially result in a fundamentally different picture of the rebates' effects.

Table 5. Receipt of Rebates by Month

	Rebates Received (billions of dollars)
April	$4.3
May	$45.7
June	$29.8
July	$12.0

Source: CRS calculations based on data from the U.S. Treasury.

Figure 1 illustrates that there was an increase in disposable income (i.e., income net of taxes) in June that far exceeded normal monthly fluctuations. Disposable income rose 0.1% in April, 5.2% in May, and fell 2.6% in June. (The fall in June is caused by fewer rebates being paid out in June than in May. Disposable income in June was 2.4% higher than in April.) The Bureau of Economic Analysis estimates that in the absence of the rebates, disposable income would have fallen by 0.1% in May and 0.4% in June.[35] Disposable income continued to fall in July and August, and was up slightly in September. Yet, as shown in **Figure 1**, the large increase in disposable income has not yet led to any perceptible rise in consumption spending above the trend.[36] Consumption spending rose 0.1% in April, 0.3% in May, and fell 0.2% in June, 0.6% in July, and 0.4% in September. The rise in May is slightly above average, but the changes in April and June are below average. There was a large increase in personal saving from 0.3% of disposable income in April to 5% in May and 2.8% in June, suggesting that the rebates initially resulted in mostly higher personal saving. As noted previously, there may be a lag between receiving a rebate and increasing consumption. Consumption in March, the month before the rebate checks were first sent, rose 0.3%—it is debatable how much of this increase might be attributable to the anticipation of rebate checks not yet received.

Another weakness in the argument that the rebate checks have already stimulated the economy is the fact that the overall economy grew at a more rapid pace than consumption in the second and third quarters of 2008. GDP growth was 2.8%, while consumption grew by 1.2% in the second quarter. Government spending, net exports, and even non-residential investment (which typically shrinks during a recession) all grew at a more rapid pace than consumption in the second quarter, despite the boost to disposable income from the rebate checks.[37]

The effectiveness of the rebates in boosting overall spending could in theory be reduced by "leakages" into higher inflation, interest rates, or imports.[38] Prices for personal consumption expenditures rose at an annualized rate of 4.2% in the second quarter of 2008. Much of this increase was due to food and energy prices. Thus, the argument can be made that most of the rise in *nominal* consumption in the second quarter went toward price increases rather than higher consumption in *inflation-adjusted* terms. Spending on real imports fell by 6.6% in the second quarter, so that does not appear to be a source of "leakage." Likewise, interest rates in general did not show much movement during the second quarter.

The effects of the rebates on consumption cannot be determined by looking at the absolute growth of consumption in isolation. Rather, we need to compare actual growth to the growth in consumption that would have occurred in the counterfactual case without any rebates. Since there is no way of observing the counterfactual, economists must rely on economic models to conjecture about the counterfactual. One simple counterfactual would be to compare consumption following the rebates to consumption in a typical month. By this measure, the rebates seemed to have had no discernible effects so far. But there are good reasons to think that the past three months have not been typical months—namely, because of the slowdown in the economy and the resulting rise in unemployment and decline in consumer confidence.

Goldman Sachs estimates that the counterfactual would have been for consumption to have fallen by 1.5%-1.75% in the second quarter. Compared to this counterfactual, Goldman Sachs estimates the rebates to have boosted consumption by $22.5 billion to $25.2 billion and consumption growth by 3.1 to 3.3 percentage points in the second quarter. Of the total boost to spending, Goldman Sachs analysts attribute $1.7 billion to $2.3 billion to higher spending in March in anticipation of receiving the rebate checks.[39] Their counterfactual decline in consumption spending is strikingly large, however. Consumption spending has not fallen by as much as they assume (or even been negative) since the fourth quarter of 1991. Disposable income excluding the rebates does not show a similarly large decline. A less pessimistic assumption about consumption in the counterfactual would have resulted in a smaller estimate of the boost to consumption from the rebates.

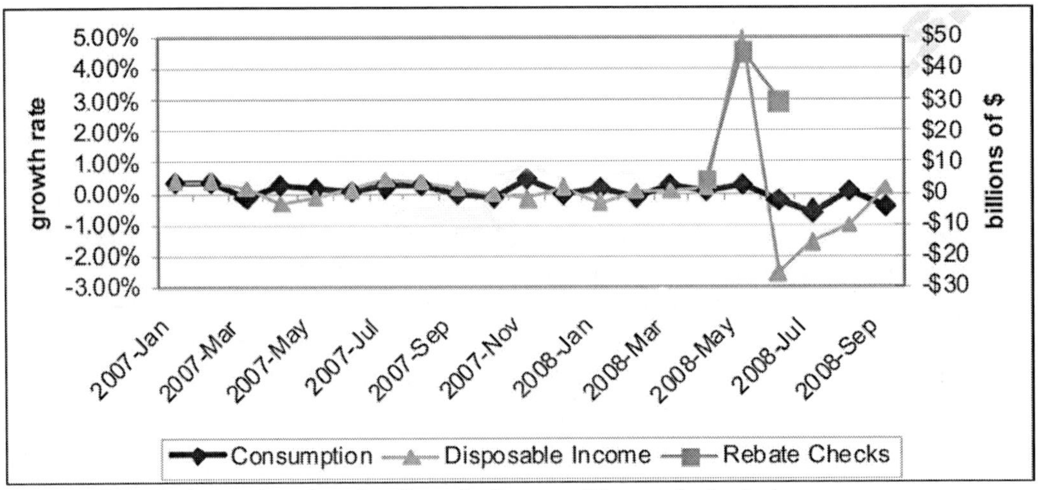

Source: CRS calculations based on data from the Bureau of Economic Analysis.

Note: Consumption and Disposable Income data are adjusted for inflation. Rebate checks are not adjusted for inflation.

Figure 1. Consumption, Disposable Income, and Rebate Checks, January 2007 to September 2008

The ultimate success of the rebates will depend partly on whether they help move consumption onto a path of sustainable growth in the future. If consumption falls after the effect of the rebates wears off, some may argue that the rebates will have at best postponed the economic downturn. Goldman Sachs predicts that by the fourth quarter of 2008 the effect of the rebates on GDP will have worn off, "at which point we (fore)see renewed stagnation in U.S. output."[40]

Economist Martin Feldstein argues that the rebates should be deemed a failure because they have had very little "bang for the buck."[41] He argues that rebates, which added nearly $80 billion to disposable income to date, have resulted in additional consumption of only $12 billion. In other words, about 15% of the money spent on the rebates served its stated purpose. (Goldman Sachs was more generous in crediting consumption spending to the rebates, concluding that the rebates added $22.5 to $25.2 billion to consumption, which is still considerably less than $80 billion.) Feldstein attributes the rebates' ineffectiveness to their having been mostly saved, and argues that a permanent tax cut would have been spent at a much higher rate than a one-time rebate. Two points can be made about Feldstein's conclusions. First, the $12 billion estimate understates the rebates' ultimate effects since somewhat more of the rebates are likely to be spent in future months. Second, the ineffectiveness of the rebates due to the saving effect is a more powerful argument for direct government spending, rather than permanent tax cuts, as a more cost-effective way to stimulate the economy in the short-term since none of government spending is saved.[42]

A study based on survey data of household non-durable consumption concluded that

> the average family spent around 20% of their rebate in the first month after receipt. Extrapolating similarly over time, our estimates imply that the receipt of the tax rebates directly raised non-durable PCE (personal consumption expenditures) by 2.4% in the second quarter of 2008 and will raise it by 4.1% in the third quarter.[43]

Their findings of relatively large effects at the household level can be reconciled to the macroeconomic data on a few grounds. First, their study examined only the consumption of nondurable goods. In the second quarter, non-durable consumption rose by 4% but consumption of durable goods fell by 3% at annualized rates. It is questionable why the effect of the rebates would be found in non-durable goods, and not durable goods. Second, the bulk of their estimated effect has not yet occurred and is based on their assumptions about future spending. Third, household survey data should be viewed with skepticism due to sample size, reporting error, and other issues.[44]

Business Tax Incentives[45]

The original House bill included two business provisions. The first was bonus depreciation, allowing 50% of investment with a life of less than 20 years (which applies mostly to equipment) to be deducted when purchased. The second addressed a provision that allowed small businesses to deduct all equipment investment when purchased, by increasing the ceiling on eligible equipment and phasing out the benefit more slowly. The Senate committee proposal had these same provisions, although it modified bonus depreciation by allowing a deduction over two years instead of one. It also added a provision that would allow companies to increase the period of time in the past that they can use to offset current net operating losses (NOLs) against past positive taxable income from two years to five, for losses generated in 2006 or 2007. The Senate committee proposal would have allowed businesses to use only one of the three provisions. The Senate committee proposal also included the extension of some energy provisions that largely relate to businesses. These provisions are compared in **Table 6**. The final bill followed the original House provisions.

The bonus depreciation provisions are the most costly of the business provisions, amounting to $43.9 billion in FY2008 and $5.4 billion in FY2009 for the House bill and $16.4 billion in FY2008 and $20.2 billion in FY2009 for the Senate committee proposal. (Apparently the election provision significantly reduces the cost of bonus depreciation in the first two years.) As with all of the provisions, which largely involve timing, revenue is gained in future years as regular depreciation deductions fall. Over 10 years, the cost is $7.4 billion in the House bill and $6.7 billion in the Senate committee proposal.[46]

The small business expensing provision, in both plans, costs $0.9 billion in FY2008 and $0.6 billion in FY2009, with the 10-year cost $0.1 billion. The net operating loss (NOL) provision in the Senate committee proposal loses $15.4 billion in FY2008, and $8.1 billion in FY2009, and then gains revenue, with the ten-year cost $5.1 billion.

Table 6. Business Tax Provisions of the House, Senate Committee and Final Plans

	House Bill (H.R. 5140)	Senate Committee Bill	Final Bill
Bonus Depreciation	For 2008, allows 50% of eligible investment (generally equipment) to be deducted when incurred	For 2008, elect to allow 50% of investment to be deducted equally over the first two years	Same as House.
Small Business Expensing	For 2008, increases the amount of eligible investment (generally equipment) expensing from $128,000 to $250,000; begin phaseout at $800,000 instead of $510,000.	For 2008, elect to increase the amount of eligible investment (generally equipment) expensing from $128,000 to $250,000; begin phaseout out at $800,000 instead of $510,000.	Same as House.
Net Operating Loss (NOL) Carryback	None	Elect to increase NOL carryback from two years to five years for losses generated from 2006 to 2008; and suspends provision that NOL cannot exceed 90% of alternative minimum taxable income.	Same as House.
Other Features	None	Taxpayer may elect only one of the three business benefits above; extends through 2009 of expired or expiring energy incentives; expands tax exempt bonds.	Same as House.

Source: CRS.

Because these benefits arise from timing, neither the initial cost nor the 10-year cost provide a good reflection of the value to the firm. For the benefit of bonus depreciation to the firm, the discounted values (using an 8% nominal interest rate) would be about $18 billion for the House bill and about $14 billion for the Senate committee proposal.

Overall, it is unlikely that these provisions would provide significant short-term stimulus. Investment incentives are attractive, if they work, because increasing investment does not trade off short term stimulus benefits for a reduction in capital formation, as do provisions stimulating consumption. Nevertheless, most evidence does not suggest these provisions work very well to induce short-term spending.[47] This lack of effectiveness may occur because of planning lags or because stimulus is generally provided during economic slowdowns when excess capacity may already exist.

Of business tax provisions, investment subsidies are more effective than rate cuts, but there is little evidence to support much stimulus effect. Temporary bonus depreciation is likely to be most effective in stimulating investment, more effective than a much costlier permanent investment incentive because it encourages the speed-up of investment. Although there is some dispute, most evidence on bonus depreciation enacted in 2002 nevertheless suggests that it had little effect in stimulating investment and that even if the effects were pronounced, the benefit was too small to have an appreciable effect on the economy.

The likelihood of the remaining provisions having much of an incentive effect is even smaller. Firms may, for example, benefit from the small business expensing, but it actually discourages investment in the (expanded) phase out range. The NOL provision, since it largely relates to events that have occurred in the past and therefore the effect is only a cash flow effect, is unlikely to have much incentive effect.

The energy provisions provide an extension through 2009 of provisions that expired at the end of 2007 or will expire at the end of 2008.[48] Their overall cost is $5.7 billion and they are unlikely to have a stimulative effect of importance, not only because of their size and because investment incentives are unlikely to be effective, but also because market participants may already be acting under the expectation that they will be extended in any case. Finally the Senate committee proposal provides an extension of tax exempt bonds for housing, that costs $1.7 billion and, similarly, would be unlikely to provide a significant short-term stimulus.

Housing Provisions[49]

The act allows the housing government-sponsored enterprises (GSEs), Fannie Mae and Freddie Mac, to purchase qualifying mortgages originated between July 1, 2007, and December 31, 2008, up to a value of $729,750 in high-cost areas. This is an increase above the permanent conforming loan limit of $417,000. The limit for any area is the greater of (1) the 2008 conforming loan limit ($417,000) or (2) 125% of the area median house price, and no higher than (3) 175% of the 2008 conforming loan limit ($729,750, which is 175% of $417,000).

Under this provision, Fannie Mae and Freddie Mac can continue to purchase loans in high-cost areas that qualify after December 31, 2008. However the GSEs are charters restrict them to acquiring loans no more than one year old.

The Federal Housing Administration (FHA) has temporary authority to insure mortgages in highcost areas up to this $729,750 limit. The authority expires December 31, 2008. The FHA permanent limit ranges from $200,160 to $362,790 in high-cost areas.[50]

H.R. 3221, Housing and Economic Recovery Act of 2008, as signed into law on July 30, 2008, would permanently increase the high cost loan limit to 115% of the area median house price, but no greater than 150% of the national conforming loan limit, beginning in 2009. The national maximum would have been $625,000 in 2008 if the bill had been effective at that time. The bill would use $417,000 as the base for future changes in the conforming loan limit, eliminating the $700 decline that was "banked" against future increases in October 2006.[51]

The FHA high cost limits would be similar to the conforming loan limit.

Many of those supporting the increases believe they provide a needed stimulus to housing and mortgage markets.[52]

Factors tending to limit the impact of the increased mortgage limits are as follows:

- Existing loan-to-value ratio limits continue to apply. This prevents homeowners who owe more on a house than its appraised value from participating in the program.
- Existing credit worthiness and debt-to-income requirements apply. This would prevent anyone not current on their mortgage from refinancing.
- The reduction of the 30% extra capital requirement to 20% could allow the GSEs to purchase and hold an additional $200 billion in mortgages. The GSEs could also purchase additional mortgages by following the suggestion in the Economic Stimulus Act of 2008 and H.R. 3221 to package these mortgages, add their guarantees, and sell mortgage-backed securities (MBS) to large investors.

These housing-related provisions of the act could narrow or eliminate the spread between loans above the permanent loan limit (but under temporary limits) and conforming loans already eligible for purchase. Recently, this spread has been in the range of 0.90% to 1.10%, as compared to a "normal" spread of approximately 0.20%. The provisions, and subsequent reduction in the spread, could:

- Help homebuyers with good credit obtain lower interest rates on loans in the affected range. The monthly payments on a 30-year fixed-rate $600,000 mortgage could fall from $3,824 to $3,377, saving $447 per month.[53] FHA's guidelines state that mortgage payments, insurance, and taxes should not exceed 29% of monthly income. According to the guidelines, a combined monthly housing expense of $3,377 would require a minimum annual household income of $140,000;
- Primarily help home buyers in areas with high home prices such as California, New York City and its suburbs, the Boston area, the Seattle area, and the Washington, DC area. Most other parts of the nation have home prices that do not cause their ceiling to increase;
- The provision raising the limit on home prices to 125% of the area median house price would raise the loan ceiling in areas with a median house price of more than $336,000. For example, in Barnstable, MA the limit is temporarily increased to $462,000;
- Likely have little impact in areas and houses where the permanent conforming loan limits still apply;
- Not count mortgages purchased by the GSEs as a result of the higher loan limit for the purpose of low-and moderate-income housing goals and underserved areas goals. HUD establishes numeric goals based on the Housing and Community Development Act of 1992;[54] and
- Help FHA compete against private sector lenders and possibly open homeownership to borrowers who, for one reason or another, could not qualify for a conforming mortgage to purchase a more expensive home.[55]

Extending Unemployment Benefits[56]

The Senate proposal included an extension of unemployment benefits, but these provisions were not included in the final economic stimulus legislation.[57] However, an extension (Emergency Unemployment Compensation, EUC08) was included in the Iraq/Afghanistan supplemental appropriations (H.R. 2642), which was passed by the Senate on June 26 and sent to the President, who signed it on June 30 (P.L. 110-252).[58] On November 21, 2008, the President signed P.L. 110-449, the Unemployment Compensation Extension Act of 2008 into law. P.L. 110-449 expands the potential duration of the EUC08 benefit from up to 13 weeks of EUC08 to a maximum of 20 weeks. It also creates a second tier of benefits for workers in states with high unemployment of up to a maximum of an additional 13 weeks of tier II EUC08 benefits (for up to a cumulative 33 weeks of EUC08 benefits).

Originally, the intent of the Unemployment Compensation (UC) program was, among other things, to help counter economic fluctuations such as recessions.[59] This intent is reflected in the current UC program's funding and benefit structure. UC is financed by federal payroll taxes under the Federal Unemployment Tax Act (FUTA) and by state payroll taxes under the State Unemployment Tax Acts (SUTA). When the economy grows, UC program revenue rises through increased tax revenues, while UC program spending falls as fewer workers are unemployed. The effect of collecting more taxes than are spent is to dampen demand in the economy. This also creates a surplus of funds or a "cushion" of available funds for the UC program to draw upon during a recession. In a recession, UC tax revenue falls and UC program spending rises as more workers lose their jobs and receive UC benefits. The increased amount of UC payments to unemployed workers dampens the economic effect of earnings losses by injecting additional funds into the economy.[60]

The limited duration of UC benefits (generally no more than 26 weeks) results in some unemployed individuals exhausting their UC benefits before finding work or voluntarily leaving the labor force for other activities such as retirement, disability, family care, or education. The Extended Benefit (EB) program, established by P.L. 91-373 (26 U.S.C. 3304, note), may extend UC benefits at the state level if certain economic situations exist within the state. The EB program, like the UC program, is permanently authorized. The EB program is currently active solely in North Carolina (up to 13 weeks) and Rhode Island (up to 20 weeks). On December 7, 2008, the EB program will be activated on in Oregon.

In addition to the current EUC08 program, Congress acted seven other times—in 1958, 1961, 1971, 1974, 1982, 1991, and 2002—to establish temporary programs of extended UC benefits. These programs extended the time an individual might claim UC benefits (ranging from an additional 6 to 33 weeks) and had expiration dates. Some extensions took into account state economic conditions; many temporary programs considered the state's TUR and/or the state's insured unemployment rate (IUR).

Recently, congressional and popular debate has examined the relative efficacy of the expansion of UC benefits and duration compared to other potential economic stimuli. In his January 22, 2008 congressional testimony, the Director of the Congressional Budget Office (CBO) stated that increasing the value or duration of UC benefits may be one of the more effective economic stimulus plans.[61] This is because many of the unemployed are severely cash constrained and would be expected to rapidly spend any increase in benefits that they may receive.[62]

Others point out that increasing either the value or length of UC benefits may, however, discourage recipients from searching for work or from accepting less desirable jobs.[63] A rationale for making an extension in UC benefits only temporary is to mitigate disincentives to work, since the extension would expire once the economy improves and cyclical unemployment declines.

A vigorous debate on how to determine when the federal government should extend unemployment benefits has been active for decades. Generally, this debate has examined the efficacy of using the IUR or TUR as triggers for extending benefits. The debate also has examined whether the intervention should be at a national or state level. Recently, serious consideration of alternative labor market measures has become increasingly common. In particular, the increase in the number of unemployed from the previous year has emerged in several proposals as a new trigger for a nation-wide extension in unemployment benefits.

Senate Committee Proposal

The bill, as passed by the Senate Finance Committee on January 30, 2008, would create a new temporary extension of UC that would entitle certain unemployed individuals to unemployment benefits that are not available under current law. (The House bill contained no provisions relating to unemployment benefits.) Individuals who had exhausted all rights to regular UC benefits under the state or federal law with respect to a benefit year (excluding any benefit year that ended before February 1, 2007) would be eligible for these additional benefits. The amount of the benefit would be the equivalent of the individual's weekly regular UC benefit (including any dependents' allowances). The temporary extension would be financed 100% by the federal government.

The number of weeks an individual would be eligible for these temporary extended UC benefits would be the lesser of 50% of the total regular UC eligibility or 13 weeks. Under a special rule, if the state is in an EB period (which has a special definition for purposes of this temporary extension), the amount of temporary extended UC benefits would be augmented by an additional amount that is equivalent to the temporary UC benefit. Thus, in those "high-unemployment" states where the EB program was triggered, temporary benefits of up to 26 weeks would be possible.[64]

Governors of the states would be able to pay the temporary extended UC benefit in lieu of the Extended Benefit (EB) payment (if state law permits). Thus, once the regular UC benefit was exhausted, a state would be able to opt for the individual to receive the temporary extended UC benefit (100% federal funding) rather than receiving the EB benefit (50% federal funding and 50% state funding).

The program would terminate on December 31, 2008. Unemployed individuals who had qualified for the temporary extended UC benefit or had qualified for the additional "high-unemployment" provision would continue to receive payments for the number of weeks they were deemed eligible. However, if the unemployed individual has not exhausted the first temporary extension of UC benefits by December 31, 2008, regardless of state economic conditions, the individual would not be eligible for an additional "high-unemployment" extension of the temporary UC benefit. If an individual exhausts his or her regular UC benefits after December 31, 2008, the individual would not be eligible for any temporary extended UC benefit. No such benefits would be payable for any week beginning after March 31, 2009.

P.L. 110-252http://www.congress.gov/cgi-lis/bdquery/R?d110:FLD002:@1(110+252), Emergency Unemployment Compensation (EUC08). The Emergency Unemployment Compensation (EUC08) program was created by P.L. 110-252 and has been amended by P.L. 110-449. This temporary unemployment insurance program provides up to 20 additional weeks of unemployment benefits to certain workers who have exhausted their rights to regular unemployment compensation (UC) benefits. A second tier of benefits exists in states with a total unemployment rate of at least 6% and provides up to an additional 13 weeks of EUC08 benefits (for a total of 33 weeks of EUC08 benefits.) The program effectively began July 6, 2008, and will terminate on March 28, 2009. No EUC08 benefit will be paid beyond the week ending August 22, 2009.

EUCO8 and EB Interactions

The EUC08 program allows states to determine which benefit is paid first. Thus, states may choose to pay EUC08 before EB or vice versa. States balance the decision of which benefit to pay first by examining the potential cost savings to the state with the potential loss of unemployment benefits for unemployed individuals in the state. It may be less costly for the state to choose to pay for the EUC08 benefit first as the EUC08 benefit is 100% federally financed (whereas the EB benefit is 50% state financed).[65] However, if the state opts to pay EUC08 first, individuals in the state might receive less in total unemployment benefits if the EB program triggers off before the individuals exhaust their EUC08 benefits. Both North Carolina and Rhode Island have opted to pay EUC08 benefits before EB.

A Second Stimulus Package?[66]

Some of the proposals included in earlier stimulus packages or discussed in the course of the debate have become part of a second stimulus package. A second stimulus plan (H.R. 3997) was proposed involving $50 to $60 billion in additional spending on infrastructure, unemployment benefits, Medicaid and nutrition programs. The bill passed the House on September 26 (as H.R. 7110) and included $36.9 billion on infrastructure ($12.8 billion highway and bridge, $7.5 billion water and sewer, $5 billion Corps of Engineers); $6.5 billion in extended unemployment compensation, and $14.5 billion in Medicaid, and $2.7 billion in food stamp and nutrition programs. A similar bill has not been able to pass the Senate and the President has indicated that he would veto the House bill. Earlier, a bill relating to housing relief was passed.

The Senate budget resolution set aside $35 billion for a second package, which is allocated between taxes and spending.[67] The accompanying Committee Print discussed the unemployment benefit extension discussed above as part of a potential future package, along with two other spending programs: expanding food stamps and aid to the states. It also discussed spending on ready-to-go infrastructure investments discussed during the stimulus debate, additional spending on LIHEAP (Low Income Energy Assistance Program) and WIC (Special Supplemental Nutrition Program for Women Infants and Children), and the summer jobs program.

The resolution also discussed a current proposal under consideration to address housing issues, the Foreclosure Prevention Act of 2008 (S. 2636). This proposal was passed by the

Senate as H.R. 3221 on April 10. It was not a broad stimulus package, but was largely targeted at the housing sector. It included some regulatory and direct spending provisions; in the latter case, primarily a $4 billion authorization for state and local governments to redevelop abandoned and foreclosed homes.

It also included some tax reductions. The largest of these (in short run revenue cost) was a provision similar to that enacted by the Senate for the first stimulus bill, allowing firms to elect an extended net operating loss carryback provision and a temporary suspension of the alternative minimum tax limitation for bonus depreciation and small business expensing for 2008 and 2009. The net operating loss carryback period was extended to four years. This provision cost $25 billion from FY2008-2010, although it would raise revenues thereafter with a total cost of $6 billion over ten years. The bill also included liberalization of tax-exempt mortgage revenue bonds, a tax credit for buyers of homes in foreclosure, a temporary deduction for property taxes by homeowners who do not itemize (capped at $500 for single and $1000 for couples), and an election to refund certain corporate credits in lieu of other business provisions. There were also some limited provisions for areas still recovering from hurricanes and from storms and tornadosin Kansas. Altogether, the package would have cost $22 billion over ten years.

The House also considered housing legislation, H.R. 5720, which had been reported out of the Ways and Means Committee. That provision has a more limited number of tax incentives. It includes a credit for first-time homebuyers (to be repaid over 15 years) as well as the property tax deduction in the Senate bill (but with lower caps of $350 and $700), along with some provisions affecting the low-income housing credits and tax exempt bonds for housing. The bill provided revenue offsets, however, and is therefore revenue neutral. On May 8, the House combined the tax legislation with other housing legislation and passed its version of H.R. 3221. The measure was delayed in the Senate, but the perceived need for a rapid legislative response to the GSE's problems resulted in Senate passage (where the provisions have been negotiated with the House; the net operating loss provision was eliminated and the tax credit is now similar to the House bill) of the bill on July 10. A final vote was taken by the House on July 23 and by the Senate on July 26, with the bill signed on July 30 by President Bush, who had withdrawn his veto threat (related to non-tax provisions). The tax benefits are, however, generally offset.

There continued to be indications that interest remained in the House in a possible second stimulus bill; House Speaker Pelosi indicated such an interest in a press conference to mark the payment of rebates, on April 25, 2008. A letter to the speaker by 30 members on April 17 suggested a wide variety of spending programs including unemployment benefits, food stamps, and infrastructure. On June 12, Senator Charles Schumer indicated that a second stimulus package should contain provisions other than spending increases. On July 15, House Speaker Pelosi indicated she intends to push a second stimulus bill in through Congress in September, and that a second rebate is a possibility, but should not exclusively dominate the package. She reiterated her plan for a second stimulus on July 31, when the new GDP growth rates were released. The Senate is considered a $24 billion supplemental spending bill which would include spending on infrastructure, energy programs, and disaster aid.

In the week of September 22, following the request of the administration for authority to purchase assets, Congressional leaders indicated that a stimulus bill, which could include extension of unemployment benefits, infrastructure spending, and spending on home heating oil, food stamps and health care, would also be considered. Recent proposals of this nature proposed spending of around $50 billion. The bill, H.R. 7110, passed the House on September 26, but a Senate proposal for a $56.2 billion plan has not obtained enough votes to pass the Senate.

Congress returned after the election to consider a second stimulus package; the unemployment compensation extension was passed, but not the other elements. Discussions now suggest a potentially much larger package supported by Congressional leaders and the President Elect that could be in excess of $500 billion. It could include additional tax cuts as well as spending programs. There is also discussion of additional assistance to the states, which, because of balanced budget requirements, tend to cut spending in downturns.

Fiscal stimulus is only effective if the money is spent, and many economists also view fiscal policy as less effective than monetary policy in an open economy. Tax cuts may be less effective than spending because some of the tax cut may be saved. Tax cuts that are temporary, that appear in a lump sum rather than in withholding, or that are aimed at higher income individuals are thought more likely to be saved. For example, some evidence suggests that only two thirds of the 2001 tax rebate was spent.

The challenge to spending programs is that there may be a lag time for planning and administration before the money is spent. For that reason, infrastructure spending is often discussed in the context of "ready-to-go" projects where all of the planning is in place and the only missing factor is funding. Some analysts suggest that aid to state and local governments may be more quickly spent because these governments are likely to cut back on spending in downturns, and the aid may forestall these cuts.[68]

These delays in spending are less of a concern if the downturn appears likely to be protracted or the recovery slow.

Comparing the Macroeconomic Effects of Various Proposals[69]

The relative effectiveness of different proposals in stimulating the economy has been evaluated along a number of lines that will be discussed in this section.[70]

Bang for the Buck. In terms of first-order effects, any stimulus proposal that is deficit financed would increase total spending in the economy.[71] For second-order effects, different proposals could get modestly more "bang for the buck" than others if they result in more total spending. If the goal of stimulus is to maximize the boost to total spending while minimizing the increase in the budget deficit (in order to minimize the deleterious effects of "crowding out"), then maximum bang for the buck would be desirable. The primary way to achieve the most bang for the buck is by choosing policies that result in spending, not saving.[72] Direct government spending on goods and services would therefore lead to the most bang for the buck since none of it would be saved. The largest categories of direct federal spending are national defense, health, infrastructure, public order and safety, and natural resources.[73]

Higher government transfer payments, such as extended unemployment compensation benefits or increased food stamps, or tax cuts could theoretically be spent or saved by their recipients.[74] While there is no way to be certain how to target a stimulus package toward recipients who would spend it, many economists have reasoned that higher income recipients would save more than lower income recipients since U.S. saving is highly correlated with income. For example, two-thirds of families in the bottom 20% of the income distribution did not save at all in 2004, whereas only one-fifth of families in the top 10% of the income distribution did not save.[75]

Presumably, recipients in economic distress, such as those receiving unemployment benefits, would be even more likely to spend a transfer or tax cut than a typical family. As discussed previously, business tax incentives can be crafted so that they can be claimed only in response to higher investment spending, but businesses may be unwilling to increase their investment spending when faced with a cyclically-induced decline in demand for their products.[76]

Mark Zandi of *Moody's Economy.com* has estimated multiplier effects for several different policy options, as shown in **Table 7**.[77] The multiplier estimates the increase in total spending in the economy that would result from a dollar spent on a given policy option. Zandi does not explain how these multipliers were estimated, other than to say that they were calculated using his firm's macroeconomic model. Therefore, it is difficult to offer a thorough analysis of the estimates. In general, many of the assumptions that would be needed to calculate these estimates are widely disputed (notably, the difference in marginal propensity to consume among different recipients and the size of multipliers in general), and no macroeconomic model has a highly successful track record predicting economic activity. Thus, the range of values that other economists would assign to these estimates is probably large. Qualitatively, most economists would likely agree with the general thrust of his estimates, however—spending provisions have higher multipliers because tax cuts are partially saved, and some types of tax cuts are more likely to be saved by their recipients than others. As discussed above, a noticeable increase in consumption spending has not yet accompanied the receipt of the rebates from the first stimulus package.

Timeliness. Timeliness is another criterion by which different stimulus proposals have been evaluated. There are lags before a policy change affects spending. As a result, stimulus could be delivered after the economy has already entered a recession or a recession has already ended. First, there is a legislative process lag that applies to all policy proposals—a stimulus package cannot take effect until bills are passed by the House and Senate, both chambers can reconcile differences between their bills, and the President signs the bill. Many bills get delayed at some step in this process. As seen in **Table 8**, many past stimulus bills have not become law until a recession was already underway or finished.

Second, there is an administrative delay between the enactment of legislation and the implementation of the policy change. For example, although the stimulus package was signed into law in February, the first rebate checks were not sent out until the end of April, and the last rebate checks were not sent out until July. When the emergency unemployment compensation (EUC08) program began in July 2008 there was about a three week lag between enactment and the first payments of the new EUC08 benefit. Many economists have argued that new government spending on infrastructure could not be implemented quickly enough to stimulate the economy in time since infrastructure projects require significant planning. (Others have argued that this problem has been exaggerated because existing plans or routine maintenance could be implemented more quickly.) Others have argued that although federal spending cannot be implemented quickly enough, fiscal transfers to state and local governments would be spent quickly because many states currently face budgetary shortfalls, and fiscal transfers would allow them to avoid cutting spending.[78]

Table 7. Zandi's Estimates of the Multiplier Effect for Various Policy Proposals

Policy Proposal	One-year change in real GDP for a given policy change per dollar
Tax Provisions	
Non-refundable rebate	1.02
Refundable rebate	1.26
Payroll tax holiday	1.29
Across the board tax cut	1.03
Accelerated depreciation	0.27
Extend alternative minimum patch	0.48
Make income tax cuts expiring in 2010 permanent	0.29
Make expiring dividend and capital gains tax cuts permanent	0.37
Reduce corporate tax rates	0.3
Spending Provisions	
Extend unemployment compensation benefits	1.64
Temporary increase in food stamps	1.73
Revenue transfers to state governments	1.36
Increase infrastructure	1.59

Source: Mark Zandi, *Moody's Economy.com.*

Table 8. Timing of Past Recessions and Stimulus Legislation

Beginning of Recession	End of Recession	Stimulus Legislation Enacted
Nov. 1948	Oct. 1949	Oct. 1949
Aug. 1957	Apr. 1958	Apr. 1958, July 1958
Apr. 1960	Feb. 1961	May 1961, Sep. 1962
Dec. 1969	Nov. 1970	Aug. 1971
Nov. 1973	Mar. 1975	Mar. 1975, July 1976, May 1977
July 1981	Nov. 1982	Jan. 1983, Mar. 1983
July 1990	Mar. 1991	Dec. 1991, Apr. 1993
Mar. 2001	Nov. 2001	June 2001

Source: Bruce Bartlett, "Maybe Too Little, Always Too Late," *New York Times*, Jan. 23, 2008.

Finally, there is a behavioral lag, since time elapses before the recipient of a transfer or tax cut increases their spending. For example, the initial reaction to the receipt of rebate checks was a large spike in the personal saving rate (see above). It is unclear how to target recipients that would spend most quickly, although presumably liquidity-constrained households (i.e., those with limited access to credit) would spend more quickly than others. In this regard, the advantage to direct government spending is that there is no analogous lag. Although monetary policy changes have no legislative or administrative lags, research suggests they do face longer behavioral lags than fiscal policy changes because households and business generally respond more slowly to interest rate changes than tax or transfer changes.

Long-term Effects. As discussed above, while a deficit-financed policy change can stimulate short-term spending, it can also reduce the size of the economy in the long run through the crowding out effect on private investment. Stimulus proposals can minimize the crowding out effect by lasting only temporarily—an increase in the budget deficit for one year would lead to significantly less crowding out over time than a permanent increase in the deficit. Among policy options, increases in public investment spending would minimize any negative effects on long-run GDP since decreases in the private capital stock would be offset by additions to the public capital stock. Also, tax incentives to increase business investment would offset the crowding out effect since the spending increase was occurring via business investment.

Should Stimulus be Targeted?

It is clear that the slowdown has been concentrated in housing and financial markets to date. Some economists have argued that as long as problems remain in these depressed sectors, then generalized stimulus will only postpone the inevitable downturn. (As noted above, separate legislation to support housing and financial markets were recently enacted.) For example, Goldman Sachs predicts that by the fourth quarter of 2008 the effect of the rebates on GDP will have worn off, "at which point we (fore)see renewed stagnation in U.S. output."[79] Other economists argue that if the current housing bust is being caused by the unwinding of a bubble, then it could be detrimental for the government to interfere with natural market adjustment which is bringing those markets back to equilibrium that, in the long run, is both necessary and unavoidable. And some would argue that the best way to help a troubled sector is by boosting overall demand.

INTERVENTIONS FOR FINANCIAL FIRMS AND MARKETS[80]

Problems in financial markets became more acute in September 2008. Troubled assets on bank balance sheets, especially mortgage-backed securities (MBS), caused financial markets to freeze, as evidenced by spiking spreads between U.S. Treasury securities and other interest rates. Policymakers had been intervening for financial firms on a case-by-case basis. In the Spring, the Federal Reserve had provided a backstop for the sale of Bear Stearns. Financial turmoil following the decision of the government to decline such aid for Lehman Brothers, but to assist AIG, has created dissatisfaction with the case-by-case approach. Policymakers responded by passing a broad plan authorizing Treasury to spend up to $700 billion (P.L. 110-343).[81] Treasury is authorized to purchase any asset that may help to restore confidence in financial markets and stabilize credit markets.[82] Although the original draft Treasury proposal focused on purchasing illiquid mortgage-related assets from financial institutions, the plan as passed included a much broader definition of troubled asset. This broader definition encompasses any asset, including stock in banks, that Treasury in consultation with the Federal Reserve believes is necessary to provide financial stability. Following passage, Treasury committed to purchase $150 billion of preferred shares of the nine largest banks in order to inject capital into the financial system.[83] Treasury has formally announced that it has abandoned plans to remove troubled MBS from bank balance sheets, but has also announced plans to use some of the funds to intervene in consumer-based asset-backed securities (ABS) markets such as credit card receivables, auto loans, and student loans.[84]

Case-by-Case Interventions

One factor that may have contributed to financial market instability was the uncertainty created by case-by-case interventions in financial markets. Market participants were unsure which institutions would qualify for government assistance. Justifications for intervention appeared to rely on one of two arguments. First, institutions might receive aid if they were considered too big to fail. Second, institutions might receive aid if they perceived as too complex to unwind in traditional bankruptcy proceedings.

Too Big to Fail. The government sponsored enterprises (GSEs), Fannie Mae and Freddie Mac, were placed in a conservatorship.[85] Arguably, the GSEs were considered too big to fail because their combined portfolios exceeded $1 trillion. In addition, it was believed that their role in mortgage finance was essential in the housing market, which was a source of instability for the rest of the banking system.

The terms of this conservatorship included significant commitments of taxpayer financing. The Treasury promised to purchase sufficient preferred stock to insure institutional solvency. In addition, the Federal Reserve promised to directly lend funds to the GSEs at pre-determined interest rates. While the rescue of the GSEs would not affect smaller firms not believed to be too big to fail, the conservatorship of Fannie Mae and Freddie Mac triggered trillions of dollars of credit derivatives that referenced the GSEs. The potential repercussions of these credit derivatives may have created uncertainty as to the financial health of other firms.

Too Complex to Fail. In addition to a too-big-to-fail test, some have argued for a too-complex-tofail test. Firms may be too complex, in this view, if an attempt to unwind their financial commitments can cause too much uncertainty for the balance sheets of other financial firms. Because financial firms are highly leveraged, the failure of a major counterparty to their contracts could significantly damage their solvency. Because credit derivatives are traded, many firms might not know how exposed they are to particular counterparties until the derivatives are triggered.[86] Furthermore, there is no assurance that counterparties have adequate resources to fulfill their commitments.

Great uncertainty surrounded the too-complex-to-fail test. The Federal Reserve was willing to provide a financial backstop to the resolution of Bear Stearns but declined to do so for Lehman Brothers, even though both firms participated significantly in credit derivatives markets.[87] It appeared that the too-complex-to-fail test would not be applied in the future. However, three days later, the Federal Reserve provided a bridge loan to insurer AIG, partly due to AIG's positions in credit derivatives markets.[88] Financial markets promptly lost confidence and policymakers expressed dissatisfaction with a case-by-case approach.

Broad Based Intervention

Dissatisfaction with a case-by-case approach led some policymakers to advocate for a more systemic approach, but there was some disagreement concerning the merits of alternative responses. Conceivably, a systemic plan could be crafted to (1) remove existing illiquid assets from bank balance sheets,[89] (2) inject capital into banks by purchasing equity shares,[90] (3) increase the liquidity of existing troubled assets by insuring them, (4) stabilize existing mortgagerelated securities markets by lowering default rates by purchasing loans likely to default, and (5) support consumer credit markets by purchasing newly issued MBS and ABS. Treasury's initial draft plan focused on the first option, removing existing illiquid assets. Some Congressional leaders argued for the second option, purchasing equity positions in banks. Others in Congress argued for the third option, insuring existing illiquid assets. In the end, the draft plan was amended to be general enough to encompass any of these approaches or any combination. Although implementation of the plan has been evolving since its passage, the focus of the Treasury action to date has been on purchasing equity in banks.

Remove Illiquid Assets. Although subsequently abandoned, the initial draft plan was to purchase up to $700 billion of troubled mortgage-related assets from financial institutions which was adopted This option would attempt to remove devalued and illiquid assets from the balance sheets of financial firms at the same time to clean up the entire system. One advantage of this approach is that many firms become healthy in one swoop. Financial firms will have the ability to make new loans, not because of more capital, but because their existing capital would not be encumbered by bad assets. This approach is similar to the Resolution Trust Corporation (RTC) during the savings and loan crisis. The RTC was created to resolve insolvent thrifts.

It has the advantage of dealing with large amounts of bad debts in a short period of time. It has the disadvantage of putting the government in an awkward position. First, the government will be the holder of vast amounts of mortgage debt. The Treasury proposal says that assets should be resolved to protect the taxpayer; however, this creates a conflict of interest for those policymakers that would want to see more debt forbearance for distressed borrowers. Second, the government could also hold vast interests in real estate. If the government sells it quickly to terminate the issue then home prices could collapse. If the government holds on to the assets then the government could be in the position of being a landlord for extended periods of time. Finally, this approach may have the unintended effect of penalizing firms that acted prudently by cleaning up the balance sheets of their competitors but not of themselves.

Problems in accurately pricing the securities could complicate this approach. On the one hand, auctions can be designed to attempt to make sure that the government does not "overpay" for the illiquid securities.[91] On the other hand, the inclusion of mandatory warrants in EESA complicates the calculation of the worth of the securities to the firms that hold them. A firm considering selling some securities must not only attempt to evaluate the worth of the security, but must also try to calculate the impact of government warrants that could dilute future shareholder positions. Furthermore, the impact on the value of individual securities would be complicated by the number of securities that the firm might consider to sell because the amount of warrants is not directly related to the amount of securities sold. A firm planning to sell many securities would discount the impact of the warrants (similar to spreading fixed costs) compared to firms that might plan to sell fewer securities. As a result, not all securities of the same intrinsic risk-weighted value would be treated the same in a potential EESA auction. In the end, Treasury decided to abandon purchasing existing illiquid mortgage-related assets.

Broad Based Injection of Capital. Rather than assuming bad assets, the government could attempt to heal bank balance sheets by injecting good assets. The government could purchase preferred stock in financial firms, an action that has already begun following the passage of P.L. 110-343. In a similar approach, the government acquired warrants to for this purpose for Fannie Mae and Freddie Mac.[92] This approach has several advantages. It would leave the decisions of which assets to keep and which to dispose of to firm managers who would presumably have greater expertise. Second, it would not require the government to become the administrator of large accumulations of real estate assets. Third, if the program successfully revives financial markets then the stock will compensate the government for the cost of the program.

This approach is similar to the Reconstruction Finance Corporation (RFC) during the 1930s. The RFC was created to loan funds directly to banks, railroads, and other firms during the great depression. During the Hoover administration, the RFC primarily intervened by providing loans to banks and trusts. The names of recipient banks were announced which may have had the perverse effect of identifying weak banks, which subsequently suffered runs on their deposits. FDR made several changes, one of which allowed the Comptroller of the Currency to reorganize national banks without a receivership. The Comptroller could then have the RFC subscribe to new preferred shares of stock in the bank.

Currently, Treasury has purchased preferred shares in large banks and has set up an application system for smaller banks that may wish to participate. On October 28, 2008, Treasury purchased $125 billion in preferred shares in the 9 largest banks representing approximately 55% of the assets in the banking system.[93] In return, Treasury is to receive dividends of 5% for the first five years followed by dividends of 9% in following years, in addition to warrants for additional stock purchases.[94] The banks must pay dividends to Treasury before any dividends can be paid to junior or equal shareholders. Smaller banks may apply for Treasury funds equal to $25 billion or 3% of risk-weighted assets, whichever is smaller.

End Notes

[1] See CRS Report RL34707, *Auction Basics: Background for Assessing Proposed Treasury Purchases of Mortgage-Backed Securities*, by D. Andrew Austin.

[2] Testimony of Interim Assistant Secretary for Financial Stability Neel Kashkari before the House Committee on Oversight and Government Reform, Subcommittee on Domestic Policy, November 14, 2008.

[3] David M. Herszenhiorn, "Chances Dwindle on Bailout Plan for Automakers," *New York Times*, November 14, p. A1.

[4] Federal Reserve Board Press Release, October 14, 2008.

[5] Buinyamin Appelbaum, FDIC Details Plan to Alter Mortgages, Washington Post, November 14, 2008, p. A1.

[6] See CRS Report R40003, *U.S. Motor Vehicle Industry: Federal Financial Assistance and Restructuring, coordinated* by Stephen Cooney, et al. for further discussion.

[7] This section was prepared by Marc Labonte of the Government and Finance Division.

[8] National Bureau of Economic Research, *The NBER's Recession Dating Procedure*, January 7, 2008.

[9] Blue Chip, *Economic Indicators*, vol. 33, no. 10, October 10, 2008; no. 11, November 10, 2008 and no. 12, December 10, 2008. The consensus was that the recession will be deeper and last longer than the 2001 recession and perhaps deeper and longer than any post-World-War-II contraction.

[10] Michael Grynbaum, "Home Prices Sank in 2007, and Buyers Hid," *New York Times*, January 25, 2008. Prices are compiled by the National Association of Realtors.

[11] For more information, see CRS Report RL34244, *Would a Housing Crash Cause a Recession?*, by Marc Labonte.

[12] See, for example, Frederic Mishkin, "Housing and the Monetary Transmission Mechanism," working paper presented at the Federal Reserve Bank of Kansas City symposium, August 2007.

[13] See CRS Report RL34182, *Financial Crisis? The Liquidity Crunch of August 2007*, by Darryl E. Getter et al.

[14] See CRS Report RL34427, *Financial Turmoil: Federal Reserve Policy Responses*, by Marc Labonte.

[15] David Cho and Neil Irwin, "No Bailout: Feds Made New Policy Clear in One Intense Weekend," *Washington Post*, September 16, 2008, pp. A1, A6-A7.

[16] Glenn Kessler and David S. Hilzenrath, "AIG at Risk; $700 Billion in Shareholder Value Vanishes," *Washington Post*, September 16, 2008; U.S. Seizes Control of AIG With $85 Billion Emergency Loan, *Washington Post*, September 17, 2008, pp. A1, A8.

[17] See CRS Report RS22957, *Proposal to Allow Treasury to Buy Mortgage-Related Assets to Address Financial Instability*, by Edward V. Murphy and Baird Webel.

[18] For more information, see CRS Report RL31608, *The Effects of Oil Shocks on the Economy: A Review of the Empirical Evidence*, by Marc Labonte.

[19] For more information, see CRS Report RL34072, *Economic Growth and the Business Cycle: Characteristics, Causes, and Policy Implications*, by Marc Labonte.

[20] Crowding out is likely to be less of a concern if the economy enters a recession since recessions are typically characterized by falling business investment.

[21] If foreign borrowing prevents crowding out, the future size of the economy will not decrease but capital income will accrue to foreigners instead of Americans.

[22] For more information, see CRS Report RS21409, *The Budget Deficit and the Trade Deficit: What Is Their Relationship?*, by Marc Labonte and Gail E. Makinen.

[23] See, for example, "Options for Responding to Short-term Economic Weakness," Testimony of CBO Director Peter Orszag before the Committee on Finance, January 22, 2008.

[24] See CRS Report RL32747, *The Economic Implications of the Long-Term Federal Budget Outlook*, by Marc Labonte.

[25] In March 2008, CBO projected the budget deficit for FY2008 compared to FY2007 to increase to $193 billion, largely reflecting the stimulus package of $153 billion, offset by some other small reductions. Note also that, in January, CBO estimated that if supplemental military spending to maintain current troop levels overseas and an alternative minimum tax patch are enacted, and expiring tax provisions are extended, the 2008 deficit could increase by $98 billion in total compared to 2007. This projection was made in the absence of stimulus legislation and would increase the $56 billion deficit increase by $42 billion.

[26] For interest rate changes see CRS Report 98-856, *Federal Reserve Interest Rate Changes: 2001-2008,* by Marc Labonte and Gail E. Makinen.

[27] For more information, see CRS Report RL30354, *Monetary Policy and the Federal Reserve: Current Policy and Conditions*, by Gail E. Makinen and Marc Labonte.

[28] Fed Chairman Ben Bernanke may have hinted at the latter case when he testified that "fiscal action could be helpful in principle, as fiscal and monetary stimulus together may provide broader support for the economy than monetary policy actions alone." Quoted in Ben Bernanke, "The Economic Outlook," testimony before the House Committee on the Budget, January 17, 2008.

[29] This section was prepared by Jane Gravelle, Government and Finance Division.

[30] Joint Committee on Taxation, See JCX-6-08 and JCX-9-08, http://www.house.gov/jct/.

[31] See CRS Report RL34341, *Tax Rebate Refundability: Effects and Issues*, by Jane G. Gravelle.

[32] See CRS Report RS22790, *Tax Cuts for Short-Run Economic Stimulus: Recent Experiences*, by Jane G. Gravelle.

[33] According to the Tax Policy Center, 18 million households over the age of 65 would receive no rebate under the House bill. See Tax Policy Center, Table T08-0030, at http://www.taxpolicycenter.org/numbers/displayatab.cfm?Docid=1742&DocTypeID=4.

[34] The remaining quarter of rebates were received since June 30 or will be received between now and next April as additional tax returns are filed.

[35] Bureau of Economic Analysis, "Income Growth Affected by Rebates," news release, August 4, 2008.

[36] All figures discussed in this paragraph measure the change since the previous month and have been adjusted for inflation.

[37] Inventory reduction was a large drag on growth in the second quarter, which suggests that producers responded to higher consumption by reducing inventories rather than increasing production.

[38] For an explanation of the relationship between fiscal stimulus and these factors, see CRS Report RL34072, *Economic Growth and the Business Cycle: Characteristics, Causes, and Policy Implications*, by Marc

Labonte, *Economic Growth and the Business Cycle: Characteristics, Causes, and Policy Implications,* by Marc Labonte.

[39] Goldman Sachs, "Rebates Helped Avoid a Drop in Real Spending Last Quarter," *U.S. Daily Financial Market Comment*, August 5, 2008.

[40] Ibid.

[41] Martin Feldstein, "The Tax Rebate Was a Flop. Obama's Stimulus Plan Won't Work Either," *Wall Street Journal*, August 6, 2008, p. A15.

[42] See CRS Report RS21136, *Government Spending or Tax Reduction: Which Might Add More Stimulus to the Economy?,* by Marc Labonte.

[43] Christian Broda and Jonathan Parker, "The Impact of the 2008 Tax Rebates on Consumer Spending: Preliminary Evidence," working paper, July 29, 2008.

[44] J. Steven Landefeld, Eugene P. Seskin, and Barbara M. Fraumeni, "Taking the Pulse of the Economy: Measuring GDP," *Journal of Economic Perspectives*, Spring 2008.

[45] This section was prepared by Jane Gravelle, Government and Finance Division.

[46] Revenue estimates are from the Joint Committee on Taxation, See JCX-6-08 and JCX-9-08, http://www.house.gov/jct/

[47] See CRS Report RL31134, *Using Business Tax Cuts to Stimulate the Economy*, by Jane G. Gravelle, andCRS Report RS22790, *Tax Cuts for Short-Run Economic Stimulus: Recent Experiences*, by Jane G. Gravelle.

[48] The provisions include the credit for energy efficient appliances, the credit for certain non-business energy property, the suspension of the net income limit for marginal oil and gas properties, the 30% credit for residential investments in solar and fuel cells, the placed-in-service date for the tax credit for electricity produced from renewable resources, the credit for construction of energy efficient homes, the section 48 business credit, clean renewable energy bonds, and the energy efficient commercial property deduction.

[49] This section was prepared by Eric Weiss, Government and Finance Division.

[50] FHA limits are available from HUD's website at https://entp.hud.gov/idapp/html/hicost1.cfm.

[51] Office of Federal Housing Enterprise Oversight, Department of Housing and Urban Development, "Notice of Final Examination Guidance—Conforming Loan Limit Calculations; Response to Comments," 73 *Federal Register*, 16895-16899, March 31, 2008. http://www.ofheo.gov/media/guidance/CLLGuidanceFR32608.pdf

[52] James R. Haggerty and Damian Paletta, "Details Lacking on Mortgage-Relief Plan," *Wall Street Journal*, January 26, 2008, p. A6.

[53] Interest rates are based on mortgage rates reported by Bankrate.Com at http://www.bankrate.com/brm/graphs/graph_trend.asp?tf=91&ct=Line&prods=1,325&gs=275,250&st=zz&c3d=False&web=brm&cc=1&prodtype=M&bgcolor=&topgap=&bottomgap=&rightgap=&leftgap=&seriescolor=.

[54] 12 U.S.C. 4562-4564 and 4566.

[55] For more information on FHA, see CRS Report RS22662, *H.R. 1852 and Revisiting the FHA Premium Pricing Structure: Proposed Legislation in the 110th Congress*, by Darryl E. Getter, andCRS Report RS20530, *FHA-Insured Home Loans: An Overview*, by Bruce E. Foote and Katie Jones.

[56] This section was prepared by Julie M. Whittaker, Domestic Social Policy Division.

[57] For further discussion of proposals, see CRS Report RL34460, *Current Law and Selected Proposals Extending Unemployment Compensation*, by Julie M. Whittaker.

[58] See CRS Report RS22915, *Temporary Extension of Unemployment Benefits: Emergency Unemployment Compensation (EUC08)*, by Julie M. Whittaker for information on the new temporary benefit.

[59] See, for example, President Franklin Roosevelt's remarks at the signing of the Social Security Act http://www.ssa.gov/history/fdrstmts.html#signing.

[60] For a detailed examination of how the federal government has extended UC benefits during recessions see CRS Report RL34340, *Extending Unemployment Compensation Benefits During Recessions*, by Julie M. Whittaker.

[61] See CBO Testimony of Peter Orszag on Options for Responding to Short-Term Economic Weakness before the Committee on Finance United States Senate on January 22, 2008, http://www.cbo.gov/ftpdocs/89xx/doc8932/01-22-TestimonyEconStimulus.pdf.

[62] For another paper that takes this position see the following: Elmendorf, Douglas W. and Jason Furman, *If, When, How: A Primer on Fiscal Stimulus,* January 2008, http://www.brookings.edu/papers/2008/0110_fiscal_stimulus_elmendorf_furman.aspx.

[63] For example, Shrek, James and Patrick Tyrell, *Unemployment Insurance Does Not Stimulate the Economy*, Web memo #1777, January 2008: http://www.heritage.org/Research/Economy/wm1777.cfm#_ftn1. Martin Feldstein in testimony before the Senate Committee on Finance on January 24, 2008 stated that "(w)hile raising unemployment benefits or extending the duration of benefits beyond weeks would help some individuals ... it would also create undesirable incentives for individuals to delay returning to work. That would lower earnings and total spending." http://www.senate.gov/~finance/hearings/testimony/2008test/012408mftest.pdf

[64] The bill would temporarily change the definition of an EB period only for the purposes of the bill. Regardless of whether a state had opted for section 203(f) of the Federal-State Extended Unemployment Compensation Act of 1970, an EB period would be in effect for such state in determining the level of temporary extended UC

benefits in the state. The bill would temporarily change that trigger by removing the requirement that the TUR be at least 110% of the state's average TUR for the same 13-weeks in either of the previous two years. The bill would also change the base EB trigger described in section 203(d) only for purposes of the bill, reducing it from an IUR of 5% to an IUR of 4%.

[65] Some recipients may find jobs before becoming eligible for EB. In addition, the state may trigger off of the EB program before some recipients exhaust EUC08.

[66] This section was prepared by Jane Gravelle, Government and Finance Division.

[67] See *Concurrent Resolution of the Budget for 2009, Senate Report to Accompany S.Con.Res. 70*, Senate Print 110-039, March 2008, p. 6.

[68] See CRS Report 92-937, *Counter Cyclical Job Creation Programs*, for a discussion of some of these issues.

[69] This section was prepared by Marc Labonte, Government and Finance Division.

[70] For a more detailed analysis, see Congressional Budget Office, *Options for Responding to Short-Term Economic Weakness*, January 2008.

[71] There may be a few proposals that would not increase spending. For example, increasing tax incentives to save would probably not increase spending significantly. These examples are arguably exceptions that prove the rule.

[72] Policies that result in more bang for the buck also result in more crowding out of investment spending, which could reduce the long-term size of the economy (unless the policy change increases public investment or induces private investment).

[73] For the purpose of this discussion, government transfer payments, such as entitlement benefits, are not classified as government spending.

[74] Food stamps cannot be directly saved since they can only be used on qualifying purchases, but a recipient could theoretically keep their overall consumption constant by increasing their other saving.

[75] Brian Bucks et al, "Recent Changes in U.S. Family Finances: Evidence from the 2001 and 2004 Survey of Consumer Finances," *Federal Reserve Bulletin*, vol. 92, February 2006, pp. A1-A38.

[76] For more information, see CRS Report RS21136, *Government Spending or Tax Reduction: Which Might Add More Stimulus to the Economy?*, by Marc Labonte.

[77] Mark Zandi, "Washington Throws the Economy a Rope," *Dismal Scientist*, Moody's Economy.com, January 22, 2008.

[78] Transfers to state and local governments could be less stimulative than direct federal spending because state and local governments could, in theory, increase their total spending by less than the amount of the transfer. (For example, some of the money that would have been spent in the absence of the transfer could now be diverted to the state's budget reserves.) But if states are facing budgetary shortfalls, many would argue that in practice spending would increase by as much as the transfer.

[79] Ibid.

[80] This section was written by Edward V. Murphy, Government and Finance Division.

[81] Treasury Press Release, "Paulson Outlines Comprehensive Approach to Mortgage Problems," September 22, 2008, available at http://www.treasury.gov/news/index1.html.

[82] CRS Report RL34730, *The Emergency Economic Stabilization Act and Current Financial Turmoil: Issues and Analysis*, by Baird Webel and Edward V. Murphy.

[83] U.S. Department of Treasury, "Tranche Report to Congress," November 4, 2008, available at http://www.treasury.gov/initiatives/eesa/docs/Tranche-Reportfinal.pdf.

[84] "Remarks by Secretary Henry M. Paulson, Jr. on Financial Rescue Package and Economic Update," Press Release, U.S. Department of Treasury, November 12, 2008, available at http://www.treasury.gov/press/releases/hp1265.htm.

[85] CRS Report RL34661, *Fannie Mae's and Freddie Mac's Financial Problems,* by N. Eric Weiss.

[86] CRS Report RS22932, *Credit Default Swaps: Frequently Asked Questions*, by Edward V. Murphy.

[87] CRS Report RL34420, *Bear Stearns: Crisis and "Rescue" for a Major Provider of Mortgage-Related Products*, by Gary Shorter.

[88] Federal Reserve Press Release, September 16, 2008, available at http://www.federalreserve.gov/newsevents/press/other/20080916a.htm

[89] Treasury Secretary Paulson, "Turmoil in US Credit Markets: Recent Actions regarding Government Sponsored Entities, Investment Banks and other Financial Institutions," Testimony by Secretary Henry M. Paulson, Jr. before the Senate Committee on Banking, Housing, and Urban Affairs, September 23, 2008.

[90] CRS Report RS22962, *The U.S. Financial Crisis: Lessons From Sweden*, by James K. Jackson.

[91] CRS Report RL34707, *Auction Basics: Background for Assessing Proposed Treasury Purchases of Mortgage-Backed Securities*, by D. Andrew Austin.

[92] CRS Report RS22950, *Fannie Mae and Freddie Mac in Conservatorship*, by Mark Jickling.

[93] "Remarks by Secretary Henry M. Paulson, Jr. on Financial Rescue Package and Economic Update" Press release, U.S. Department of Treasury, November 12, 2008, available at http://www.treasury.gov/press/releases/hp1265.htm.

[94] U.S. Department of Treasury, "Tranche Report to Congress," November 4, 2008, available at http://www.treasury.gov/initiatives/eesa/docs/Tranche-Reportfinal.pdf.

In: Government Interventions in Economic Emergencies ISBN: 978-1-60741-356-1
Editor: Pablo Sastre

Chapter 22

FINANCIAL TURMOIL: FEDERAL RESERVE POLICY RESPONSES

Marc Labonte

SUMMARY

The Federal Reserve (Fed) has been central in the response to the current financial turmoil that began in August 2007. It has sharply increased reserves to the banking system through open market operations and lowered the federal funds rate and discount rate on several occasions. As the turmoil has progressed without signs of subsiding, the Fed has introduced new policy tools to try to restore normality.

Through new credit facilities, the Fed first expanded lending to the banking system and then extended lending to non-bank financial firms. Lending to non-banks is a major departure from past policy, for it is the first time that financial institutions that are not member banks of the Federal Reserve System have been allowed to borrow directly from the Fed on a routine basis. As the crisis worsened, the Fed began providing credit directly to markets for commercial paper and asset-backed securities. As a result of these programs, the Fed's outstanding loans and private asset purchases have ranged from $0.5 trillion to $1 trillion in recent months. The Fed's authority and capacity to lend is bound only by fears of the inflationary consequences, which have been offset by additional debt issuance by the Treasury.

In March 2008, JPMorgan Chase agreed to acquire Bear Stearns. As part of the agreement, the Fed made a $28.82 billion loan to a limited liability corporation (LLC) it created to buy $29.97 billion of assets from Bear Stearns. The Fed has also agreed to make loans and purchase assets through an LLC from the American International Group (AIG) worth up to $112.5 billion. In November 2008, the Fed and federal government agreed to guarantee losses on $306 billion of assets owned by Citigroup. In all of these agreements, the Fed is exposed to downside financial risk if the assets purchased or guaranteed fall in value.

The statutory authority for most of the Fed's recent actions is based on a clause of the Federal Reserve Act to be used in "unusual or exigent circumstances" that had not been invoked in more than 70 years. All loans are backed by collateral that reduces the risk of losses. Any losses borne by the Fed from its loans or asset purchases would reduce the profits it remits to the Treasury, making the effect on the federal budget similar to if the loans were made directly by Treasury. It is highly unlikely that losses would exceed its other profits and capital, and require revenues to be transferred to the Fed from the Treasury.

The primary policy issues raised by the Fed's actions are the issues of systemic risk and moral hazard. Moral hazard refers to the phenomenon where actors take on more risk because they are protected. The Fed's involvement in stabilizing Bear Stearns, AIG, and Citigroup stemmed from the fear of systemic risk (that the financial system as a whole would cease to function) if either were allowed to fail. In other words, the firms were seen as "too big (or too interconnected) to fail." The Fed's regulatory structure is intended to mitigate the moral hazard that stems from access to government protections. Yet Bear Stearns and AIG were not under the Fed's regulatory structure because they were not member banks.

INTRODUCTION

On August 9, 2007, liquidity abruptly dried up for many financial firms and securities markets. Suddenly some firms were able to borrow and investors were able to sell certain securities only at prohibitive rates and prices, if at all. The "liquidity crunch" was most extreme for firms and securities with links to subprime mortgages, but it also spread rapidly into seemingly unrelated areas.[1] The Federal Reserve (Fed) was drawn into the liquidity crunch from the start. On August 9, it injected unusually large quantities of reserves into the banking system to prevent the federal funds rate from exceeding its target.

It has been observed that the most unusual aspect of the crisis is its persistence for more than a year. Over that time, the Fed has aggressively reduced the federal funds rate and the discount rate in an attempt to calm the waters. When this proved not to be enough, the Fed greatly expanded its direct lending to the financial sector through several new lending programs, some of which can be seen as adaptations of traditional tools and others which can be seen as more fundamental departures from the status quo.[2] Most controversially, in March 2008, the Fed was involved in the "bailout" of the investment bank Bear Stearns, which was not a member bank of the Federal Reserve system (because it was not a depository institution), and, therefore, not part of the regulatory regime that accompanies membership.[3] In August, Fannie Mae and Freddie Mac, the housing government-sponsored enterprises (GSEs) were taken into conservatorship by the government.[4] In September, the investment bank Lehman Brothers filed for bankruptcy (it did not receive emergency government assistance) and the financial firm American International Group (AIG), which was also not a member bank, received a credit line from the Fed in order to meet its obligations. Lending to non-members requires emergency statutory authority that had not previously been used in more than 70 years.[5] In November 2008, the Fed and federal government agreed to guarantee losses on $306 billion of assets owned by Citigroup.

One of the original purposes of the Federal Reserve Act, enacted in 1913, was to prevent recurrence of financial panics. To that end, the Fed has been given broad authority over monetary policy and the payments system, including the issuance of federal reserve notes as the national currency. As with any statutory delegations of authority, the Fed's actions are subject to congressional oversight. Although the Fed has broad authority to independently execute monetary policy on a day-to-day basis, questions have arisen as to whether the unusual events of recent months raise fundamental issues about the Fed's role, and what role Congress should play in assessing those issues. This chapter reviews the Fed's actions since August 2007 and analyzes the policy issues raised by those actions.

TRADITIONAL TOOLS

The Fed, the nation's central bank, was established in 1913 by the Federal Reserve Act (38 Stat. 251). Today, its primary duty is the execution of monetary policy through open market operations to fulfill its mandate to promote stable economic growth and low and stable price inflation. Besides the conduct of monetary policy, the Federal Reserve has a number of other duties: it regulates financial institutions, issues paper currency, clears checks, collects economic data, and carries out economic research. Prominent in the current debate is one particular responsibility: to act as a lender of last resort to the financial system when capital cannot be raised in private markets to prevent financial panics. The next two sections explain the Fed's traditional tools, open market operations and discount window lending, and summarizes its recent use of those tools.

Open Market Operations and the Federal Funds Rate

Open market operations are carried out through the purchase and sale of U.S. Treasury securities in the secondary market to alter the reserves of the banking system.[6] By altering bank reserves, the Fed can influence short-term interest rates, and hence overall credit conditions. The Fed's target for open market operations is the federal funds rate, the rate at which banks lend to one another on an overnight basis. The federal funds rate is market determined, meaning the rate fluctuates as supply and demand for bank reserves change. The Fed announces a target for the federal funds rate and pushes the market rate toward the target by altering the supply of reserves in the market through the purchase and sale of Treasury securities.[7] More reserves increase the liquidity in the banking system and, in theory, should make banks more willing to lend, spreading greater liquidity throughout the financial system.

When the Fed wants to stimulate economic activity, it lowers the federal funds target, which is referred to as expansionary policy. Lower interest rates stimulate economic activity by stimulating interest-sensitive spending, which includes physical capital investment (e.g., plant and equipment) by firms, residential investment (housing construction), and consumer durable spending (e.g, automobiles and appliances) by households. Lower rates would also be expected to lead to a lower value of the dollar, all else equal. A lower dollar would stimulate exports and the output of U.S. import-competing firms. To reduce spending in the economy (called contractionary policy), the Fed raises interest rates, and the process works in reverse.

Central banks across the world, including Europe, Japan, and the United States acted quickly to restore liquidity to the financial system following August 9, 2007. On a normal day, the Fed might need to buy or sell a couple billion dollars of Treasury securities to keep the federal funds rate within a few one-hundredths of a percent of its target. Suddenly on August 9, the federal funds rate approached 6%, and the Fed was forced to purchase $24 billion of Treasury securities in order to add enough liquidity to bring the federal funds rate back down to its target of 5.25%. On August 10, the Fed needed to purchase an additional $38 billion to keep the rate at its target, and issued a statement that began, "The Federal Reserve is providing liquidity to facilitate the orderly functioning of financial markets." The European Central Bank provided 156 billion euros ($215 billion) of liquidity to markets on August 9 and 10. Normalcy soon returned to the federal funds market, although other parts of the financial system remained illiquid. The Fed took similar actions on March 7, 2008, when it announced that it would be injecting up to $100 billion in liquidity for at least 28 days through open market operations. It took similar actions again in September 2008.

How should the Fed's actions in these instances be characterized? The Fed's actions cannot be classified as a policy change since it left the federal funds target rate unchanged—in the August case for over a month.[8] Nor can it be considered unusual that the Fed bought Treasury securities to keep the federal funds rate at its target—the Fed does this on a daily basis. What was unusual about the incidents was the magnitude of liquidity the Fed needed to add to keep the rate near its target.

On September 18, 2007, the Fed reduced the federal funds target rate by 0.5 percentage points to 4.75%, stating that the change was "intended to forestall some of the adverse effects on the broader economy that might otherwise arise from the disruptions in financial markets..." Since then, the Fed has aggressively lowered interest rates several times. The Fed decides whether to change its target for the federal funds rate at meetings scheduled every six weeks. In normal conditions, the Fed would typically leave the target unchanged or change it by 0.25 percentage points. From September to March, the Fed lowered the target at each regularly scheduled meeting, by an increment larger than 0.25 percentage points at most of these meetings. It also lowered the target by 0.75 percentage points at an unscheduled meeting on January 21, 2008.

As the financial turmoil persisted, the Fed became more concerned about rising inflationary pressures. Although financial conditions had not returned to normal, the Fed kept the federal funds rate steady from April 30, 2008, until October 9, 2008, when it again reduced the federal funds rate, this time by 0.5 percentage points, to 1.5%. Unusually, this rate reduction was coordinated with several foreign central banks. On October 29, 2008, the Fed reduced the federal funds rate to 1%.

The Discount Window

The Fed can also provide liquidity to member banks (depository institutions that are members of the Federal Reserve system) directly through discount window lending.[9] Discount window lending dates back to the early days of the Fed, and was originally the Fed's main policy tool. (The Fed's main policy tool shifted from the discount window to open market operations several decades ago.) Loans made at the discount window are backed by collateral in excess of the loan value. A wide array of assets can be used as collateral, but they must generally have a high credit rating. Most discount window lending is done on an overnight basis. Unlike the federal funds rate, the Fed sets the discount rate directly through fiat.

During normal market conditions, the Fed has discouraged banks from borrowing at the discount window on a routine basis, believing that banks should be able to meet their normal reserve needs through the market. Thus, the discount window has played a secondary role in policymaking to open market operations. In 2003, the Fed made that policy explicit in its pricing by changing the discount rate from 0.5 percentage points below to 1 percentage point above the federal funds rate. A majority of member banks do not access the discount window in any given year. Since the beginning of the financial turmoil, the Fed has reduced the spread between the federal funds rate and the discount rate, although it has kept the spread positive.

On August 17, 2007, the Fed took further actions to restore calm to financial markets when it reduced the discount rate from 6.25% to 5.75%. Since then, the discount rate has been lowered several times, typically at the same time as the federal funds rate. From 1959 to 2007, discount window lending outstanding never surpassed $8 billion. Discount window lending (in the primary credit category) increased from a daily average of $45 million outstanding in July 2007 to $1,345 million in September 2007. Lending continued to increase to more than $10 billion outstanding per day from May 2008, and has reached as high as $90 billion, but was superseded in economic significance by the creation of the "Term Auction Facility" in December 2007 (discussed below).

NEW TOOLS

The Fed's traditional tools are aimed at the commercial banking system, but current financial turmoil has occurred outside of the banking system as well. The inability of traditional tools to calm financial markets since August 2007 has led the Fed to develop several new tools to fill perceived gaps between open market operations and the discount window.

Traditionally, the lender of last resort function has focused on the banking system, and the Fed's relationship with the banking system is prescribed in detail by the Federal Reserve Act. Many of the new facilities are aimed at other parts of the financial system, however, and the Federal Reserve Act is largely silent on the Fed's authority outside the banking system. One exception is the broad emergency authority under Section 13(3) of the Federal Reserve Act, which the Fed has frequently invoked since the financial crisis began.

Term Auction Facility

A stigma is thought to be attached to borrowing from the discount window. In good times, discount window lending has traditionally been discouraged on the grounds that banks should meet their reserve requirements through the marketplace (the federal funds market) rather than the Fed. Borrowing from the Fed was therefore seen as a sign of weakness, as it implied that market participants were unwilling to lend to the bank because of fears of insolvency. In the current turmoil, this perception of weakness could be particularly damaging since a bank could be undermined by a run based on unfounded, but self-fulfilling fears. Ironically, this means that although the Fed encourages discount window borrowing so that banks can avoid liquidity problems, banks are hesitant to turn to the Fed because of fears that doing so would spark a crisis of confidence. As a result, the Fed found the discount window a relatively ineffective way to deal with liquidity problems in the current turmoil. It created the supplementary Term Auction Facility (TAF) in response.[10]

Discount window lending is initiated at the behest of the requesting institution—the Fed has no control over how many requests for loans it receives. The TAF allows the Fed to determine the amount of reserves it wishes to lend out to banks, based on market conditions. The auction process determines the rate at which those funds will be lent, with all bidders receiving the lowest winning bid rate. The winning bid may not be lower than the prevailing federal funds rate. Determining the rate by bid provides the Fed with additional information on how much demand for reserves exists.

Any depository institution eligible for discount window lending can participate in the TAF. Auctions through the TAF have been held twice a month beginning in December 2007. The amounts auctioned have greatly exceeded discount window lending, which averages in the hundreds of millions of dollars outstanding daily in normal times and more than $10 billion outstanding since May 2008. The TAF initially auctioned $20 billion every two weeks, but this amount was increased on several occasions to as much as $150 billion every two weeks, so that the daily loans outstanding have exceeded $100 billion since April 2008.[11] Like discount window lending, TAF loans must be fully collateralized with the same qualifying collateral. As with discount window lending, the Fed faces the risk that the value of collateral would fall below the loan amount in the event that the loan was not repaid. For that reason, the amount lent diminishes as the quality of the collateral diminishes.

Loans mature in 28 days—far longer than overnight loans in the federal funds market or the typical discount window loan. (In July 2008, the Fed began making some TAF loans that matured in 84 days.) Another motivation for the TAF may have been an attempt to reduce the unusually large divergence that had emerged between the federal funds rate and interbank lending rates for longer maturities. This divergence, which can be seen as a sign of how much liquidity had deteriorated in spite of the Fed's previous efforts, became much smaller after December. In subsequent periods of market stress, such as September 2008, the divergence reemerged. The evidence on the effectiveness of the TAF in reducing this divergence is mixed.[12]

The TAF program was announced as a temporary program that could be made permanent after assessment. Given that the discount rate is set higher than the federal funds rate to discourage its use in normal market conditions, it is unclear what role a permanent TAF would fill, unless the funds auctioned were minimal in normal market conditions. A permanent TAF would seem to run counter to the philosophy governing the discount window that financial institutions, if possible, should rely on the private sector to meet their short-term reserve needs during normal market conditions.

Term Securities Lending Facility

For many years, the Fed has allowed primary dealers (see box for definition) to swap Treasuries of different maturities or attributes with the Fed on an overnight basis through a program called the System Open Market Account Securities Lending Program to help meet the dealers' liquidity needs. (While all Treasury securities are backed by the full faith and credit of the federal government, some securities are more liquid than others, mainly because of differences in availability.) Securities lending has no effect on general interest rates or the money supply since it does not involve cash, but can affect the liquidity premium of the securities traded. Since the loans were overnight and collateralized with other Treasury securities, there was very little risk for the Fed.

WHAT IS A PRIMARY DEALER?

Primary dealers are about 20 large financial institutions who are the counterparties with which the Fed undertakes open market operations (buying and selling of Treasury securities). To be a primary dealer, an institution must, among other things, meet relevant Basel or SEC capital requirements and maintain a good trading relationship with the Fed.

On March 11, 2008, the Fed set up a more expansive securities lending program for the primary dealers called the Term Securities Lending Facility (TSLF). Under this program, up to $200 billion of Treasury securities could be lent for 28 days instead of overnight (as of September 2008). Initially, loans could be collateralized with U.S. Treasuries, government "agency" debt (including debt issued by Fannie Mae and Freddie Mac), mortgage-backed securities (MBS) issued by government agencies or private labels with an AAA/Aaa rating, agency commercial mortgage-backed securities, and agency collateralized mortgage obligations. On September 14, 2008, the Fed expanded acceptable collateral to include all investment-grade debt securities. Given the recent drop in MBS and other asset prices, this made the new lending program considerably more risky than the old one. But the scope for losses is limited by the fact that the loans are fully collateralized with a "haircut" (i.e., less money is loaned than the value of the collateral), and if the collateral loses value before the loan is due, the Fed can call for substitute collateral. The first auction on March 27 involved $75 billion of securities. In August 2008, the program was expanded to allow the primary dealers to purchase up to $50 billion of options (with prices set by auction) to swap for Treasuries through the TSLF. The TSLF was announced as a temporary facility. The facility was subsequently extended, most recently until the end of April 2009.

By allowing the primary dealers to temporarily swap illiquid assets such as MBS for highly liquid Treasuries, "[t]he TSLF is intended to promote liquidity in the financing markets for Treasury and other collateral and thus to foster the functioning of financial markets more generally," according to the Fed.[13] Given the timing of the announcement—less than a week before the failure of one of its primary dealers, Bear Stearns—critics have alleged that the program was created, in effect, in an attempt to rescue Bear Stearns from its liquidity problems. But it should be noted that the new program did not involve Bear Stearns' most illiquid and devalued assets. As will be discussed below, the Fed would take much larger steps to aid Bear Stearns later the same week.

Primary Dealer Credit Facility

On March 16—a day too late to help Bear Stearns—the Fed announced the creation of the Primary Dealer Credit Facility (PDCF), a new direct lending program for primary dealers very similar to the discount window program for depository institutions. Loans are made through the PDCF on an overnight basis at the discount rate, limiting their riskiness.

Acceptable collateral initially included Treasuries, government agency debt, and investment grade corporate, mortgage- backed, asset-backed, and municipal securities. Borrowing from the facility has been sporadic, with average daily borrowing outstanding above $10 billion in the first three months, hitting zero in August 2008, and above $50 billion following the financial deterioration in September 2008. On September 14, 2008, the Fed expanded acceptable collateral to include certain classes of equities. Many of the classes of eligible assets can and have fluctuated significantly in value. Fees will be charged to frequent users.

EMERGENCY AUTHORITY UNDER SECTION 13(3) OF THE FEDERAL RESERVE ACT

The Fed has limited authority to assist non-member banks under the Federal Reserve Act. One exception where authority is granted is under paragraph 3 of Section 13 of the Federal Reserve Act. It reads,

In unusual and exigent circumstances, the Board of Governors of the Federal Reserve System, by the affirmative vote of not less than five members, may authorize any Federal reserve bank...to discount for any individual, partnership, or corporation, notes, drafts, and bills of exchange.... Provided, that before discounting any such note, draft, or bill exchange...the Federal reserve bank shall obtain evidence that such individual, partnership, or corporation is unable to secure adequate credit accommodations from other banking institutions...

It is noteworthy that this text allows emergencies to be identified by the Board of Governors and places few limits on what type of institution can receive financial assistance from the Fed or what form that assistance can take. The fact that the authority is justified only by unusual and exigent circumstances suggests that decisions made under 13(3), such as the creation of lending facilities, could not be made permanent under existing authority. As will be discussed below, on a few occasions in 2008, Section 13(3) has been invoked to lend to an entity that the Fed created.

According to the New York Fed, this authority had not been used in about 70 years prior to the Bear Stearns incident. It has been invoked numerous times in 2008, including to authorize the Primary Dealer Credit Facility, the Fed's role in the Bear Stearns merger, and the Fed's extension of credit to AIG. Financial crises can spread quickly, and Section 13(3) makes a prompt response possible. But recent events have demonstrated that it vests the Fed with the ability to take large, wide-ranging actions without Congressional approval. (It has voluntarily sought and received Treasury approval in each instance.)

Section 13(3) was amended in October 2008. P.L. 110-343 requires the Fed to report to Congress on its justification for exercising Section 13(3), the terms of the assistance provided, and regular updates on the status of the loan.

For more information, see Federal Reserve Bank of New York, "The Discount Window," Fedpoint, Aug. 2007; David Fettig, "The History of a Powerful Paragraph," Federal Reserve Bank of Minneapolis, The Region, June 2008..

The program was announced as lasting six months, or longer if events warrant. The program is authorized under paragraph 3 of Section 13 of the Federal Reserve Act. The facility was subsequently extended, most recently until the end of April 2009.

Although the program shares some characteristics with the discount window and the Term Securities Lending Facility, the fact that the program was authorized under paragraph 3 of Section 13 of the Federal Reserve Act suggests that there is a fundamental difference between this program and the Fed's normal operations. The Fed is referred to as the nation's central bank because it is at the center of the banking system—providing reserves and credit, and acting as a regulator, clearinghouse, and lender of last resort to the banking system. The privileges for banks that come from belonging to the Federal Reserve system—access to Fed credit—come with the costs of regulation to ensure that banks do not take excessive risks. Although the primary dealers are subject to certain capital requirements, they are not necessarily part of the banking system, and do not fall under the same "safety and soundness" regulatory structure as banks.

Term Asset-Backed Securities Loan Facility

In November 2008, the Fed created the Term Asset-Backed Securities Loan Facility (TALF) in response to problems in the market for asset-backed securities (ABS). According to the Fed,

> New issuance of ABS declined precipitously in September and came to a halt in October. At the same time, interest rate spreads on AAA-rated tranches of ABS soared to levels well outside the range of historical experience, reflecting unusually high risk premiums.[14]

The TALF is intended to stimulate the issuance of new securities backed by pools of student loans, automobile loans, credit card loans, and loans guaranteed by the Small Business Administration. (The Fed announced that the TALF may later be expanded to other classes of ABS, such as mortgage-related securities.) The Fed fears that if lenders cannot securitize these types of loans, eventually households will be forced to reduce consumption spending, which would exacerbate the economic downturn. For a security to be eligible for use as collateral, its issuer (not the borrower) must follow the executive compensation policies under Section 111(b) of the Emergency Economic Stabilization Act, P.L. 110-343.[15]

Rather than purchase ABS directly, the Fed will make non-recourse loans to private individuals to purchase newly issued ABS receiving the highest credit rating, using the ABS as collateral. If the ABS lose value, the losses will be borne by the Fed and the Treasury through the TARP program instead of by the borrower. The Fed will lend less than the current value of the collateral, so the Fed would not bear losses on the loan until losses exceed the value of the "haircut." The loans will have a term of one year, but can be renewed. The amount lent and the interest rate on the loans will be determined by an auction process, with maximums and minimums set by the Fed. The total amount lent will not exceed $200 billion. Any U.S. citizen or business may borrow from the Fed via a primary dealer under this program; since the Fed is lending to non-banks, the facility is authorized under Section 13(3) of the Federal Reserve Act. The facility is scheduled to cease making new loans at the end of 2009.

If the loans are not repaid, the Treasury will bear the first $20 billion in total losses on the underlying collateral, and the Fed will bear any additional losses. The Treasury's losses will be financed through the Troubled Assets Purchase Program (TARP), authorized by P.L. 110-343. TALF has some similarities to TARP as it was originally envisioned, with the primary differences being that the Fed is lending to purchase rather than purchasing assets, and the assets backing the loans are newly issued as opposed to "troubled" existing assets. Since the Treasury's funds will finance loan losses rather than asset purchases, the $20 billion will support a much larger volume of assets than would be possible through direct purchase via TARP.

Intervention in the Commercial Paper Market

Many large firms routinely issue commercial paper, which is short-term debt purchased directly by investors that matures in less than 270 days, with an average maturity of 30 days. There are three broad categories of commercial paper issuers: financial firms, non-financial firms, and pass- through entities that issue paper backed by assets. The commercial paper issued directly by firms tends not to be backed by collateral, as these firms are viewed as large and creditworthy and the paper matures quickly.

Individual investors are major purchasers of commercial paper through money market mutual funds and money market accounts. The Securities and Exchange Commission regulates the holdings of money market mutual funds, limiting their holdings to highly rated, short-term debt; thus, investors widely perceived money market mutual funds as safe and low risk. On September 16, the Reserve Fund, which is a money market mutual fund, "broke the buck," meaning that the value of its shares had fallen below face value. This occurred because of losses it had taken on short-term debt issued by Lehman Brothers, which filed for bankruptcy on September 15. Money market investors had perceived "breaking the buck" to be highly unlikely, and its occurrence set off a run on money market funds, as many investors simultaneously attempted to withdraw their investments. This run greatly decreased the demand for new commercial paper. Firms rely on the ability to issue new debt to roll over maturing debt to meet their liquidity needs.

Fearing that disruption in the commercial paper markets could make overall problems in financial markets more severe, the Fed announced on September 19 that it would create the Asset-Backed Commercial Paper Money Market Mutual Fund Liquidity Facility (AMLF). This facility would make non-recourse loans to banks to purchase asset-backed commercial paper. Because the loans were non-recourse, the banks would have no further liability to repay any losses on the commercial paper collateralizing the loan. In its first week of operation, there were daily loans of $152 billion outstanding through the AMLF. The temporary facility was subsequently extended until the end of April 2009.

Although the creation of the AMLF and the Treasury's temporary guarantee of money market mutual fund deposits had eased conditions in the commercial paper market, the market remained strained. For example, commercial paper outstanding fell from more than $2 trillion outstanding in August 2007 to $1.8 trillion on September 7, 2008, to $1.6 trillion on October

1, 2008. The yield on 30-day, AA-rated asset-backed commercial paper rose from 2.7% on September 8, 2008, to 5.5% on October 7, 2008.

Because of the importance of commercial paper for meeting firms' liquidity needs, the Fed decided to take stronger action to ensure that the market was not disrupted.[16] On October 7, it announced the creation of the Commercial Paper Funding Facility (CPFF), a special purpose vehicle (SPV) that would borrow from the Fed to purchase all types of three-month, highly rated U.S. commercial paper, secured and unsecured, from issuers. The interest rate charged by the CPFF was set at the three month overnight index swap plus 1 percentage point for secured corporate debt, 2 percentage points for unsecured corporate debt, and 3 percentage points for asset-backed paper. The CPFF can buy as much commercial paper from any individual issuer as that issuer had outstanding in the year to date. Any losses borne by the CPFF would ultimately be borne by the Fed. The Fed has hired the private company PIMCO to manage the SPV's assets. The facility is authorized under Section 13 (3) of the Federal Reserve Act, its emergency authority. It will operate until April 2009, subject to renewal by the Fed. The Fed argued that the assurance that firms will be able to roll over commercial paper at the CPFF will encourage private investors to buy commercial paper again.

The CPFF is notable on several grounds. First, it is the first Fed standing facility in modern times with an ongoing commitment to purchase assets, as opposed to lending against assets. Technically, the Fed is lending against the assets of the SPV, but the SPV was created by the Fed and is controlled by the Fed. (The arrangement is similar to the Fed's creation of Maiden Lane, a limited liability corporation, to purchase Bear Stearns' assets (discussed below), but that involved a one-time purchase.) Second, in the case of non-financial commercial paper, it is the first time in several decades that the Fed is providing financial assistance to non-financial firms.[17] Third, in the case of commercial paper that is not asset backed, it is unusual for the Fed (through the SPV) to purchase uncollateralized debt.

On October 21, 2008, the Fed announced the creation of the Money Market Investor Funding Facility (MMIFF), and pledged to lend it up to $540 billion. The MMIFF will lend to private sector SPVs that invest in commercial paper issued by highly rated financial institutions. Each SPV will be owned by a group of financial firms and can only purchase commercial paper issued by that group. These SPVs can purchase commercial paper from money market mutual funds facing redemption requests to help avoid runs such as the run on the Reserve Fund. (The Treasury has already guaranteed existing money market deposits to avoid further runs.) The Fed hopes that if money market mutual funds, in turn, do not have to worry about how to finance redemptions, they will become more willing to purchase commercial paper. Financial firms have an incentive to participate in these SPVs since mutual funds will be more willing to purchase an institution's commercial paper if it is able to sell it back to an SPV. To reduce the risk to the Fed, its lending will be equal to 90% of the value of the commercial paper the SPV purchases (the other 10% of financing will be provided by the money market fund), and done with recourse on an overnight basis at the discount rate. Since the SPVs are not member banks of the Federal Reserve System, the Fed authorized the MMIFF under Section 13(3) of the Federal Reserve Act. The MMIFF is scheduled to wind down by the end of April 2009. Upon winding down, the SPVs will receive a fixed profit, with any additional profits accruing to the Fed.

Swap Lines with Foreign Central Banks

In December 2007, the Fed announced the creation of temporary reciprocal currency agreements, known as swap lines, with the European Central Bank and the Swiss central bank. These agreements let the Fed swap dollars for euros or Swiss francs for a fixed period of time. Since September 2008, the Fed has extended similar swap lines to central banks in several other countries. In October 2008, it made the swap lines unlimited in size. The swap lines are currently authorized through the end of January 2009.

The swap lines are intended to provide liquidity to banks in non-domestic denominations. For example, many European banks have borrowed in dollars to finance dollar-denominated transactions, such as the purchase of U.S. assets. Normally, foreign banks could finance their dollar-denominated borrowing through the private inter-bank lending market. As banks have become reluctant to lend to each other through this market, central banks at home and abroad have taken a much larger role in providing banks with liquidity directly. But through normal lending channels, banks can only borrow from their home central bank, and central banks can only provide liquidity in their own currency. The swap lines allow central banks to provide needed liquidity in other currencies.

Payment of Interest on Bank Reserves

Banks hold reserves to meet daily cash-flow needs and requirements imposed by the Fed. At times over the past year, the Fed has faced conflicting goals—it seeks to ensure that banks have enough reserves to remain liquid, but it also seeks to maintain its target for the federal funds rate to meet its economic goals. The federal funds rate is the market rate in the private market where a bank with excess reserves lends them overnight to other banks. At times, ensuring that all banks have adequate reserves has resulted in an overall level of reserves in the market that has pushed the federal funds rate below its target. In other words, the only way for the Fed to make sure that each bank has enough reserves has been to oversupply the banking system as a whole with liquidity at the given federal funds target.

To avoid this problem, Congress authorized the Fed to pay interest on bank reserves in the Emergency Economic Stabilization Act of 2008 (H.R. 1424/P.L. 110-343). By setting an interest rate on bank reserves close to the federal funds rate, the Fed would in effect place a floor on the rate. In theory, the federal funds rate would not fall below the interest rate on reserves because banks would rather hold excess reserves to earn interest than lend them out to other banks at a lower interest rate.[18] Paying interest on reserves may also encourage banks to hold more reserves overall, which may somewhat reduce banks' liquidity problems during the current period of heightened uncertainty.

The interest rate on excess reserves was initially set at 0.75 percentage points less than the federal funds rate. Immediately after the Fed began paying interest, the federal funds rate was still falling below the target, and some days was even below the interest rate on reserves. In response, the Fed subsequently changed the interest rate, most recently in November 2008 to 0.1 percentage points less than the federal funds rate. Even after this change, the actual federal funds rate continued to fall below the target rate.

Paying interest on reserves does not encourage banks to increase overall lending to firms and households, however, because it increases the attractiveness of holding reserves. Thus, it is not a policy that stimulates the economy, at least in any direct sense; on the contrary, it prevents the increase in liquidity to banks from stimulating the economy by preventing the federal funds rate from falling.

P.L. 110-343 gave the Fed permanent authority to pay interest on reserves. Once financial conditions return to normal, the liquidity benefits from paying interest will be less important (since banks will again be able to meet reserve needs through the federal funds market), and the primary remaining benefit would be a reduction in the volatility of the federal funds rate. The Fed previously intervened in the federal funds market on a daily basis to keep the market rate close to the target, sometimes unsuccessfully. The volatility partly resulted from banks devoting resources to activities that minimize reserves, such as "sweep accounts."

Paying interest on reserves reduces the Fed's profits, and thus reduces its remittances to the Treasury, thereby increasing the budget deficit, all else equal. It can be viewed as a transfer from the federal government to the banks, although in the long run, competition makes it likely that the banks will pass on the benefit to depositors in the form of higher interest paid on deposits. From Congress's perspective, the benefit of a less volatile target rate and less resources spent minimizing reserves would have to be weighed against the lost federal revenue, over time. The decision to pay interest on required, as well as excess, reserves also increases the cost of the policy without any additional benefit to liquidity or reduced volatility (because banks must keep required reserves even if no incentive is offered).

Assistance to Individual Financial Institutions

Over the course of the year, several financial firms that were deemed "too big to fail" received financial assistance from the Fed. This assistance went beyond its traditional role of acting as a lender of last resort by providing loans to illiquid but solvent firms.[19]

The Fed's Role in the JPMorgan Chase Acquisition of Bear Stearns

The investment bank Bear Stearns came under severe liquidity pressures in early March, in what many observers have coined a non-bank run.[20] On Friday, March 14, JPMorgan Chase announced that, in conjunction with the Federal Reserve, it had agreed to provide secured funding to Bear Stearns, as necessary. Through its discount window, the Fed agreed to provide $13 billion of back-to-back financing to Bear Stearns via JPMorgan Chase. It was a non-recourse loan, meaning that the Fed had no general claim against JPMorgan Chase in the event that the loan was not repaid and the outstanding balance exceeded the value of the collateral. Bear Stearns could not access the discount window directly because, at that point, only member banks could borrow directly from the Fed. This loan was superseded by the events of March 16, and the loan was repaid in full on March 17.

On Sunday, March 16, after negotiations between the two companies, the Fed and the Treasury, JPMorgan Chase agreed to acquire Bear Stearns. As part of the agreement, the Fed will purchase up to $30 billion of Bear Stearns' assets through Maiden Lane, a new Limited Liability Corporation (LLC) based in Delaware that it has created and controls. After the merger was completed, the loan was finalized on June 26, 2008. Two loans were made to the LLC: the Fed lent the LLC $28.82 billion, and JPMorgan Chase made a subordinate loan to the LLC worth $1.15 billion, based on assets initially valued at $29.97 billion.[21] The Fed's loan will be made at an interest rate set equal to the discount rate (2.5% when the terms were announced, but fluctuating over time) for a term of 10 years, renewable by the Fed.[22] JPMorgan Chase's loan will have an interest rate 4.5 percentage points above the discount rate.

Using the proceeds from that loan, the LLC will purchase assets from Bear Stearns worth $29.97 billion at marked to market prices by Bear Stearns on March 14. The Fed reported that

> The portfolio supporting the credit extensions consists largely of mortgage-related assets. In particular, it includes cash assets as well as related hedges. The cash assets consist of investment grade securities (i.e. securities rated BBB- or higher by at least one of the three principal credit rating agencies and no lower than that by the others) and residential or commercial mortgage loans classified as "performing". All of the assets are current as to principal and interest (as of March 14, 2008). All securities are domiciled and issued in the U.S. and denominated in U.S. dollars. The portfolio consists of collateralized mortgage obligations (CMOs), the majority of which are obligations of government-sponsored entities (GSEs), such as the Federal Home Loan Mortgage Corporation ("Freddie Mac"), as well as asset-backed securities, adjustable-rate mortgages, commercial mortgage-backed securities, non-GSE CMOs, collateralized bond obligations, and various other loan obligations.[23]

The CEO of JPMorgan Chase testified that JPMorgan Chase "kept the riskier and more complex securities in the Bear Stearns portfolio...We did not cherry pick the assets in the collateral pool (for the LLC)."[24] These assets are owned by the LLC, which will eventually liquidate them to pay back the principal and interest owed to the Fed and JPMorgan Chase. The LLC's assets (purchased from Bear Stearns) are the collateral backing the loans from the Fed and JPMorgan Chase. A private company, BlackRock Financial Management, has been hired to manage the portfolio. Neither Bear Stearns nor JPMorgan Chase owes the Fed any principal or interest, nor are they liable if the LLC is unable to pay back the money the Fed lent it. The New York Fed explained that the LLC was created to "ease administration of the portfolio and will remove constraints on the money manager that might arise from retaining the assets on the books of Bear Stearns."[25] JPMorgan Chase and Bear Stearns did not receive the $28.82 billion from the LLC until the merger was completed.[26]

It was announced that the Fed is planning to begin liquidating the assets after two years. The assets will be sold off gradually, "to minimize disruption to financial markets and maximize recovery value."[27] As the assets are liquidated, interest will continue to accrue on the remaining amount of the loan outstanding. Thus, in order for the principal and interest to be paid off, the assets will need to appreciate enough or generate enough income so that the rate of return on the assets exceeds the weighted interest rate on the loans (plus the operating costs of the LLC). **Table 1** shows how the funds raised through the liquidation will be used. Any difference between the proceeds and the amount of the loans is profit or loss for the Fed, not JPMorgan Chase. Because JPMorgan Chase's $1.15 billion loan was subordinate to the Fed's $28.82 billion loan, if there are losses on the total assets, the first $1.15 billion of losses will be borne, in effect, by JPMorgan Chase, however. As of November 2008, the value of the assets had already been written down by nearly $3 billion, exceeding the maximum losses borne by JPMorgan Chase.[28] The interest on the loan will be repaid out of the asset sales, not by JPMorgan Chase.

Table 1. Use of Funds Raised by Liquidation of Bear Stearns Assets

Payments from the liquidation will be made in the following order:
(1) operating expenses of the limited liability corporation
(2) $29 billion principal owed to the Federal Reserve
(3) interest due to the Federal Reserve on the $29 billion loan
(4) $1 billion principal owed to JPMorgan Chase
(5) interest due to JPMorgan Chase on $1 billion subordinated note
(6) non-operating expenses of the limited liability corporation
(7) remaining funds accrue to Federal Reserve

Source: Federal Reserve Bank of New York.

Note: Each category must be fully paid before proceeding to the next category.

The CEO of JPMorgan Chase testified that "we could not and would not have assumed the substantial risks of acquiring Bear Stearns without the $30 billion facility provided by the Fed."[29] The primary risk was presumably that the value of mortgage-related assets would continue to decline. Had the transaction been crafted as a typical discount window loan directly to JPMorgan Chase, JPMorgan Chase would have been required to pay back the principal and interest, and it (rather than the Fed) would have borne the full risk of any depreciation in value of Bear Stearns' assets.

The Fed's statutory authority for its role in both Bear Stearns transactions comes from paragraph 3 of Section 13 of the Federal Reserve Act. In his testimony, New York Fed President Timothy Geithner stated that the Fed did not have authority to acquire an equity interest in Bear Stearns or JPMorgan Chase.[30] Yet the LLC controlled by the Fed acquired assets from Bear Stearns, and the profits or losses from that acquisition will ultimately accrue to the Fed. It is unclear why the Fed decided to create and lend to a LLC to complete the transaction, rather than engaging in the transaction directly. Although the Fed did not buy Bear Stearns' assets directly, there are certainly important policy questions raised by the Fed's creation and financing of an LLC in order to buy Bear Stearns' assets. Typically, the Fed lends money to institutions and receives collateral in return to reduce the risk of suffering a loss. When the loan is repaid, the collateral is returned to the institution. In this case, the Fed made a loan, but to a LLC they created and controlled, not to a financial institution. From the perspective of JPMorgan Chase or Bear Stearns, the transaction was a sale (to the LLC), not a loan, regardless of whether the Fed or the LLC was the principal.

Assistance to American International Group (AIG)

Initial Loan

On September 16, 2008, the Fed announced, after consultation with the Treasury Department, that it would lend up to $85 billion to the financial institution American International Group. AIG had experienced a significant decline in its stock price and was facing immediate demands for $14 billion to $15 billion in collateral payments due to recent downgrades by credit rating agencies, according to press reports.[31] The Fed and Treasury feared that AIG was also "too big to fail" because of the potential for widespread disruption to financial markets that would result.

The Fed announced that AIG could borrow up to $85 billion from the Fed over the next two years. On September 18, the Fed announced that it had initially lent $28 billion to AIG.[32] The interest rate on the funds drawn is 8.5 percentage points above the London Interbank Offered Rate (LIBOR), a rate that banks charge to lend to each other. AIG will also have to pay a (lower) interest rate on any funds that it is does not draw from the facility. In return, the government will receive warrants that, if exercised, would give the government a 79.9% ownership stake in AIG. The Fed will name three independent trustees to oversee the firm for the duration of the loan.

The lending facility is backed by the assets of AIG's non-regulated subsidiaries (but not the assets of its insurance company). In other words, the Fed can seize AIG's assets if the firm fails to honor the terms of the loan. This reduces the risk that the Fed (and ultimately, taxpayers) will suffer a loss. The risk still remains that if AIG turned out to be insolvent, its assets would be insufficient to cover the amount it had borrowed from the Fed. Since AIG has been identified as too big to fail, it is unclear how its assets could be seized in the event of non-payment without precipitating failure.

Second Loan

On October 8, the Fed announced that it was expanding its assistance to AIG and swapping cash for up to $37.8 billion of AIG's investment-grade, fixed-income securities. These securities, belonging to AIG's insurance subsidiaries, had been previously lent out and unavailable as collateral at the time of the original agreement. It has been reported that as AIG's loans matured, AIG realized losses on investments it had made with the collateral and some counterparties stopped participating in the lending program.[33] As a result, AIG needed liquidity from the Fed to cover these losses and counterparty withdrawals.

Although this assistance resembles a typical collateralized loan (the Fed receives assets as collateral, and the borrower receives cash), the Fed characterized the agreement as a loan of securities from AIG to the Fed in exchange for cash collateral. It appears the arrangement was structured this way because New York insurance law prevents AIG from using the securities as collateral in a loan.[34] The terms of the agreement are unavailable at this time.

Revised Agreement[35]

On November 10, 2008, the Federal Reserve and the U.S. Treasury announced a restructuring of the federal intervention to support AIG. Since the initial loan, some, notably AIG's former CEO Maurice Greenberg, had criticized the terms as overly harsh, arguing that the loan itself might be contributing to AIG's eventual failure as a company. As evidenced by the additional borrowing after the September 16 loan, AIG had continued to see cash flow out of the company, particularly to post collateral for the credit default swaps that were arguably the primary cause of the financial problems in the company. The revised agreement points to the tension between making the terms of the assistance undesirable enough to deter other firms from seeking government assistance in the future, compared to making the terms of assistance so punitive that it exacerbates the financial problems of the recipient firm. It also points to the fact that once a firm has been identified as too big to fail, government assistance to the firm can become open-ended, as the original amounts offered were quickly revised upward.

The November 10 restructuring eased the payment terms for AIG and had three primary parts: (1) a $40 billion direct capital injection, (2) restructuring of the $85 billion loan, and (3) a $52.5 billion purchase of troubled assets.

Loan Restructuring

The initial $85 billion loan facility from the Federal Reserve was reduced to $60 billion, for a time period extended to five years, and the financial terms are eased considerably. Specifically, the interest rate on the amount outstanding is reduced by 5.5 percentage points (to Libor plus 3%) and the fee on undrawn funds is reduced by 7.75 percentage points (to 0.75%).

Purchase of Troubled Assets

While P.L. 110-343 provided for the government purchase of troubled assets, the purchases related to AIG are being done by limited liability corporations (LLCs) created and controlled by the Federal Reserve. This structure is similar to that created by the Federal Reserve to facilitate the purchase of Bear Stearns by JPMorgan Chase in March 2008. There are two LLCs set up for AIG—one for residential mortgage-backed securities (RMBS) and one for collateralized debt obligations (CDO).

The RMBS LLC will be lent up to $22.5 billion by the Federal Reserve and $1 billion from AIG to purchase RMBS from AIG's securities lending portfolio. The AIG loan is subordinated and AIG will bear the first $1 billion in losses should there be future losses on these securities. AIG and the Federal Reserve will "share" in any future gains, though it is unclear exactly how such gains would be shared. The previous $37.8 billion loan securities lending loan facility is to be repaid and terminated with the proceeds from this LLC plus additional AIG funds if necessary.

The CDO LLC will be lent up to $30 billion from the Federal Reserve and $5 billion from AIG to purchase CDOs on which AIG has written credit default swaps. The $5 billion loan from AIG is subordinated and AIG will bear the first $5 billion in future losses on these securities. AIG and the Federal Reserve will "share" in any future gains, though it is unclear exactly how such gains would be shared. The Federal Reserve also indicates that the credit default swaps will be unwound at the same time that the CDOs are purchased. Many credit default swaps, however, are purchased by entities not holding the underlying CDOs; it is unclear how, or if, such credit default swaps written by AIG will be addressed.

Direct Capital Injection

Through the Troubled Asset Relief Program (TARP), the Treasury purchased $40 billion in preferred shares of AIG. In addition to $40 billion in preferred shares, the Treasury also receives warrants for common shares equal to 2% of the outstanding AIG shares. TARP was authorized by Congress in H.R. 1424/P.L. 110-343 and the Capital Purchase Program (CPP) under TARP was first announced by Treasury Secretary Paulson on October 14, 2008. AIG would be the first announced non-bank to receive TARP funds. The $40 billion in preferred AIG shares now held by the Treasury are slated to pay a 10% dividend per annum, accrued quarterly.[36] Participation in TARP triggers restrictions on executive pay as required by Congress, including a restriction on "golden parachutes" and a requirement for clawbacks on previously provided bonuses in the case of accounting irregularities. According to the

November 10, 2008, AIG filings with the Securities and Exchange Commission, the amount of shares held in trust for the benefit of the U.S. Treasury will be reduced by the shares and warrants purchased under TARP, so the total equity interest currently held by the U.S. government equals 77.9% plus warrants to purchase another 2%.

Legal Authority

All Fed assistance to AIG is authorized under Section 13 (3) of the Federal Reserve Act, the same emergency authorization used for the Bear Stearns loan. This authorization was needed because the Fed cannot normally lend to a financial firm that is neither a depository institution nor a primary dealer.

Guarantee of Citigroup's Assets

Similar to Bear Stearns and AIG, Citigroup faced a sudden drop in its stock price in late 2008. Its stock price fell from $23 per share on October 1, 2008, to $3.77 on November 21, 2008, amidst investor concern about its losses. Stepping in before a potential run began, the Federal Reserve and federal government announced on November 23 that it would purchase an additional $20 billion of Citigroup preferred shares through TARP and guarantee a pool of up to $306 billion of Citigroup's assets. These assets were described as "loans and securities backed by residential and commercial real estate and other such assets."[37] The guarantee is in place for 10 years for residential assets and 5 years for non-residential assets. Citgroup will exclusively bear up to the first $29 billion of losses on the pool. Any additional losses will be split between Citigroup and the government, with Citigroup bearing 10% of the losses and the government bearing 90%. The first $5 billion of government's losses will be borne by the Treasury using TARP funds; the next $10 billion will be borne by the FDIC; all further losses will be borne by the Fed through a non- recourse loan. Citigroup will pay the federal government a fee for the guarantee in the form of preferred stock. The assets will remain on Citigroup's balance sheet, and Citigroup will receive the income stream generated by the assets.

In the cases of Bear Stearns and AIG, management was replaced and shareholders equity was diluted to limit moral hazard problems associated with government assistance.[38] Similar steps were not taken in the case of Citigroup.

POLICY ISSUES

Cost to the Treasury

Unlike all other institutions, currency (Federal Reserve notes) is the Fed's primary liability. Along with its holdings of Treasury securities, its assets are the loans it makes (through the discount window and the new programs detailed above) and the private assets it hold through LLCs (e.g., for AIG and the Bear Stearns takeover). Its loans and asset purchases are financed by increasing its liabilities (Federal Reserve notes), and does not inherently impose any cost to the Treasury. Indeed, if the loans are repaid, they would increase the profits of the Fed, which in turn would increase the Fed's remittances to the Treasury.[39] Even if the loans are not repaid, they are fully collateralized (in some cases, over collateralized), so the Fed would not suffer losses unless the collateral had lost value. In addition, some of the loans discussed above are made with recourse, which means that the firms are liable if the collateral loses value.

The Fed had net income of $38.4 billion and remitted $34.6 billion to the Treasury in 2007. In the past, most of the Fed's net income has derived from the interest on its Treasury securities holdings, not its loans. The earnings and any losses the Fed took on its loans would increase or reduce its net income, respectively. If loan losses caused an overall net loss, the Fed's capital (the excess of its assets compared with its liabilities) would be reduced. The Fed had capital of $36.9 billion at end of 2007, half of which was paid-in capital of member banks and the other half was surplus. The Fed has not had an annual net operating loss since 1915. However, the Fed's assets became more risky in 2008 due to the shift in its assets from U.S. Treasuries to direct loans and due to the increase in its assets and liabilities relative to its capital.

Thus, any potential losses on loans to the Fed would not involve taxpayer dollars unless the losses exceeded the sum of its other earnings and its capital. For example, in October 2008, the Fed's capital would be depleted if its realized net losses were equal in value to 3.5% of its holdings of securities (U.S. Treasuries and loans). However, any losses could result in a smaller remittance of earnings to the Treasury than would have occurred had the Fed not made the loans. Therefore, the ultimate cost to the government is the same whether loans to the financial sector are made through the Fed or the Treasury. Although the Fed has taken steps to minimize the risk that recent activities will result in losses, Members of Congress have raised the question of whether taxpayers should be exposed to additional fiscal risks without congressional approval, particularly since some of the Fed's actions have similarities to those authorized under TARP.

How Much Can the Fed Lend? Will the Fed Run Out of Money?

As direct loans from the Fed have multiplied, some observers have questioned at what point the Fed's lending power will be exhausted. The Fed cannot "run out of money" to lend because it controls the monetary base, through which it expands or contracts the amount of money outstanding to suit its needs. There are no statutory limits on the size of the money supply (and, thus, how much it can loan); the ultimate constraint on the monetary base, and thus its willingness to lend, comes from the part of its congressional mandate requiring stable prices (i.e., a low and stable rate of price inflation.) If the Fed allows the money supply to become too large, then price inflation will become uncomfortably high (discussed in the section below on "Stagflation?"). In the 12 months ending in August 2008, inflation (as measured by the consumer price index) had risen 5.4%—significantly higher than the Fed's self-identified "comfort zone." Thus, the Fed is reluctant to allow its loans to result in a significant expansion in the money supply.[40] (As commodity prices fell later in 2008, the inflation rate also fell.)

When the Fed makes loans to private financial firms, it increases the money supply unless offset by open market operations, namely, the sale of Treasury securities. In practice, before September 2008, the Fed had kept the monetary base relatively constant by selling enough Treasury securities to offset the additional loans it makes. (When the Fed sells Treasury securities, it removes the money it receives from circulation.) On the Fed's balance sheet, both Treasury securities and loans outstanding are assets. Thus, as loans outstanding have risen, its holdings of Treasury securities have declined. For example, in September 2007, 88% of its assets were Treasury securities held outright and less than 1% were loans to the financial system. In November 2008, 23% of its assets were Treasury securities, 32% were loans, and 16% were private securities (mostly commercial paper).

Some have worried that, if this trend continued, the Fed would eventually hold too few Treasury securities to be able to conduct open market operations.[41] This scenario is not imminent—as of October 2008, the Fed still held about $480 billion in Treasury securities (although some of those are lent through the TSLF). Nevertheless, to safeguard against any risk of this eventuality, the Treasury announced the Supplementary Financing Program on September 17, 2008. Under this program, the Treasury will temporarily auction more new securities than it needs to finance government operations and will deposit the proceeds at the Fed. As of December 2008, about $500 billion had been borrowed by the Treasury and deposited at the Fed through this program. Congress authorized this borrowing only indirectly by raising the statutory debt limit, most recently in P.L. 110-343.

This program has two effects. First, it supplies more Treasuries to investors when there is excess demand because of a "flight to quality." (The Treasuries issued under the program are indistinguishable to investors from regularly-issued securities.) Second, it allows the Fed to take on more loans without requiring a reduction to its Treasury holdings in order to offset the effects on the money supply. (The increase in the money supply is offset because the money received by the Treasury is held at the Fed and not allowed to circulate.) Ultimately, the program will not affect the Treasury's fiscal position, however, because it will increase the profits of the Fed, which are then remitted to the Treasury.

The fact that the Fed has been "sterilizing" the effects of its loans on the money supply may be limiting the effects of those loans on financial conditions. In essence, the Fed has two methods for providing the financial system with liquidity—open market operations or direct loans. The Fed has increased the role of direct loans to directly meet individual financial institutions' liquidity needs. But the Fed has to offset the effects of the direct loans on the money supply to meet its goals for inflation. Thus, the loans do not provide additional overall monetary stimulus to the economy when sterilized.[42] Since the Fed is sterilizing the loans because of its concerns with inflation, the utility of the program is fundamentally a question of whether the Fed has achieved the proper balance between stabilizing the financial sector and providing price stability, two topics that are discussed below.

Why Have the Fed's Actions Not Successfully Restored Financial Normalcy?

The Fed's actions since 2007 have been primarily focused on restoring liquidity to the financial system—lending to financial firms to convert their illiquid assets into cash or U.S. Treasury securities. But as financial conditions have deteriorated in spite of increasing Fed intervention, it has become apparent that the problems facing financial firms are not exclusively related to liquidity.

The crux of the firms' problem stems from the large losses on some of their assets, particularly mortgage-related assets.[43] This has caused a number of problems for the firms related to *capital adequacy,* which is the difference between the value of their assets and the value of their liabilities. First, losses and write-downs associated with those assets have reduced the firms' existing capital. According to Bloomberg, financial firms had written down losses of $501 billion on mortgage-related assets and raised $353 billion in capital to compensate as of August 2008.[44] Second, in the current environment, investors and creditors are demanding that firms hold more capital relative to assets than before so that firms can better withstand any future losses.

Third, the losses to date have impaired the firms' ability to raise enough new capital. Firms can raise new capital through retained earnings, which have been greatly reduced for many firms by the poor performance of their assets, or by issuing new capital (equity) and selling it to new investors. But in current market conditions, investors have been reluctant to inject new capital into struggling firms. Part of the explanation for this is that current losses have made the firms less profitable. But another part of the reason is that investors fear that there will be further losses in the future that would reduce the value of their investment, and perhaps even cause the firm to become insolvent. Uncertainty about future losses is partly caused by the opacity surrounding the assets that have been declining in value, which makes it hard for investors to determine which assets remain overvalued and which are undervalued. The result for companies such as Bear Stearns, Lehman Brothers, AIG, Washington Mutual, and Wachovia was a downward spiral in their stock price, which had two self-reinforcing characteristics. First, there was little demand for existing stock since its worth would either be diluted by new capital (raised privately or through government intervention) or lost in insolvency. Second, new capital could not be attracted because the fall in stock value had left the market capitalization of the firms so low. If a firm's capital is completely depleted, there is no longer a buffer between its assets and liabilities, and it becomes insolvent.

Many large financial firms, including the firms that have failed, are heavily dependent on short-term borrowing to meet their current obligations. As financial conditions have worsened, some of the firms that have had the problems described above have had problems accessing short-term borrowing markets that in normal conditions could be taken for granted. In an atmosphere where creditors cannot perceive which firms have insufficient capital, they become unwilling to lend for even short intervals. This is the essence of the liquidity problem—although the firms' assets may exceed their liabilities, without access to short-term borrowing, the firm cannot meet its current obligations because it cannot convert its assets into cash quickly enough (at least not if it wishes to avoid "fire sale" prices).

The Fed has always been the "lender of last resort" in order for banks to avoid liquidity problems during financial turmoil. To borrow from the Fed, a financial firm must post collateral. In essence, this allows the firm to temporarily convert its illiquid assets into cash, enabling the firm to meet its short-term obligations without sacrificing its assets. The Fed has always lent to commercial banks (depository institutions) through the discount window.[45] As discussed above, it has extended liquidity to non-bank financial firms in 2008 through new lending facilities.

Borrowing from the Fed increases liquidity but it does not change a firm's capital position since it now has a liability outstanding to the Fed. So borrowing from the Fed cannot solve the problems of undercapitalization that some firms currently face. Indeed, the Fed will generally not lend to firms that are not creditworthy because it wants to provide liquidity only to firms that are solvent, and thus able to repay.[46]

H.R. 1424, which was signed into law on October 3 (P.L. 110-343), created the Troubled Assets Relief Program (TARP). Thus far, the Treasury has announced it would use TARP funds to address the capital adequacy problem directly by providing $250 billion in capital to banks directly through preferred share purchases by TARP.[47]

If TARP proves insufficient to restore financial calm, some have asked whether there is any program that the Fed could operate to address the financial firms' capital adequacy problems. All of the Fed's standing lending facilities involve collateralized lending, and as discussed above, any program involving collateralized lending would not change a firm's capital position. According to one legal analysis, there is no express statutory authority for the Fed to purchase corporate bonds, mortgages, or equity.[48] But the Fed's assistance in the Bear Stearns merger with JPMorgan Chase took a form that has some similarities to the TARP proposal. In the case of Bear Stearns, the Fed created a limited liability corporation called Maiden Lane, and lent Maiden Lane $28.82 billion. Maiden Lane used the proceeds of that loan and another loan from JPMorgan Chase to purchase mortgage-related assets from Bear Stearns. Thus, although the Fed created and controlled Maiden Lane, the assets were purchased and held by Maiden Lane, not the Fed. Similar to TARP, Maiden Lane plans to hold the assets until markets recover, and then sell the assets to repay its loans to the Fed and JPMorgan Chase. Maiden Lane was created under the Fed's Section 13(3) emergency authority.[49]

The Fed was presumably granted broad emergency powers under Section 13(3) so that it had the flexibility to deal with unforeseen circumstances. Nonetheless, too broad of a reading of its powers could provoke displeasure in Congress or legal challenges. Creating TARP within the Treasury through legislation rather than the Fed through emergency powers avoided the argument whether such a program extended beyond the Fed's intended role.

Lender of Last Resort, Systemic Risk, and Moral Hazard

Since its early days, one of the Fed's main roles has been to act as a lender of last resort to the banking system when private sources of credit become unavailable. The lender of last resort function can be seen from the perspective of an individual institution or the financial system as a whole.[50] From the perspective of the individual institution, discount window lending is meant to provide funds to institutions that are illiquid (cannot meet current obligations out of current cash flow) but still solvent (assets exceed liabilities) when they cannot access funds from the private market. Discount window lending was unable to end bank runs, however—bank runs did not cease until the creation of federal deposit insurance. The experience of the Great Depression suggested that bank runs placed intolerably high costs on the financial system as a whole, as they led to widespread bank failures.[51] Discount window lending is not meant to help insolvent institutions, with one exception explained below.

Access to discount window lending and deposit insurance creates moral hazard for financial institutions—they can take on more risk than the market would otherwise permit because of the government safety net. To limit moral hazard, institutions with depository insurance and access to the discount window are subject to a safety and soundness regulatory regime that includes capital requirements, reserve requirements, bank examinations, and so on.

The exception to the rule that insolvent institutions cannot access the discount window is when the institution is deemed "too big to fail." Institutions that are too big to fail are ones that are deemed to be big enough that their failure could create *systemic risk*, the risk that the financial system as a whole would cease to function smoothly.[52] A systemic risk episode could impose heavy costs on the overall economy, as the bank panics of the Great Depression demonstrated. Although too big to fail institutions are not offered explicit guarantees, it can be argued that they have implicit guarantees since the government would not be willing to allow a systemic risk episode. This accentuates the moral hazard problem described above. There is no official governmental classification of which financial institutions are too big to fail, presumably since maintaining uncertainty over which institutions are too big to fail could help reduce the moral hazard problem. But the lack of official designation arguably creates a vacuum in terms of policy preparedness. (Making the problem more complex, as one report described the situation, "Officials grimly concluded that while Bear Stearns isn't too big to fail, it was too interconnected to be allowed to fail in just one day." It is unclear how to judge which institutions are too interconnected to fail.)[53]

As the cases of Bear Stearns, Fannie Mae and Freddie Mac, and AIG illustrate, some of the modern-day financial institutions that are too big to fail are not depository institutions that fall under the strict regulatory umbrella that accompanies membership in the Federal Reserve system. This highlights the shift in financial activity from a bank-dominated financial system at the time of the Fed's creation to a system whose health now depends on many types of institutions. The Fed was set up to be a lender of last resort to only the banking system. In the current crisis, it has been able to extend its lender of last resort functions to non-bank financial institutions only because of its Section 13 (3) emergency powers. A policy issue going forward is whether the extension of these functions should be made permanent, and if so, what types of regulatory safeguards should accompany it. Because Section 13(3) is intended for emergencies, it grants authority that is broader and more open-ended than the Fed's normal authority.

It is possible that part of the reason these institutions failed is because they took on excessive risks in the belief that they were too big to fail. Although that theory can be debated, it is clearer that the precedent of the Fed's role in the Bear Stearns acquisition may strengthen the perception of other institutions and investors that any financial firm, regardless of whether it is a depository institution, will be bailed out in the future if it is too big to fail, or merely too interconnected to fail. If so, it could be argued that the Bear Stearns episode may have increased moral hazard going forward. The government's decision not to intervene to prevent the failure of the investment bank Lehman Brothers in September 2008, but to subsequently assist AIG and Citigroup may have created further market uncertainty regarding which institutions the government views as too big to fail. Lehman Brothers was larger than Bear Stearns and involved in similar business activities. Others have argued that the decision to let Lehman Brothers fail proves that Lehman Brothers was too big to fail, since it set off a wave of unrest in money markets (see above), interbank lending markets, and the market for credit default swaps.[54]

The government assistance to Bear Stearns, Fannie Mae and Freddie Mac, and AIG all include clauses that significantly reduced the value of existing shareholder equity. This was partly justified in terms of reducing moral hazard—investors would be reluctant to buy equity in too big to fail companies that were taking excessive risks if the government demanded a reduction in existing shareholder value. But government assistance in all of these cases made creditors and other counterparties whole. In these cases, the moral hazard problem manifests itself in a willingness of creditors to lend to, and counterparties to transact with, a firm they know to be taking excessive risks, thereby potentially allowing the firm to take more risks. More recent government assistance to Citigroup was provided without similar measures to replace management or dilute shareholders. Market participants may view this decision as a signal that the government is no longer placing emphasis on avoiding moral hazard.

Going forward, policymakers must determine whether new regulation is needed to limit moral hazard since there may be no credible way to maintain a policy that prohibits the rescue of future institutions that are too big to fail even if such a policy were desired. The current situation raises three broad points about systemic risk. First, risk is at the foundation of all financial intermediation. Policymakers may wish to curb excessive risk taking when it leads to systemic risk, but too little financial risk would also be counterproductive for the economy. (Indeed, some would argue that part of the underlying problem for the financial system as a whole at present is that investors are currently too risk averse.) Second, many analysts have argued that part of the reason that so much financial intermediation has left the commercial banking system is to avoid the costs of regulation.[55] This point applies to future regulatory changes as well. An attempt to increase regulation on banks could lead more business to move to hedge funds, for example. Third, financial markets have become significantly more complex and fast-moving in recent years. Many of the financial instruments with which Bear Stearns, Lehman Brothers, and AIG were involved did not exist until recently. For regulation to be effective in this environment, it faces the challenge of trying to keep up with innovation. If used prudently, many of these innovations can reduce risk for individual investors. Yet the Bear Stearns example implies that innovation may also lead to more interconnectivity, which increases systemic risk.

Effects on the Allocation of Capital

In normal conditions, the Fed primarily influences economic conditions through the purchase and sale of U.S. Treasury securities on the secondary market. This enables the Fed to influence overall economic conditions without favoring any particular financial firm or asset, thus minimizing its effect on the market allocation of capital.

As the Fed has shifted to an increasing reliance on more direct intervention in the financial system in 2008, its actions have had growing consequences for the allocation of private capital. By purchasing commercial paper and Bear Stearns' assets (via pass-through entities), the Fed has increased the relative demand for those assets. In a time when liquidity is scarce, access to Fed borrowing confers an advantage on banks and primary dealers over other types of institutions. It may also arguably retard the process of weeding out bad institutions, since reputation is needed to access private liquidity, but not Fed liquidity. On the other hand, during a panic both good and bad firms can be shut out of credit markets.

Other Fed programs adopted in 2008 also affect the allocation of capital. As discussed above, assisting Bear Stearns and AIG after their mistakes may encourage inefficiently high risk taking by other firms that are deemed "too big to fail." Punitive conditions attached to the assistance mitigate but do not eliminate these effects.[56] Allowing primary dealers to temporarily swap their illiquid assets for Treasuries protects those who invested poorly. Assistance to the commercial paper market confers and advantage to those firms that access that market, which are generally large and have high credit ratings. The Fed has attempted to push down yields on certain assets that it feels have become inefficiently high (e.g., through the Term Asset Backed Securities Lending Facility), but it may be that at the height of the boom yields on these assets had become inefficiently low because investors underestimated their riskiness. The Fed's efforts could eventually reintroduce inefficient underpricing of risk.

The Fed's short-term goal is to avoid the downward spiral in conditions that could lead to a panic, causing serious disruptions to the credit intermediation process for all firms, prudent or otherwise. But in the long run, once financial stability has been restored, these distortions to the market allocation of capital could result in economic inefficiencies. There is also a risk that the Fed's activities could "crowd out" private lenders and investors in the market for bank reserves and commercial paper, leading to less robust private markets. Even if some of the Fed's current programs are allowed to expire, if investors believed that they would be revived during the next downturn, capital allocation would be altered.

Liquidity Trap?

Some economists have argued that the Fed's recent string of newly created programs points to increasing desperation on its part to "right the ship." Although monetary policy is credited with having contributed to an unusual degree of economic stability since at least the mid-1980s, some argue that it has been rendered ineffective by the current outlook. The argument is that lower interest rates will not boost spending because the economy is stuck in a credit crunch in which financial institutions are unwilling to lend to creditworthy borrowers because of balance sheet concerns. The capital of financial firms has been depleted by investment losses. In turn, financial firms are said to be hoarding capital and unable to access credit markets because of fears of future losses. Following September 2008, banks greatly increased their reserve holdings, which could potentially be a troubling sign. Borrower demand may increase in response to lower rates, but as long as institutions are trying to rebuild their balance sheets, they will remain reluctant to extend credit. This problem is sometimes referred to as a "liquidity trap." Liquidity traps are rare in modern times, but the decade of economic stagnation suffered by Japan in the 1990s after the bursting of its financial bubble is cited as an example. Interest rates were lowered to almost zero in Japan, and the economy still did not recover quickly.[57]

There are some problems with this line of reasoning at present. First, liquidity traps are seen as an extreme form of recession, but while the U.S. economy has entered a recession, the fall in economic output has so far been mild compared to previous recessions. Second, liquidity traps are most likely to occur when overall prices of goods and services are falling (called *deflation*). The Fed cannot reduce the federal funds rate below zero. When prices are falling, real interest rates are higher than nominal interest rates, so it is more likely that a very low nominal interest rate would still be too high in real terms to stimulate economic activity. But inflation has been above average in 2008, although falling more recently.[58] Inflation would not be expected to be persistently high if the economy were in a liquidity trap. Third, there is a more benign, well- documented explanation for why the Fed's expansionary policy has not yet stimulated economic activity—monetary policy always suffers lags between a reduction in interest rates and corresponding increases in economic activity.

While a liquidity trap cannot be ruled out, it is premature to conclude the economy is stuck in one at this point in time. Liquidity traps are a threat when monetary policy has been kept too tight, but the Fed has eased monetary policy aggressively since the crisis began.

Stagflation?

Other critics have argued that the Fed has created the opposite problem of a liquidity trap—rising inflation due to excessive liquidity. They argue that the economy has entered a period of stagflation, where falling or negative economic growth is accompanied by high or rising inflation.[59]

Typically, one would expect an economic slowdown to be accompanied by a decline in the inflation rate. Excess capacity in the capital stock and rising unemployment would force firms and workers to lower their prices and wage demands, respectively. But critics believe the economy is in a situation where a modest but persistent increase in inflation in recent years has led individuals to come to expect higher inflation, and factor that expectation into their price and wage demands. Couple those higher inflation expectations with rising commodity prices and the recent unusual large liquidity injections by the Fed, and critics argue that inflation will rise even if the economy slows. They point to the experience of the 1970s, when inflationary expectations became so ingrained that inflation continued to rise despite a fairly deep recession, as a potential parallel to the current situation.

Data suggest that the fear of stagflation is premature—both unemployment and inflation remain relatively low at present. It is true that in the long run inflation is primarily a monetary phenomenon, and if the Fed's recent monetary stance were maintained for too long, it would not be consistent with stable inflation. But in the near term, if unemployment and excess capacity rose, that would be expected to take much of the pressure off of the inflation rate. Furthermore, commodity prices fell in the second half of 2008, reversing the immediate upward pressure on prices. Ironically, if the Fed's actions succeed in reviving the economy, then the probability that its actions would boost inflation would increase. The key to maintaining a stable inflation rate is finding the proper balance between the disinflationary pressures of the slowdown and the inflationary pressures of expansionary monetary policy. The large amounts of liquidity that the Fed has added to the system must be removed soon enough that inflation does not rise, but not so soon that a nascent financial recovery is stubbed out. Given the uncertainty facing policymakers at present, finding the proper balance is extremely difficult.[60]

Concluding Thoughts

Although turmoil plagues financial markets periodically, the current episode is notable for its breadth and persistence. It is difficult to make the case that the Fed has not responded to the current turmoil with alacrity and creativity. The Fed's inability to restore normalcy is not necessarily a sign that its policy decisions have been wrongheaded—the Fed can provide the financial sector with additional liquidity, but it cannot force institutions to use that liquidity to expand their lending or investing.

The Fed's response has raised statutory issues that Congress may wish to consider in its oversight capacity. Namely, the Fed's role in the Bear Stearns acquisition, the AIG loan, the creation of the Primary Dealer Credit Facility (a sort of discount window for a group of non-member banks), and its intervention in the commercial paper market involved emergency authorities that had not been used in more than 70 years. This authority was needed because the actions involved financial institutions that were not member banks of the Federal Reserve System (i.e., depository institutions). But because the authority is broad and open-ended, the Fed's actions under this authority are subject to few legal parameters. The authority allows lending to non-member banks, but the loan in the Bear Stearns agreement is to a LLC that the Fed created and controls, and is being used to purchase Bear Stearns' assets. These actions raise an important issue—if financial institutions can receive some of the benefits of Fed protection, in some cases because they are "too big to fail," should they also be subject to the costs that member banks bear in terms of safety and soundness regulations, imposed to limit the moral hazard that inevitably results from Fed and FDIC (Federal Deposit Insurance Corporation) protections?

Some policymakers have begun to question whether an institution largely independent from the elected branches of government should be able to (indirectly) place significant taxpayer funds at risk by assisting the financial sector through use of its emergency powers. Furthermore, without Congressional input, hundreds of billions of dollars of borrowing by the Treasury (through the Treasury Supplementary Financing Program) has allowed the Fed to increase its lending capacity without detrimental effects on inflation. But as long as there is no government program to systematically manage financial difficulties at too big to fail institutions, the Fed is the only institution that can step in quickly enough to cope with problems on a case-by-case basis. While some had believed TARP provided the type of systemic approach that would allow the Fed to return to a more traditional role, the Fed's subsequent creation of lending facilities to support the commercial paper market suggests that TARP cannot cover all unforeseen contingencies.

End Notes

[1] For more information see CRS Report RL341 82, *Financial Crisis? The Liquidity Crunch of August 2007,* by Darryl E. Getter et al.

[2] Current amounts of Fed lending outstanding can be found at Federal Reserve, "Factors Affecting Reserve Balances of Depository Institutions," statistical release H.4. 1, updated weekly.

[3] Many of the loans and new programs described below are operated through the Federal Reserve Bank of New York, under the authorization of the Board of Governors. This report uses the term Federal Reserve, and does not distinguish between actions taken by the Board and actions taken by the Federal Reserve Bank of New York. The Federal Reserve System is composed of the Board of Governors and twelve regional banks (one of which is the New York Fed).

[4] The Fed authorized lending to Fannie Mae and Freddie Mac on July 13, 2008, but this authority was not used at that point, as it was soon superseded by the authority granted to Treasury to offer the GSEs financial assistance. On September 19, 2008, the Fed announced that it would also purchase (for the first time since 1981) debt obligations of Fannie Mae, Freddie Mac, and the Federal Home Loan Banks through open market operations. On November 25, 2008, the Fed announced that it would purchase up to $100 billion of the direct obligations and $500 billion of the mortgage- backed securities issued by Fannie Mae, Freddie Mac, and Ginnie Mae, however.

[5] Federal Reserve Bank of New York, "The Discount Window," *Fedpoint,* August 2007.

[6] Some of the Fed's purchase and sale of Treasury securities are made outright, but most are made through repurchase agreements, which can be thought of as short-term transactions that are automatically reversed at the end of a predetermined period, typically lasting a few days. Since the Fed must constantly adjust the

amount of bank reserves available to keep the federal funds rate near its target, repurchase agreements give the Fed more flexibility to make these adjustments.

[7] For more information, see CRS Report RL30354, *Monetary Policy and the Federal Reserve: Current Policy and Conditions,* by Gail E. Makinen and Marc Labonte.

[8] Although no change in the targeted rate was announced, the Fed allowed the actual federal funds rate to fall below 5% on most days over the next month.

[9] For more background, see James Clouse, "Recent Developments in Discount Window Policy," *Federal Reserve Bulletin*, November 1994, p. 965.

[10] For more information, see Olivier Armantier et al, "The Federal Reserve's Term Auction Facility," Federal Reserve Bank of New York, *Current Issues in Economics and Finance,* vol. 14, no. 5, July 2008; Charles Carlstrom and Sarah Wakefield, "The Funds Rate, Liquidity, and the Term Auction Facility," Federal Reserve Bank of Cleveland, *Economic Trends*, December 14, 2007.

[11] The dates, terms, and amounts of future TAF auctions can be accessed at http://www.federalreserve.gov/monetarypolicy/tafschedule.htm.

[12] See James McAndrews et al, "The Effect of the Term Auction Facility on the London Inter-bank Offered Rate," Federal Reserve Bank of New York, Staff Report no. 335, July 2008; John Taylor and John Williams, "A Black Swan in the Money Market," Federal Reserve Bank of San Francisco, working paper 2008-04, April 2008.

[13] Board of Governors of the Federal Reserve System, press release, March 11, 2008.

[14] Board of Governors of the Federal Reserve System, press release, November 25, 2008.

[15] For more information, see CRS Report RL34730, *The Emergency Economic Stabilization Act and Current Financial Turmoil: Issues and Analysis,* by Baird Webel and Edward V. Murphy.

[16] Financial firms experiencing any disruption to their liquidity needs in the commercial paper market were already eligible to borrow from the Fed on a collateralized basis.

[17] See David Fettig, "Lender of More Than Last Resort," Federal Reserve Bank of Minneapolis, *The Region,* December 2002.

[18] See Todd Keister et al, "Divorcing Money From Monetary Policy, Federal Reserve Bank of New York, *Economic Policy Review*, September 2008.

[19] This section discusses the special assistance that the troubled firms received from the Fed. The same firms may also have subsequently accessed Fed resources through its normal lending facilities. All lending through facilities is confidential, so knowledge of such activity is limited to self-reporting by the firms. For example, the CEO of JPMorgan Chase testified to Congress that Bear Stearns had borrowed an additional $25 billion from the Fed. (Source: Kara Scannell and Sudeep Reddy, "Officials Say They Sought to Avoid Bear Bailout," *Wall Street Journal,* April 4, 2008, p. A1.) Similarly, AIG announced that it had accessed the Commercial Paper Funding Facility. (Source: "U.S. Treasury, Federal Reserve and AIG Establish Comprehensive Solution for AIG," AIG press release, November 10, 2008.)

[20] For more information, see CRS Report RL34420, *Bear Stearns: Crisis and "Rescue" for a Major Provider of Mortgage-Related Products*, by Gary Shorter.

[21] Federal Reserve Bank of New York, "New York Fed Completes Financing Arrangement Related to JPMorgan Chase's Acquisition of Bear Stearns," press release, June 26, 2008. A subordinate loan is one where the principal and interest are not repaid until after the primary loan is repaid. The originally announced terms of the loans were for up to $29 billion from the New York Fed and $1 billion from JPMorgan Chase. After more thoroughly reviewing the assets the LLC would receive, the Fed changed the terms of the loan.

[22] Federal Reserve Bank of New York, "Summary of Terms and Conditions Regarding the JPMorgan Chase Facility," press release, March 24, 2008. Many of the details of the loan, including the size, were not announced on March 16.

[23] Timothy Geithner, "Testimony Before the Senate Committee for Banking, Housing and Urban Affairs," April 3, 2008, Annex II.

[24] Jamie Dimon, *Testimony Before the Senate Committee on Banking, Housing, and Urban Affairs*, April 3, 2008.

[25] Federal Reserve Bank of New York, "Summary of Terms and Conditions Regarding the JPMorgan Chase Facility," press release, March 24, 2008.

[26] Timothy Geithner, "Testimony Before the Senate Committee for Banking, Housing and Urban Affairs," April 3, 2008, p. 17.

[27] Federal Reserve Bank of New York, "Statement on Financing Arrangement of JPMorgan Chase's Acquisition of Bear Stearns," press release, March 24, 2008.

[28] Federal Reserve, *Factors Affecting Reserve Balances of Depository Institutions*, press release H.4. 1, September 11, 2008. Information on the portfolio will be updated quarterly and announced through this press release.

[29] Jamie Dimon, *Testimony Before the Senate Committee on Banking, Housing, and Urban Affairs,* April 3, 2008.

[30] Timothy Geithner, "Testimony Before the Senate Committee for Banking, Housing and Urban Affairs," April 3, 2008, p. 13.

[31] See, for example, "U.S. to Take Over AIG in $85 Billion Bailout; Central Banks Inject Cash as Credit Dries Up," *Wall Street Journal*, September 17, 2008, pp. A1-A6.

[32] Federal Reserve, "Factors Affecting Reserve Balances," press release H.4.1, September 18, 2008.

[33] Liam Pleven et al, "AIG Bailout Hit By New Cash Woes," *Wall Street Journal,* October 9, 2008, p. A1.

[34] N.Y. Ins. Law, Sec. 1410.

[35] This section was prepared with Baird Webel, analyst in Financial Economics.

[36] Full details of the preferred shares can be found on the Treasury website athttp://ustreas.gov/press/releases/ reports/ 111008aigtermsheet.pdf.

[37] "Joint Statement by Treasury, Federal Reserve, and the FDIC on Citigroup," joint press release, November 23, 2008.

[38] For a full discussion, see the section below entitled "Lender of Last Resort, Systemic Risk, and Moral Hazard".

[39] Assuming that the interest rate on the loans exceeded the rate of return on the Treasuries that the Fed would have purchased if the loans had not occurred.

[40] Were the amount of loans to increase significantly because financial conditions became significantly worse, it is unlikely that the Fed would continue to fear that a larger money supply would have unacceptable consequences for inflation. If so, the Fed could become less concerned about taking steps to offset the loans' effects on the money supply.

[41] It should be noted that a portfolio of Treasury securities is only needed to tighten monetary policy. Expansionary monetary policy involves the purchase of Treasury securities.

[42] As financial conditions deteriorated after September 2008 and the Fed increased its assets to support the financial system, the Fed's liabilities increased significantly because of an increase in bank reserves. Thus, the Fed did not sterilize this increase. Normally, this would have been inflationary, but it appears that the increase in reserves was caused by a desire by banks to increase their reserves rather than their lending. If so, there may not be inflationary consequences to the increase in the Fed's assets.

[43] For more information, see CRS Report RS22963, *Financial Market Intervention,* by Edward V. Murphy and Baird Webel.

[44] Yalman Onaran, "Banks' Subprime Losses Top $500 Billion on Writedowns," Bloomberg, August 12, 2008.

[45] In normal conditions, borrowing from the discount window is allowed but discouraged, and banks are expected to meet their liquidity needs through private markets. Soon after the financial turmoil began, the Fed began to encourage discount window borrowing.

[46] In addition, the Fed faces some statutory limitations on lending to undercapitalized banks under normal circumstances. See, for example, Section 10B of the Federal Reserve Act.

[47] For more information, see CRS Report RL34730, *The Emergency Economic Stabilization Act and Current Financial Turmoil: Issues and Analysis,* by Baird Webel and Edward V. Murphy.

[48] David Small and James Clouse, "The Scope of Monetary Policy Actions Authorized under the Federal Reserve Act," Federal Reserve, FEDS working paper no. 2004-40, July 2004, p. 29.

[49] The Fed also created the Term Asset Backed Liquidity Facility (TALF) to lend to private investors to purchase illiquid assets of the same types that TARP was originally intended to purchase. TALF is also aimed at improving liquidity, and does not affect the capital adequacy problem, however.

[50] For more information, see CRS Report RS21986, *Federal Reserve: Lender of Last Resort Functions,* by Marc Labonte.

[51] In this context, it is interesting to note that the Bear Stearns failure has been described as a non-bank run, meaning Bear Stearns was undermined because it was shunned by its counterparties and investors, analogous to a bank being shunned by its depositors. The defining characteristic of a run is that the fear of failure becomes self-fulfilling since it deprives an institution of the resources it needs to avoid failure.

[52] For more information, see CRS Report RL34412, *Containing Financial Crisis,* by Mark Jickling.

[53] Greg Ip, "Central Bank Offers Loans to Brokers, Cuts Key Rate," *Wall Street Journal,* March 17, 2008, p. A1.

[54] Chairman Bernanke argued that the Fed did not have the authority to assist Lehman Brothers because Lehman Brothers could not offer the Fed adequate collateral for a loan of the size needed, which according to Bernanke, would have been much larger than the assistance for Bear Stearns. See Ben Bernanke, "Current Economic and Financial Conditions," speech at the National Association for Business Economic Annual Meeting, October 7, 2008.

[55] This problem in relation to investment banking has to some degree been overtaken by events, as none of the five largest investment banks still exist in their original form. Lehman Brothers has entered bankruptcy, Bear Stearns and Merrill Lynch have merged with commercial banks, and Goldman Sachs and Morgan Stanley have reorganized as bank holding companies that are regulated by the Fed.

[56] For example, the decision to make creditors whole in the case of Bear Stearns and AIG reduces incentives for creditors to curb lending to other institutions deemed "too big to fail."

[57] While the term liquidity trap was often applied to Japan, it is theoretically defined as a situation where household demand for money becomes so great that normal sized changes in the money supply do not affect interest rates. Under this strict definition, it is not clear that Japan, or any other economy, has experienced a liquidity trap.

[58] Asset prices have been falling lately, but they are not included in standard measures of inflation, which measures the prices of goods and services.

[59] See CRS Report RL34428, *Understanding Stagflation and the Risk of Its Recurrence,* by Brian W. Cashell and Marc Labonte.

[60] For more information, see CRS Report RL34562 , *Slow Growth or Inflation? The Federal Reserve's Dilemma,* by Brian W. Cashell and Marc Labonte.

In: Government Interventions in Economic Emergencies ISBN: 978-1-60741-356-1
Editor: Pablo Sastre

Chapter 23

REGULATION OF NAKED SHORT SELLING

Mark Jickling

SUMMARY

Short sellers borrow stock, sell it, and hope to profit if they can buy back the same number of shares later at a lower price. A short sale is a bet that a stock's price will fall. A short sale is said to be "naked" if the broker does not in fact borrow shares to deliver to the buyer. When executed on a large scale, naked short sales can equal a large portion of total shares outstanding, and can put serious downward pressure on a stock's price. Critics of the practice characterize it as a form of illegal price manipulation. The Securities and Exchange Commission (SEC) in 2004 adopted Regulation SHO, a set of rules designed to control short selling abuses, focusing on small-capitalization stocks where the number of shares held by the public was relatively small. Until the current financial crisis, the SEC did not view short selling of large, blue-chip stocks as a problem. In July 2008, however, the SEC temporarily banned naked short sales of the stock of Fannie Mae, Freddie Mac, and 17 other large financial institutions. On September 18, 2008, the SEC banned all short selling of the shares of more than 700 financial companies in an emergency action that expired on October 8, 2008. On October 1, the SEC adopted a rule requiring short sellers' brokers to actually borrow shares to deliver to buyers, within the normal three-day settlement time frame.

Short selling was best described by Daniel Drew, the Gilded Age speculator and robber baron: "He that sells what isn't his'n, must buy it back or go to prison." Short sellers borrow shares from a broker, sell them, and make a profit if the share price subsequently drops, allowing them to buy back the same number of shares for less money. In other words, short selling is a bet that the price of a stock will fall.

Short sellers have always been unpopular on Wall Street. Like skeletons at the feast, they seem to stand against rising share values, expanding wealth, and general prosperity. However, most market participants recognize that they provide a valuable service to the extent that they identify companies and industries that are overvalued by investors in the grip of irrational exuberance. By bringing such valuations down to earth, short selling can prevent economically wasteful over-allocation of resources to those firms and sectors.

MANIPULATION BY SHORT SELLERS

Another persistent complaint against short sellers is that they cause artificial price volatility. A form of manipulation common in the 19th century was the "bear raid" — a gang of speculators would sell a stock short, causing the price to drop. They would follow with another wave of short sales, depressing the price still further, and so on, until the stock's price was driven to the floor.

In the 1930s, the Securities and Exchange Commission (SEC) adopted a regulation to prevent bear raiding. The "uptick rule"[1] stated that a short sale may occur only if the last price movement in a stock's price was upward. This prevents short sellers from piling onto a falling stock and setting off a downward price spiral. In the words of a standard securities law textbook, the tick test (and related rules) "seem pretty well to have taken the caffeine out of the short sale."[2] In 2007, the SEC concluded that growth in the market made the rule unnecessary, and it was repealed.[3]

However, in recent years, complaints about manipulative short selling have reappeared. Many shareholders and officers of smaller firms have identified "naked" short selling as a source of price manipulation and have criticized the SEC's enforcement record. At the same time, the SEC has identified short selling in connection with spreading rumors as an abuse that may raise fears about the solvency of the target firm and cut off its access to credit, potentially leading to the destruction of the firm, as was the case with Bear Stearns in March 2008.

NAKED SHORTING

A short sale always involves the sale of shares that the seller does not own. The buyer, however, expects to receive real shares. Where do those shares come from? Normally, they are borrowed by the broker from another investor or from a brokerage's own account. This is usually not difficult to do if the shares are issued by a large company, where millions of shares change hands daily and where many shares are not registered to the actual owners, but are held in "street name," that is, in the broker's account. With smaller corporations, however, the number of shares in circulation may be limited, and brokers may find it difficult to locate shares to deliver to the buyer in a short sale transaction.

When shares are not located to "cover" a short sale, the short position is said to be naked. If shares are not found by the time the transaction must be settled, there is a "failure to deliver" shares to the buyer. If it occurs sporadically and on a small scale, naked short selling does not raise serious manipulation concerns. However, when the number of shares sold short represents a significant fraction of all shares outstanding, there may be a strong impact on the share price. In such cases, when naked short selling creates a virtually unlimited quantity of shares, a market based on supply and demand can be seriously distorted. The SEC notes that "naked short sellers enjoy greater leverage than if they were required to borrow securities and deliver within a reasonable time period, and they may use this additional leverage to engage in trading activities that deliberately depress the price of a security."[4]

The case against naked short selling has been that by permitting short sales to occur when there is no possibility of actually delivering shares to the buyers, brokers and dealers accommodate manipulation. When naked short selling drives prices down, holders of the stock understandably feel cheated. They do not believe the stock is overvalued; they are not selling; but the price drops anyway.

It is important to note that naked short selling is not always evidence of intent to manipulate prices. Under certain circumstances, a market maker[5] may engage in naked short selling to stabilize the market. For example, assume that there is a sudden flurry of buy orders for a stock. The market maker may judge the buying interest to be temporary and not justified by any real news about the company's prospects. It may be the result of a questionable press release or a rumor in an Internet chat room. The market maker may choose to sell short to avoid what in its view would be an unjustified run-up in the stock's price. In this situation, naked short selling by the market maker may protect investors against manipulation.

It is also worth noting that while restrictions on short selling discourage certain forms of manipulation, they may encourage or facilitate others. Manipulations that involve artificially inflating stock prices are probably more common than techniques (like naked shorting) that seek to depress them. Rumors, false press releases, and unexpected purchases may all cause sudden run-ups of stock prices, which may be followed (in the classic "pump-and-dump" fraud) by sudden collapse, as the manipulators sell their shares to the unwary. Without short selling as a counterweight, the magnitude and duration of such fraudulent run-ups are likely to be greater

Until July 2008, the SEC viewed the problem of naked shorting as largely confined to smaller firms, particularly small-capitalization "penny" stocks listed on the Nasdaq bulletin board market (OTCBB).[6] In these companies, the bulk of outstanding shares may be owned by corporate insiders or by securities dealers who act as market makers, so that relatively few shares are available for purchase on the open market. This means that transactions have a proportionately greater impact on the stock price than do trades of the same size in the shares of a larger company, making manipulation easier. In addition to OTCBB stocks, however, smaller companies listed on the exchanges or the Nasdaq national market may also be vulnerable to short selling abuse.

REGULATION SHO

After several years of deliberation, the SEC in 2004 adopted rules designed to control abusive naked short selling. Regulation SHO[7] took effect on January 3, 2005. The new regulation replaced existing exchange and Nasdaq rules with a uniform national standard. Under Regulation SHO, a broker may not accept a short sale order from a customer, or effect a short sale for its own account, unless it

- has either borrowed the security, or made a bona fide arrangement to borrow it; or
- has reasonable grounds to believe that it can locate the security, borrow it, and deliver it to the buyer by the date delivery is due; and
- has documented compliance with the above.

The appearance of a stock on an exchange's "easy to borrow" list constituted reasonable grounds for believing that the stock can be located. Stocks on such lists tend to be highly capitalized, with large numbers of shares in circulation.

If a broker executes a short sale, and then fails to deliver shares to the purchaser, further restrictions on short selling may come into force. If the "fail to deliver" position is 10,000 shares or more, for five consecutive trading days, and the position amounts to at least 0.5% of total shares outstanding, the stock becomes a *threshold security*. The exchanges and Nasdaq are now required to publish daily lists of threshold securities. Regulation SHO specifies that if a fail to deliver position in a threshold security persists for 13 trading days, the broker (or the broker's clearing house) must close the short position by purchasing securities of like kind and quantity. After the 13 days have elapsed, the broker may not accept any more short sale orders until the fail to deliver position is closed by purchasing securities.

The rules include exemptions for market makers engaged in bona fide marketmaking activities, and for certain transactions between brokers.

EFFECTS OF REGULATION SHO

The adoption of Regulation SHO has not put an end to investor complaints about naked short selling. Complaints are heard that the SEC is not enforcing the rules vigorously enough, that short selling continues, and that some brokers evade the 13-day requirement by passing fail to deliver positions from one to another.[8]

The SEC staff has monitored the incidence of fail to delivers after the effective date of Regulation SHO, and, in July 2006, Chairman Cox reported that the rule "appears to be significantly reducing fails to deliver without disruption to the markets."[9] Nevertheless, some further amendments to Regulation SHO were considered.

In July 2006, the SEC proposed rules to close two "loopholes" in Regulation SHO, which it called responsible for the persistence of fail to deliver positions in certain stocks. Under the proposed rules, the current exemption for options market makers would be restricted. Second, a "grandfather" provision in the original rule — which exempted short positions that had been established before a stock was placed on the threshold securities list from the requirement that fail to deliver positions be closed out after 13 consecutive trading days — would be eliminated.

In August 2007, the SEC adopted the proposed rule abolishing the grandfather provision. When a stock goes onto the threshold list, all short positions in the stock will be subject to the 13-day close-out requirement. The SEC did not adopt the proposal relating to options market makers.

THE 2008 EMERGENCY ORDERS

As financial companies came under pressure from tight credit markets in late 2007 and 2008, concerns emerged about manipulative short sellers spreading rumors about firms' creditworthiness and liquidity. Despite regulators' assurances that Bear Stearns, a leading investment bank, had adequate capital and liquidity reserves, the firm was destroyed in March 2008 by the equivalent of a bank run: market participants, fearing that the firm might not be able to meet its obligations, refused to extend credit. The Federal Reserve was forced to arrange a hasty merger with JP Morgan Chase, which acquired Bear Stearns on condition that the Fed purchase $29 billion of risky mortgage assets.

All large financial firms finance their operations by issuing short-term debt, which must be continually refinanced, or rolled over. Thus, they are vulnerable to "nonbank runs" — they cannot survive long if markets lose confidence and become unwilling to provide new funds. In July 2008, share prices of Fannie Mae and Freddie Mac, the two giant government-sponsored enterprises that hold about $1.5 trillion in mortgage-backed assets, plunged, and fears arose that they might go the way of Bear Stearns. On July 15, the SEC issued an emergency order banning naked short sales of the shares of Fannie, Freddie, and 17 other large financial institutions.[10]

Under the terms of the order, no short sale of the stock of any of the 19 listed firms may occur unless the seller has actually borrowed (or arranged to borrow) the stock and delivers the stock to the buyer on the regular settlement date.

The SEC explained the rationale for its unusual action:

> False rumors can lead to a loss of confidence in our markets. Such loss of confidence can lead to panic selling, which may be further exacerbated by "naked" short selling. As a result, the prices of securities may artificially and unnecessarily decline well below the price level that would have resulted from the normal price discovery process. If significant financial institutions are involved, this chain of events can threaten disruption of our markets.
>
> The events preceding the sale of The Bear Stearns Companies Inc. are illustrative of the market impact of rumors. During the week of March 10, 2008, rumors spread about liquidity problems at Bear Stearns, which eroded investor confidence in the firm. As Bear Stearns' stock price fell, its counterparties became concerned, and a crisis of confidence occurred late in the week. In particular, counterparties to Bear Stearns were unwilling to make secured funding available to Bear Stearns on customary terms. In light of the potentially systemic consequences of a failure of Bear Stearns, the Federal Reserve took emergency action.[11]

The SEC's intervention has been criticized by some who believe that financial stocks have been battered not by false rumors, but by realistic assessments of firms' underlying financial weakness. Short selling, in this view, is simply market discipline at work. One view is that the SEC's objective of raising financial stock prices itself amounts to market manipulation.[12]

The SEC's original order, issued on July 15, was extended through August 12, 2008.

On September 18, 2008, as financial stocks plunged, the SEC issued another, much more sweeping emergency order. All short selling (naked or not) of the shares of more than 700 financial firms was banned. The rationale was the same as for the earlier action: whatever benefits short selling might provide in terms of price efficiency were far outweighed by the possible damage to the financial system and the economy if major firms were swept away by panic. The emergency order expired October 8, 2008.

On October 1, 2008, in addition to extending the short sale ban announced on September 18, the SEC adopted a rule that in effect banned naked short selling in all stocks.[13] This order, in the form of an interim final rule, requires that when a failure to deliver shares within the normal three-day settlement period occurs, the seller's broker must immediately purchase or borrow securities and close out the fail to deliver position by no later than the beginning of trading on the next business day. Failure to comply means that the broker cannot sell that stock short either for its own account or for customers, unless the shares are not only located but also pre-borrowed.

The SEC also adopted Rule 10b-21, a naked short selling anti-fraud rule, covering short sellers who deceive broker-dealers or any other market participants about their intention or ability to deliver securities in time for settlement. The rule makes clear that such persons are violating the law when they fail to deliver.

End Notes

[1] Rule 10a-1(a). The rule technically applies only to exchange-listed stocks, but a comparable rule was extended to Nasdaq National Market System stocks in 1994.

[2] Louis Loss, *Fundamentals of Securities Regulation* (Boston: Little Brown, 1983), p. 717.

[3] Release No. 34-55970, "Regulation SHO and Rule 10a-1," June 28, 2007. See also CRS Report RL34519, *The Uptick Rule: The SEC Removes a Limit on Short Selling*, by Gary Shorter.

[4] Release No. 34-48709, "Short Sales: Proposed Rule," October 28, 2003.

[5] Market makers are dealers who stand ready to buy or sell a stock at any time and who publish the prices at which they are willing to trade. They are the key intermediaries on the Nasdaq; on the New York Stock Exchange, they are called specialists.

[6] The uptick rule does not apply to OTCBB stocks.

[7] Release No. 34-50103, "Short Sales: Final Rule," July 28, 2004, available at [http://www.sec.gov/rules/final/34-50103.htm].

[8] "Of Stocks and Socks: Senator Bennett Bores In On SECs Dismal Naked Short Sales Record," *FinancialWire*, March 14, 2005, p. 1.

[9] Chairman Christopher Cox, "Opening Statement at the Commission Open Meeting," July 12, 2006.

[10] "SEC Enhances Investor Protections Against Naked Short Selling," Press Release 2008-143, July 15, 2008. Available at [http://www.sec.gov/rules/other/2008/34-58166.pdf]. Ten of the 17 were foreign firms.

[11] Ibid.

[12] Lawrence Summers, "How to Build a U.S. Recovery," *Financial Times*, August 7, 2007, p. 5.

[13] Securities and Exchange Commission, "Amendments to Regulation SHO," [Release No. 34-58773], Oct. 1, 2008. See [http://www.sec.gov/rules/final/2008/34-58773.pdf].

CHAPTER SOURCES

The following chapters have been previously published:

Chapter 1 – This is an edited, reformatted and augmented edition of a United States Congressional Research Service publication, Report Order Code RL34707, dated October 14, 2008.

Chapter 2 - This is an edited, reformatted and augmented edition of a United States Congressional Research Service publication, Report Order Code RL33235, dated January 17, 2006.

Chapter 3 – This is an edited, reformatted and augmented edition of a United States Congressional Research Service publication, Report Order Code RL34420, dated April 9, 2008.

Chapter 4 – This is an edited, reformatted and augmented edition of a United States Congressional Research Service publication, Report Order Code RL34412, dated November 24, 2008.

Chapter 5 - This is an edited, reformatted and augmented edition of a United States Congressional Research Service publication, Report Order Code RS22956, dated October 15, 2008.

Chapter 6 - This is an edited, reformatted and augmented edition of a United States Congress Joint Economic Committee publication, Research Report #110-29, dated December 2008.

Chapter 7 - This is an edited, reformatted and augmented edition of a United States Congress Joint Economic Committee publication, Research Report #110-32, dated December 2008.

Chapter 8 - This is an edited, reformatted and augmented edition of a United States Congressional Research Service publication, Report Order Code RL34713, dated November 20, 2008.

Chapter 9 - These remarks were delivered as Testimony of Peter R. Orszag, Director, Congressional Budget Office (CBO), before the Committee on the Budget, U.S. House of Representatives, dated September 24, 2008.

Chapter 10 - This is an edited, reformatted and augmented edition of a United States Congressional Research Service publication, Report Order Code RS22961, dated September 29, 2008.

Chapter 11 - This is an edited, reformatted and augmented edition of a United States Congressional Research Service publication, Report Order Code RS22960, dated September 29, 2008.

Chapter 12 - This is an edited, reformatted and augmented edition of a United States Congressional Research Service publication, Report Order Code RS2292, dated September 29, 2008.

Chapter 13 - This is an edited, reformatted and augmented edition of a United States Congressional Research Service publication, Report Order Code RS22963, dated September 29, 2008.

Chapter 14 - These remarks were delivered as Statement of Ben S. Bernanke, Chairman, Board of Governors of the Federal Reserve System, before the Committee on Financial Services, U.S. House of Representatives, dated September 24, 2008.

Chapter 15 - These remarks were delivered as Testimony by Henry M. Paulson, Jr., United States Treasury Secretary, before the House Committee on Financial Services, U.S. House of Representatives, dated September 24, 2008.

Chapter 16 - This is an edited, reformatted and augmented edition of a United States Congressional Research Service publication, Report Order Code RL34423, dated April 18, 2008.

Chapter 17 - These remarks were delivered as a press release by Henry M. Paulson, Jr., United States Treasury Secretary, dated September 19, 2008.

Chapter 18 - These remarks were delivered as a press release by Henry M. Paulson, Jr., United States Treasury Secretary, dated November 12, 2008.

Chapter 19 - This is an edited, reformatted and augmented edition of a United States Congressional Research Service publication, Report Order Code RS22957, dated September 22, 2008.

Chapter 20 - This is an edited, reformatted and augmented edition of a United States Congressional Research Service publication, Report Order Code RS22959, dated September 26, 2008.

Chapter 21 - This is an edited, reformatted and augmented edition of a United States Congressional Research Service publication, Report Order Code RL34349, dated December 17, 2008.

Chapter 22 - This is an edited, reformatted and augmented edition of a United States Congressional Research Service publication, Report Order Code RL34427, dated December 4, 2008.

Chapter 23 - This is an edited, reformatted and augmented edition of a United States Congressional Research Service publication, Report Order Code RS22099, dated October 30, 2008.

INDEX

9

A

B

C

D

E

F

G

H

I

J

K

L

M

N

O

P

S

T

U

V

W

Y